MIND
COMPUTATION

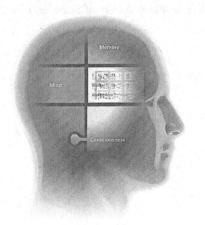

Series on Intelligence Science

Series Editor: Zhongzhi Shi *(Chinese Academy of Sciences, China)*

Published

Vol. 1   Advanced Artificial Intelligence
        by Zhongzhi Shi (Chinese Academy of Sciences, China)

Vol. 2   Intelligence Science
        by Zhongzhi Shi (Chinese Academy of Sciences, China)

Vol. 3   Mind Computation
        by Zhongzhi Shi (Chinese Academy of Sciences, China)

Series on Intelligence Science ▶▶ Vol. 3

MIND COMPUTATION

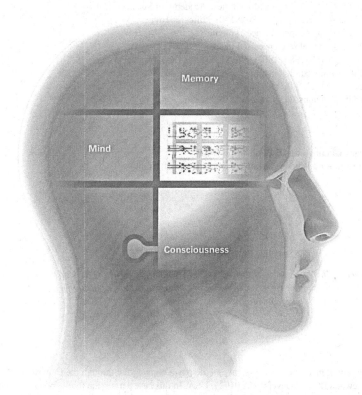

Zhongzhi SHI

Chinese Academy of Sciences, China

 **World Scientific**

NEW JERSEY · LONDON · SINGAPORE · BEIJING · SHANGHAI · HONG KONG · TAIPEI · CHENNAI · TOKYO

Published by

World Scientific Publishing Co. Pte. Ltd.

5 Toh Tuck Link, Singapore 596224

USA office: 27 Warren Street, Suite 401-402, Hackensack, NJ 07601

UK office: 57 Shelton Street, Covent Garden, London WC2H 9HE

Library of Congress Cataloging-in-Publication Data

Names: Shi, Zhongzhi, author.

Title: Mind computation / Zhongzhi Shi (Chinese Academy of Sciences, China).

Description: [Hoboken] New Jersey : World Scientific, [2016] |

    Series: Series on intelligence science ; volume 3 |

    Includes bibliographical references and index.

Identifiers: LCCN 2016032985 | ISBN 9789813145801 (hc : alk. paper)

Subjects: LCSH: Computational intelligence. | Cognition.

Classification: LCC Q342 .S48 2016 | DDC 153.901/51--dc23

LC record available at https://lccn.loc.gov/2016032985

British Library Cataloguing-in-Publication Data

A catalogue record for this book is available from the British Library.

Desk Editor: Dipasri

Typeset by Stallion Press

Email: enquiries@stallionpress.com

Printed in Singapore

My father Zelin Shi
My mother Fengpei Jiang

About the Author

 Zhongzhi Shi, Professor at the Institute of Computing Technology, Chinese Academy of Sciences. Fellow of CCF, CAAI. IEEE senior members, AAAI, ACM members. He has wide research interests, mainly including intelligent science, artificial intelligence, cognitive science, multi-agent systems, machine learning, and neural computing. He has been responsible for 973,863 key projects of NSFC. He has been awarded with various honors, such as National Science and Technology Progress Award (2012), Beijing Municipal Science and Technology Award (2006), the Achievement Award of Wu Wenjun artificial intelligence science and technology by CAAI (2013), and the Achievement Award of Multi-Agent Systems by China Multi-Agent Systems Technical Group of AIPR, CCF (2016). He has published 16 books, including *Mind Computation, Intelligent Science, Advanced Artificial Intelligence, Principles of Machine Learning*, and *Neural Network*. He has also published more than 500 academic papers. He presently serves as chair of the machine learning and data mining group, IFIP TC12. Earlier he had served as Secretary-General of China Computer Federation and vice chair of Chinese Association of Artificial Intelligence.

Preface

The grand challenge in artificial intelligence is to build human-level intelligent systems. At present, brain science and cognitive computing are extremely active research fields. European Union, USA, and other nations have set up great research projects, and invested enormous funds research. Intelligence science, which the author advocates actively, is an interdisciplinary subject covering brain science, cognitive science, artificial intelligence, etc. for the creation of intelligence theory and development of brain-like computing technology.

Mind computation is a hot spot of current intelligence science research. Mind refers all spiritual activities of people, including thinking, reasoning, memory, learning, emotion, decision, will, consciousness, and so on. Mind computation is a computing process using psychological symbols. It is the information processing course of the brain. The computational nature of the mind is the bridge and link between human spiritual activity and the artificial system simulation. The computational process of the mind provides a theoretical basis for explaining the behavior of human beings. Through research for a long time, the author has proposed the mind model CAM (Consciousness And Memory) for a general framework of the brain-like computing intelligent systems.

Consciousness and memory play key roles in the intelligent activity of the human brain. At the time of celebrating 125th anniversary of the publication *Science*, 125 most challenging scientific problems were published in the July 1, 2005 issue of the quarter journal. In the next quarter century, people will be committed to research and solving these problems. Question 2 is "what is the biological basis of consciousness?" and question 15 is "how to store and extract the memory". Therefore, the mind model CAM will be developed and perfected with the development of consciousness and memory.

The whole book centers on the mind model CAM and describes the theoretical foundation of mind computation systematically. The book is composed of nine chapters. Chapter 1 is the introduction, which briefly introduces the issues of philosophy, biological basis and computing representation etc. Chapter 2 discusses the criteria of mind modeling and describes the architecture of mind model CAM. Chapter 3 expounds the working mechanism and components of memory, including long-term memory, short-term memory, and working memory. Chapter 4 discusses the mechanism and function of consciousness, from the perspective of engineering, to realize the possibility of consciousness. Chapter 5 discusses the visual perception, which focuses on the perception of objects and spatial perception. Chapter 6 focuses on the neural structure of the motor control, the EEG signal analysis, and kinematic neural coding of motion control especially, and kinematic decision mode. Chapter 7 deals with the processing of psychological language and natural language, and the language cognition will be combined with the psychological language model and neural science. Chapter 8 focuses on learning, including reinforcement learning, deep learning, introspective learning, and brain cognitive data analysis. Finally, Chapter 9 summarizes the latest progress in the brain-like computing and proposes the roadmap for the development of intelligence science.

The research on mind computation is at an initial stage, and some concepts and approaches still remain to be further investigated. I expect this book will provide some fresh perspective and thought in brain-like intelligence to build truly brain-like intelligent systems.

Zhongzhi Shi

Acknowledgment

I would like to take this opportunity to thank my family, in particular my wife, Zhihua Yu, and my children, Jing Shi and Jun Shi, for their support in the course of writing the book. I would also like to thank the Institute of Computing Technology, Chinese Academy of Sciences, for providing a good atmosphere to do research on intelligence science.

This book has summarized scientific achievements of recent years of the Laboratory of Intelligence Science, Institute of Computing Technology, Chinese Academic Sciences, and also contains domestic and foreign research efforts. I would like to acknowledge the especially helpful discussion with McClelland, J. L. (Intelligence and Brain Computing Center, Stanford University), Van Essen, David (St. Louis Branch School of University of Washington), Meier, K. (Heidelberg University of Germany), Rosenbloom, P. S. (University of Southern California), Laird, J. E. (University of Michigan), Eliasmith, C. (University of Waterloo, Canada), Baader, F. (Dresden University Technology), Mitchell, T. M. (Carnegie Mellon University), Forbus, K. D. (Northwestern University), Weng, J. (Michigan State University).

The research works described in this book have been supported by National Key Basic Research Development Program (973) "Cognitive computing model for brain computer collaborative" (No. 2013CB329502), "Content understanding and semantic representation of unstructured information (image)" (No. 2007CB311004); National Natural Science Foundation of China "Cloud computing based massive data mining" (No. 61035003), "Intelligent computing model based on perceived learning and language cognition" (No. 60435010) and other funding.

I am also most grateful to my colleagues and students for their great help, in particular Liang Chang, Xue Han, Qingyong Li, Zhixin Li, Huifang Ma, Gang Ma, Chunqi Shi, Xiaofeng Wang, and Xi Yang. My special thanks to Tsinghua University Press for publishing this book in Chinese in 2015. I am most grateful to the editorial staff and designers from World Scientific Publishing who provided all the support and help in the course of my writing this book.

Contents

Chapter 1

Introduction

In the 21st century, intelligence science, brain science and cognitive science are becoming mainstream disciplines of scientific research. One of the challenges faced by human science is how to understand the relationship between mind and brain. It is also the goal of intelligence science exploration. Mind issue is one of the most fundamental and significant issues of intelligence science research [421]. This chapter focuses on mind-related issues of philosophy, biological basis, computation representation and so on.

1.1 Mind

"Mind" is a polysemous word in English. With respect to substance or body, it means the heart or the spirit. When we talk about sense, it means sanity or normal consciousness. It can also be used as intelligence, understanding, thought, opinion, intention, view, idea, memory and so on. In philosophy, "mind" is generally translated as soul. In intelligence science, "mind" means a series of cognitive abilities, which enable individuals to have consciousness, sense the outside world, think, make judgment and remember things. The mind is a human characteristic, however, other living creatures may also have mind.

The phenomenon and psychological aspects of the mind have long been intertwined. The phenomenon concept of mind is a consciously experienced mental state. This is the most confusing aspect of the mind. The other aspect is the psychological concept of mind, which is a causal or an explanatory basis of behavior. In this, a mental state is defined as a condition where the state plays an appropriate causal role in terms of behavior formation or it at least plays a proper role in terms of behavior interpretation.

In accordance with the concept of phenomenology, mind is depicted by the way it experiences sensations and the sensory qualities of seeing, hearing, etc., while, in accordance with the concept of psychology, the mind is depicted by its behavior. There is no competition between these two mind concepts. None is a correct analysis of the mind. They are different fields of phenomena, both of which are quite real.

A particular mind concept can often be analyzed as a phenomenology concept a psychology concept, or as a combination of both. For example, sensing is best seen as a phenomenology concept in its core meaning. There is a sense that there is a certain sensing status. On the other hand, learning and memory are best viewed as psychological concepts. Roughly speaking, when learning something, it is appropriate for the mind to adjust its capacity to respond to certain environmental stimuli. In general, phenomenological characteristics of the mind are depicted by those subjects with the characteristics. While psychological characteristics of the mind are represented by those roles, which are associated with the causal relation or explanation of behavior.

Soft computing founder Zadeh stated [534] that the role model for fuzzy logic is the human mind. It can emulate human reasoning and its ability to form concepts to provide methods for processing fuzzy information granulation and computing with words. Thus, it plays an important role in real-world fields which utilize partial knowledge, partial certainty, partial truth and approximate expression. Accordingly, it was concluded, "Fuzzy information granulation is an integral part of human cognition. This conclusion has a thought-provoking implication for AI. Without the methodology of fuzzy IG in its armamentarium, AI cannot achieve its goals." Zadeh emphasized fuzzy information processing capabilities of the human mind.

The states of mind refer to psychological states, including faith, ability, intentions, expectations, motivation, commitment and so on. It is an important factor in determining intelligent social behavior and individual behavior. The concept of the human mind is related to thoughts and consciousness. It is the product of human consciousness development at a certain stage. Anthropologists believe that all creatures have some kind of mind. Mind development went through four stages: (a) Simple reflection stage: For example, the pupil shrinks when the eyes are stimulated by strong light, which cannot be controlled by consciousness; (b) Reflex stage: Pavlov's famous experiment showed that stimuli can result in outflow of dog saliva; (c) Tool stage: Chimpanzees can get fruits from the tree using sticks; (d) Symbol stage: It is the ability to use language symbol to communicate with the outside world, which only humans can do. Therefore, in comparison with the animal mind at a relatively early stage, human mind is the product of mind development at the highest stage. The generation and development of *human intelligence* cannot be separated from the symbolic language of mankind.

1.2 Philosophy Issues of Mind

For a long time, people are trying to understand the mind from the perspective of philosophy, religion, psychology and cognitive science, and to explore its unique nature. Many famous philosophers studied this domain, including Plato, Aristotle, Descartes, Leibniz, Kant, Heidegger, Searle, Dennett, etc. Some psychologists, including Freud and James, had also set up a series of influential theories about the nature of the human mind from the perspective of psychology in order to represent and define the mind. In the late 20th century and early 21st century, scientists established and developed a variety of ways and methods to describe the mind and its phenomena in the field of cognitive science. In another field, artificial intelligence began to explore the possibility of the existence of nonhuman mind by combining control theory and information theory. They also looked for the method of realizing the human spirit on the machine.

In recent years, mind philosophy developed rapidly, and has become a fundamental and pivotal subject in the field of philosophy. Earlier, the movement from modern philosophy to contemporary philosophy had gone through "Copernicus revolution" and linguistic philosophy replaced epistemology to become a symbol of contemporary philosophy. Then, mental philosophy became the foundation of contemporary genres. If we say that the solution to the problem of ontology and epistemology cannot be separated from linguistic philosophy, then that of linguistic philosophy depends on the exploration and development of the mental philosophy. For example, to explain the meaning, reference, nature, characteristics of the language, it is definitely required to resort to the intention of the mental state (but it is not the only factor). It is amazing to see the rapid progress in this domain with large number of works, depth and vastness of problems, novel and unique insights, and fierce debates.

The study of mind philosophy is mainly about the form, scope, nature, characteristics, relationship between mind and body, psychological content and its source, and the philosophical reflection [166] on the explanatory model of folk psychology. With the deepening of cognition, mental philosophy has changed or is changing the traditional psychology. As the psychological phenomenon is an important part of the cosmic structure, the newest exploration has touched the fundamental cosmic view, such as collateral, dependence, decision, covariance, reduction, rule and so on. There are indications that the development of mental philosophy will be one of the most important sources and forces of the future philosophy. From this point of view, the philosophy of mind is not a narrow mental knowledge, but a profound domain with stable core, fuzzy boundary, open character and broad future. At present, the focus is as follows:

(1) Mind–body problem

Mind–body problem means the nature of psychological phenomenon and the relationship between the mind and the body. The current debate is mainly concentrated in the reductionism, the functionalism, and the dilemma of realizationism and physicalism.

The problem of the nature is the relationship between the brain and the nervous system. Mind–body dichotomy discusses whether the mind is independent of human flesh to some extent (dualism) and whether the flesh is from physical phenomena and can be regarded as physical phenomena including neural activity (physicalism). It also discusses that the mind is not consistent with our brain and its activity. The other question is whether it is only the man who has the mind, or some or all of the animals and all creatures also have the mind, or whether even a man-made machine would have the mind.

Regardless of the relationship between the mind and the body, it is generally believed that the mind makes the individual subjective and intentional of the environment. Accordingly, an individual can perceive and respond to the stimulation by a certain medium. At the same time, the individual can think and feel.

(2) Consciousness

The consciousness here is in a limited sense, meaning the common awareness, which runs through the human being's various psychological phenomena. Around consciousness, scientists have formed a special and independent research field, some of whom also put forward the concept of "consciousness". There are numerous problems of consciousness, which can be classified into two kinds: "difficult problem" and "easy problem". The former refers to the problem of "experience" that attracts much more attention.

(3) Sensibility

It is the subjective characteristic or phenomenological nature of people experiencing the psychological state of feeling. Nonphysicalists argue that physicalism has been able to assimilate all kinds of counterexamples except the qualia. Sensibility is the new world of the psychological world, a nonphysical thing that cannot be explained by the physical principle. However, physicalists will give that back tit for tat, struggling to move physicalism forward.

(4) Supervenience

It is a new problem and a new paradigm in mental philosophy of referring to the characteristic that psychological phenomenon is interdependent on physical phenomenon. Definitely, it can also be generalized to other relations or attributes, so as to become a universal philosophical category. Throughout its study, people try to further grasp the essence and characteristic of mental phenomena and its status in the cosmic structure. They also want to look for the product of a middle path between reductionism and dualism. All these relate to the crucial problem of decision, reduction, inevitability, psychophysical law in mental philosophy and cosmology.

(5) The language of thought

The language of thought refers to the "machine language", different from the natural language, which is the real medium of the human brain. It seems to many people that natural language has echoism so it cannot be processed by the brain.

(6) Intentionality and content theory

This is an old but new problem, which is the intersection of linguistic philosophy and mental philosophy. Many people think that the meaning of natural language is related to the mental state, and the latter is rooted in the semantic of both language of thought and mental representation. But what is the semantic of language of thought? What is the relationship between it and the function of mental state? What is the relationship between it and the syntactic of psychological statement? All these are the focuses of debates.

(7) Mental representation

Mental representation is the expression of information, which is stored and processed by people. The information is attained when they acquaint themselves with the world and their own. These studies deeply reach the internal structure, operation and mechanism of the mental world.

(8) Machine mind

It is the problem about the "other mind", i.e., is there any other mind except human mind? If it exists, how can we recognize and prove that? What is the basis, reason and process of that? What is the foundation to judge whether the object like robot is intelligent? The debate focuses on the skepticism and analogous argumentation of the "other mind".

The mental philosopher has been arguing about the relationship between the phenomenological consciousness and the brain and mind. Recently, neural scientists and philosophers discussed the problem of neural activity in the brain that constitutes a phenomenological consciousness and how to distinguish between neural correlates of consciousness and nervous tissue? What levels of neural activity in the brain can constitute a consciousness? What might be a good phenomenon for study, such as binocular rivalry, attention, memory, emotion, pain, dreams and coma? What should consciousness know and explain in this field? How to apply tissue relationship to the brain, mind and other relationships like identity, nature, understanding, generation and causal preference? The literature [313] brings together the interdisciplinary discussion of the problems by neural scientists and philosophers.

In 2004, Chinese scholars held the first "Mind and Machine" Seminar in Xiamen. In 2007, the Institute of Artificial Intelligence, the School of Information, Xiamen University, founded the journal, *Mind and Computation*. In October 2014, the 11th "Mind and Machine" Seminar, discussed consciousness issue from different angles among philosophy, brain science, psychology, linguistics, neuroscience, psychiatry and artificial intelligence. The conference set three themes: philosophy of consciousness, science of consciousness and project of consciousness.

Experimental philosophy [239] is a new concept in the 21st century. In just over a decade, like a powerful cyclone, it shook the philosophers' dream about the rationality of traditional research methods and sparked a reflection on philosophical methodology. With the heated debate, its influence spread around the world rapidly. In order to promote the development of experimental philosophy in China, the first Experimental Philosophy Seminar with the 11th "Mind and Machine" Conference was held. The subject was "Experimental Philosophy — China and the World", which included the comparison of methodology between experimental philosophy and traditional philosophy, the philosophical reflection on experimental philosophical movement, the research progress, the interdisciplinary research, the research between Chinese and Western cultures and experimental philosophy, and the cultivation of special talents.

1.3 Biological Basis of Mind

Human brain is the most complex material in the world. It is the physiological basis of human intelligence and mental activity. Brain science studies the relationship between brain structure and function, the relationship between brain and behavior, the relationship between brain and mind. It also studies the evolution of brain, biological composition, neural network and its law. The function of the nervous system and brain is to receive information from both internal and external environments, and to process, analyze and store the information and then to control the body to make proper response. Therefore, nervous system and brain are two kinds of information processing systems.

Computational neuroscience uses mathematical analysis and computer simulation to simulate and study the nervous system at different levels: from the real biological physical model, their dynamic interaction and neural network, to the brain tissue and quantification theory of neural type calculation. From the calculation perspective, it tries to understand the brain and study nonprocedural, adaptability aspects, the brain's style of processing information, in order to explore new information processing mechanisms and ways for developing the brain. Its development will have an important influence on intelligence science, information science, cognitive science and neuroscience.

Computational neuroscience research has a long history. In 1875, the Italy anatomist Golgi made out a single nerve cell using the staining method. In 1889, Cajal founded the neuron theory and argued that the nervous system was composed of relatively independent nerve cells. Based on Cajal's neuron theory, Sherrington proposed the concept of synaptic connections between neurons in 1906 [413]. Lapique presented the integrate-and-fire neuron model in 1907. In the 1920s, Adrian proposed the nerve action potential. In 1943, McCulloch and Pitts proposed the M–P neural network model [306]. In 1949, Hebb came up with the rules of neural network learning [2006]. In 1952, Hodgkin and Huxley proposed the Hodgkin–Huxley model [215], describing the changes of cell's current and voltage. In the 1950s, Rosenblatt proposed the perceptron model [382]. Since the 1980s, the research of neural computing has made progress. Hopfield imported Lyapunov function (called the "computational energy function") and gave out the criterion of network stability [216], which can be used for associative memory and optimizing calculation. Amari did a lot of research on the basis of neural network theory, including statistical neural dynamics, neural field dynamics theory and associative memory, especially some foundation work in information geometry [11].

Computational neuroscience research tries to reflect the following basic characteristics of the brain: (a) Cerebral cortex is a large and complex system connecting a wide range of regions; (b) Calculation of the human brain is built on the basis of simulating parallel processing in large scale; (c) The human brain has strong fault tolerance and associative ability and is good at generalizing, analogizing and promoting activities; (d) The brain function is restricted by congenital factors, but acquired factors like experience, learning and training play an important role, suggesting that the human brain has strong self-organization and adaptivity. A lot of human intelligent activities are not carried out by logical reasoning, but by training.

At present, the understanding of how the human brain works is still superficial. Brain science research has become the hotspot in the current world. The European Commission announced in January 28, 2013 that the human brain plan was elected to "New Flagship Technology in the future" projects. It also established a special

R&D program, with 1 billion euros for R&D funds in the next 10 years. The project plans 200 interdisciplinary scholars of 80 top research institutes to interpret human emotion, consciousness and thought united by more than a million cranial nerves. These complex operations will be achieved through a supercomputer simulation in multi-layer phenomenon. The U.S. President Barack Obama announced a significant program with 3-billion-dollar investment on April 2, 2013. This program intends to carry out the research on the activity map and consciousness of human brains within the next 10 years. It was officially named "Brain Research through Advanced Innovative Neurotechnologies (BRAIN)" program. National Institutes of Health, Defense Advanced Research Projects Agency and National Science Foundation will participate in the study together, hoping to find out the treatment for Alzheimer's disease and other related diseases of the brain.

1.4 Intelligence Science Issues of Mind

In order to explore the fundamental theory of intelligence, especially the mechanisms of the mind, literature [421] proposed the interdisciplinary subject "Intelligence Science" in 2003. It is composed of brain science, cognitive science, artificial intelligence and studies the basic theory and implementation technique of intelligence. At the molecular level, cellular level and behavior level, brain science includes research in the mechanism of human brain intelligence, establishing brain model to reveal the nature of the human brain. Cognitive science is the study of human perception, learning, memory, thought, consciousness and other human brain mental activity processes. Artificial intelligence research imitates, extends and expands human intelligence, realizing machine intelligence through artificial methods and technology. With the help of crossover study, it hopes to explore new concepts, new theories, new methods and create a new era of intelligence science.

Modern cognitive science is supported by six related disciplines: philosophy, psychology, linguistics, anthropology, computer science and neuroscience. Research on the human cognition forms the six core branches of cognitive science first: Cognitive Philosophy, also known as mind philosophy, studies cognition from the human mind process, including consciousness, thought, understanding, inference and logic; cognitive psychology, an important branch of cognitive science, studies the detection, processing, acquisition and memory of information in the early stages, also known as the information processing psychology. In recent years, connection theory and multi-functional system theory have become the main theory of cognitive psychology; cognitive linguistics is an important basic subject of cognitive science, having gone through the first generation of Chomsky's rationalism and psychologism. Now, the second generation is empiricism represented by Lakoff, suggesting that cognitive linguistics is changing the linguistic foundation of cognitive science; cognitive anthropology studies the influence of different culture on cognition from culture and evolution; cognitive computer science, known as artificial intelligence, is the most successful field of cognitive science but faces new challenges. It needs to learn from human intelligence and understand human intelligence again; cognitive neuroscience utilizes modern science and technologies, including computed tomography (CT), positron-emission tomography (PET), nuclear magnetic resonance (NMR) and functional magnetic resonance imaging (fMRI) to study the physiological function of brain cognition and a series of new cognitive science theories were proposed.

In the early 1960s and 1970s, Newell and Simon studied the way humans deal with various problems and proposed the problem space–computational model (PSCM), which can describe the process [336] of problem solution. Newell and Simon analyzed task environment and intelligent beings' possible behavior, leading them to put forward the concept of problem space and its hypothesis: The problem space is the basis of reasoning, solution and decision [335]. The PSCM tries to refine the basis of the problem space, so as to become the basis of cognitive structure.

In 1987, according to the PSCM's framework, Newell *et al.* presented a general problem–solution structure called Soar [250] hoping that all weak methods could be implemented in the structure.

Soar is the abbreviation of "State, Operator and Result", which means that the basic principle of the method is to make the operator work on the state and achieve new results. Soar is a theoretical cognitive model, which is not only from the perspective of psychology for modeling human cognition, but also from the perspective of knowledge engineering for proposing a general problem–solution structure. Its learning mechanism is to acquire a general knowledge of search control from the external experts' guidance. External guidance may be a direct recommendation or a direct simple question. The system transforms the high-level information given by external guidance into internal representation and learns about the search block.

Production memory and decision-making process form the processing structure. Production rules are stored in the production memory and its decision of search control is divided into two stages. The first stage uses all rules in working memory in parallel, determining the priority and deciding which part of the context to change and how to change. The second stage is decision-making: determining the part and object in the stock context to change.

Components of Soar are called objects, including state, state space, operator and target. All of these objects are stored in a library, called Stock, divided into four parts.

In addition, there is the current context which is divided into four parts. Each part of the context can store one element of the corresponding parts of Stock at most. For example, the state part of the current context can store a state of Stock, called current state and so on. A portion of the current context may be empty regarded as an undefined part at that time. For example, if there is no operator to work on the current state, the operator of the current context is not defined. Why are state and state space divided into two separate parts? This is because in the process of solving the problem, it is possible to change the form of the problem, so as to move from one state to another.

Another famous cognitive system is adaptive control of thought (ACT), which was proposed by the American psychologist Anderson in 1976 [16]. It was named ACT-R in 1993. The general framework of the ACT production system is composed of three parts: declarative memory, procedural memory and working memory.

(1) Declarative memory: A semantic network with different activation intensity composed of interconnected concept.
(2) Procedural memory: A series of procedural memory of production rules.
(3) Working memory: It contains the current activated information.

The model of human cognition above is still very superficial. To further study the mind, it faces the following scientific issues in Intelligence Science.

1.4.1 Working mechanism of brain neural network

The brain is a network of neurons, and the connection among the neurons depends on synapse. The neuron is composed of a special neural network to exert brain's function. The interaction plays a key role in achieving stable equilibrium, resolving complexity and processing information of neural circuit functions. At the same time, the receptors and ion channels in the neuronal membrane are very crucial for controlling neuron excitability, regulating synapse function and the dynamic balance of various neurotransmitters and ions. Understanding the structure of the brain's neural network and the formation mechanism of complex cognitive function is the basis in understanding the brain, its development and utilization.

In a sense, the cognition and behavior of human beings are the embodiments of the brain function, and they coordinate the performance of the activities in the nervous system. Cognition and behavior depend on the nervous system, especially in the human brain. Therefore, in order to understand the nature of cognition and behavior, it is a non-negligible and irreplaceable part to explain the mechanism of molecules, cells and neural circuits in the cognitive process. The joint research of cognition, behavior and related molecule, cell and circuit, the combination of macro- and microdimensions, is also an important mode and strategy in the development of brain and cognitive science at present and in the next 20 years. The questions are: How is the neural network formed? How can we construct the central nervous system? In the process of neural network formation, the study of nerve cell differentiation, neuron migration, synapse plasticity, neuron activity and neurotransmitter, ion channel, neural circuit and information integration, will provide a powerful neurology basis for the calculation and research of neural network.

1.4.2 Perception process and perception theory

Perception is the process of people's sensation and awareness of objective things. Sensation is the human brain's reflection of an object's individual attributes that directly act on the sense organs. An object has many individual attributes, such as color, sound, smell, taste, temperature, etc. When these individual attributes directly act on the eyes, ears, nose and tongue, they cause vision, hearing, smelling, taste and tactual changes in the brain. From the view of information processing, sensation is the process of transforming information to the human brain such that the human brain receives the information.

Awareness is the human brain's reflection of objective things' entirety that directly acts on the sense organs. For example, seeing a red flag and hearing a song are awareness. In the process, the human brain is involved in information processing with various sensory experiences, and interprets things. From the perspective of information processing, awareness is the human brain's organization and interpretation of sensory information.

The expression and integrality of perceptual information, and the organization and integration of perception are the basic problems in research. So far, four kinds of perception theories have been established:

(1) The constructivist's study focuses on the factors of learning and memory, arguing that all perception is influenced by people's experiences and expectations.
(2) Gibson's ecology concentrates on all inherent context information in the stimulation mode suggesting that perception is direct without any reasoning process, intermediate variable or association.
(3) The Gestalt theory explores that the whole is greater than the sum of its parts, laying particular stress on the nativism factor of perceptual organization.
(4) The action theory emphasizes the feedback effect of percipient's action in his environment.

1.4.3 Memory

Memory is past experience. It can produce accurate internal representation in brain, and extract, utilize them correctly and efficiently. Memory involves the acquisition, storage and extraction of information, which determines the synergy of different brain regions. In the formation stage of initial memory, the brain is required to integrate multiple dispersed features or combine multiple knowledge organizations, so as to form the unified representation. In space, the memory with different characteristics may be stored in different brain regions and neurons; and in time, memory is divided into three classes, short-term, middle-term and long-term memory. Extraction is required to focus, monitor and verify in order to select the relevant information effectively and suppress the irrelevant information. The control of memory process and related neural mechanism has become a hot scientific problem. The in-depth study of memory's neurophysiological mechanism can not only improve people's understanding of their intelligence activities, but also provide theoretical basis or reference for the establishment of efficient and intelligent information processing system.

Memory can be divided into many types, such as visual, olfactory, spatial memory even linguistic memory. Different memory systems have corresponding specific brain structures. In the development of different stages of memory formation, there is mutual support and transformation between different memory systems, meaning that its coordination is the neural basis of animal intelligence and adaptation. So, the neural mechanism of its formation and operation is an important scientific problem.

The study on the structure and function of working memories has great significance in understanding the nature of human intelligence. In 1974, Baddeley and Hitch, based on the simulation experiment of short-term memory disturbance, proposed "3-system" concept of working memory, using "working memory" rather than "short-term memory" [44]. Baddeley believes that working memory refers to a system that provides temporary storage space and processing of necessary information for complex tasks like understanding of speech, learning and reasoning, which can store and process information at the same time. This is different from short-term memory that only emphasizes storage function [44]. Working memory is divided into three subcomponents: central executive, visual processing system and phonological loop. A large number of behavioral studies and neuropsychological evidence show the existence of three subcomponents, and the related structure and function of working memory are constantly enriched and perfected. People find that the working memory is close to language comprehension ability, attention and reasoning. Working memory may be the answer to intelligence.

1.4.4 Learning

Learning is not only a basic cognitive activity, an accumulation of experience and knowledge, but also the process of grasping and understanding front–back relation outside in order to improve the performance of system behavior. Learning theory is the research and interpretation of essence, process, and rules of learning along with the various constraint conditions of learning. In the course of studying the learning theory, because of different philosophical basis, theoretical backgrounds, research methods, a variety of theoretical perspectives and theoretical schools have been formed, including the behavioral school, the cognitive school and the humanistic school.

Some scholars utilize the relationship between stimulus and response to explain learning as a habit formation process, which is to establish an unprecedented relationship between a certain stimulus and an individual. The binding process of stimulus and response is the learning exactly. Therefore, the theory is called the stimulus–response theory, or the behavior school. Learning theories of behavior emphasize the observable behavior, and consider that pleasure or pain results in many times changes in individual behavior. The existing theories, including Pavlov's classic conditioning theory Watson's behaviorist perspective, Thorndike's connectionism, Skinner's operating conditioning theory, and Bandura's social learning theory, can be regarded as representative theories of the behavioral school.

In addition, some scholars do not agree with the view that learning is a habit formation process, emphasizing the role of understanding in the learning process. They believe that learning is a process of individual cognition to the relationship between things in their environment. Therefore, the theory is called cognitive theory. Cognitive school suggests that learning is the change of internal cognition, a more complex process than the stimulus–response binding. The existing theories, including the learning theory of Gestalt school, Tolman's cognitive theory, Piaget's schema theory, Vygotsky's internalization theory, Bruner's cognition discovers theory, AuSubel's meaningful learning theory, Gagnè's information-processing learning theory and constructivist learning theory can be regarded as representative theories of the cognitive school.

Maslow and Rodgers proposed the humanist learning theory, arguing that we must understand the world of behavior in order to understand human behavior. This means, we should view things from the perspective of the actors. In other words, humanistic psychologists try to explain and understand the behavior from the perspective of behavior rather than the observer.

Introspective learning is the learning process of self-reflection, self-observation and self-understanding. With the support of domain knowledge and case base, the system can automatically carry out the selection and planning of the machine learning algorithm for better knowledge discovery of mass information.

Implicit learning is a course of acquiring complicated knowledge unconsciously about any stimulus environment. In implicit learning, people are not aware of or stating the rules that control their behavior, but they master the rules. After the mid-1980s, implicit learning has become the most popular topic in the field of psychology, especially in the learning and cognitive psychology domain, and it has become one of the most important issues that will have a profound impact on the development of cognitive psychology.

The basis of learning neurobiology is the synaptic plasticity change between nerve cells, which has become a very active research field in neuroscience. Synaptic plasticity means that when the presynaptic fiber and its associated postsynaptic cell excite at the same time, synaptic connection will be strengthened. In 1949, a Canadian psychologist Hebb proposed the Hebb learning rule. He assumed that the related synapsis changes in the learning process result in the enhancement of synaptic connection and synaptic transmission. The rule became the basis of connectionist learning.

1.4.5 Cognitive mechanisms of language processing

During the human evolution, the use of language made the function of two brain hemispheres differentiate. Due to the language hemisphere, the humans became different from other primates. Some studies show that the left hemisphere is related to serial, sequential and logical analysis information processing and the right hemisphere is related to concurrent, visual, nonsequential information processing.

Language is a system composed of pronunciation as shell, vocabulary as material and grammar as rule. Language is usually divided into two categories: spoken language and written language. The form of spoken language is the voice while the expression of written language is the figure. Spoken language is far more ancient than the written language. An individual learns spoken language first, and then the written language.

Language is the most complex, the most systematic and the most widely used symbol system. Linguistic signs not only express specific objects, states or actions, but also represent abstract concepts. Chinese language with its unique lexical and syntactic system, writing system and voice tonal system, is significantly different from the Indo-European languages, having a unique style of pronunciation, figure and meaning combination. The concept is the thought form that reflects the special attribute of things, so concept is close to word. The emergence and existence of the concept must be attached to the word. Words can express other things, because people have the corresponding concept in their mind. Therefore, word is the language form of concept and concept is the content of word.

At the three levels of nerve, cognition and computation, the study of Chinese vocabulary gives us a good opportunity to open the door of intelligence. The cognitive psychology of Chinese vocabulary has been studied for many years and has achieved some world-class research results. However, these researches focus on the Chinese characters and vocabulary and need to be further discussed in the higher levels like syntax and sentence processing. The study of the whole speech chain is not enough, especially in the mechanism of the brain's language processing. In the field of intelligent system, China has paid much attention to the processing of Chinese information in computer. It has invested a lot of money to support the R&D of computational linguistics, machine translation and natural language understanding system, getting a number of important results. However, on the whole, there are many outstanding questions about the intelligent processing of language information, which must be based on the research of cognitive science, and it is possible to make a breakthrough guided by the new theory.

In 1991, Mayeux and Kandel proposed a new language information processing model based on the Wernicke–Geschwind model [295]. Language information from auditory input is transferred to the angular gyrus by the auditory cortex, then to Wernicke's area and finally to Broca's area. Language information from visual input is transferred directly from the visual association cortex to Broca's area. The visual and auditory perception of one word are independently processed by different accesses of the feeling mode. Each of these paths independently reaches Broca's area and the high-level region related to language meaning and language expression. The mechanism of language processing for each step in the brain needs to be further studied.

Using the method of mathematics to study language, we need to find out the form, model and formula of language structure, so that the grammatical rules of language can be characterized in a systematic and formal way. In 1956, the famous American linguist Chomsky proposed the formal grammar of language and established the theoretical foundation of language information processing. In the 1960s, he proposed the transformation-generative grammar theory and the concept of surface structure and deep structure. Since then, he devoted himself to the research on proving the psychological reality of Chomsky's syntactic theory, which has become the mainstream in the study of psychological linguistics.

1.4.6 Cognitive mechanisms of thought

Thought is a conscious human brain's self-conscious, indirect and general reflection on the essence and internal regularity of objective reality, showing through implicit or explicit language or action. Thought is endowed by complicated brain mechanism, processing the objective relationship, contact in multilayer, revealing the inherent nature of things. So, thought is an advanced form of understanding.

The main form of human thought includes abstract (logic) thought, image (intuitive) thought, perception thought and inspiration (insight) thought. With scientific abstract concept, abstract thought reflects on the essence of things and the profound development of the objective world, so that people attain much more knowledge through the understanding activity than through the direct perception of sensory organs. Based on the perceptual knowledge, through concept, judgment and reasoning, abstract thought can reflect the nature of things and reveal internal relation.

Image thought is a kind of basic thought that utilizes certain form, method and tool to create and describe the image, based on the experience and memory of objective image system transmitted by image information. Figurativeness is the most basic characteristic of image thought. Image thought is a reflection of things' image. Its form is a figurative concept such as image, intuition and imagination. Its expression includes a perceptible graphics, figure, pattern or figurative symbol. Image thought's figurativeness makes it have vitality, intuition and integrity. Different from the abstract thought that processes end-to-end information, image thought can invoke more image material and combine them together to form a new image, or jump from one image to another. Its information processing is not sequential but parallel, in two or three dimensions. It can make the subject of thought quickly grasp the overall problem. Image thought is one of the breakthroughs in the research of intelligence science.

The study of thought is very important in the understanding of human's cognitive and intellectual nature, which will have significant scientific meaning and application value. By studying the thought model at different levels, we can research its rule and method, so as to provide principle and model for the new intelligent information processing system.

1.4.7 Intelligence development

Intelligence is the integration of various stable psychological characteristics, which ensure that people successfully carry out the cognitive activities. It is composed of five basic elements, including observation, memory, thinking ability, imagination and attention. It is not the simple additive result of five basic factors, but the integration of various factors, whose core is thinking ability. Therefore, intelligence is a complete and unique psychological structure composed of these five factors. In intellectual activity, these psychological compositions are interrelated and the intelligence level is different individually.

Intelligence can be regarded as a comprehensive cognitive ability, including learning ability, adaptive ability, abstract reasoning ability, etc. This kind of ability, based on heredity, is formed by the individual with the influence of the external environment. It is performed through absorbing, storing and utilizing knowledge in order to adapt to the environment.

A human's intelligence is not innate, but a process of formation and development. Generally, individual intelligence develops with age. Based on his long-term clinical research in the field of children's intellectual development, like language, thought, logic, reasoning, concept formation and moral judgment, Piaget created the intellectual development theory with the core of the intellectual development stage theory.

1.4.8 Emotion system

As one of the founders of artificial intelligence, Minsky proposed the relationship between computer intelligence and emotion: The problem is not whether the intelligent machine can have emotion, but how a machine can be smart without emotion. Therefore, letting the computer have feelings makes the computer more intelligent. Picard defines "affective computing" as "the computation related to emotion, triggered by emotion or that can affect emotion" [364]. Affective computing is one of the foundations of building a harmonious man–machine environment, aiming to give the computer the ability of recognition, understanding, expression and the ability to adapt to human emotion, improving the quality and efficiency of man–machine interaction.

At present, affective computing research is widely popular. MIT affective computing research group developed a wearable computer to identify human emotion in real situations. They also studied the emotional feedback mechanism in man–machine interaction and developed a robot capable of expressing emotion using body language. The Swiss government has set up the Emotion Science Center, where psychology, neuroscience, philosophy, history, economics, sociology and law cooperate with each other for the research and application of affective computing. The Japanese Ministry of Education had supported the funding of "the Science, Psychology Research of Emotional Information" key project. University of Geneva established the Emotion Research Laboratory, and University of Brussels established a research group of the emotional robot. University of Birmingham carried out the study of "Cognition and Emotion". Affective computing is also included in the study planning by EU. In addition to providing a new way for the development of artificial intelligence, the study of affective computing has important value in understanding a human's emotion as well as a human's thought. The research on emotion itself and the interaction between emotion and other cognitive processes is becoming a hotspot of intelligence science.

1.4.9 Consciousness

Consciousness is the organism's awareness of objective things like outside world, mental activity and physiological activity. Consciousness is the core problem of intelligence science research and the brain mechanism of consciousness is the common research object at various levels of brain science. The human consciousness is mainly carried out in the brain. In order to reveal the scientific law of consciousness and construct the brain model of consciousness, we not only need to study the cognitive process, but also study the unconscious cognitive process (the process of automatic information processing) and the procedure of two kinds of processes transforming one another in the brain. At the same time, self-consciousness and situation awareness is also a problem that needs attention. Self-consciousness is the individual's awareness of their own existence, the self-perceived organization system and the way that the individuals view themselves, including three kinds of psychological elements: self-perception, self-experience and self-control.

Situation awareness is the internal representation of individuals facing the ever-changing external environment. In the complex and dynamic environment of social information, situation awareness is the key factor that influences people's decision and performance. The cognitive principle of consciousness, the neurobiology basis of consciousness and the information processing of consciousness and unconsciousness are the problems that we need to focus on.

1.4.10 Mind model

Mind is all of human being's spiritual activities, including emotion, will, feeling, perception, image, learning, memory, thought, intuition and so on. Modern scientific method is frequently utilized to study the form, process and law of human irrational psychology and rational cognition's integration. The technology of establishing the mind model is often called the mind modeling, with the purpose of exploring and studying the mechanism of human's thoughts in some ways, especially the human information processing mechanism, which also provides the design of corresponding artificial intelligence system with new architecture and technology.

Mind problem is a very complex nonlinear problem, and the mind world must be studied by the modern scientific method. Intelligence science is researching on a psychological or mind process, but it is not a traditional psychological science. It must look for the evidence of neurobiology and brain science, so as to provide a certainty basis for the mind problems. The mind world is different from the world described by modern logic and mathematics: The latter is a world without contradiction, while the mind world is full of contradiction; logic and mathematics can only use deductive reasoning and analytical methods to understand and grasp the possible world, while the human's mind can master the world in many ways such as deduction, induction, analogy, analysis, synthesis, abstraction, generalization, association and intuition. So, the mind world is more complex than the latter. Then, from the poor, noncontradictory, deductive and relatively simple possible world, how can we enter the infinite, contradictory, using multiple logic and cognitive approach, more complex mind world? This is one of the basic issues in intelligence study.

In the 20th century, the combination of biology and information resulted in the formation and development of bioinformatics. The results of bioinformatics studies on the related genes not only have important theoretical value, but can also be applied directly to industrial and agricultural production and medical practice. In the 21st century, the combination of biology and information will promote the development of intelligence science. In December 2001, National Science Foundation and Ministry of Commerce came forward to organize experts and scholars from government departments, research institutions, universities and industries for gathering in Washington and discussing Converging Technologies to Improve Human Performance problem. Based on the papers and conclusions presented in this conference, in June 2002, National Science Foundation and the United States Department of Commerce together came up with 468 pages of Converging Technologies Report [382]. The report suggests the following: cognitive science, biology, information science and nanotechnology are developing rapidly at present; the combination and integration of four science and related technologies is the convergence technologies, whose union is nano-bio-info-cogno in simplified English, NBIC for short. Cognitive domain includes cognitive science and cognitive neuroscience. Biological area includes biotechnology, biomedical and genetic engineering. Information field includes information technology and advanced computing and communications. Nano area includes nanoscience and nanotechnology. The integration of each discipline's research methods and technology will accelerate the development of intelligence science and related disciplines, and ultimately promote the development of society. Converging technology development will significantly improve life quality, enhance and expand people's ability, the whole society's innovation ability and the level of national productivity. Besides, it will also strengthen the country's competitiveness and provide a more powerful guarantee for national security.

1.5 The Structure of Mind

In 1967, Project Zero, which was initiated by the U.S. philosopher Goodman, was set up in Harvard Graduate School of Education. It attracted a large number of psychologists and educators. In 1970s, led by famous psychologists Perkins and Gardner, Project Zero thoroughly became a psychological program. The developmental psychology study group, which was led by Gardner, mainly studied the developmental characteristics of using symbols between normal children and talented children. And they wanted to discuss a great question: *The nature of human's potential and its actualization.* Their study results were assembled as the book *Frames of Mind* in 1983 by Gardner [167].

Gardner studied a large amount of individuals, including talented individuals, child prodigies, patients with brain damage, mentally deficient people with special abilities, normal children, normal adults, experts in different fields and people in different cultures. Analyzing the studies, he came up with a new theory about intelligence along with its properties and structures — *The Theory of Multiple Intelligences.* The theory considers intelligence as "a biopsychological potential to process information that can be activated in a cultural setting to solve problems or create products that are of value in a culture", which does not emphasize on IQ. Intelligence is not inherent. Every individual has the capacity to improve and extend his or her own intelligence. Every individual's intelligence is multivariate, and it has its own distinctive combination of intelligence. According to *The Theory of Multiple Intelligences*, there are eight kinds of intelligences:

(1) Linguistic intelligence

Linguistic intelligence is the capacity to use spoken or written language effectively. It involves not only the susceptibility to both spoken and written language, but also the capacity of learning a language and achieving certain goals by using the language.

(2) Logical–mathematical intelligence

Logical–mathematical intelligence is the capacity for effectively using numbers and reasoning. It involves the capacity of logical reasoning and calculation. Capacities for analyzing with a scientific method and critical thinking are also involved.

(3) Musical intelligence

Musical intelligence is the capacity to detect, identify, modify and express music. This intelligence includes the susceptibility to rhythm, pitch, melody and timbre as well as the appreciation ability.

(4) Bodily–kinesthetic intelligence

Bodily–kinesthetic intelligence is the capacity to express one's thoughts and feelings with his or her body and to handle objects skillfully. This intelligence includes special physical skills, such as balance, coordination, agility, power, elasticity, speed and capacity caused by sense of touch.

(5) Spatial intelligence

Spatial intelligence is the capacity to sense the visual space accurately and to express what you've sensed. This intelligence includes colors, stripes, shapes, forms, spaces and the susceptibility among them. The abilities to visualize both visual sense and space with one's mind eye as well as to identify the direction in a spatial matrix are also included.

(6) Interpersonal intelligence

Interpersonal intelligence is the capacity to sense and distinguish others' moods, feelings, temperaments and motivations. It includes the susceptibility to facial expression, voice and action, as well as the capacity to identify the hints of different interpersonal relationships and to react to those hints. Individuals who have interpersonal relationships have the capacity to understand one's purpose, motivation and aspiration, and to cooperate with others effectively.

(7) Intrapersonal intelligence

This refers to having a deep understanding of the self and being able to act properly. This intelligence includes the capacities of knowing oneself, realizing one's own moods, intentions, motivations and temperate, as well as possessing self-discipline and self-esteem. It involves self-understanding and the ability to find an effective work pattern based on one's own characteristic, and to adjust one's own life.

(8) Naturalist intelligence

Naturalist intelligence refers to interests in natural scene (plants, animals, minerals, astronomy, etc.), showing strong care for nature, an acute observation and identification capacity. It helps identifying whether a certain individual is a member of the group (or species) and in recognizing the members in certain species. In addition, it helps to find out the existence of other species that are similar to them and show their formal or informal relations by using figures or grams.

Shearer studied how to improve the cognitive ability by applying multiple intelligences. He started to write Multiple Intelligences Developmental Scales (MIDAS) in 1987. Apart from the US and Canada, MIDAS has been promoted in many countries, including Spain, France, China, South Korea, Singapore, Malaysia and Indonesia. The Theory of Multi-Intelligences is not merely an intelligence theory, but a philosophy of education.

1.6 The Modularity of Mind

The modularity of mind, which studies the modularization of mind, aims at explaining how the mind operates. The research hypothesis is that the human mind consists of multiple modules that are functionally independent and interact with each other. Based on the hypothesis, the modularity of mind studies the common mechanism of the human's mind.

In mid-1950s, cognitive psychology treated mind process as an information processing task. It studied the internal mechanism of mind activity widely and thoroughly and significant achievements were made during the studies. The cognitive psychology proposes to study the structure and process of mind's activity itself and to study the mind's mechanism beyond the physiological mechanism.

The US mind philosopher Fodor proposed a hypothesis on language of thought and a theory on modularity of mind. "How can we express our thought?" Based on the question, Fodor published the book, *The Language of Thought* in 1975 [147]. What is the language of thought? According to Fodor's view, the medium of thought is an innate language that is distinct from all spoken languages and is semantically and expressively complete. The so-called Mentalese is supposed to be an inner language that contains all of the conceptual resources necessary for any of the propositions that humans can grasp, think or express — in short, the basis of thought and meaning. Fodor's hypothesis can be divided into four parts:

(1) Representational realism: Thinkers have explicit representational systems; to think a thought with a given content is to be appropriately related to a representation with the right meaning. In fact, it is also the main function which the thought language represents. Otherwise, the representation of the internal mind will detach with the external objects and situations.
(2) Linguistic thought: It is also the main part of language of thought's hypothesis. It refers to the associativity between syntax and semantics in the representational system. In short, it can clearly express the meaning of proposition by using syntactic function of the representational system.

(3) Nativism: It refers to the inherent existence of a mental language that is processed by humans since there is a special gene which can determine it.

(4) Semantic completeness: It refers to the fact that this language is expressively semantically complete. In fact, this characteristic infers the associativity between syntax and semantics. Otherwise, the syntactic operation will become meaningless and this syntax will not be able to express the thought.

Mind Philosopher Aydede believes that "LOTH is an empirical thesis about the nature of thought and thinking. According to LOTH, thought and thinking are done in a mental language, i.e., in a symbolic system physically realized in the brain of the relevant organisms." [32] Aydede presents the main characteristics and levels of the language of thought hypothesis. He believes that it can be characterized as the conjunction of the following three theses:

(1) Representational Theory of Mind (RTM): It includes *Representational Theory of Thought* and *Representational Theory of Thinking*.

(2) Mind representations: It includes two parts. First, the representations of the system have a combinatorial syntax and semantics. Second, the operations on representations are causally sensitive to the syntactic/formal structure of representations defined by this combinatorial syntax.

(3) Functionalist materialism: It is easy to understand. The subject and the object of representations can be realized by the physical properties and the neurophysiological properties.

According to Kaye, specific mental representations occur in similar language representational systems. Productivity, systematicity and semantical combinatorial are the primary features that should be considered [234]. There are two advantages of emphasizing that the language of thought is linguistic. First, if the language of thought is linguistic, it can be analyzed from the language structure and can give an expression of mental operation. Second, if the language of thought is led by linguistic rules, the referential relations between mind and world can be ensured. Based on this concept, the productivity and systematicity of language will be ensured. If we extend the concept of productivity, we can find that it has something to do with language structure. In other words, we can make many sentences with different meanings by knowing a few sentence patterns. It is the productivity of language structure that makes it happen. When it comes to systematicity, it involves the operation of thought. The reason why propositional system can be calculated is that there is an integration among the propositions. And it exactly becomes the basis of logical operations of mental representations. However, there is a question: How to combine both syntax and semantics? If we admit that the concept is the basic unit of semantics rather than the proposition, then how does thought put those concepts that have semantic content into the proper structures? In other words, how does semantic content combine with the syntax structure? It is a very difficult question.

As a functionalist, Fodor must offer mental representations an operating mechanism and a platform. Only by having those requirements can language of thought hypothesis have a firm foundation of ontology. In 1983, Fodor published *The Modularity of Mind* [149]. Fodor believes that mind's cognitive system can functionally be divided into three systems: sensory system, input system and central system. The sensory system can translate the stimulation signal into a corresponding neural signal. The input system can set the operating range for central mechanism by encoding the mental representations. It is the medium between perceived inputs and central cognitive mechanism. Central system's function is to establish the faith and to think. Only the input system has the modularity while the central system does not.

Fodor points out that there are nine properties in modularity of mind: domain specificity, obligatory firing, limited accessibility, fast speed, informational encapsulation, shallow outputs, fixed neural architecture, special damage mode and characteristic ontogeny [149]. Domain specificity and information encapsulation are the basic and main properties of the modularity. Fodor believes that domain specificity refers to a module that only processes the special information corresponding to its function. It only "calculates" the specific inputs which are restrained "from bottom to top" (those from the sensory system). It only focuses on the information that is related to its special processing capacity.

Informational encapsulation is the key property of a system. Fodor believes that informational encapsulation is the essence of the modularity. The other parts of mentality can neither influence nor understand the internal operation of a module. The higher level of representations cannot give feedback to the lower level of analysis. The operation of the input system is independent of any other background information. It is immune from the subject's expectation, faith and function.

Fodor presented *The Modularity of Mind*, which makes a broad impact on psychology, especially on cognitive psychology. Some psychologists speak highly of it. It brings a brand new research method and content to psychology. However, parts of the theory were queried by some psychologists, which can fulfill some of the views from the modularity of mind. These are the views:

(1) Module is both innate and acquired

"Innateness" is the key factor of the module, which is Fodor's view. He points out that the module system is closely linked to the neural hardware structure. Module, which is the "hardware", has a fixed neural system, and innately has an original "modular" structure. A. Karmiloff-Smith believes the relativity of innateness and posteriority as well as that inheritance and environment are the fundamental theoretical problems in developing psychology. Just like most of the developing psychologists, Karmiloff-Smith emphasizes the importance of interaction between innateness and posteriority as well as between inheritance and environment. Giving a counterexample of human's skill-learning process, she believes that not all the modules are innate and lots of modules are formed during the modularized process [233]. She believes that infants' input type of mind calculation is limited due to the limited amount of innate domain specific modules. However, as time goes by, some brain circuits are selected to calculate in certain domains, so that it can form a relative-encapsulation module.

(2) Central system has modularity

Fodor believes only the input system has modularity while the central system's typical function is to enhance faith by reasoning in domain specificity. So, the central system has no modularity. Some researchers argue that the input system has modularity while the central system is non-modularity, which implies that the essence of mind is non-modularity. What's the point of modularity of mind and its corresponding theories? So they propose a thorough and integrated theory of modularity of mind, in which there is a modular relation between low-level process and high-level process (or between input system and central system). Both properties and processes of the mind or the cognitive system totally have modularity.

(3) Modularity exists not only in sensory-input system, but also in other psychological systems

Fodor's modularity of mind is discussed in the category of the cognitive system. But some researchers, especially those in evolutionary psychology, believe modularity is not only the property of sensory-input system, but also, and mainly, the property of mind mechanism.

1.7 The Society of Mind

Kelly, the founding editor of the magazine *Wired* in the United States, in 1994 wrote a book named *Out of Control: The New Biology of Machines, Social Systems and the Economic World* [235]. This book has 24 chapters, of which the third chapter is "Machine with An Attitude." Kelly pointed out, "Natural evolution insists that we are apes; artificial evolution insists that we are machines with an attitude.... As humans, we find spiritual refuge in knowing that we are a branch in the swaying tree of life spread upon this blue ball. Perhaps someday we will find spiritual wholesomeness in knowing we are a link in a complex machine layered on top of the green life. Perhaps we'll sing hymns rhapsodizing our role as an ornate node in a vast network of new life that is spawning on top of the old." Kelly praised Minsky, "He spared no effort in advocating loading intelligence of human brain into computers." Minsky advocated, "We need to endow machines with wisdom, so that they have self-consciousness!" [235].

Minsky published a book named *The Society of Mind* [318] in 1985. In this book, he pointed out that intelligence does not exist in the central processor, but is generated from the collective behavior of many machines closely linked to each other with a special purpose. Minsky indicated that the mind is composed of many small processors called agents. Each agent can only do simple tasks and has no mind. Intelligence is generated when these agents constitute the society. A variety of mind phenomena emerge from the highly associated interactive mechanism of the brain. Dennett said, "Meaning emerges from distributed interaction of lots of little things, none of which can mean a damn thing."

The Mobile Robot Laboratory, which was founded by the famous US Robotics expert Brooks, has developed a whole set of distributed control methods, including the following:

(1) Do simple things first.
(2) Learn to do simple things accurately.
(3) Add a new level of activities on the results of simple tasks.
(4) Do not change simple things.
(5) Let the new level work as accurately as simple levels.
(6) Repeat the above steps and analogize unlimitedly.

The set of methods embodies "getting smart from dumb things."

In *The Society of Mind*, Minsky presented that it was possible to transplant consciousness into the machine. At least since the 1930s, people have known that there is movement of electrons in the human brain. This implies that people's memories and even personalities may exist in the form of electronic pulses. In principle, it is possible to measure these pulses by utilizing some electronic equipment and copying them from another medium (e.g., the memory base). As a result, as the "I" in nature, the "I" in the memory can be stored in the computer memory. The memory can be copied, transported and digitally operated. It becomes the digital show of the true self. Thus, even in the computer, "I" can still get the same experience as obtained previously. With the digitalization of self-consciousness, it can be copied and removed from the memory. In addition, there is a reverse process, in which the self-consciousness outside our bodies, including self-consciousness of other people and self-consciousness processed by machines, can be moved into the self-mind to form new self-consciousness.

1.8 Automata Theory

1.8.1 Overview

Automata theory explores the mathematical model, including the function and structure of digital systems as well as the relationship between them. These models have played a very important role in many application areas of computer science. For example, the theory of finite automata is applied to text processing, compiler programming and hardware design. Context-free grammar is applied to programming languages and artificial intelligence. As a mathematical concept in automata theory, an automaton is an abstract model of discrete systems. The following part will give a general overview of the development of automata theory.

In 1936, British scientist Turing published his famous paper "On Computable Numbers, with an Application to the Entscheidungs problem" [493]. In this paper, he presented an abstract computational model to accurately define computable functions, which initiates the abstract theory of automata. From 1935 to 1938, the Soviet mathematician Shostakov and American mathematician Shannon independently applied Boolean algebra to the analysis and synthesis of relay contact circuit. Their established switching network theory, also known as logic automata theory, initiated the structure theory of automata.

In 1943, American neurophysiologists McCulloch and Pitts proposed the self-organizing theory of automata [306]. They assumed that the neuron model followed the "all-or-none" law. When the number of simple neurons is big enough and their connection weights are properly set, McCulloch and Pitts have proved that the constructed nets with synchronous operations can compute any computable function in principle. It has a significant impact on von Neumann. In 1945, von Neumann successfully designed and developed the Electronic Discrete Variable Automatic Computer (EDVAC) [504], which was called von Neumann machine. von Neumann machine has become the main mode of modern general purpose electronic digital computer.

In 1948, von Neumann compared all kinds of artificial automata with natural automata and proposed to establish the general theory of automata for summarizing common laws. He also proposed the self-organizing theories including the self-reproduction theory and the self-repair theory. von Neumann made a detailed analysis on modern automata and pointed out that the function of automata was transforming and processing information. As the foundation of automata theory, the theory of sensitive automata is a statistical one [505]. In 1956, the famous book *Automata Studies* edited by Shannon and McCarthy was published [408].

Automata theory developed rapidly during the 1950s and 1960s. A variety of abstract automata were proposed, including finite automata [237], infinite automata [315], probabilistic automata [408], fuzzy automata [391], cellular automata [507] and so on. Based on the McCulloch–Pitts neural network model, Kleene presented the concept of regular events in 1951. He proved that regular events can be represented by neural networks or finite automata and that all the events represented by neural networks or finite automata must be regular events.

In 1956, Chomsky drew the thought of finite state Markov process from Shannon's work. He utilized finite state automata in characterizing the language syntax. Moreover, he defined the finite state language as a language generated by the finite state grammar. The early studies initiated the research area of "formal language theory". It defined formal language as a sequence of symbols using algebra and set theory. It also established the correspondence between formal language and automata [84]. Chomsky first proposed a context-free grammar in natural language research. The research work skillfully combines mathematics, computer science, and linguistics together and greatly promotes the study on language problems using mathematical methods.

From a mathematical point of view, Chomsky proposed the new definition of the language, which can be applied to both natural language and artificial language of logic and computer programming theory [85]. In the paper "Formal Properties of Grammar", he uses one section to introduce programming language and discuss the compiler issues related to programming languages. In the research on the formal grammar of composition and structure [85], these problems were put forward from a mathematical point of view, and explored from the perspective of theoretical computer science. Paper [89] proposed, "We will be concerned here with several classes of sentence-generating devices that are closely related, in various ways, to the grammars of both natural languages and artificial languages of various kinds. By a language we will mean simply a set of strings in some finite set V of symbols called the vocabulary of the language. ...Regarding a grammar as specifying programming language, the string would be called programs." Chomsky placed the natural language and programming language on the same plane. From the perspective of mathematics and computer science, he investigated the basic concepts of linguistics (e.g., "language" and "glossary") with a unified point of view, and got a highly abstract understanding.

Due to the development requirements of the theories of pattern recognition, artificial intelligence, and large systems, automata have attracted more and more people's attention. Many scholars have attempted to establish a unified theory of automata. Therefore, the algebraic theory of automata has made great progress. Much academic research is focused on the category theory of automata. Automata theory is mainly composed of the abstract theory, the structure theory and the self-organization theory.

1.8.1.1 *Abstract theory*

Within the abstract theory of automata, we take the automaton as a mathematical system and study its general mathematical properties without considering its structure and the specific form of its input and output signals. For the abstract theory, we only study state changes and generated output signals of automata when the input signals arrive. From a mathematical point of view, the abstract theory of automata is the machine algorithm theory, in which the possibility is restricted in advance. It is the foundation of modern programming theory.

In 1936, Turing proposed that the Turing machine can be used to define the classes of computable function, which initiated the research on the abstract theory. The abstract theory contains much important research content, including the semigroup theory (formed in the 1960s), the algebraic theory (developed later) and the category theory of automata. In the late 1950s, some researchers proposed that automata can be taken as a speech recognizer. It established the correspondence between formal language and automata. They utilized automata in generating recognition programs of corresponding grammar. As a result, they achieved grammar compiling and generated a compiler of the compiler. As the model of computation process, automata can be used to study the theories of algorithms, programs and computational complexity. This is also within the category of the abstract theory, for which the main development direction is to establish the unified theory of automata.

1.8.1.2 *Structure theory*

The structure theory of automata is the further development of the abstract theory of automata. Research focuses of structure theory are on automata integration, methods of constructing automata from cellular automata and methods of encoding cell signal transmitted in input and output channels.

Due to the urgent need for designing novel computers, the structure theory of digital automata has been developed rapidly. General-purpose electronic digital computer can be regarded as a class of digital automata within a wider range. The structure theory of digital automata involves issues related to Boolean algebra, propositional calculus, predicate calculus and the information theory. For digital automata, the structural theory is directly related to the integration issues, including abstract integration, combination integration, structure integration, component integration and reliability integration.

There are two categories of methods for constructing automata using cellular automata: (a) Cascade method. It is to use serial, parallel and hybrid methods to link a number of cellular automata into one automaton. This automaton can have tree, star and net topologies. The inverse problem of the cascade method is the cascade decomposition problem. The cascade decomposition of automata is equivalent to the decomposition of large-scale systems. For the finite state automaton, the cascade decomposition problem is related to its semi-group structure. Accordingly, this problem can be resolved by the semi-group structure theory and the group divisibility theory. The cascade decomposition theorem of finite state automata has been proven. (b) Neighborhood connection method. It has been developed into cellular automata theory now. It has been widely applied to parallel computers and the LSI with the consistent structure.

1.8.1.3 *Self-organization theory*

The self-organization theory is the result of the development of the abstract theory and the structure theory of automata. Self-organizing theory involves many aspects, including neural networks, artificial intelligence, pattern recognition and so on. Sometimes, it also utilizes the achievements of cooperative learning, the dissipative structure theory, the super-cycle theory, etc. The pioneering work on neural networks, proposed by McCulloch and Pitts in 1943, has a profound influence on the development of the neural network theory. It promoted the early research work on the self-organization theory. Fu, Tanaka, Santos *et al.* applied the concept of fuzzy neurons to automata theory in 1969 [391]. It promoted the new development of research on the neural network theory. Moreover, people began to utilize the automata theory to study the behavior of complex and large systems.

In the study on the self-organization theory, von Neumann proposed a series of creative concepts. In 1948, he presented the concept of self-breeding machine. He proposed the iterative array of associated finite automata for studying pattern recognition of characters. In 1952, he made his famous redundancy technology, which organized a highly reliable automaton out of unreliable automata with a large number of parallel connections. This technology developed into the fault-tolerant automata theory later. Based on the theory, he proposed a new concept of von Neumann cell space, which developed into the cellular automata theory later.

1.8.2 Finite state automata (FSA)

FSA is an abstracted computational model for studying the calculation process of limited storage and some language classes. A finite state automaton has a finite

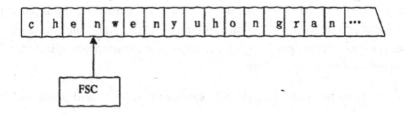

Fig. 1.1. The physical model of finite state automaton

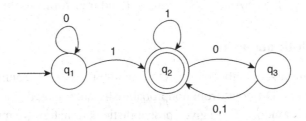

Fig. 1.2. Finite state automata

number of states, which can migrate to zero or more states. A finite state automaton can be represented as a state transition diagram. An example of the physical model of FSA is shown in Figure 1.1.

A finite state automaton can be defined as a 5-tuple,

$$FA = (Q, \Sigma, \delta, q_0, F),$$

where

Q is a finite set of states;
Σ is the alphabet or a set of symbols on the input tape;
$q_0 \in Q$ is the initial state;
$F \subset Q$ is a set of accept states (end states);
δ is the state transition function of $Q \times \Sigma \rightarrow Q$, which is

$$\delta(q, x) = q'$$

and means that the state will transform from q to q' if symbol x is scanned.

Figure 1.2 gives an example of a finite state automaton. There are three states, including q_1, q_2 and q_3, where q_1 and q_2 are the start state and accept state, respectively. Herein, the lines with arrows represent the state changes.

When the finite state automaton accepts an input string 1101, it will process and give the output of accept or reject. The string 1101 is loaded sequentially from left to right. Starting from the state q_1, the next state is decided by the input symbol. The last input symbol directs the finite automaton to the final state. If the final state is an accept state, the output is accepted, otherwise the output is rejected. We can list the handling procedure as follows:

(1) Starting from the state q_1, the FSA accepts the input 1 and transforms to the state q_2.
(2) In the state q_2, the FSA accepts the input 1 and stays in the state q_2.
(3) In the state q_2, the FSA accepts the input 0 and transforms to the state q_3.
(4) In the state q_3, the FSA accepts the input 1 and transforms to the state q_2.

1.8.3 Probabilistic automata

Probabilistic automata mainly do research on automata with environmental or internal random factors. Different from nonprobabilistic automata, the action of probability automata is random. For a given probabilistic automaton, we must first define the conditional probability function of automaton's next action (e.g., state transition, the output of a letter, rewriting letters, etc.), when the automaton is in a state with an input letter. Then, we give probability distribution of initial states of the automaton. Generally, the probability distribution is represented by a random vector $\pi = (\pi_1, \pi_2, \ldots, \pi_n)$, where each π_i is non-negative and the sum is equal to 1. Herein, n is the number of automaton state, and π_i represents the probability of the automaton in the ith state at the beginning. Probabilistic automata are used to represent communication channels and digital circuits with unreliable elements.

1.8.4 Cellular automata (CA)

CA provide a powerful method for simulating complex phenomena including self-organizing structure. The basic idea of the cellular automata model is as follows: There are many complex structures and processes in nature. In the final analysis, it is caused by the simple interaction of a large number of basic constituent units. Therefore, we probably simulate the evolution process of any complex thing using a variety of cellular automata.

In 1948, von Neumann proposed the self-organization theories including the self-propagation and the self-repair theories. He found two different methods for giving genetic description of organism:

(1) Interpret instructions to construct descendants;
(2) Copy data to the created description copies without interpretation and then pass data to descendants.

von Neumann gave constructive proof of the possibility of the self-replicating machine. He required the self-replicating machines to have calculated universality and construction universality.

The cellular automaton is developed on the concept of von Neumann cell space. It consists of a large number of identical cells, which are connected with each other according to the neighborhood association method and can form a variety of topology configuration patterns. Within the cellular automaton, a cell is a finite state automaton. Each cell can obtain input information from neighboring cells or the external environment. The output information of each cell can be passed to an adjacent cell or the external environment. Thus, the cellular automaton can be used to study the architecture of parallel computers and the design of large-scale integrated circuit (LSI).

The state set of the simplest one-dimensional cellular automata has two elements $\{0, 1\}$. The neighborhood of a cell is a region of radius 1. This means, each cell has the left and the right cells as its neighbors. Since the state set only has two states $\{0, 1\}$, any cell and its two neighbors totally have eight kinds of the state combination, including 111, 110, 101, 100, 011, 010, 001 and 000.

Assuming cell c_i is currently considered, it is in the state $s_{i,t}$ at time t, its two neighbors are in states $s_{i-1,t}$ and $s_{i+1,t}$, at time t, and the next state of c_i is $s_{i,t+1}$ at time $t + 1$. Accordingly, the transition rule can be represented by the following function:

$$s_{i,t+1} = f(s_{i-1,t}, s_{i,t}, s_{i+1,t}),$$

where $s_{i,t} \in \{0, 1\}$ for any i and t.

Considering the cellular automaton in two-dimensional space, we use V to denote a set of cell states the element v_0 of which is a stationary state. If we define f as the function $V^*V^* \ldots {}^* V \rightarrow V$ satisfying $f(v_0, v_0, \ldots, v_0) = v_0$, (V, v_0, f) is called m-neighbor cellular automaton with the transition function f. After establishing the following transition rules, we can construct the growth of the cellular automaton in two-dimensional space.

$$
\begin{array}{llll}
f(0, 1, 2, 7, 6) = 1 & f(7, 0, 0, 0, 2) = 3 & f(2, 0, 0, 2, 3) = 7 & f(1, 0, 2, 3, 2) = 6 \\
f(0, 1, 2, 3, 2) = 1 & f(3, 1, 2, 1, 1) = 0 & f(7, 0, 2, 1, 2) = 0 & f(1, 0, 7, 2, 2) = 3 \\
f(4, 0, 2, 0, 2) = 2 & f(2, 0, 0, 2, 4) = 0 & f(2, 0, 2, 6, 2) = 4 & f(2, 0, 0, 1, 4) = 2 \\
f(4, 0, 2, 6, 2) = 2 & f(2, 0, 4, 6, 2) = 4 & f(1, 2, 4, 2, 6) = 4 & f(4, 1, 2, 2, 2) = 0 \\
f(2, 0, 0, 4, 2) = 0 & f(2, 0, 2, 4, 2) = 0 & f(2, 0, 1, 2, 4) = 2 & f(6, 0, 2, 4, 2) = 4 \\
f(7, 0, 0, 2, 1) = 0 & f(0, 1, 2, 7, 2) = 4 & &
\end{array}
$$

The first argument of the function f above represents the state of the center cell. The following four arguments are the states of four neighbors in clockwise direction in order to generate a minimum of 4-bit digits. Herein, we give the propagation process of signal 0 and signal replication at time T, T+1 and T+2.

$$
\begin{array}{ccc}
2\,2\,2\,2\,2\,2 & 2\,2\,2\,2\,2\,2 & 2\,2\,2\,2\,2\,2 \\
1\,0\,3\,1\,1\,1 \rightarrow & 1\,1\,3\,1\,1\,1 \rightarrow & 1\,1\,0\,1\,1\,1 \\
2\,2\,1\,2\,2\,2 & 2\,2\,1\,2\,2\,2 & 2\,2\,0\,2\,2\,2 \\
\,2\,1\,2\,\,* & *\,2\,1\,2\,*\,* & *\,2\,1\,2\,*\,* \\
\,2\,1\,2\,\,* & *\,2\,1\,2\,*\,* & *\,2\,1\,2\,*\,* \\
\text{Time T} & \text{Time T} + 1 & \text{Time T} + 2
\end{array}
$$

In 1968, the Dutch biologist Lindenmayer proposed dynamic cellular automata, which are called L-systems [278]. For dynamic cellular automata, cells can be divided into daughter cells, regardless of initial position of the cells in the array. The format of dynamic association has attracted the attention of theoretical biologists, which can be used as the model for growth and development of life.

1.9 Turing Machine

In 1936, British scientist Turing submitted his famous paper "On Computable Numbers, with an Application to the Entscheidungs problem". He put forward an abstract computation model, which could accurately define the computable function. In this pioneering paper, Turing gave "computable" a strict mathematical definition and put forward the famous "Turing machine". The Turing machine is an abstract model, rather than a material machine. It can produce a very easy but compute-powerful computing device, which can compute all the computable functions that you've ever imagined. Its physical structure is similar to the finite state machine's. Figure 1.3 shows that the Turing machine has a finite state controller (FSC) and an external storage device that is an infinite tape which can randomly extend rightwards. (The top left is the tape head, identified as "⊢".) A tape is divided into cells. Each cell

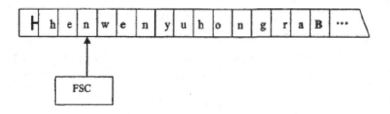

Fig. 1.3. Turing machine's physical model

can be blank or contain a symbol from some finite alphabet. For the sake of convenience, we use a special symbol **B**, which is not in the alphabet, to represent the blank symbol. FSC interconnects with the tape by using a head that can read and write. Generally, symbol **B** will be marked at the right.

At any moment, FSC is in a certain state. The read/write head will scan every cell. According to the state and the symbol, the Turing Machine will have an action for changing the state of FSC. It will erase the symbol on cells which has been scanned and write a new symbol for it. (The new symbol might be the same as the previous one, which makes the cell content stay the same.) The read/write head will move left or right at one cell or the head is stationary.

The Turing machine can be defined as a 5-tuple

$$TM = (Q, \Sigma, q_0, q_a, \delta),$$

where

Q is a finite set of states;

Σ is a finite set of alphabet symbols on the tape, with the augmented set $\Sigma' = \Sigma \cup \{B\}$;

$q_0 \in Q$ is the initial state;

$q' \in Q$ is an accept state;

δ is the state transition function of $Q \times \Sigma' \to Q \times \Sigma' \times \{L, R, N\}$, which is

$$\delta(q, x) = (q', w, \{L, R, N\}).$$

Generally, the transition function (or rules of the Turing Machine) will be marked as

$$\langle q, x, q', w, \{L, R, N\}\rangle,$$

where $x, w \in \Sigma \cup \{B\}$ means that if symbol x is scanned, the state will transform from q to q' and the new symbol w will be written. The read/write head will move to the left (L), right (R), or not move (N).

1.10 Computational Theory of Mind

In philosophy, computational theory of mind is one of the most significant frameworks in studying the human mind. The computationalism theories of mind were formed when we took this framework to study the unique phenomenon of the human mind. This theory is named as "the computational theory of mind". In 1960, Putnam published the book *Minds and Machines*. It discusses the heart–body-related mind and analogical problem of the Turing machine. He firstly came up with the computational theory of mind [377]. Putnam explicitly pointed out that the universal Turing machine is an abstract machine, which has nearly infinite implementations in physics. In his 1967's papers *The Nature of Mental States* [378], he treated mental state as the same as functional state. He believed pain is not a state of brain, meaning, it is not the physical–chemical state of brain (or even the entire neural system). He believed it is the functional state of the entire organism. And he further explained the view of multiple-implementation of mental state. Putnam believed the different states of the Turing machine assign the corresponding functional states, which can correspond with different mental states. Harnish pointed out in his book *Minds, Brains, Computers: An Historical Introduction to the Foundations of Cognitive Science* that "Compared to Turing", it is more likely Putman who made a key step from "intelligence of computation" to "computational theory of intelligence" [202].

Block and Fodor expended the thought of Putnam's Turing machine (or probabilistic automata) to the general computing system [57]. Fodor expanded and refined the computational theory of mind, discussing the language of thought [147], modularity of mind [149], folk psychology and analysis of propositional attitude [150], narrow content and intentional conclusion [152], finishing the construction of the computational theory of mind. Fodor tried to regulate the relations, operations and representations that the computational theory of mind involves.

(1) In the computational theory of mind, relations are computable.
(2) In the computational theory of mind, operations are computable.
(3) In the computational theory of mind, representations are computable.

With regard to the relations and operations of computation, Fodor believes it must follow the formal constraints. He considers that thinking and other mental processes mainly consist of computations operating on the syntax of representations [148].

Representations also have semantics. In other words, representations have "mental contents", because they express the propositions and point to something. The general computational theory of mind can be expressed as follows:

(1) Cognitive state is a computational relation of computational mental representations with specific contents.
(2) Cognitive process (the change of cognitive state) is a computational operation of computational mental representations with specific contents.

So far, there has been a general computational theory of mind. As a digital computational theory of mind, there are two reasonable conditions required:

(1) Structures: One of the additional restrains of the digital computational theory of mind is that the computational structure (memory and control) must be digital.
(2) Representations: The other additional restrain of digital computational theory of mind is that the representations must be digital. This is the reason why it is called the digital computational theory of mind.

According to these two conditions, we can state the basic digital computational theory of mind by using the digital regulations of the computational theory of mind as follows:

(1) Cognitive state is a computational relation of computational mental representations with specific contents.
(2) Cognitive process (the change of cognitive state) is a computational operation of computational mental representations with specific contents.
(3) The structures and representations of computation are digital.

The computational theory of mind mainly includes the following discussions of some basic questions:

(1) Establish various feature models by applying computational model and algorithm. Try to actualize these models into all kinds of intelligent machines, making them into artificial "minds".
(2) In order to understand the features of mind, we provide them with a one-way metaphor according to features of some computer product models. We try to reveal the nature of mind, so as to achieve a scientific and reasonable recognition of the human mind.

Philosopher Thagard from University of Waterloo, Canada is an advocator of computational theory of mind. He considers the principle of cognitive science as "Computational Representational Understanding of Mind" (CRUM). Mind functions are like a computer, the most appropriate understanding of thought is to view it as representational structures of mind and the computational programs that run on those structures [477].

Regarding some basic facts of explanations of mind, representations and computations might not be totally appropriate. However, judging various successes of the knowledge representational theory, we will see that inspiring progresses of understanding the computational representations of mind are made. Without any doubt, computational representational understanding of mind is the most theoretically and experimentally successful way to study the mind so far. Although not everyone agrees with the computational representational understanding of mind, it is not difficult to tell from authoritative academic journals of psychology and other areas that computational representational understanding of mind is the main method for cognitive science.

The success of computational representational understanding of mind benefits from drawing an analogy between it and the computer. Analogy is very useful for putting forward a new science thought. To analogize computers to minds provides us with a powerful way to understand the mind, which is overwhelmingly better than analogizing telephone switchboards to them. Readers who have computer science background must be familiar with conclusions, such as that a computer program consists of data structures and algorithms. Modern programming languages include a series of data structures, such as a string "abc", a number "3", and other more complicated structures like tables (ABC) and trees. An algorithm–mechanical program can be defined as an operation on various data structures. For instance, pupils learning long division are learning an algorithm that operates on digits. The other simple algorithm can be defined as the transposition of a table such as turn (ABC) into (CBA). This program can consist of two smaller subprograms. First, we pull out an element from a table. Then, we put this element into the beginning of the other table, where the computer will get (A) first, then (BA), till (CBA). Similarly, the computational representational understanding of mind has mental representations, which is similar to a data structure. Computer programs are similar to algorithms. "Running programs = data structures + algorithms" is similar to "c = mental representations + computational procedures". That is the orthodox analogy of cognitive science, though it twists an analogy which is based on human brains a little bit.

Connectionists put forward a new understanding on representations and computations. They analogize data structures to neurons and it connects while analogizing algorithms to activations of neurons and spreading activations. Such an understanding is a complicated three-dimensional analogy among minds, brains and computers. Each of the three can provide the other two with a new understanding. There is no unique model about computation of mind because different computers and programming methods suggest different operation modes of mind. The computers which most of us use today are serial processors, executing one instruction at a time. But our brains and some newly developed computers are parallel processors, executing multiple instructions at a time.

If you have much knowledge of computer, it will be natural for you to understand the mind from the perspective of computers, even though you disagree that mind is fundamentally a computer. Readers who have never written a computer program but used a recipe can consider another analogy. A recipe usually includes two parts: a material table and a set of instructions of deploying the materials. A dish is the result of applying cook's instructions to materials while an executable program is the result of applying algorithms to data structures like digits and tables. As well as a thought is the result of applying computational programs to mental representations. It is farfetched to analogize thoughts to recipes because the material is not a representation, while a cook's instructions need to be interpreted by people.

Guided by the principle of computational representational understanding of mind, mind researchers have six representative accesses: logic, rules, concepts, analogies, images and connections. Logical access concentrates on "Why will people reason?" Their arguing point is "Do people have mental representations that are similar to propositions in logic? Do people have deductions on operating such propositions and inductive programs? Does applying deductions and inductive programs to propositions produce reasoning?" Maybe, we should admit that the representation and computation of logic access is stronger than any other. But so far, its psychological plausibility is controversial. People know nothing about the neurological plausibility in logical rules. Connectionism's unique explanation of mind is that "People have representations which are formed by the connecting units of active and inhibitory neurons. People have handlers of spreading activation and the way of correcting connection. People also have the behavior of applying the program of spreading activation and learning the units to produce intelligences." Although connectionism can explain a lot of psychological phenomena, and artificial neural network and human brain's structure have something in common, when compared to the real brain neural network, it is clear that there is a big gap between them.

Thagard comes up with five criteria of evaluating the model of mental representations: representational power, computational power, psychological plausibility, neurological plausibility and practical applicability. A high representational model should be able to express more information on the power of solving the problems, the power of learning and the power of language. A computational power of the system refers to the capacity for finishing high-efficient computations. Psychological plausibility requires a good mental representational theory, accounting for the humans not only all kinds of capacities qualitatively, but also for the matching degree with its corresponding psychological experiment results. Neurological plausibility refers to the fact that a good mental representational theory should correspond with neuroscientific experiment results. A high-applicability representational theory should have application value in practice.

Although the representational–computational research principle makes progress in cognitive science, it has seven challenges. Thagard has concluded as follows [477]:

(1) Brain: The computer model of mind neglects the essential differences between biological brain's activation mode and the Turing machine's operation mode.

Human's thought might not be the standard computation. Brain works in different ways.

(2) Emotions: There is growing evidence that emotions are not the antithesis of the rational ability of human glory. Rationality is not completely independent of emotions. On the contrary, emotions play an important role in human's thoughts and decisions because emotions provide the rational thinking activity with motivation, direction, value and meaning.

(3) Consciousness: Consciousness is the "crown" of evolution and the development of the biological mind. However, due to the specificity of the subjective feeling, conscious experiment became the taboo of science study for a long time. This situation started to change dramatically in the 1980s. This change marked the prosperity of modern "consciousness study".

(4) Body: Human being is a living organism. The nature of mind is embodied. The body's formation of organism and interaction between the body and the environment determine the way of cognizing the organism and feeling the world. Edelman believes that it is not enough to say mind involves body. The most important thing is to understand how to involve.

(5) World: Physical environment is not the pure supplier of sensory stimulation. World is the object and we can get hold of its regulations. World is everything we think and every clear-sensory natural environment and field. Is analytical unit of cognition merely a cognitive agent or a bigger cognitive system including environment? What is the border between mind and environment? These questions are beginning to be discussed and studied under the topics of cognitive system, distributed cognition, expanded cognition and expanded mind.

(6) Power system: Mind is a computational procedure with power system's emergent property and function, rather than with symbols. Power system's outlook of cognition requires a paradigm shift.

(7) Society: All the intelligent beings are social beings. Human's sociality is full of cultural connotations. Apart from specific biological basis, human's cognition and mind are developing in social culture. Leaving the specific stimulations of social culture, human's mind will stop at an extremely limited biological level.

These seven challenges incisively reflect the disagreements and correcting trends of the traditional mind model from various kinds of paradigm's competition of cognitive science in the recent 20 years. According to this, Thagard's response is not disruptive, but constructive. In his opinion, there is no need to abandon CRUM regarding its difficult situation. An expanded and complementary solution should be taken. The most important thing is to emphasize the effects of multilateral integrations: First, we need an interdisciplinary integration of philosophy, psychology, artificial intelligence, linguistics, neurosciences, anthropology, even biology and power system theory. Second, we need to promote the integration in experiments. For instance, solving the consciousness problem not only needs to value experimental data of both behavioral sciences and neurosciences, but also pay attention to the data from our conscious experience. Similarly, the data of molecular biology will be more and more important. Third, it is a theoretical integration brought by computational thought and simulation.

Chapter 2

Mind Model CAM

In this chapter, we focus on the mechanism of consciousness and memory which is guiding us to create the mind model "Consciousness And Memory (CAM)", which can be taken as a general framework of brain-like intelligent systems.

2.1 Introduction

As you know, a typical computer consists of processor, memory, file system and I/O devices. Memory stores data and programs; processor executes the program instructions to implement basic operations, which transform the data in memory and determines the next instruction to be executed. To enable the computer system to not only coordinate work efficiently and reliably, but also provide users an easy way to have a computer-friendly environment, the computer operating system usually has processor management, memory management, device management, file management, operations management and other functional modules, which cooperate together to accomplish all the functions of the operating system.

In the view of mind computation, mind system structure is similar to computer architecture. It has memories, processing and control components, data representation, and input/output devices. These components play the roles of supporting knowledge representation, acquisition, and knowledge utilization for the general computers to achieve goals. The key difference between the structure of the general computer system and the mental system is that the computational task of the computer is fixed and independent, while in the mind system the knowledge of the intelligent agent is interrelated and can be increased by learning. Although learning amends and supplies the new knowledge to the mind system, it does not change the architecture of the mind system. Moreover, through learning, the way of knowledge change is defined. System architecture can change gradually, but the time scale of

43

these changes is much greater than a single task. While people can build a mind system architecture to solve a specific problem, a mind system structure is designed to create a general and automated agent which can solve a variety of problems, by using a wide range of knowledge. For the mind system architecture, one of the major challenges is to coordinate many of the functions of intelligent systems, such as perception, reasoning, planning, language processing and learning, in order to build a unified mind system.

In 1936, Turing proposed the Turing machine model [493]. This is the first landmark of mind model research, which lays the theoretical foundation for a modern computable computer. After nearly 80 years of research, several mind models were proposed.

Simon is one of the founders of artificial intelligence and computer-based mathematical theorems. After the 1950s, Simon's research underwent a major shift and gradually turned to the field of cognitive psychology and artificial intelligence. Simon considered economics, management, psychology and other disciplines that study the same subject, which is "people's decision-making process and the problem-solving process." To truly understand the decision-making process within the organization, it is necessary to have a profound understanding of humans and their thinking processes. Therefore, with the help of computer technology, Simon and Newell began to do experiments to simulate human behavior, psychology and artificial intelligence, which led to a new research field named cognitive research. Simon believes that there is correspondence between the human thought process and computer running process, as essentially both are procedures involving processing of series of symbols. Thus, computers can be used to simulate the working of the human brain. He even boldly predicted that what the human brain can do can also be accomplished by the computer. The advent of artificial intelligence software, such as "Elementary Perceiver And Memorizer (EPAM)" and "General Problem Solver (GPS)", partly proved Simon's prophecy. In 1958, Simon and Newell proposed the heuristic problem-solving method [456]. In [136], a method for purpose analysis is introduced, which recursively accomplishes the subgoals to achieve problem-solving.

In 1976, American psychologist Anderson proposed a theoretical model to interpret the mechanism of information processing in the human brain, which is referred as adaptive control of thought (ACT) model [16]. The original meaning of ACT is "adaptive control thinking". Anderson integrated human associative memory (HAM) model with the structure of the production systems to build a production system to simulate the human cognitive process. This has a great significance in the study of artificial intelligence. The ACT model emphasizes the control process of high-level thinking and has developed the following version of systems:

1978: ACT
1993: ACT–R
1998: ACT–R 4.0
2001: ACT–R 5.0
2004: ACT–R 6.0

In the 1970s, Newell and Simon assured humans as an information processing system, known as a physical symbol system [332]. They emphasize the object of study is a specific material system. Physical symbol system consists of memory, a set of operations, control, inputs and outputs. It takes input using sensors and such inputs are usually modified to produce new expressions. Well, its external behavior is composed of output, which is a function of the input. In 1976, Newell and Simon made a physical symbol system hypothesis [335] that forms the theoretical basis for traditional artificial intelligence.

Based on similarity between the human brain and the computer in functionality, Atkinson and Shiffrin proposed a process-oriented cognitive model in 1971. In 1982, based on the process-oriented cognitive model, cognitive-memory-based information processing model was proposed.

The pioneering work on neural network-based mind modeling was started by McCulloch and Pitts [306]. In 1986, Rumelhart and McClelland published the book *Parallel Distributed Processing: Explorations in the Microstructure of Cognition* [302]. The book plays an important role for promotion of mind modeling based on neural network.

In the early 1980s, Newell and Rosenbloom believed that by acquiring knowledge about the model from the task environment, the system performance could be improved. Chunks can serve as model basis for human behavior simulation. By observing the problem-solving process, experience chunks can be obtained. These chunks can be used to substitute various subgoals in complex processes and significantly improve the performance of the system for problem-solving. This laid the foundation of empirical learning. In 1987, Newell, Laird and Rosenbloom proposed a general problem-solving structure Soar [250], hoping to be able to make all kinds of weak methods in the structure of this problem-solving.

Agent is able to support the interaction with dynamic environment and collaborative work execution. In 1993, paper [330] proposed an agent-based mind model CIRCA to ensure real-time dynamic response. In 1998, Franklin and his colleagues developed the IDA system [156]. In 2006, Franklin and Baars worked together to introduce the global workspace theory of consciousness into the IDA [157], and later the IDA concept was spread out into the LIDA cognitive model. Langley made the Icarus mind system [253]. The system follows five general principles of advanced intelligent systems: (a) perception and action is the basis of cognition; (b) concepts and skills have different cognitive structure; (c) long-term memory is organized in a hierarchy; (d) hierarchies of skills and concepts are formed in a cumulative way; (e) long-term memory and short-term memory have a good correspondence.

In 1997, Sun Rong proposed Clarion [472]. Clarion is a hybrid structure. It uses a symbolic component to process explicit knowledge reasoning and uses connective component based on connectionism to handle implicit knowledge. The implicit knowledge learning process is achieved through neural networks, reinforcement learning, or other machine learning methods. The combination of symbolic method and subsymbolic methods is very powerful, which possesses the metacognitive and motivational modules. However, it still misses episodic memory, learning and curiosity, etc.

In 2002, the US National Institute of Standards and Technology proposed a 4D/RCS (Real-time Control Systems) architecture for unmanned ground vehicle systems [6]. In the architecture, an unmanned ground vehicle (UGV) system software definition and an organization reference model are provided. Furthermore, it defines approaches for multi-task analysis, planning, execution and coordination. Hierarchical sensor processing and real-time execution are involved. 4D/RCS is not learning-based, but is based on the fixed structure and algorithms to simulate the qualitative structure of the corresponding portions of the brain and then use it to enhance learning.

In 2012, Eliasmith of University of Waterloo, Canada, led the research team to develop a unified network of artificial brain semantic pointer architecture called Spaun [135]. Spaun is made up of 2.5 million of neurons, which simulates a series of intracranial subsystems, including the prefrontal cerebral cortex, the basal ganglia and the thalamus. Spaun can perform eight types of tasks, including drawing, counting, answering questions and performing fluent reasoning.

The European Commission on January 28, 2013 announced that the Human Brain Project is selected as the "Future Emerging Technology Flagship project" and will get 1 billion euros in R&D funding in the next 10 years. It plans to invite more than 200 scholars from 80 of the world's leading interdisciplinary research units to jointly interpret the trillion neurons linking human emotions, consciousness and thought. These complex computations will be implemented by the supercomputer-based multi-layer simulation.

On April 2, 2013, US President Obama announced the beginning of "the use of advanced and innovative neural brain research technology (BRAIN)" major program, to conduct a research program to unveil the mysteries of the human brain. It is expected that $3 billion would be invested in the next 10 years. The research scientists named this research program as "brain activity map" project.

2.2 Criteria of Mind Modeling

There is a close relationship between research on brain-like computation of intelligence science and mind computation theory. Generally, it utilizes a model to indicate how the mind works and understands the working mechanism of the mind. In 1980, Newell firstly proposed the criteria of the mind model [331]. In 1990, Newell described the human mind as a set of functional constraints and proposed 13 criteria for mind modeling [334]. In 2003, based on Newell's 13 criteria, Anderson put forward the Newell test [24] to determine the knowledge requirement of the human mind implementation, as well as conditions for better working. In 2013, a paper [433] analyzed the standard mental model. In order to build a better mind model, the following is a comprehensive discussion on mind modeling standards.

2.2.1 Agile action

Newell reiterated that the first criterion is "behavior plays a role of environment function flexibly" in the book "Unified Cognitive Theory" [334] published in 1990. In 1980, Newell was very clear that this is a universality of computation and is the most important criterion. For Newell, the flexibility of human behavior indicates computing universality. Environmental behavior is an arbitrary function. It is clear that this is the computation universality, which, for the human mind, is the most important criterion.

Newell believes that the human mind and the flexibility of modern computers possess same features. He realized that the creation of this ability and the representation of computation universality are in the same difficulty level. For example, the limits of memory prevent the human computation ability to be equivalent to a Turing machine (with infinite tape) and frequent sliding prevents humans to show perfect behavior. However, Newell realized that the flexibility of human cognition should be the same as computation universality. This is similar to the fact that the modern computer is regarded as being equivalent to a Turing machine, even though it has physical limitations and accidental errors.

When the computation universality is the fact of human cognition, even if the computer has a specialized processor, it should not be regarded as opposed to the implementation of a variety of specific cognitive functions. Moreover, it should not be opposed to humans to learn some things that are easier than other devices. Emphasis is on the natural language in the language field, learning the natural language is much easier than the unnatural language. Common artifact is only a small part of the unnatural system. When humans approach universal computation, only a very small part of feasible computable functions is acquired and executed.

Assessment rating: To determine whether a theory is well regulated, it should be relatively straightforward to find out if it is a universal computation. This is not to say that the theory should claim that it would be easy to find all equivalences, or that human's performance will never be wrong.

2.2.2 Real-time

For a cognitive theory, mere flexibility is not enough, it must explain how humans can solve problems under real-time conditions, where "real-time" means the human's time. As people can understand the neural network, cognition increased restrictions. Real-time implies similar restriction on learning and implementation. If you learn something, it takes a life time. In principle, this study process is not good.

Assessment rating: if a theory has specific constraints which can swiftly deal with the implementation process, then for any particular case of human cognition, whether it is able to make a decision in real-time is relatively insignificant. It is impossible to prove that the theory satisfies all the real-time constraints of human cognition. To know whether it can satisfy all constraints, one must look at the specific situation.

2.2.3 Adaptive behavior

Humans do not just perform amazing mental computations, but they also choose the computation meeting their requirements. In 1991, Anderson proposed two levels of adaptability: one level is the basic system structure process and related forms, providing useful features. The other level is regarding the entire system as a whole, whether its entire computation meets people's needs.

Assessment rating: Newell complained that short-term memory models do not have the adaptive ability. In Soar system, whether real-world behavior functions are permissible is discussed.

2.2.4 Large-scale knowledge base

The key point of human adaption is that humans can access a lot of knowledge. Perhaps, the biggest difference between human cognition and various expert systems is that in most cases human can access necessary knowledge to take action. However, large-scale knowledge can cause problems. Not all knowledge is equally reliable or equivalently relevant. For the current situation, relevant knowledge can quickly become irrelevant. Successfully storing all the knowledge and retrieving the relevant knowledge within a reasonable time may have a serious problem.

Assessment rating: In order to assess this criterion, it is necessary to determine the change of performance according to knowledge scale. Similarly, determining if a theory is well regulated is based on the fact that whether this standard follows a formal analysis. Of course, we should not expect this scale to have no effect on performance.

2.2.5 Dynamic action

In the real world, the problem-solving is not as simple as solving a maze or Towers of Hanoi problem. Changes in the world cannot be as we expected, and they cannot be controlled. Even when we try to control the world with human action, there will be unexpected results. Processing dynamic, unpredictable environment is a prerequisite for the survival of all organisms. Given that the humans have established complexity of their own environments, the need for the dynamic response is a major cognitive problem. Handling dynamic behavior requires theoretical and cognitive theory of perception and action. Context awareness due to the structure of cognitive work emphasizes how the outside world appears [180, 471]. Supporters of this position argue that all knowledge is the reaction to the outside world. This is well comparable with earlier thoughts that cognition can ignore the outside world [94, 95].

Assessment rating: How can one create a system test "accident"? Of course, such a typical laboratory experiment is conducted by the tedious work. These systems need to be inserted into the uncontrolled environment in some testing cases. In this regard, a suite of promising tests cases is carried out in which cognitive intelligence agents are established in the systems and inserted into real or synthetic environment. For example, Newell's Soar system successfully simulates pilots in air force mission. The simulation includes 5,000 agents containing pilots [225].

2.2.6 Knowledge integration

Newell regards this criterion as "symbol and extraction". Newell comments on this standard in his book in 1990: "The mind can use symbols and extraction. We know that, just watch yourself." He seems to never admit that there is a debate on this issue. Newell believes external symbols, like symbols, equations, have little dispute about its existence. He thinks symbols are a specific case of list processing language. Many symbols have no direct meaning. It is different from the effect of philosophy discussion or computation. According to Newell, symbol as grading criteria is impossible to be installed. However, if we pay attention to the definition of the physical symbol, they will understand the rationality of this criterion [334].

Assessment rating: It is recommended that the assessment focuses on whether the theory can generate the combination of ability with which humans perform intelligent activities, such as reasoning, inductive, metaphors and analogies. It is always possible that the manipulation system produces any specific inference, and a limited normal ability of the intellectual combination, otherwise large-scale knowledge is rare. The system should be able to reproduce the mental composition of people daily, which is located elsewhere within the body system. Remote access requirement has constraints of computation systems, which stems from the fact that action is always triggered from local body, coupled with only limited knowledge in limited space, which can be encoded, and the human mind includes a large amount of knowledge. Thus, coding knowledge must be spread out in space, it is stored in the place where process is needed. Symbol is a tool for remote access [334]. Symbols provide a tool for reasoning about the most intimate knowledge of the concept of human reason.

2.2.7 Natural language

Natural language is the basis of human symbol manipulation; on the contrary, it should be assessed to what extent the symbol manipulation is the basis of natural language. Newell thinks that language depends on symbol manipulation.

Assessment rating: As an important part of the test, the community has established a language processing test. It is a bit like reading a message, and answering questions. This will involve parsing, comprehension, reasoning and the past knowledge about the current text.

2.2.8 Consciousness

Newell acknowledged the importance of consciousness for the entire human cognition. Newell lets us consider all the criteria, and not carefully choose one of them to consider.

Assessment rating: Cohen and Schooler edited the book *Scientific Approaches to Consciousness* [96], which contains subliminal perception, implicit learning, memory, and metacognitive processes. It is suggested that the assessment of a theory according to this criterion is to measure its ability to produce these phenomena and explain why they are human cognitive functions.

2.2.9 Learning

Learning seems to be another uncontrollable criterion in human cognition theory. A satisfying cognitive theory must explain the cognitive ability of human beings to obtain their competitiveness.

Assessment rating: Simply asking whether this theory is able to learn is not enough, because people must be able to have many different kinds of learning abilities. It is recommended to take Squire's classification [467] as a measure to determine whether the theory can explain the range of human learning. The main directories of Squire's classification are semantic memory, episodic memory, skills, startup and conditions. It may not be clearly distinct from theory classes and there may be more learning approaches, but this also represents more human learning ranges.

2.2.10 Development

Development is the first of the three constraints that are initially listed by Newell for cognitive system architecture. Although, in the ideal world, people think associated functions and emerging cognitions are fully mature, human cognition is constrained to organism extension and response to experience.

Assessment rating: Similar to language criterion, there are also problems in development progress. It seems there is no good characterization of the entire dimension of human development. Compared with the language, because human development is not an ability, but a constraint, there is no recognized test criterion. However, there are many test methods for child development in the world.

2.2.11 Evolution

Human cognitive ability must be promoted through evolution. There are a variety of content-specific capabilities, such as the ability to detect cheaters [102], or the constraints of natural language [365]. Evolution occurs at a particular time in the history of human evolution. The change of evolutionary constraints is comparison constraint. What is the difference between architecture of human cognition and other mammals? We have confirmed that cognitive plasticity is one of the characteristics of human cognition, as well as other languages have been identified as prescribed features. According to the unique cognitive attributes, what is the human cognitive system?

Assessment rating: Newell thought it difficult to take what evolutionary constraints for representation. Evolutionary constraint grading is a very deep problem, because there is few data on the development of human cognition. From the view of human adaptation to environment (criteria 3), the reconstruction of choice pressure history seems likely to become construction criteria [152]. The best we can do is loosen the theory, taking the evolutionary and comparative methods into consideration.

2.2.12 Brain

The last constraint is cognition realization based on the nervous system. According to a recent research progress, the data of special brain area that can be used to do cognition constraints theory research has greatly increased.

Assessment rating: The establishment of this theory requires enumeration and proof. Enumeration can map the building block of cognitive architecture to the brain structure; Proof is the module of mapping of computational brain structures to cognitive architecture. Unfortunately, knowledge of brain function has not developed to this step. However, there is enough knowledge to partially implement such tests. Even as part of the test, this is quite demanding.

2.3 Cognitive Mind Modeling

So far, there are many mind modelling methods, including symbolic-based model, neural network-based on connectionism mind modeling, agent-based mind modeling, math-based mind modeling, computer simulation-based mind modeling, and hybrid mind modeling. This chapter is divided into three sections describing cognitive mind model, connectionism mind modeling and agent-based modeling.

2.3.1 Physical symbol system

The physical symbol system consists of a set of symbol entities, which are the physical modes and can be used as components of the symbol structural entities [331]. The system can be operated with 10 operations, including setup, modify, copy, delete and so on, to generate additional symbol structures.

In 1976, Newell and Simon put forward the hypothesis that the physical symbol system is necessary and proposed sufficient conditions for intelligent actions in their speech during the ACM Turing Award [337]. Based on this assumption, we can deduce the following conclusion: people are intelligent and therefore man is a physical symbol system; computer is a physical symbol system, so it will have intelligence; the computer can simulate the human, or it can simulate the human brain functions.

The goal of cognitive mind is to support the development of the human behavior model and behavioral data matching reaction time, error rate, and fMRI results. The advantage of using cognitive structure to build the human behavior model is that the cognitive model provides processes and structures that are consistent with human behavior. ACT-R and Soar are typical examples.

2.3.2 ACT-R

In 1983, Anderson elaborated the basic theory of ACT-R from every aspect of psychological processing activities in the book *Cognitive Structure*. The general framework of ACT consists of three memory components: working memory, declarative memory and procedural memory (Figure 2.1) [17]:

- declarative memory is semantic network composed by interconnected concepts with different active intensities,
- procedural memory is a series of production rules of procedural memory, and
- working memory contains the information that is currently active.

Declarative knowledge is represented by chunks. Chunk is similar to a graph structure. Each chunk can encode a group of knowledge. Declarative knowledge is able to be reported and not closely associated with the context. However, procedural knowledge usually cannot be expressed. It is automatically used and is targeted to be applied to a specific context. It was tested that a variety of methods can be used to store information in declarative memory and then extract the stored information. The matching process is to find the correspondence between the information in working

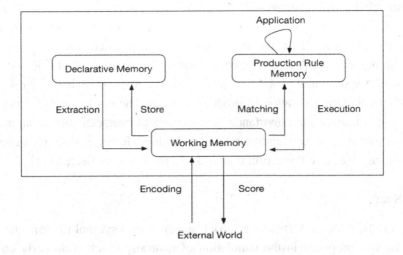

Fig. 2.1. Architecture of ACT

memory and conditions of production rules. The execution process is to put the actions generated by successfully matched production rules to the working memory. Matching all production activities before execution is also known as production applications. The last operation is done by the working memory. Then the rule execution is achieved. Through the "application process", the procedure knowledge can be applied to its own processing. By checking existing production rules, new production rules can be learned. To the greatest extent, Anderson explained skill acquisitions as knowledge compilation. It is the realization of transformation of declarative knowledge to procedural knowledge. Knowledge compilation has two subprocesses: procedure programming and synthesis.

Procedure programming refers to the process of transforming declarative knowledge into procedural knowledge or production rules. Problem-solvers initially solve the problem, such as mathematics or programming, according to knowledge obtained from books. In the process of problem-solving, the novice will combine weak problem-solving methods, such as the hill-climbing method or the method-goal analysis, to produce many subgoals and produce declarative knowledge. When repeatedly solving an event in the problem, some special declarative knowledge will be extracted repeatedly. At this moment, a new production rule is generated. While an application can learn new production rules indicating that according to the ACT theory the process of learning is "learning from doing". Program knowledge can be described as a mode (IF part of production rule), and the action to be performed is described as an action (THEN part of production rule). This declarative knowledge to procedural knowledge transformation process will also lead to reduction of processing on test speech. Related to this, the degree of automation on problem-solving will be increased.

In ACT-R, learning is realized by the growth and adjustment of microknowledge units. This knowledge can be combined to produce complex cognitive processes. In the learning process, the environment plays an important role because it established the structural problem object. This structure can assist in chunk learning and promote the formation of production rules. The importance of this step is that it re-emphasizes the importance of the essential characteristics in an analytical environment for understanding human cognition. However, since the demise of behaviorism, cognitive revolution rose and this point was neglected [18].

2.3.3 Soar

In late 1950s, a memory structure model, which uses a symbol to mark the other symbols, was proposed in the simulation of neurons, which is an early concept of chunks. A lot of chess cases are preserved in the experience memory block of the chess master mind. In early 1980s, Newell and Rosenbloom believed that by acquiring knowledge about the model problem in the task environment, the system performance could be improved. Chunk can be regarded as model basis for human behavior simulation. By observing the problem-solving process, acquiring experience chunks, and substituting various complex processes in subgoals, the speed of problem-solving can be significantly improved. Therefore, the foundation for experiential learning was established. In 1987, Newell, Laird and Rosenbloom proposed a common problem-solving structure called Soar. They hoped that the various weak methods would be implemented in this problem-solving structure.

Soar is abbreviation of State, Operator and Result. It means that the basic principle of weak methods implementation is repeated to apply operator to the state, in order to obtain new results (Figure 2.2) [250]. Soar is a theoretical cognitive model. It modeled human cognition from a psychological point of view and proposed a general problem-solving structure from a knowledge engineering point of view. The learning mechanism in Soar is provided by the guidance of outside experts to

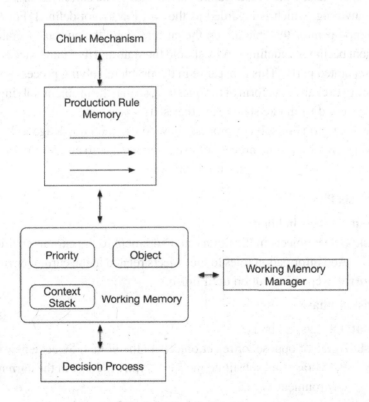

Fig. 2.2. Soar framework

obtain a general knowledge of the search control. External guidance can be direct advice. It can also be an intuitive simple question. The system puts high level information of external guidance into an internal representation and learns to search chunks.

Production memory and decision-making process form the process structure. Production rules are stored in the production memory. The search control decisions in the production memory consist of two stages. The first stage is the stage of detailed inference, all rules are applied to working memory in parallel, the priorities of rules are determined, in order to decide which part of context will be changed. The second stage is the decision-making stage that determines which parts of objects in the context stack will be changed.

In Soar, all components are named as objects. These components include the state, state space, operators and objectives. All of these objects are stored in stocks. The stock is divided into four sections. There is a current environment, which is also divided into four parts. Each part is mostly stored up to one element in the corresponding part of stocks. For example, the state of the current environment can store one stock state, which is called the current state. The current environment may not store anything, which is regarded as the part that is not defined. For example, if there is no operator that can act on the current state, the current operator of the environment becomes undefined. Why should the state and the state space be divided into two separated parts? This is because in the problem-solving process sometimes it is necessary to change the form of the question, so that the problem-solving process can be transferred from one state to another state space.

In the Soar problem-solving process, how to use the knowledge in knowledge space is very important. The process of using knowledge to control Soar running is roughly an analysis–decision–execution process.

1. Analysis Phase

> **Input**: Objects in library.
> **Task**: Select objects in the library and add them to the current environment;
> Add information roles to the objects related to the current environment.
> **Control**: Repeat execution until finish.

2. Decision Phase

> **Input**: Objects in library.
> **Task**: Agree or oppose, or reject objects in the library. Select a new object in the library and substitute the same type of object in the current environment.
> **Control**: Agree and oppose are executed simultaneously.

3. Execution Phase

Input: Current state and current operator.

Task: Apply the current operator to the current state.

If a new state is generated, the new state will be appended to the library and use it to substitute the current environment.

Control: This is atomic action that cannot be further divided.

During Soar system running, in the analysis phase, the task tries to extend the knowledge about the current object, for using knowledge in the decision-making stage. Decision stage is mainly a vote done by executing rules and the rules can be executed simultaneously. Voters do not pass information to each other, thus they do not affect each other. Vote consists of agree, oppose and reject. For each received agree vote, one point is added. For each received negative vote, one point is subtracted. If a reject vote is received, then the object will not be selected. In the execution phase, if each part of the current environment is defined, then the current operator is applied to the current state. If the execution is successful, the old state is replaced by the new state. The operator becomes undefined and re-executes the analysis phase.

Analysis phase and decision-making phase are implemented through the production system. The form of production system is

$$C_1 \wedge C_2 \wedge \ldots \wedge C_n \to A,$$

whether C_i is true depends on the current environment and objects in the library, A is an action. Its content includes increasing the object information and voting results.

Whenever a problem-solver cannot successfully solve a problem, the system enters advice space to request the experts' guidance. Experts give guidance in two ways. One way is the direct command mode; then the system expands all the operators and the state at the same time. An expert designates the operator according to the situation. The designated operator needs to be evaluated, namely, the system establishes a subgoal and uses the expert designated operator to solve a subgoal. If the goal has a solution, the evaluation confirms that the operator is feasible, and the system will accept the command and return to verify whether using this operator for goal solving is correct. By synthesizing the confirmation process, the general conditions of the use of expert advice can be learned, and this is chunk.

Another way is an indirect and simple form; the system firstly parses the original problem into an internal tree structure representation according to the syntax, along with the initial state, then requests expert advice. Experts give an intuitive problem by external instruction. The given problem should approximate the original problem. The system establishes a subgoal to solve this simple problem. After the solving process is executed, an operator sequence is obtained. The learning mechanism learns chunks from subgoal solving processes. As the chunks can directly solve the original problem, thus there is no longer a need to request guidance for solving original problem.

In the Soar system, chunk learning mechanism is the key of learning. It uses the working memory unit to collect conditions and build chunks. When the system generates a subgoal according to expert advice or simple problems, the current state is firstly stored in working memory unit w-m-e. When the subgoals give solutions, the initial state of the system is removed from w-m-e. When the subgoal is solved, the system retrieves the initial state of subgoal from w-m-e deletes the solution operator obtained from the operator or the simple problem as a result of the action. Then production rules are generated, which are chunks. If the subgoals are sufficiently similar to the original problem, the chunk will be applied directly to the original problem. Learning strategy transfers learned experience from one problem to another problem.

Chunk composition process is based on the interpretation of the subgoals to consult external guidance, and then put expert instruction or intuitive simple problem into a machine-executable form, which uses the method of teaching of learning. Finally, solving intuitive problem is to use the original problem, which involves some of the ideas from analogy learning. Therefore, we can say, learning in the Soar system is the comprehensive application of several learning methods.

2.4 Connectionism-based Mind Modeling

2.4.1 Connectionism

Modern connection mechanism begins in the pioneering work of McCulloch and Pitts. In 1943, they published their papers in a neural modeling group [304]. In the classical thesis, McCulloch and Pitts combined neural physiology and mathematical logic to describe a neural network. Their neuron model follows have it or not model law. If there are enough number of such simple neurons, connection weights and synchronous operations are properly set, and any computable function can be computed by this network in principle, McCulloch and Pitts had proved such conclusion. This is a significant result and it marks the birth of connectionism.

In 1986, Rumelhart and McClelland published the book *Parallel Distributed Processing: Explorations in the Microstructure of Cognition* [302], which proposed connectionism parallel distributed processing architecture. The architecture consists of eight components:

(1) A set of processing units;
(2) Activate state of processing unit;
(3) Output function of processing unit;
(4) Connection mode of processing unit;
(5) Transfer rules;
(6) Activation rule for combining input of processing unit and current state to generate activate values;
(7) Learning rule for connection strength adjustment through experience;
(8) The system running environment.

Connectionism mechanism has great similarities in information processing and brain information processing.

2.4.1.1 *Large-scale parallel processing*

Similar to connectionism computation models, information processing in the brain may be in a massively parallel manner. Neurons in the brain transfer signal at a rate of approximately 1/1,000 s. If there is a serial program for processing, then in 1/10 s one can only run 100 instructions. It is impossible to complete the basic operations like visual recognition and language understanding. Usually, a very complex process can be accomplished within a few hundred milliseconds. Human brain perception processing, memory retrieval, most language processing, intuitive reasoning and other processing can be completed within this time frame. This means that the time of task processing in the human brain must be in less than 100 steps. This 100-step limit in program instructions was mentioned by Feldman [144].

2.4.1.2 *Content-based addressing*

Similar to the connective computational theory model, brain use can get all the information by using part of information content. The manner of addressing is by content rather than by the address.

2.4.1.3 *Distributed storage*

Similar to the connective computational theory model, it seems there is no fixed address in the brain to store specific memory, but the information is distributed in many regions of the brain. For some single memory, it is estimated that about

700,000–7,000,000 neurons are involved in storing memory traces. Some others estimated that 1,000 neurons are involved.

2.4.1.4 *Adaptability*

Neural network embeds an ability to adjust connection weights to adapt to external changes. In particular, a trained neural network can easily be retrained to adapt to the small environment change. Furthermore, when it is in a time-varying environment, the weights of the network can be designed to change over time. It is used for pattern recognition, signal processing and neural network-coupled control and has become an effective tool for adaptive pattern recognition, adaptive signal processing and adaptive control. As a general rule, the system has a better self-adaptive ability, it will run in a time-varying environment with more robust performance.

2.4.1.5 *Fault tolerance*

A hardware implemented neural network has a natural potential of fault tolerance, its performance declines under some negative cases. For example, when a neuron or a connection is corrupted, the memory of the stored pattern is impaired in quality. However, due to the distributed information storage, such damage is decentralized. Therefore, in principle, the performance of a neural network shows a slow degradation rather than catastrophic failure.

Mind model is different from the brain model. Relatively good mind model should be very close to the brain model. Connectionism mechanism-based mind model can simulate the overall brain structure and brain functions. Connectionism mind has following similarities with brain structure:

(1) Unit in connective mind model is similar to the brain neuron.
(2) Connections and weights in the connective mind model are similar to neuron axons, dendrites and synapses.
(3) Connective mind model and brain are organized in a hierarchical manner.
(4) Brain learning can be achieved by adjusting connections strength, similar to the connective mind model as well.
(5) Parts of brain show a parallel excitatory and inhibitory characteristic, similar to some connective mind model as well.

2.4.2 Adaptive Resonance Theory

The American College of Cognitive and Neural Systems at Boston University conducted long-term studies of brain models. As early as 1976, Grossberg proposed

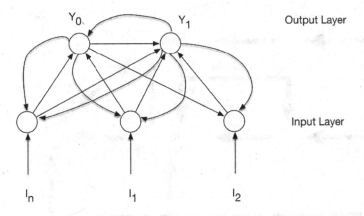

Fig. 2.3. Basic structure of ART

an adaptive resonance theory (ART) [181]. The top-down expectations control predictive encoding and matching, in order to concentrate, synchronize and gain attention feature representation, and to effectively resist completely forgetting the fast learning.

Inspired by the collaboration competition network interaction model, Grossberg proposed the ART theory model. He believed that continuous nonlinear network model can be created by analyzing adaptive behavior of the network. This network can be implemented by a short-term memory (STM) and long-term memory (LTM). STM is the activation value of neurons, which is not processed by the s function. LTM is the weights.

The basic structure of the ART is shown in Figure 2.3. It consists of input neurons and output neurons. Forward weight and sample input are used to obtain neuron output and this output is the matching metric; neuron activation with the largest matching metric is enhanced through lateral inhibition between neurons, while by not matching the measure the maximum level of neuronal activity will gradually weaken. There is feedback connection between neuron input and neuron output for comparison learning. Similarly, it also provides mechanism to compare the maximum neuron output with input mode.

Figure 2.4 shows the ART model, which consists of two subsystems: attentional subsystem and orienting subsystem, also known as adjustment subsystem. These two complementary subsystems are functional subsystems. The ART model handles the familiar and unfamiliar events with interaction of the two subsystems and control mechanisms. In the attention subsystem, F_1, F_2 are composed by short-term memory, namely STM-F_1 and STM-F_2. Connection between F_1 and F_2 is long-term memory (LTM). Gain control has two functions. One function is to discriminate bottom-up

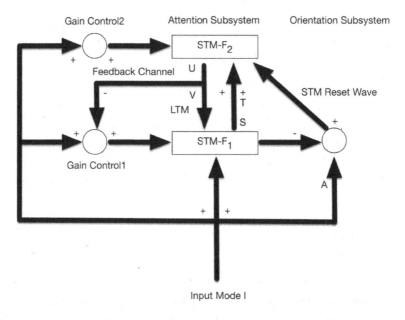

Gain Control2   Attention Subsystem   Orientation Subsystem

Fig. 2.4.   ART framework

and top-down signal in F_1; another function is that when the input signal gets into the system, F_2 can be the threshold function for input coming from F_1. Adjustment subsystem is composed by A and STM reset wave channels.

Attention subsystem aims to handle the familiar events. This subsystem establishes the internal representation of familiar events, in order to respond to related familiar events. Actually, this is coding for active mode STM. Meanwhile, this subsystem also produces top-down expectation samples from F_2 to F_1 to help to stabilize the code of learned familiar event.

The function of adjustment subsystem is to generate response to unfamiliar events. When an unfamiliar event is inputted, isolated attention subsystem cannot generate the code for the unfamiliar event. Therefore, adjustment subsystem is established to handle an unfamiliar event. When there is an unfamiliar event input, adjustment subsystem immediately generates a reset wave to adjust F_2, so that the attention system can generate a new code for the unfamiliar event. In fact, when the bottom-up input mode and the top-down triggered mode from F_2 does not match expectations in F_1, adjustment subsystem will send a reset signal to the F_2. It re-selects the activation unit in F_2. Canceled output mode initially be sent from F_2.

In short, the functions of the attention subsystem are to complete bottom-up vector competitive selection, and complete the similarity comparison between bottom-up vector and top-down vector. The function of the orientation subsystem is to test the degree of similarity of the expectation vector V and the input vector I. When the similarity is lower than a given standard value, competition winners are canceled this time, and the winners from other categories are chosen. The ART model completes the self-organization process by interaction of the attention subsystem and the adjustment subsystem.

ART theoretical model proposed by Grossberg has the following main advantages:

(1) It is able to carry out real-time learning and adapt to nonstationary environment.
(2) For the learned object, it has quick recognition ability and is able to quickly adapt to the new object that does not learn.
(3) It has the ability to self-normalize, according to the proportion of certain characteristics in the whole environment. Sometimes, they are used as key features; sometimes they are considered as noise.
(4) It is an unsupervised learning, and does not require prior knowledge of the sample results. If a mistake is made to the environment, "alertness" is automatically raised to quickly identify the object.
(5) Capacity does not limit the number of input channels. Stored objects do not require each other's orthogonality.

In 2011, on the basis of the ART model, Versace designed a MoNETA (modular neural exploring traveling agent) software [499]. It is the brain on a chip. The difference between MoNETA and other artificial intelligence systems is that it does not need to be explicitly programmed. Like the mammalian brain, it has the same adaptability and utility. Dynamic learning can be performed in various environments.

Currently, the mind models with human level are based on connectionism mechanism. Its goal is to support the development of intelligent systems with a wide range of behavioral and cognitive ability to create a complete, integrated brain-like intelligent system. The architecture emphasizes knowledge rich behavior, multiple long-term memory and learning and can solve a wide variety of problems. Eliasmith at University of Waterloo developed an artificial brain pointer semantic architecture unified network called the Spaun [135]. It simulates neurons that link to each other. The linkage is same as the neuron network in human brain. The basic idea is to make these subsystems run in a manner that is very similar to the real operation of the brain. The thalamus portion of the brain processing visual input, the data stored in the neurons and the basal ganglia to the prefrontal cortex of the brain are responsible for processing tasks execution notification and completing the required functions.

2.5 Agent Mind Modeling

The aim of agent mind modeling is to support the development of artificial intelligence agents, dynamic interaction with the environment and a combination use of artificial intelligence technology, including reactivity, goal-driven behavior and planning. Agent system architecture emphasizes the integration of a variety of technologies, as well as programmability and flexibility. They do not need to integrate all human cognitive abilities, such as large-scale knowledge base, natural language and ubiquitous learning. Typically, it uses traditional programming specified fine-grained procedural knowledge. CIRCA [330] is an example of the architecture of the early-agent system, stressed to ensure real-time responsiveness. The IDA built by Franklin is a typical distributed agent system [156]. In the introduction of a global workspace theory of consciousness (2006), IDA was promoted to cognitive model LIDA [157]. The LIDA system structure is shown in Figure 2.5 [465]. Intelligent data analysis can be divided into nine steps:

(1) Perception stimulus input is filtered by preconscious perception, intended to get involved to generate sensing object.
(2) The current perceptual object is moved to preconscious working memory and integrated with objects in the previous cycle that have not been attenuated to higher level perception structure.
(3) The current structure of working memory can induce transient episodic memory and declarative memory, resulting in partial contact with long-term working memory.
(4) The combination of long-term working memory contents competes with consciousness to make the consciousness to put system resources to the most urgent and important tasks.
(5) Conscious broadcast is created by global working space method, which makes it possible to complement with learning and other internal resources. Based on some empirical resource, it is assumed that the broadcast time requires 100 ms.
(6) Memory on programs needs to respond to the contents of conscious broadcast.
(7) Create other (unconscious) response schemes, such as reproduce the selection mechanism, binding variable, activating transfer.
(8) Behavior selection mechanism selects a response for cognitive cycle.
(9) Intelligent data analysis generates response to internal or external environment.

The LIDA cognitive cycle can be divided into three phases: understanding phase, attention (awareness) phase and action selection phase. It starts at the top left corner in Figure 2.5, generally in a clockwise flow. The understanding phase begins with

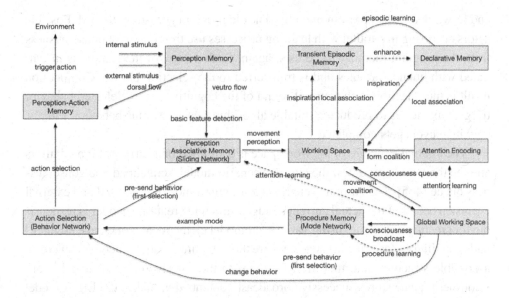

Fig. 2.5. LIDA system architecture

stimulation input, which activates the primary feature detector in the perception memory. The output signal is sent to the perception associative memory, where a higher level of function detector exists for detecting the more abstract entities such as objects, classes, actions, events and others. The generated perception is moved to the working space, where transient episodic memory generating local association and declarative memory will be made trail markers. These local association and perception are combined to produce the current context model to express what the intelligent agent thinks has happened in the current situation.

Attention encoder forms connections between portions in the current scenario. The attention phase starts and the formed connections are transferred to the global workspace.

After competition in global workspace, most prominent, most relevant, most important and most urgent connections are selected. Their content becomes conscious content. Then, the content of these consciousness is broadcasted to the whole space and the action selection phase is launched. Action selection phase in the LIDA cognitive cycle is also a learning phase. This learning phase is performed by several processing operations executed in parallel. The new joint of entities and strengthening over the old consciousness will occur along with distribution of consciousness to associative memory. Events in consciousness broadcasting are codes for transient episodic memory, which lead to new memory generation. Feasible action plans, along with their background and expected results, are published by consciousness and forwarded to the program memory. The old program gets strengthened. Possible actors occurring in parallel with learning processes use the content of consciousness from the program memory to be used again. Such a copy of the sample is instantiated with bound variables and is transferred to the selection phrase. Competition result is the selection in the current round of the cognitive cycle. Selected behavior triggers memories to produce a suitable algorithm to perform this behavior. Finally, cognitive cycle gets completed.

The internal structure of the workspace is composed of a variety of input buffers and the three main modules: the current scenario model, scratchpad and consciousness queue [465]. The current scenario is a structural model of internal and external events on behalf of the actual current storage. Structure creation encoder is responsible for creating a structure using various submodel elements of workspace. Scratchpad is auxiliary space in workspace, where the structure creation encoder can create a possible structure, and then transfer them to the current scenario model. Consciousness queue stores successive broadcast contents that makes the LIDA model capable of understanding and operating the time-related concepts.

2.6 CAM Architecture

In the mind activities, memory and consciousness play an most important role. Memory stores various important information and knowledge; consciousness makes humans possess the concept of self, according to the needs, preferences-based goals, and perform all kinds of cognitive activity according to memory information. Therefore, the main emphasis on mind model CAM is on memory functions and consciousness functions [428]. Figure 2.6 shows the architecture of the mind model CAM, which includes 10 main modules, a brief introduction is given in the following subsections:

(1) Vision

Human sensory organs include vision, hearing, touch, smell and taste. In the CAM model, visual and auditory are focused on. Visual system of the organism has visual perception ability. It uses visible light to build the perception around the world. According to the image, the process of discovering what objects are in the surrounding scenery and where the objects locate in includes the discovery of the useful symbolic description for image. Visual system has the ability to reconstruct a three-dimensional (3D) world from a 2D projection of the outside world. It should be noted that the various objects in the visible light spectrum can be perceived in a different location.

The process of outside objects imaging in retina is actually the light stimulus transformed by retinal photoreceptor cells (rods and cones) into electrical signals,

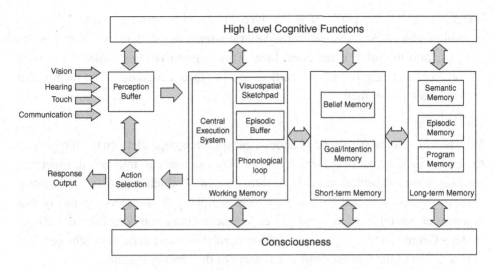

Fig. 2.6. Architecture of mind model CAM

which with the help of retinal ganglion cells spread within the bipolar cells for the formation of nerve impulses, which is otherwise known as visual information. Visual information is transmitted to the brain via the optic nerve. Bipolar cells can be regarded as the Level 1 neurons of visual transduction pathway neurons; ganglion cells are Level 2 neurons. Many ganglion cells send out nerve fibers composed of the coarse optic nerve, the optic nerve at the back end of the eye leaving the eye back into the cranial cavity. At this time, the left and right sides of the optic nerve cross. The cross-section is called the optic chiasm. Optic tract in the bottom of the brain is connected to the lateral geniculate body. Lateral geniculate body is an important visual information transmission intermediate station, which contains the Level 3 neurons. They emit a large number of fibers that are composed of the so-called radiation. Fiber optic radiation is projected to the visual center of the occipital lobe — the visual cortex. Visual information only reaches the visual cortex of the brain and is processed, analyzed and then finally forms the subjective visual experience.

Visual cortex refers to the part of cerebral cortex that is responsible for processing visual information. It is located in the rear of the occipital lobe of the brain. Human visual cortex includes the primary visual cortex (V1, also known as the striate cortex) and extrastriate cortex (V2, V3, V4, V5, etc.). Primary visual cortex is located in the 17th area. Extrastriate cortex comprises 18 area and 19 area.

The output of the primary visual cortex (V1) forwards to the two pathways, respectively, to become the dorsal and ventral stream flow. Dorsal stream begins with V1, through V2, into the dorsal medial area and the temporal area (MT, also known as V5), then arrives in the inferior parietal lobule. Dorsal stream is often referred to as "space path". It is involved in spatial location and related motion control of objects, such as saccades. Ventral stream begins with V1, followed by V2, V4, into the inferior temporal lobe. This passage is often called a "content access", participating object recognition, such as face recognition. The path is also related to long-term memory.

(2) Hearing

Why humans can hear sound and understand speech is dependent on the integrity of the entire auditory pathway, which includes the external ear, middle ear, inner ear, auditory nerve and central auditory. Auditory pathway, which is outside of the central nervous system, is called the auditory outer periphery. The auditory pathway that is inside of central nervous system is called the auditory center or central auditory system. Central auditory spanning brainstem, midbrain and thalamus of the cerebral cortex is one of the longest central pathways of the sensory system.

Sound information is conducted from the surrounding auditory system to the central auditory system. Central auditory system has processing and analysis functions for sound, such as functions to feel the tone, pitch, intensity and determine the orientation of sound. There are specialized cells that are able to respond to beginning and ending of sound. Auditory information spreading to the cerebral cortex has connections with the language center of the brain, which manages the "read", "write" and "speak".

(3) Perception buffer

Perception buffer, also known as sensory memory or instantaneous memory, is the first direct impression of sensory information to the sensory organ. Perception buffer can only cache information from all the sensory organs from tens to hundreds of milliseconds. In the perception buffer, the information may be noticed and become significant after encoding process. Proceed to the next phase of processing and if unnoticed or not encoded, the sensory information will automatically subside.

A variety of sensory information is stored in the perception buffer in its unique form for a time period and continues to work. These sensory information forms are visual representation and sound representation, which are named as video image and sound image. Imagery can be said to be directly and primitively memorized. Imagery can only exist for a short period of time; even the most distinctive visual image can only be kept for tens of seconds. Perception memory has the following characteristics:

(1) The memory is very transient;
(2) The ability to handle same amount of energy like receptors on the anatomy and physiology;

(3) Encode information in a straightforward way. Transiently save all kinds of signals coming from the sensory organs.

(4) Working memory

Working memory consists of central executive system, visuospatial sketchpad, phonological loop and episodic buffer. Central executive system is the core of working memory, which is responsible for associating various subsystems and long-term memory, making attention to resource coordination, strategy selection and planning, and so on. Visuospatial sketchpad is mainly responsible for the storage and processing of visual–spatial information. It contains visual and spatial subsystems. Phonological loop is responsible for the sound-based storage and control of information, including sound storage and pronunciation control. By silent read, the characterization of faded voice can be reactivated in order to prevent a recession, and can also transfer words in a book into speech. Episodic buffer stores connected information across the region, in order to form a visual, spatial and verbal integrated unit in chronological order, such as a story or a movie scene memory. Episodic buffer also associates with long-term memory and semantic memory.

(5) Short-term memory

Short-term memory stores beliefs, goals and intentions. They respond to rapidly changing environment and operations of the agents. In short-term memory, perceptual coding scheme and experience coding scheme for related objects is prior knowledge.

(6) Long-term Memory

Long-term memory is the container with large capacity. In long-term memory, information is maintained for a long time. According to stored contents, long-term memory can be divided into semantic memory, episodic memory and procedural memory.

(1) Semantic memory stores words, concepts and general rules by reference to the general knowledge system. It has generality and does not depend on time, place and conditions. It is relatively stable and is not easy to be interfered by external factors.

(2) Episodic memory stores personal experience, it is the memory about events that take place in a certain time and some place. It is easy to be inferred by a variety of factors.

(3) Procedure memory refers to technology, process, or "how to" memories. Procedural memory is generally less likely to change, but can be automatically exercised unconsciously. It can be a simple reflex action, or a combination of

more complex series of acts. Examples of procedural memory include learning to ride a bicycle, typing, using the instrument or swimming. Once internalized, the procedure memory can be very persistent.

(7) Consciousness

Consciousness is a complex biological phenomenon. A philosopher, physician, psychologist may have a different understanding about the concept of consciousness. From a scientific point of view of intelligence, consciousness is a subjective experience. It is an integration of outside world, physical experience and psychological experience. Consciousness is a brain possessed "instinct" or "function"; it is a "state", a combination of the number of brain structures for a variety of organisms. In CAM, the consciousness is concerned about automatic control, motivation, metacognitive, attention and other issues.

(8) High-level cognitive function

High-level cognitive functions include learning, memory, language, thinking, decision-making and emotion. Learning is the process of continually receiving stimulus from the nervous system, accessing new behaviors, habits and accumulating experiences. While memory refers to maintenance and reproduction of behavior and knowledge by learning. It refers to the intelligent activities that we perform every day. Language and higher-order thinking is the most important factor that differs among humans and animals. Decision-making is the process of finding the most optimal solution through analysis and comparison of several alternatives. It can be a decision made under uncertain conditions to deal with the occasional incidence. Emotion is attitudinal experience arising in humans when objective things meet or do not meet their needs.

(9) Action selection

Action selection means to build a complex combination of actions by the atomic action, in order to achieve a particular task in the process. Action selection can be divided into two steps. The first step is atomic action selection, which is choosing the relevant atomic actions from the action library. Then, using planning strategies, the selected atomic actions are composed to form complex actions. Action selection mechanism could be implemented by the spike basal ganglia model.

(10) Response Output

Response output is classified from the overall objective. It can be influenced by surrounding emotion or motivation input. Based on the control signal, the primary motor cortex directly generates muscle movements, to achieve some kind of internally given motion command.

2.7 CAM Cognitive Cycle

Cognitive cycle consists of the basic steps of cognitive-level mind activity. Human cognition is recurring brain events of the cascade cycle. In CAM, each of the cognitive cycles perceives the current situation according to the goal in motivation, which is intended to be achieved. Then an internal or external flow of actions is constituted in order to respond to the goal that it wants to reach [442], as shown in Figure 2.7. CAM cognitive cycle is divided into three phases, which are perception, motivation and action planning. In the perception phase, the process of environmental awareness is realized by sensory input. Sensory input and information in working memory are taken as a clue, then a local association is created with automatic retrieval of episodic memory and declarative memory. Motivation phase is focused on the learner's needs on beliefs, expectations, sorting and understanding. According to the motivation factors, such as activation, opportunities, continuity of actions, persistence, interruption and preferential combination, the motivation system is built. Action plan will be achieved through action selection and action planning.

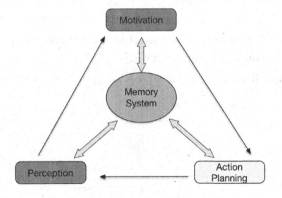

Fig. 2.7. CAM cognitive cycle

2.7.1 Perception phase

Perception phase is to achieve environmental awareness or understanding, and organizing and interpreting of the sensory information processing. Sensory organ receives external or internal stimulus. This is the beginning of creation in the perception phase. Awareness is the event feeling, perception, consciousness states or ability. In this level of consciousness, sensory data can be confirmed by the observer, but does not necessarily mean understanding. In biological psychology, awareness is defined as a human's or animal's perception and cognitive response to external conditions or events.

2.7.2 Motivation phase

Motivation phase in CAM should determine the explicit goals according to the need. A target includes a set of subgoals, which can be formally described as

$$G_t = \{G_1^t, G_2^t, \ldots, G_n^t\} \quad \text{at time } t.$$

2.7.3 Action planning phase

Action planning is the process of building a complex action composed by atomic actions to achieve a particular task. Action planning can be divided into two steps: first is action selection, which is to select the relevant action from the action library; then use planning strategies to integrate the selected actions together. Action selection is to instantiate the action flow, or select an action from a previous action flow. There are many action selection methods, most of them based on similarity matching between goals and behaviors. Planning provides an extensible and effective method for action composition. It allows an action request to be expressed as a combination of objective conditions, and regulates a set of restrictions and preferences, under which a set of constraints and preferences exists. In CAM, we use the dynamic logic to formally describe the action and design action planning algorithms.

Chapter 3

Memory

Memory is the psychological process of accumulation, preservation and extraction of individual experience in the human brain. As a result of memory, people can maintain a reflection of the past, generate new reflections on the basis of past reflections thus make reflections more comprehensive and deep. That is, by having the memory, human beings could accumulate and expand their experiences. Memory is psychological continuation in time, and links up former and later experiences to enable the psychological activity to be a developing and unified process, which forms the psychological characteristics of a person. Memory is a fundamental aspect of the reflecting function.

3.1 Overview

Memory is a psychological process that human beings accumulate, preserve and it helps to extract individual experiences in their brains. In terms of information processing, memory is the process that human brains encode in the storage and retrieval of information. A person will have impressions in his mind about the objects he ever perceived, the questions he ever thought, the emotions he ever experienced and the activities he ever engaged. Under certain conditions, these impressions will be aroused and used to deal with new activities. The whole process, including the storage of information in the mind and the extraction and application of the information, is called memory.

Memory consists of three basic processes: input information into the memory (also called encoding), storage information in the memory (called retaining) and extract information from the memory (called extraction). Encoding is the first basic process of memory, which turns the information from the sensory information into the form that the memory system can receive and use. In general, a person can obtain information from the outside by his sensory organs. This information will be first transformed into various memory codes, which are called mental representations of objective physical stimulations. Attention plays an important role in the encoding process. It affects the processing level of the encoding process or affects the forms of expression. For example, given a Chinese character, you may pay attention to its structure, its pronunciation or its meaning, and correspondingly in the encoding process, different codes will be generated such as visual code, sound code or semantic code. The strength of the encoding process will directly affect the persistence of the memory. Of course, a strong emotional experience can also enhance the effect of a memory. In short, the encoding of information has a direct impact on the storage and extraction of a memory. In general, the effect of a memory can be enhanced if the information is encoded by many forms.

The information that has been encoded must be preserved in the brain, and can be extracted after a certain period of time. However, the preservation of information is not always automatic. In most cases, in order to use the information in the future, we must strive to find ways to preserve information. Information that has been stored may also be undermined and be forgotten. In their study of memory, psychologists try to find factors affecting the storage of memory so as to fight against forgetting.

The information stored in the memory is meaningless unless it is extracted to be applied. There are two forms of extraction: recall and recognition. The word "remember" used in daily life just refers to recall. Recognition means that there is some original stimulus in front of us and we have many clues to use; the only thing we need to do is to determine the degree of familiarity for these clues. In some cases, we cannot remember some materials which we have studied; does it mean that these materials have completely disappeared from our brain? The answer is no. Memory traces will not disappear completely. This answer can be proved by an experiment of relearning. If we let a participant to study a material twice, and each time ask him to achieve the same level of proficiency, then the number of exercises used in the second study must be less than the number of exercises used in the first study; the difference between the two times or the number of times shows the information kept in memory.

The memory system of human beings is extremely similar to the storage system of a computer. In a computer system, the storage system is organized in three levels: cache, main memory and auxiliary memory. In these three levels, the speed is decreased but the capacity is increased. Similarly, according to the length of memory time, there are three types of human memories: working memory, short-time memory and long-term memory.

In order to formally describe the mechanisms of information processing in various memory modules, we will make use of the dynamic description logic (DDL). In the following subsection, we give an introduction to the DDL.

3.2 Basis of the DDL

The DDL extends description logics by introducing a dimension on actions [438]. With DDL, knowledge on actions can be described based on the domain knowledge specified by description logics, and can be reasoned about with an effective reasoning engine. With DDL, domain knowledge is described by ontology based on described logics, states of the world are described by assertions of description logics, and each atomic action is specified by two sets of assertions for describing its preconditions and effects respectively. Starting from atomic actions, complex actions with sequence, choice and iteration structures can also be described by DDL [77]. It has been proved that reasoning problems in DDL are sound, complete and decidable [79].

3.2.1 Notations

Definition 3.1 (Primitive symbols). Primitive symbols of DDL consist of

- Concept names: $C_1, C_2, \ldots$;
- Role names: $R_1, R_2, \ldots$;
- Individual constants: $a, b, c, \ldots$;
- Individual variables: $x, y, z, \ldots$;
- Concept constructors: $\neg, \sqcap, \sqcup, \exists$ and $\forall$;
- Formula constructors: $\neg, \wedge$ and $\rightarrow$;
- Action names: $A_1, A_2, \ldots$;
- Action constructors: $; , \cup, *, ?$.

Definition 3.2 (Concepts). Concepts of DDL are defined inductively as follows:

- Each concept name P is a concept;
- If C, D are concepts, then $\neg C$, $C \sqcap D$ and $C \sqcup D$ are all concepts;
- If C is a concept and R is a role name, then $\forall R.C$, $\exists R.C$ are concepts.

Definition 3.3 (Formulas). Formulas of DDL are defined inductively as follows:

- Let C be a concept, R be a role name and a, b be individual constants. Assertions of the forms $C(a)$ and $R(a, b)$ are formulas;

- If φ and ψ are formulas, then $\neg\varphi, \varphi \wedge \psi, \varphi \rightarrow \psi$ are all formulas;
- If φ is a formula and α is an action, then $[\alpha]\varphi$ is a formula.

Definition 3.4 (Instance Substitution). Let $a_1, \ldots, a_n$ be individual constants and let $x_1, \ldots, x_n$ be individual variables satisfying $x_i \neq x_j$ for every pair $i, j \in \{1, \ldots, n\}$ with $i \neq j$. A finite set of the form $\{a_1/x_1, \ldots, a_n/x_n\}$ is called an instance substitution.

Definition 3.5 (Formula Instantiation). Let φ be a formula containing individual variables, and let $x_1, \ldots, x_n$ be all the individual variables contained in φ. Let φ be a formula generated by applying an instance substitution on φ. Then φ is called an instance of φ.

Definition 3.6 (Atomic Action). Atomic action of DDL is a triple $A(x_1, \ldots, x_n) = (P_A, E_A)$, where

- A is the name of the atomic action;
- $x_1, \ldots, x_n$ are individual variables for specifying the objects that the action will operate on;
- P_A is a finite set of ABox assertions which might contain individual variables and is used for describing the preconditions of the action;
- E_A is a finite set of ABox assertions which might contain individual variables and is used for describing the effects of the action.

Definition 3.7 (Instance of Atomic action). Let $A(x_1, \ldots, x_n) \equiv (P_A, E_A)$ be an atomic action and let $a_1, \ldots, a_n$ be individual constants. Then we use $A(a_1, \ldots, a_n)$ to denote an action generated by applying the instance substitution $\{x_1/a_1, \ldots, x_n/a_n\}$ on all the formulas contained in P_A and E_A, and call $A(a_1, \ldots, a_n)$ an instance of $A(x_1, \ldots, x_n)$.

Definition 3.8 (complex action). Let α be an atomic action and φ be a formula. Complex actions of DDL are constructed by the following syntax rule:

$$\pi, \pi' \rightarrow \alpha | \varphi? | \pi \cup \pi' | \pi; \pi' | \pi^*.$$

Actions of the forms $\varphi?, \pi \cup \pi', \pi; \pi', \pi^*$ are respectively called test action, choice action, sequential action and iterated action. By using complex actions, we can model all the control flows in general computer programs.

A knowledge base in DDL consists of three parts: TBox, ABox and ActBox. TBox is a set of general concept inclusion axioms which provide a description for domain knowledge. ABox is a set of assertions for describing the current state. ActBox is a set of action definitions for describing atomic actions and complex actions.

3.2.2 Semantics of the DDL

The semantic model of DDL is a combination of the interpretation of description logics and the model of dynamic logic. A DDL model is of the form $M = (W, T, \Delta, I)$, where W is a non-empty finite set of models, T is a function which maps each action name α to a binary relation $T(\alpha) \subseteq W \times W$, Δ is a non-empty set of individuals and I is a function. The function I associates with each state $w \in W$ a DL-interpretation $I(w) = < \Delta, \cdot^{I(w)} >$, where the function $\cdot^{I(w)}$ maps each concept name A to a set $A^{I(w)} \subseteq \Delta$, maps each role name R to a binary relation $R^{I(w)} \subseteq \Delta \times \Delta$ and maps each individual constant a to an individual $a^{I(w)} \in \Delta$.

Given a DDL model $M = (W, T, \Delta, I)$, the semantics of roles, concepts, formulas and actions are defined inductively as follows:

1. $(\neg C)^{I(w)} = \Delta \backslash C^{I(w)}$;
2. $(C \sqcap D)^{I(w)} = CI(w) \sqcap D^{T(w)}$;
3. $(\forall R.C)^{I(w)} = \{x|$ for all $y \in \Delta$: if $(x, y) \in R^{I(w)}$ then $y \in C^{I(w)}\}$;
4. $I(w) \models C(p)$ iff $p^{I(w)} \in C^{I(w)}$;
5. $I(w) \models R(p, q)$ iff $(p^{I(w)}, q^{I(w)}) \in R^{I(w)}$;
6. $I(w) \models \neg\phi$ iff $I(w)\phi$;
7. $I(w) \models \pi \vee \psi$ iff $I(w) \models \pi$ or $I(w) \models \psi$;
8. $I(w) \models <\pi>\phi$ iff there exists some state $w' \in W$ such that $(w, w') \in T(\pi)$ and $I(w') \models \phi$;
9. $T(\phi?) = \{(w, w)|I(w) \models \phi\}$;
10. $T(\pi_1 \cup \pi_2) = T(\pi_1) \cup T(\pi_2)$;
11. $T(\pi 1; \pi 2) = \{(w, w')|$ there exists some $w'' \in W$ with $(w, w'') \in T(\pi_1)$ and $(w'', w') \in T(\pi_2)\}$;
12. $T(\pi^*) =$ the reflexive and transitive closure of $T(\pi)$.

3.2.3 Inference in the DDL

Definition 3.9 (Clash). Let C be a concept, R a role and a, b individuals. A clash is one of the following forms:

- $\{\bot(a)\}$;
- $\{C(a), \neg C(a)\}$;
- $\{R(a, b), \neg R(a, b)\}$.

Definition 3.10 (Completed formula set). A formula set is called completed if no expansion rule can be applied to it.

Expansion rules used in the decision procedure are listed as follows:

- $\sqcap$-rule: if $C_1 \sqcap C_2(x) \in F$, and either $C_1(x) \notin F$ or $C_2(x) \notin F$, then put $C_1(x)$ and $C_2(x)$ into F;
- $\sqcup$-rule: if $C_1 \sqcup C_2(x) \in F$, and both $C_1(x) \notin F$ and $C_2(x) \notin F$, then put $C_1(x)$ or $C_2(x)$ into F;
- $\exists$-rule: if $\exists R.C(x) \in F$, and there is no y with both $R(x, y) \in F$ and $C(y) \in F$, then put $C(y)$ and $R(x, y)$ into F;
- $\forall$-rule: if $\forall R.C(x) \in F$, $R(x, y) \in F$, and $C(y) \notin F$, then put $C(y)$ into F;
- action-rule: if $[\alpha]C(x) \in F$ with $\alpha = (P_\alpha, E_\alpha)$, then remove all the formulas occurring in P_α from F, put all the formulas occurring in E_α into F and put $C(x)$ into F.

The above algorithm is an extension of the classical Tableau decision algorithm for description logics. It has been proved to be sound and complete.

Definition 3.11 (Consistency of an action). An action $A(y_1, \ldots, y_n) \equiv (P_A, E_A)$ is consistent if there exists an instance $A(a_1, \ldots, a_n)$ of it such that both the formula set $P_A(a_1, \ldots, a_n)$ and the formula set $E_A(a_1, \ldots, a_n)$ are consistent.

In the DDL, the definition of atomic actions provides a schema for describing a general knowledge of actions. Before making use of this knowledge, we need to guarantee that all of these actions are consistent.

Definition 3.12 (Executability of action). An atomic action $A(a_1, \ldots, a_n) \equiv (P, E)$ is executable on the states described by an ABox A with respect to a TBox T, if and only if the formula $\text{Conj}(A) \to \text{Conj}(P)$ is valid with respect to T.

In the above definition, the notion $\text{Conj}(A)$ denotes the conjunction of all the formulas contained in the set A. If the formula $\neg(\text{Conj}(A) \to \text{Conj}(P))$ is unsatisfiable w.r.t. T, then we can get that the formula $\text{Conj}(A) \to \text{Conj}(P)$ is valid w.r.t. T and consequently the action $A(a_1, \ldots, a_n)$ is executable on A w.r.t. T.

Definition 3.13 (Projection of action). A formula φ is a consequence of applying an action π on the states described by an ABox A w.r.t. a TBox T, if and only if the formula $\text{Conj}(A) \to [\pi]\varphi$ is valid w.r.t. T.

Now we can introduce the definition of action plan.

Definition 3.14 (Action plan). Starting from the initial states described an ABox A_1, a sequence of actions $Seq = (P_1, E_1), (P_2, E_2), \ldots, (P_n, E_n)$ is a plan for the target states described an ABox A_2 w.r.t. a TBox T if the sequential action $(P_1, E_1);(P_2, E_2); \ldots; (P_n, E_n)$ can be executed on A_1 and the formula $\text{Conj}(A_2)$ is a consequence of applying $(P_1, E_1);(P_2, E_2); \ldots; (P_n, E_n)$ on A w.r.t. T.

According to the above definition, we can design planning algorithms for the planning problem.

3.3 Long-term Memory

Information maintained for more than one minute is referred to as long-term memory. The capacity of long-term memory is greatest among all memory systems. Experiments are needed to illustrate the capacity, storage, restore and duration of long-term memory. The result measured that the duration of how long one thing can be memorized is not definite. Memory cannot last for a long time because the attention is unstable; if accompanied with repetitions, however, memory will be retained for a long time. The capacity of long-term memory is infinite. Eight seconds are needed to retain one chunk. Before it is recovered and applied, information stored in long-term memory needs to be transferred into short-term memory.

Long-term memory can be divided into procedural memory and declarative memory, as shown in Table 3.1. Procedural memory keeps the skill about operating, which mainly consists of perceptive-motor skill and cognitive skill. Declarative memory stores the knowledge represented by the symbol to reflect the essences of things. Procedural memory and declarative memory are similar memories that reflect someone's experience and action influenced by previous experience and action. Meanwhile, there are differences between them. First, there is only one way for representation in procedural memory which needs skill research. The representation of declarative information can be various and is different from action completely. Second, with respect to true or false question of knowledge, there is no difference between true and false to skilled procedure. Only the knowledge of cognation of world and the relationship between the world and us helps identify the truth from falsehood. Third, the study forms of these two kinds of information are different. Procedural information needs certain exercise, and declarative information needs

Table 3.1. System of long-term memory

Long-term memory system		Other names	Cognitive active style	Information extraction method
Declarative memory	Semantic memory	Factual memory	Space, Relation	Explicit
	Episodic memory	Event memory	Time, Location	Explicit
Procedural memory		Not declarative memory	Sport Skill	Implicit
			Cognitive Skill	Implicit

only a chance practice. Finally, a skilled action works automatically, but the reparation of declarative information needs attention.

Declarative memory can be further divided into episodic memory and semantic memory. Episodic memory is a person's personal and biographical memory. Semantic memory stores the essential knowledge of the incident that the individual understands or in other words — the world knowledge. Table 3.2 shows the differences between these two kinds of memories.

Long-term memory is divided into two systems in terms of information encoding: image system and verbal system. Image system stores information of specific

Table 3.2.   Comparison of episodic memory and semantic memory

Characteristics of distinction	Episodic memory	Semantic memory
Information domain		
Input source	Sensory	Understanding
Unit	Event, episodic	Truth, concept
System	Time	Conceptive
Reference	Oneself	World
Facticity	Personal belief	Consistent of society
Operation domain		
Content of memory	Experiential	Symbol
Symbolization of time	Yes, direct	No, indirect
Feeling	Important	Not very important
Reasoning ability	Low	High
Context dependent	High	Low
Susceptible	High	Low
Store and read	Depend on intention	Automatically
Retrieval method	According to time or place	According to object
Result of retrieval	Memory structure changed	Memory structure unchanged
Retrieval principle	Concerted	Open
Content recalled	Past memory	Knowledge represented
Retrieval report	Feel	Know
Order of develop	Slow	Fast
Children amnesia	Hindered	No hindered
Application domain		
Education	Independent	Dependent
Generality	Low	High
Artificial intelligence	Unclear	Very good
Human intelligence	Independent	Dependent
Experience proven	Forgotten	Semantic analyze
Lab topic	Given scene	Generic knowledge
Legal evidence	Yes, witness	No, surveyor
Memory lose	Dependent	Independent
Binary	No	Yes

objects and events by image code. Verbal system uses verbal code to store verbal information. The theory is called two kinds of coding or dual coding because these two systems are independent while related to each other.

3.3.1 Semantic memory

Semantic memory was proposed by Quillian in 1968 [379]. It is the first model of semantic memory in cognitive psychology. Anderson and Bower, Rumelhart and Norman all had proposed various memory models based on semantic network in cognitive psychology. In this model, the basic unit of semantic memory is a concept that has certain characteristics which are also concepts in fact, but they are used to explain other concepts. In the semantic network, information is represented as a set of nodes, which are connected with each other by arc with a mark that represents the relationship between nodes. Figure 3.1 is a typical semantic network. ISA link is used to represent layer relationship of concept node and to link the node representing a specific object with the relevant concept. ISPART links the global and partial concepts. For example, in Figure 3.1, Chair is a part of Seat.

3.3.1.1 *Hierarchical network model*

The hierarchical network model for semantic memory was proposed by Quillian *et al.* In this model, the primary unit of long-term memory is a concept. Concepts are related to each other and then form a hierarchical structure. As shown in Figure 3.2, the dot denoted as (squares) is a node representing the concept and the line with arrow point expresses the dependence between the concepts. For instance, the higher hierarchical concept of bird is animal, while its lower hierarchical concepts are

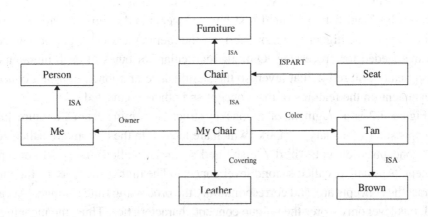

Fig. 3.1. Semantic network

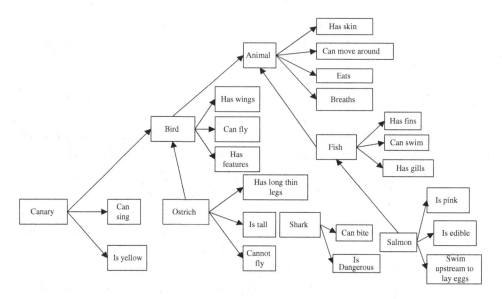

Fig. 3.2.   Hierarchical network model of semantic memory

canary and ostrich. The lines represent the relation between concept and attribute to designate attribute of each hierarchical, e.g., has wing, can fly and has feather are features of bird. Nodes represent each hierarchical concept; concept and feature are connected with lines to construct a complicated hierarchical network in which lines are association with certain significance in fact. This hierarchical network model stores features of concepts in corresponding hierarchical structure, which only stores the concepts with same hierarchy, while the common attributes of every concept in same hierarchy are stored in higher hierarchy. There is a fragment of the concept system in Figure 3.2, canary and shark in the lowest level are called zero level concepts, bird and fish are called first level concepts and animal is called second level concept. The higher and more abstract the hierarchical concept, the longer is the time needed for processing. Only the particular attributes of each hierarchical concept can be stored in that layer, so the significance or connotation of a concept is dependent on the features of that concept and others connected.

Figure 3.2 is a fragment of a concept structure coming from literature [97]. Concepts such as "canary", "shark" which are located in the bottom are called zero level concepts. Concepts "bird", "fish" and so on are called first level concepts. Concept "Animal" is called second level concept. The higher the level is, the more abstract the concepts are, and correspondingly the processing time is longer. At each level, this level only stores the unique concept characteristics. Thus, the meaning of a concept associates with other characteristics determined by the concept.

3.3.1.2 *Spreading activation model*

Spreading activation model was proposed by Collins *et al.* [98]. It is also a network model. Different from the hierarchical network model, this model organizes concepts by semantic connection or semantic similarity instead of the hierarchical structure of the concept. Figure 3.3 reveals a fragment of the spreading activation model. The squares are nodes of network representing a concept. The length of lines refers to the compact degree of relation, e.g., shorter length indicates that the relation is close and there are more common features between two concepts, or if there are more lines between two nodes by common features then it means their relation is compact; connected concepts denote their relations.

As a concept is stimulated or processed, the network node that this concept belongs to is active and activation will spread all around along lines. The amount of this kind of activation is finite, so if a concept is processed for a long time, the

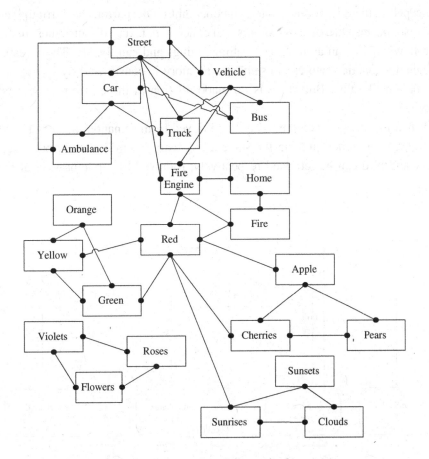

Fig. 3.3. Fragment of spreading activation model

time of spread activation will increase and familiarity effect may be formed; on the other hand, activation also follows the rule that energy decreases progressively. This model is a modification of the hierarchical network model, which considers that attributes of every concept may be in same or different hierarchies. Relation of concept-length of lines illustrates the category size effect and other effects in the form of spreading activation. This model may be the humanized hierarchical network model.

3.3.1.3 *Set theoretic model*

The set theoretic model was proposed by Meyer [312]. In this model, as demonstrated by Figure 3.4, the basic semantic unit is also a concept. Every concept is represented by a set of information or factors which can be divided as example set and attribute set or feature set. Example set means several examples of a concept, e.g., example set of a concept bird includes robin, canary, pigeon, nightingale, parrot, etc. Attribute set or feature set means attributes or features of a concept, e.g., a bird's attributes includes the following: it is an animal, has feathers, wings and can fly, etc. These features are called semantic features, so semantic memory is constructed by innumerable information like this. But, there is no made relation in these information sets or concepts.

When information is intended to be retrieved from semantic memory to judge a sentence, e.g., when judging the sentence "canary is bird", the attributes set of canary and bird can be retrieved respectively, followed by a comparison of these

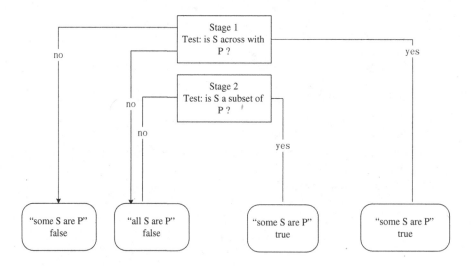

Fig. 3.4. Predicate cross model

two attribute sets and a decision dependent on the overlap degree of these two sets. The more common the attributes of two sets, the higher the overlap degree they have. As the overlap degree is high, affirm judgment can be made, or a negative judgment may result. Because attribute sets of canary and bird overlap highly, affirm judgment can be made speedily. As the feature sets of canary and animal overlap highly too, the judgment of "canary is animal" is also affirmed. But, this decision needs more time because common attributes of canary and animal are less than canary and bird. So, the set theoretic model can also illuminate the category size effect. But it is different with logic level or line used by the hierarchical network model and the spreading activation model where this model illuminates the category size effect by overlap degree of attributes set of two concepts.

3.3.1.4 *Feature comparison model*

The feature comparison model was proposed by Smith *et al.* [463]. In this model, concepts in long-term memory are represented by a set of attributes or features. But, there is a large difference with the set theoretic model; whether it distinguishes attributes or features of a concept or not depends upon their importance and considering their importance as equal in fact. Feature comparison model divides every semantic feature of a concept into two kinds. One kind is defining feature that is a necessary feature for defining a concept. The other is specificity feature, which is not necessary for defining a concept while has some representation function. Figure 3.5 shows features and their comparison of robin and bird. Features in the figure range from top to down depending on their independence; the higher the site, the more is the import. In the figure, defining features of superior concept (bird) are less than

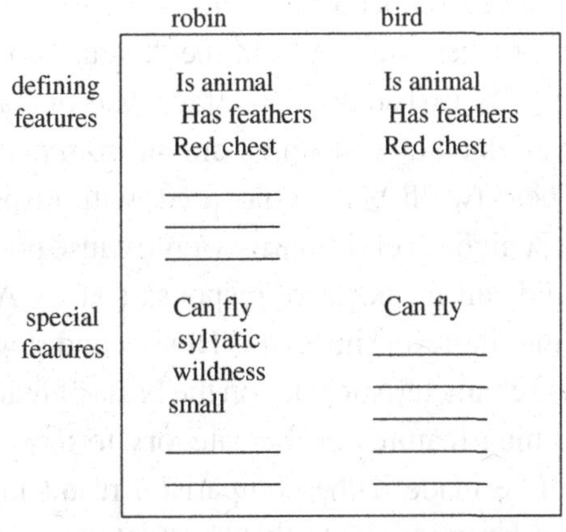

	robin	bird
defining features	Is animal Has feathers Red chest ———— ———— ————	Is animal Has feathers Red chest
special features	Can fly sylvatic wildness small ———— ————	Can fly ———— ———— ———— ————

Fig. 3.5. Features of concept

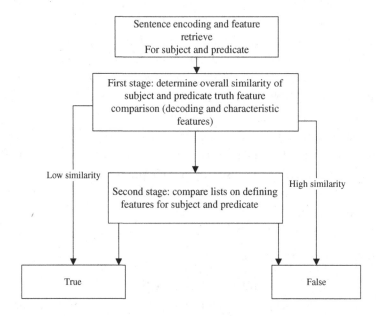

Fig. 3.6. Information processing stage for the feature comparison model

the subordinate concept (robin). But, defining features of the subordinate concept must include all of those superior concepts besides their particular features. Defining feature and specificity feature can be seen as two ends of a semantic feature continuum. Degree of defining or importance of semantic feature is changed continuously. Any point can choose to separate an important feature from others that are not very important. Feature comparison model emphasizes the action of defining feature.

Feature comparison model considers that if the more common semantic features are especially features between concepts, the closer the relation would be.

The two information processing stages in the "feature comparison" model are illustrated in Figure 3.6. At the first comparison stage, lists of features for the instance and category are retrieved, including features drawn from characteristic as well as defining dimensions. These two lists are compared, with respect to all features, to evaluate their similarity. A high-level similarity would cause positive response (true), and little similarity would call for negative response (false). A second comparison stage is necessary for a middle-level similarity. This second stage separates the more defining features from the characteristic ones on the basis of feature weights and then compares the set of defining features of the category to those of the test instance. A positive response can be made if the comparison result matched; otherwise, a negative response would be made. Note that the first stage of the model may be characterized as holistic, intuitive and error prone, whereas the second stage is selective as it considers defining features logically in that it bases its decision on a procedure that evaluates only defining features and relatively error free.

The feature comparison model could provide a reasonable explanation for the typicality. It is clear and effectual to explain various experiment results based on the similarity of semantic characteristics. However, it raises a new problem, that is, how to distinguish the features drawn from characteristics from those drawn from defining dimensions. Additionally, there is a counterexample that questions the validity of this model. The main difficulty for the semantic memory model research is that this model could not be observed directly. Therefore, all the conclusions are drawn from passive operation. Such operation could be performed in two parts: structure or process. These two parts have different concerns, leading to plenty of different models.

3.3.1.5 *Human association memory*

The greatest advantage of the human associative memory model is that this model could represent semantic memory as well as episodic memory; it could process the semantic information and the nonverbal information. What is more, this model could make proper explanation of the practice effect and imitated the computer very well. But it could not explain the phenomenon of the familiarity effect. The comparison process is composed of several stages and figures where the basic unit of semantic memory is a proposition, rather than a concept.

Proposition is composed of associations, which in turn, are composed of two concepts. There are four different kinds of association. (a) Context–fact association. The context and fact are combined into associations, in which facts refer to events that happened in the past and context means the location and exact time of the event. (b) Subject–predicate association. Subject is the principal part of a sentence and the predicate is intended to describe the specialties of the subject. (c) Relation–object association. This construction served as predicate. Relation means the connection between some special actions of subject and other things, while object is the target of actions. (d) Concept–example association. For instance, furniture–desk is a concept–example construction. Proper combination of the above constructions could make up a proposition. The structures and processes of HAM can be described by the propositional tree. When a sentence was received, for example, "The professor asks Bill in the classroom", it could be described by a propositional tree (see Figure 3.7). It is composed of nodes and labeled arrows. The nodes are represented by lower case letters and the labels on the arrows by upper case letters, while the arrows represent various kinds of association. Node A represents the idea of proposition, which is composed of facts and associations between contexts. Node B represents

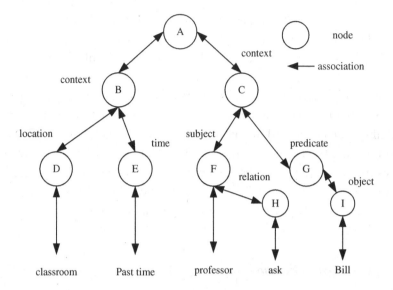

Fig. 3.7. Propositional tree of the HAM model

the idea of the context, which could be further subdivided into a location node D and a time code E (past time, for the professor had asked). Node C represents the idea of fact and it leads by arrows to a subject node F and a predicate node G, which could in turn be subdivided into a relation node H and an object node I. At the bottom of the propositional tree are the general nodes that represent our ideas of each concept in the long-term memory, such as classroom, in the past, professor, ask, Bill. They are terminal nodes for their indivisibility. The propositional tree is meaningless without these terminal nodes. These concepts are organized in a propositional tree according to the propositional structure, rather than their own properties or semantic distance. Such organization approach possesses a network quality. The long-term memory could be regarded as a network of propositional trees, which also demonstrates the advantage of the HAM model that it could represent both semantic memory and episodic memory and combine them together. This propositional tree could comprise all kinds of personal events as long as the episodic memory information is represented with proposition, which is absent in the memory models mentioned above. HAM propositional structure enables one proposition implanted into another and combines into a more complicated proposition. For example, the two propositions, that 'Professor asked Bill in classroom' and 'it makes the examination over on time', could be combined into a new proposition. In this situation, these two original propositions become the subject and the predicate of the new proposition, respectively. This complicated proposition could also be represented with the propositional tree.

According to the HAM model, four stages are needed to accomplish the process of retrieval information to answer a question or understand a sentence. These stages are:

(1) Input a sentence.
(2) Analyze the sentence and generate a propositional tree.
(3) Search from each related node in the long-term memory, until a propositional tree that matched the input proposition is found.
(4) Match the input propositional tree with that found in the long-term memory.

3.3.1.6 *ELINOR model*

ELINOR model was proposed by Lindsay, Norman and Rumelhart [386]. According to this theory, three kinds of information are stored in the long-term memory, including concept, event and scene. Concepts refer to some special ideas that are defined by kinds of relations: is, will be, be kind of. Memory is organized around events. Event is a scene that is composed of actions, actors and objects. Thus, an event could be regarded as various relations around actions. Concepts construct the events. In the ELINOR model, all the concepts, events and scenes are represented by propositions. Scene is combined by several events with temporal connections, which could illustrate the events' order. Take this sentence for example, 'Mom prepared the breakfast for her child and the child went to school with schoolbag after eating'. Among these three kinds of information, events play the most important role and are the basic unit of the ELINOR model. Human memory is organized around events, which in turn are constructed by concepts. Except the three relations of concept, ELINOR also includes more relations, which enable it to represent complex items, make a deep analysis of information and combine semantic and episodic memory together.

ELINOR is a network model. It could include multi-connections and represents various kinds of information. However, its operation process is not clear and the output is difficult to predict; thus it is tough to make reasonable comparisons with other models.

3.3.1.7 *Ontology memory model*

Ontology defines the basic terms and their relationships in thematic areas composed of vocabulary, as well as a combination of these terms and relations to define vocabulary extension rules. Ontology is a description about the important concepts which are to be formalized in a specific area, then to be shared. In the mental model CAM, according to the concept of the field, attributes and relationships in the domain, we formalized the concepts. Field concept offers interesting model entities. They are usually organized into a classification tree, where each node represents a concept, and each concept is specific to its parent node. Each concept in classification is associated with a set of instances. By the definition of taxonomy, if an instance is an instance of a concept, it belongs to conceptual ancestor. Each concept is associated with a set of attributes. In CAM, we use the DDL to represent the ontology [444].

3.3.2 Episodic memory

Episodic memory was proposed by Canadian psychologist Tulving. In his book *Elements of Episodic Memory* published in 1983, Tulving discussed the principle of episodic memory specifically [492].

The base unit of episodic memory is a personal recall behavior. Personal recall behavior begins with an event or reproducing (remember experience) subjectively of experience produced by scene, or change to other forms which keep information, or adopt the combination of them. There are a lot of composition elements and the relation among the elements about recall. The composition elements, which are elements of episodic memory, can be divided into two kinds: one observes the possible incident, and another kind is composition concepts of the hypothesis. The elements of episodic memory consist of encode and retrieval. Encode is about the information of the incident of the experience in a certain situation at some time of day; it points out the process of transform to the traces of memory. Retrieval is mainly about the form and technique of retrieval. The elements of episodic memory and their relations are demonstrated in Figure 3.8.

Nuxoll and Laird first introduced scene memory into Soar episodic in such a way that a scene memory can support a variety of cognitive function agents [342]. In CAM, the plot fragment is stored in the basic module of scenario memory. Plot segment is divided into two levels: one is the logical level of abstraction, and the other is the original level, shown in Figure 3.9. The abstraction level is described by the logic symbols. In the original stage, it includes a description of the object abstraction level, which is related to perceptual information. In order to effectively represent and organize the plot fragments, we use DDL for representation in the abstract level, and make use of ontology in the original level. Furthermore, we use object data map (ODG) to describe plot fragments.

Figure 3.10 depicts the structure of the film Waterloo Bridge object data graph, in which the plot by URI fragments is associated with other objects. Figure 3.10 shows the three objects: M_2, W_2 and movie Waterloo Bridge. In addition, the object W_2 is wearing a blue skirt. The film also associates with the two main characters M_1 and W_1 and W_1 is shown in a white coat.

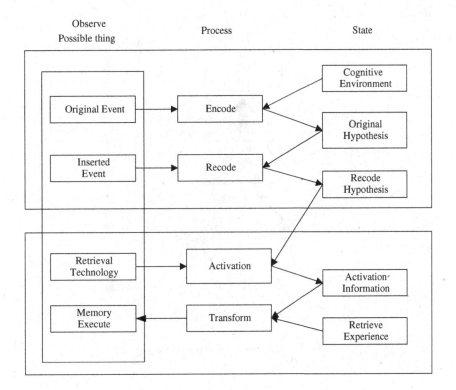

Fig. 3.8. The elements of episodic memory and their relations

In Soar, the plot is the case retrieval model-based reasoning, where based on past experience, solutions to problems are found [251]. According to the clues that back episodes, we follow this idea to build a case-based system. To simplify the system, we restrict the plot to be like a change sequence. Then, the plot retrieval model is used to solve the most relevant search event question. In the abstract level plot, it can accurately represent the contents of the event, thus matching the level of abstraction between the tips and the plot. In CAM, the conversion sequence is formally defined as a possible sequence of the world plot and clues, suggesting the tableau by DDL inference algorithm. One possible sequence of the world is a directed acyclic graph $Seq = (W_p, E_p)$ where each $w_i \in W_p$ represents a possible world and each edge $e_i = (w_i, w_j)$ indicates that the action a_i is executed in w_i and consequently causes the translation from world w_i to world w_j.

With DDL, a plot e_p implicitly indicates c if the formula $e_p \rightarrow c$ is valid. Therefore, we can check whether $e_p \rightarrow c$ is about the implication relations of effective process between plot and clues. The inference procedure is described in Algorithm 3.1.

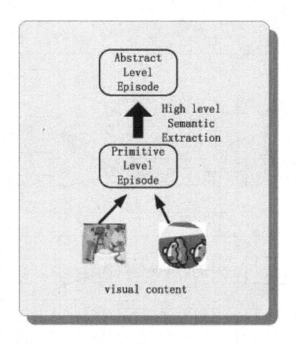

Fig. 3.9.   Fragments of two level stages

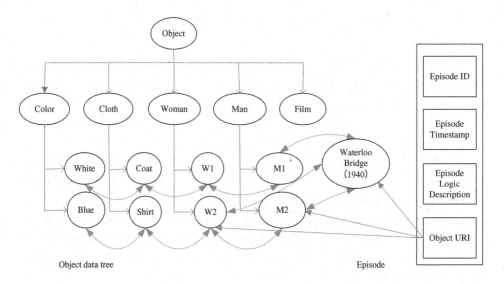

Fig. 3.10.   Figure of object data

Algorithm 3.1. CueMatch(e, c)

    Input: episode$e$,cue$c$

    Output: whether$c \preceq_p e$ hold

    (1) *length*(e) < *length*(c) then

    (2) return false;

    (3) end

    (4) n_e:=*first_node*(e);

    (5) n_c:=*first_node*(c);

    (6) if *MatchPossibleWorld*(n_e; n_c) then

    (7) a_e:=*Null*;

    (8) a_c:=*action*(n_c);

    (9) if $\neg(Pre(a_e) \rightarrow Pre(a_c))$ *unsatisfiable according DDL tableau algorithm* then

    (10) n_{tmp}:= n_e;

    (11) while *next_node*(n_{tmp}) $\neq$*Null* do

    (12) a_e:= (a_e; *action*(n_{tmp}));

    (13) if *MatchAction*(a_e; a_c) then

    (14) Let *sub$_e$* be the sub sequence by removing a_e from e;

    (15) Let *sub$_c$* be the sub sequence by removing a_c from c;

    (16) if *CueMatching*(*sub$_e$*; *sub$_c$*) then

    (17) return true;

    (18) end

    (19) end

    (20) n_{tmp}:=*next node*(n_{tmp});

    (21) end

    (22) end

    (23) end

    (24) Remove n_e from e;

    (25) return *CueMatching*(e; c);

Function MatchPossibleWorld(w_i, w_j)

Input: possible worlds w_i, w_j

Output: whether$w_i \models w_j$hold

    (1) f_w :=*Conj*(w_i) $\rightarrow$ *Conj*(w_j);

    (2) if $\neg f_w$ *is unsatisfiable according to DDL tableau algorithm* then

    (3) *return* true;

(4) else
(5) *return* false;
(6) end

Function MatchAction(α_i, α_j)
Input: actionα_i, α_j
Output: whether$\alpha_i \models \alpha_j$ hold

(1) if $\alpha_i == null \ or \ \alpha_j == null$ then
(2) *return* false
(3) end
(4) $f_{pre} := Conj(Pre(\alpha_i)) \rightarrow Conj(Pre(\alpha_j))$;
(5) $f_{eff} := Conj(Eff(\alpha_i)) \rightarrow Conj(Eff(\alpha_j))$;
(6) if $\neg f_{pre}$ *and* $\neg f_{eff}$ *are unsatisfiable according to DDL Algorithm* then
(7) *return* true;
(8) else
(9) *return* false;
(10) end

In Algorithm 3.1, the function length returns the length of a possible sequence of the world. The length of a possible world sequence is determined by the number contained in the sequence of nodes. When function returns (n), the implementation of the action is done in a possible world of order N inside. Function's next node returns n' in the possible world's sequence. The next node, n, by performing the operation (n) reaches the possible sequences of a world. Algorithm 3.1 step 14, through the sequence of actions constructors ';' produces a combined action, connecting the two movements α and action (ntmp). To simplify the algorithm, we assume that the action (NULL;) $== \alpha$. In Algorithm 3.1, MatchPossibleWorld() and MatchAction() are also functions. We use DDL tableau algorithm to decide whether the negation of the formula is satisfiable or not.

3.3.3 Procedural memory

Procedural memory refers to the memory of how to do things, including the perception skills, cognitive skills, motor skills and memory. Procedural memory is the memory of inertia, also known as memory skills, it is often difficult to use language to describe such memories and we often need several attempts to gradually explain them.

Procedural memory is the memory of procedural knowledge, i.e., "know why" is about the skills of knowledge and understanding of "how to" memories. Individuals achieve the degree of automation and refinement via full practice, then one can do two things at the same time without feeling laborious, such as use a mobile phone and drive while the program remains natural and smooth. This way the driving is not affected due to the call.

Procedural knowledge presumes knowledge of its existence only by means of some form of indirect jobs. It includes inspiration, methods, planning, practices, procedures, strategies, techniques and tricks to explain "what" and "how". It is not only about how to do something or gain knowledge about the link between stimulus and response, but also about the behavior of the program or basic skills learning. For example, people know how to drive a car, how to use the ATM, how to use the Internet search target information.

In the ACT-R, usage of production systems in Soar and other systems of procedural knowledge representation is actually a "condition–action" rule, where procedures of an act occur if certain conditions are met. Output refers to the coupling condition and action, resulting in an action under the rules of a condition, it consists of the condition items "if" (if) and the action item "then" (then).

We adopt the DDL for describing procedural knowledge of CAM. In order to be compatible with the action formalism proposed by Baader *et al.* [33], we extend the atomic action definition of DDL to support occlusion and conditional post-conditions. With respect to a TBox T, extended atomic action of DDL is a triple $\alpha \equiv (P, O, E)$ [79], where:

— $\alpha \in N_A$;
— P is a finite set of ABox assertions for describing preconditions;
— O is a finite set of occlusions, where each occlusion is of the form $A(p)$ or $R(p, q)$, with A a primitive concept name R a role name and $p, q \in N_I$;
— E is a finite set of conditional post-conditions, where each post-condition is of the form φ/ψ, with φ an ABox assertion and ψ a primitive literal.

In the above definition, the set of pre-conditions describes the conditions under which the action is executable. For each post-condition φ/ψ, if φ holds before the execution of the action, then the formula ψ will hold after the execution. Occlusions describe the formulas that cannot be determined during the execution of the action.

As an example, an action named BuyBookNotified(Tom, Kin) is specified as follows:

BuyBookNotified(Tom, Kin)≡
({*customer(Tom), book(KingLear)*} ,{} ,
{*instore(KingLear)/bought(Tom, KingLear)*,
instore(KingLear)/¬instore(KingLear),

instore(KingLear)/noti fy(Tom, Noti fyOrderSucceed),
¬instore(KingLear)/noti fy(Tom, Noti fyBookOutOf Stock) })

According to this description, if the book *KingLear* is at the store before the execution of the action, then, after the execution of the action, the formulas *bought(Tom, KingLear)*, ¬ *instore(KingLear)* and *notify(Tom, NotifyOrderSucceed)* will hold, otherwise the formula *notify(Tom, NotifyBookOutOfStock)* will be true, which indicates that Tom is notified that the book is out of stock.

The difference between declarative memory and procedural memory is that declarative memory works for the description of things, such as "self-introduction", which is an explicit memory, while procedural memory works for technical actions, such as "cycling", which is an implicit memory. The organs for procedural memory are cerebellum and striatum and the most essential part is the deep cerebellar nuclei.

3.4 Short-term Memory

According to the temporal length of memory operation, there are three types of human memory: sensory memory, short-term memory and long-term memory. The relationship among these three can be illustrated by Figure 3.11. First of all, the information from the environment reaches the sensory memory. If the information is observed, they will enter the short-term memory. It is in short-term memory that the individual will restructure the information for use and response. In order to analyze the information in short-term memory, you will be out in the long-term memory storage of knowledge. At the same time, short-term memory can preserve information, if necessary, same information can also be deposited in long-term memory. In Figure 3.11, the arrows indicate the flow of information storage in three runs in the direction of the model.

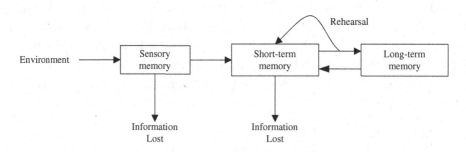

Fig. 3.11. Memory system

3.4.1 Short-term memory encoding

Information encoded in sensory memory will enter into short-term memory, through further processing, and then enter into long-term memory in which information can be kept for a long time. Information in short-term memory is generally kept for 20–30 s, but if you repeat them, they can continue to save. Delay in repeating information can lead to its disappearance.

Short-term memory stores information being used, which has an important role in psychological activities. First, short-term memory plays the role of consciousness, so that we know what we are receiving and what we are doing. Second, short-term memory enables us to integrate the information from sensory to a complete image. Third, short-term memory acts as a temporary register when thinking and solving problems. For example, when we do math problems, before every next step, we temporarily store calculation results of the previous step for final use. Finally, short-term memory keeps the current policy and wishes. All this allows us to take a variety of complex behaviors until reaching the ultimate goal. Because of the important role of short-term memory, in most of the current study, it is renamed as working memory. In contrast to the large amount of information available in sensory memory, the ability of short-term memory is quite limited. If you give the participants a string of numbers, such as 6–8–3–5–9, he can recite it immediately. If it is more than seven-digit string of numbers, most people would not be able to recite it very well. In 1956, American psychologist Miller made it clear that short-term memory capacity is 7 ± 2 chunks. Chunk means several little units that were united into a familiar and heavy unit of information processing, also means that the unit is normally made up like this. Chunk is a course and a unit. Knowledge experience and chunk: The function of the chunk is to reduce the stimulus unit in the timely memory and to increase the information contained in each unit. The more knowledge that people own, the more messages in each chunk. Similar to a chunk, but not divided by meaning. There is no meaning connection between all kinds of composition. In order to remember a long figure, we can divide figures into several groups. So, it is an effective method where we can reduce the quantity of independent elements in figures. This kind of organization is called a chunk, which plays a great role in long-term memory.

It has been proposed that information was stored in short-term memory according to its acoustical characteristic. In other words, even if a message is received by vision, it will encode according to the characteristic of acoustics. For example, when you see a group of letters B–C–D, you are recognizing them according to their pronunciation [bi:]–[si:]–[di:], but not according to their shape to encode.

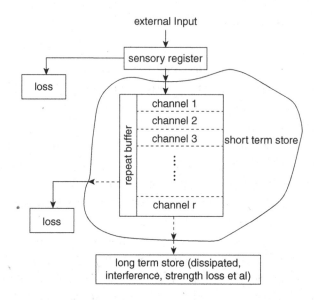

Fig. 3.12. Repeat buffer in short-term memory

Short-term memory encoding of humans may have strong acoustical attribute, but cannot get rid of the code of other properties either. Monkey cannot speak, but can do the work of short-term memory too. For example, after seeing a figure, it will select one of two colorful geometric figures.

Figure 3.12 provides repeat buffer in short-term memory. Short-term memory consists of several troughs. Every trough is equivalent to an information channel. Informational unit coming from sensory memory enters into different troughs separately. The repeating process of buffer selectively repeats the information in the troughs. The information repeated in the troughs will be entered into the long-term memory. The information which is not be repeated will be cleared out from the short-term memory and disappear.

The duration of information in various troughs is different. The longer the time the information is kept in the trough, the more chances that it may enter in the long-term memory, and the more chances that it may be washed and squeezed out by new message coming from the sensory memory. Comparatively, the long-term memory is a real storehouse of information, but information can be forgotten by subside, interference and intensity.

3.4.2 Information extraction

It is quite complicated to retrieve the course of short-term memory. It involves a lot of questions that arise from different hypotheses. There is no identical view so far.

3.4.2.1 *The classical research by Sternberg*

It is indicated by Sternberg's research results that the information retrieval in short-term memory is through the way of series scanning, which is exhaustive to realize. We can interpret it as the model of scanning.

Sternberg's experiment is a classical research paradigm. The premise of the experiment is that until participants scan all items in the short-term memory; they will judge items of test as "yes" or "no", then the reaction time of participants' correct judges should not change with the size of memory (as shown by Figure 3.13(a)) . The experimental result is shown in Figure 3.13(b). The reaction time will be lengthened with the size of the memory. It means the scanning of short-term memory does not carry on parallel scanning, but carries on serial scanning.

Sternberg's theory must solve another problem: if the information retrieval in short-term memory is serial scanning instead of parallel scanning, then, where should the scanning begin, and how should it expire. He thinks the information retrieval is serial scanning even though participants are busy enough with their own affairs. Meanwhile, the course of judgment includes comparing and decision-making process. So, when participants are judging, they will not be self-terminating.

3.4.2.2 *Direct access model*

According to Wickelgren's research, retrieving items in short-term memory is not through comparing. People can lead to the position of items in short-term memory directly, and retrieve directly.

Direct access model thinks that the retrieval of information does not require scanning in short-term memory, the brain can directly access the position where items are needed to draw them directly. This model thinks that each item in short-term memory has certain familiar value or trace intensity. So, according to these

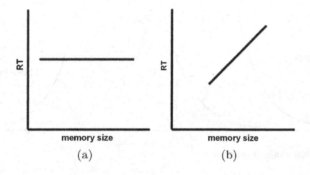

Fig. 3.13.   Scanning test by Sternberg

standards, people can draw a judgment. There is a judgment standard within the brain, if the familiarity is higher than this standard, then it will generate "yes", if lower than this standard, then will generate "no". The higher the degree of deviation from the familiarity with the standard value, the faster that people can give a yes or a no response.

Direct access model can explain the serial position effect (primacy and recency effect). But how does short-term memory know the position of the items? If retrieval of information belongs to direct access, why does the reaction time linearly increase when the numbers of items increase?

3.4.2.3 *Dual model*

According to the study by Atkinson and Juola, the retrieval process of information has already included scanning and direct access in the course of short-term memory. In brief, both ends are direct, and the middle part refers to scanning (as shown in Figure 3.14).

Search model and direct access model both have their reasonable aspects, while there is a deficiency also. So, someone attempts to combine the two together. Atkinson and Juola put forward that information retrieval of the double model in short-term memory is an attempt [30]. They imagine that each word that was input can

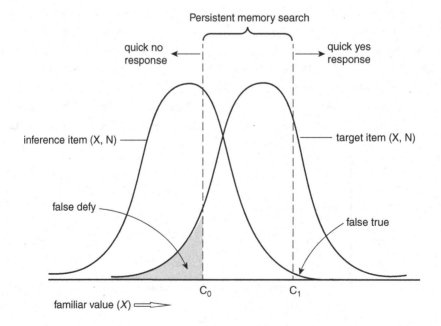

Fig. 3.14. Dual model

be encoded according to their sensorial dimensionality, called sensory code; words have meanings, called concept codes. Sensory code and concept code form a concept node. Each concept node has a different level of activation or familiar value.

There are two standards of judging within the brain; One is "high-standard" (C1) — if the familiar value of a certain word is equal or higher than this standard, people can make a rapid "yes" response; another one is a low standard (C0) — if the familiar value of a certain word is equal or lower than this standard, people can make a rapid "deny" response. Atkinson and Juola consider this as a direct access course. However, if a survey word whose familiar value is lower than a "high-standard" and is higher than "the low standard", it will carry on serial search and make a reaction. So, the reaction times will spend more.

The study of short-term memory also shows that there are some relationships between the processing speed and the materials property or the type of information. The speed of process increases with increasing of the memory capacity. The bigger the capacity of the material, the faster it will scan.

The experimental result indicates that the processing speed in short-term memory has the relationship with materials properties or information type. In 1972, Cavanaugh through calculating the average experimental results to some kind of material in different researches obtained the average time of scanning one item and contrasted the corresponding capacity of short-term memory (see Table 3.3). An interesting phenomenon can be found from the table: the processing speed is raised with increase of the memory capacity. The bigger the capacity of the material, the faster is the scan. It is difficult to explain this phenomenon clearly. When imagining in short-term memory, information is signified with its characteristic. But the storage space of short-term memory is limited, the larger each average characteristic in quantity is, the smaller is the quantity of short-term memory that can be stored.

Table 3.3. Processing speed and memory capacity in different types of materials

	Processing speed (MS)	Memory capacity (item)
Figure	33.4	7.70
Color	38.0	7.10
Letter	40.2	6.35
Words	47.0	5.50
Geometric figure	50.0	5.30
Random figure	68.0	3.80
Pointless syllable	73.0	3.40

Cavanaugh then thought that each stimulus' processing time is directly proportional to its average characteristic quantity. If the average characteristic quantity is heavy, then it will need more time to process, otherwise fewer times will be needed. Also, there are many doubtful points in this kind of explanation. But it connected the information retrieval of short-term memory, memory capacity and information representation. This is really an important problem. The processing speed reflects the characteristic of the processing course. Behind processing speed difference of different materials, the cause may be because of memory capacity and information representation, etc. and thus has different course about information retrieval.

For the forgetting process of short-term memory, it is shown by the Peterson–Peterson method that:

(1) Information can be kept for 15–30 s in short-term memory;
(2) If not repeated, then this information in short-term memory will be forgotten rapidly (as shown in Figure 3.15);
(3) If the quantity in short-term memory does not change, then the change of material property will have no influence on short-term memory.

3.4.3 Short-term memory in CAM

The short-term memory stores temporary information by using the agent BDI model, namely, beliefs, targets and intent description [378]. The agent will be used to store the memory of the world cognitive-beliefs, mainly used for storing the information of the external environment and internal environment. This information provides the necessary basis for the thinking activity. The target/intention of memory storage is the state that agent desired or wants to maintain.

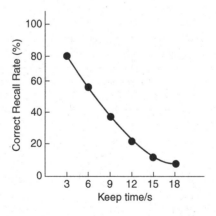

Fig. 3.15. The forgetting rate in short-term memory without repeat

3.4.3.1 *Belief*

Belief represents a kind of information; a part of the information agent can be obtained from the environment, a part of the information can be generated from their own internal environment. This information constitutes the knowledge base of the agent itself. We usually regard the belief as the agent's knowledge base, the knowledge base contains abundant contents, mainly the basic axioms, objective facts, objective data, etc. Belief knowledge can be seen as a three tuple $K = \langle T, S, B \rangle$, where T is the description of concepts and definitions in the field, S is the description of facts and the relationship between the axioms. These constraints ensure consistency and integrity of the knowledge base; B is used to represent the current state of the belief set, which contains facts and data. As time goes by, changes in the environment and the state of the agent itself change the contents of B dynamically.

3.4.3.2 *Target*

The target represents an agent's desire and the target drives the agent to produce action on external environment. As time goes on, the agent will have a lot of desires. But sometimes these desires are consistent, sometimes they are contradictory. Therefore, the agent should handle it carefully, with all the desires to form a coherent desire. The conflict desire in the agent will be removed from the desire set according to the algorithm in the system. In a target-based design, the target has different types. Some of the targets are the maintain-type, i.e., the target is to maintain a certain state of the system. Some of the targets are the achieve-type, the target which the system has not achieved before to need the agent output its actions to the external environment according to the existing state, so as to achieve its desired target.

The state of the object allows us to model the agent in multiple ways. Agent is not only a passive response to the external environment, i.e., when the external environment changes, but they should also take a series of actions to maintain its balance. At the same time, the agent cannot be influenced by the external environment and should take the initiative to complete some targets. Agent's target needs to be generated; there are three kinds of approaches:

(1) Determined by the system designer in the stage of system design or in the stage of system initialization;
(2) Generated automatically according to the dynamic changes of the environment;
(3) Generated by the agent internally.

3.4.3.3 *Intention*

Intention is one of the most accomplished or the most appropriate target(s) to achieve; it is the target that the main body is going to achieve and it is the intent of the thinking state for specific implementation through planning. Planning is a sequence of actions that the agent constructs in order to complete its cognitive tasks. In the BDI cognitive model, there are three main parts in the action plan, which are target builder, target decomposition and target action planner. Target builder is responsible for generating the target that the system needs to solve. The target decomposition is responsible for extracting the relevant information from the memory and the target can be decomposed into small targets. The main task of the target action plan is to plan each subgoal and generate the action sequence to achieve the target. The generated action sequence is stored in an action buffer, and the agent is executed according to the sequence of the action in the action buffer.

3.5 Working Memory

In 1974, based on experiments on imitated short-term memory deficit, Baddeley *et al.* proposed the concept of working memory [44]. In the traditional Baddeley model, working memory is composed of a central executive system and two subsidiary systems including phonological loop and visual–spatial sketchpad [46]. The phonological loop is responsible for the information storage and control on the foundation of voice. It consists of phonological storage and articulatory control process, which can hold information through subvocal articulation to prevent the disappearance of spoken representation and also switch from the written language to the spoken code. Visual spatial sketchpad is mainly responsible for storing and processing the information in visual or spatial form, possibly including the two subsystems of vision and space. The central executive system is a core of working memory and is responsible for each subsystem and their connection with long-term memory, the coordination of attention resources, the strategy choice and the plan, etc. A large amount of behavioral researches and a lot of evidences in neural psychology have shown the existence of three subcompositions, the understanding of the structure about working memory and then the function form is enriched and perfected constantly.

3.5.1 Models of working memory

Existing models of working memory can be roughly divided into two big classes. One is the European traditional working memory model, among which the representative one is the multi-composition model brought forward by Baddeley, which divided the working memory model into many subsidiary systems with independent resources, stress modality-specific processing and storage. The other one is the North American traditional working memory model, which is represented by the ACT-R model [20], emphasizing the globosity of the working memory, general resource allocation and activation. The investigation of the former mainly focuses on the storage component of the working memory model, i.e., phonological loop and visual–spatial sketchpad. Baddeley pointed out that short-term storage should be first clarified because of its easily operating nature before answering more complicated questions of processing, whereas the North American class emphasizes the working memory's role in complicated cognitive tasks, such as reading and speech comprehension. So, North American's working memory model is similar to European's general central executive system. Now, two classes of researches are approving some things about each other more and more and exert a mutual influence in respective theory construction. For example, the concept of episodic buffer is very similar to proposition representation of the Barnard's interacting cognitive model [49]. So, the two classes already demonstrate certain integrated and unified trend.

Baddeley developed his working memory theory in recent years on the basis of traditional model in which a new subsystem-episodic buffer is increased [45]. Baddeley suggested that the traditional model does not notice how the different kinds of information are combined and how the combined results maintain, so it cannot explain that the subjects could only recall about five words in the memory task in random word lists, but they can recall about 16 words in the memory task according to the prose content. Episodic buffer represents a separated storage system, which adopted a multi-modal code, offered a platform where information combined temporarily among phonological loop, visual–spatial sketchpad and long-term memory and integrated information from multiple resources into the intact and consistent situation through the central executive system. Episodic buffer, phonological loop and visual–spatial sketchpad are equally controlled by the central executive system. Though integration of different kinds of information is executed by the central executive system, it maintained and supported subsequent integration by the episodic buffer. Episodic buffer is independent of the long-term memory, but it is a necessary stage in long-term episodic learning. The episodic buffer can explain questions such as the interference effect of serial position recall, the mutual influence question among speech and visual space processing, the memory trunk and unified consciousness experience, etc. The four-component model of working memory including the newly increased episodic buffer is shown in Figure 3.16 [45].

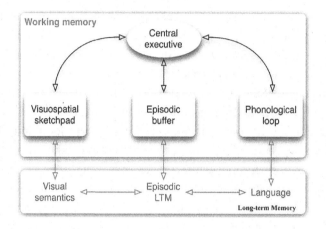

Fig. 3.16. Four-component model for working memory

The ACT-R model from Anderson can explain a large number of data with individual difference. This model regards working memory resources as one kind of attention activation, named source activation. Source activation spreads from the present focus-of-attention to the memory node related to present task, and conserves these accessible nodes. The ACT-R is a production system, and processes information according to the activation production regularity. It emphasizes that the processing activities depend on goal information, the stronger the present goal is, the higher the activation level of relevant information is, and the more rapid and accurate information processing is. This model suggests that the individual difference of the working memory capacity actually reflects the total amount of "source activation" expressed with the parameter W, which is also field-universal and field-unitary. This source activation in the phonological and visual space information is based on the same mechanism. The obvious deficiency of this model lies in the fact that it only explains with a parameter of the individual difference in the complicated cognitive task and neglects that the individual difference of working memory might be related with processing speed, cognitive strategy and past knowledge skill. But the ACT-R model emphasizes the singleness of working memory; in order to primarily elucidate the common structure in detail, it can thereby remedy the deficiency of the model emphasizing the diversity of working memory.

3.5.2 Working memory and reasoning

Working memory is closely related to reasoning and has two functions: maintaining information and forming the preliminary psychological characteristics. Representation form of the central executive system is more abstract than the two subsystems.

Working memory is the core of reasoning and reasoning is the sum of working memory ability.

According to the concept of working memory system, a dual-task paradigm is adopted to study the relationship between each component of work memory and reasoning. The *dual-task* paradigm means that two kinds of tasks are carried out at the same time: one is the reasoning task, the other is the secondary task used to interfere with every component of working memory. The tasks to interfere with the central executive system are to demand subjects to randomly produce the letter or figure, or to utilize the sound to attract subjects' attention and ask them to carry out the corresponding response. The task to interfere with the phonological loop cycle is to ask subjects pronounce constantly such as "the, the…" or to count the number in a certain order such as 1, 3, 6, 8 and so on. The task to interfere with visual–spatial sketchpad is a lasting space activity, for example, typewriting blindly in a certain order. All the secondary tasks should guarantee certain speed and correct rate, and conduct the reasoning task at the same time. The principle of the *dual-task* is that two tasks compete for the limited resources at the same time. For example, the interference to the phonological loop is to make the reasoning task and the secondary task take up the limited resources of the subsystem in the phonological loop of working memory at the same time. If the correct rate of reasoning is decreased and response time is increased in this condition, then we can confirm that the phonological loop is involved in the reasoning process. There is a series of studies which shows that the secondary task is effective for the interference of the working memory.

The relationships between reasoning and working memory were studied by Gilhooly *et al.* [174]. In the first experiment, it was found that the way of presenting the sentence influenced the correct rate of the reasoning: the correct rate was higher in visual presentations than the hearing presentation, the reason being that the load of memory in visual presentations was lower than the hearing presentations. In the second experiment, it was found that the presented deductive reasoning task visually was most prone to be damaged by the *dual-task* paradigm (memory load) used to interfere with the executive system, next by the phonological loop and least by the visual–spatial processing system. This indicates that representation in deductive reasoning is a more abstract form which is in accordance with the psychological model theory of reasoning and has caused the central executive system to be involved in reasoning activities. Probably, the phonological loop played a role too because the concurrent phonological activities with the reasoning activity slowed down, which indicated two kinds of tasks may compete for the limited resource. In this experiment, Gilhooly *et al.* found that the subjects may adopt a series of strategies in deductive reasoning, and that which kind of strategy is adopted can be inferred according to the result of reasoning. Different secondary tasks force the subjects to adopt different strategies, so their memory load is different too, vice versa. Increasing the memory load will change the strategy too because the changing strategy will cause decreased memory load. In 1998, Gilhooly explored the relationship between each component of working memory and deductive reasoning in presenting the serial sentence visually using the dual-task paradigm. Sentences presented in serial way require more storage space than those presented in simultaneous way. The result showed that visual–spatial processing system and phonological loop all participated in deductive reasoning, and the central executive system still plays an important role among them. The conclusion can be drawn that the central executive systems all participated in deductive reasoning no matter in serial or simultaneous presentation; when memory load increases, visual–spatial processing system and phonological loop may participate in the reasoning process too.

3.5.3 Neural mechanism of working memory

With the development of brain science in the recent 10 years, it has been found that there are two kinds of working memories involved in the thinking process. One is used for storing the speech material (concept) with the speech coding; the other is used for storing the visual or spatial material (imagery) with the figure coding. Further research indicates, not only concept and imagery have their own working memory, but also imagery itself has two kinds of different working memories. There are two kinds of imagery of the things: One represents the basic attribute of the things used for recognizing them, generally called "attribute imagery" or "object image"; the other one is used for reflecting the relationship of spatial and structural aspect of the things (related to visual localization), generally called "spatial image", or "relation image". Spatial image does not include the content information of the object, but the characteristic information that is used to define required spatial position information and structural relation of the objects. In this way, there are three kinds of different working memories:

(1) Working memory of storing speech material (abbreviated as the speech working memory): suitable for time logical thinking;
(2) Working memory of storing the object image (attribute image) (abbreviated as the object working memory): suitable for spatial structural thinking, which regarded the object image (attribute image) as the processing target, usually named as idiographic thinking;
(3) Working memory of storing the spatial image (related image) (abbreviated as the spatial working memory): suitable for spatial structural thinking which regarded

the spatial image (relation image) as the processing target, usually named as intuitive thinking.

It has been proved by neuroscience researchers that these three kinds of working memories and their corresponding thinking processing mechanisms have their corresponding areas of the cerebral cortex (though the localization of some working memory is not very accurate at present). According to the new development of brain science research, Blumstein of Brown University pointed out [60], the speech function is not localized in a narrow area (according to the traditional idea, the speech function only involves Broca's area and Wernicke's area of left hemisphere), but widely distributed in the areas around *lateral fissure* of the left brain, and extended toward anterior and posterior regions of frontal lobe, including Broca's area, inferior frontal lobe close to face *movement cortex* and left central front back (excluding the frontal and occipital pole). Among them, the damage of Broca's area will harm the speech expression function, and the damage of Wernicke's area will harm the speech comprehension function. But the brain mechanism related with the speech expression and comprehension function is not merely limited to these two areas. The working memory used for maintaining speech materials temporarily is regarded as generally relating to left prefrontal lobe, but the specific position is not accurate still at present.

Compared with the speech working memory, the localization of object working memory and the spatial working memory is much more accurate. In 1993, Jonides and other researchers from the Michigan University investigated the object image and the spatial image with positron emission tomography (PET) and obtained some achievement about their localization and mechanism [226]. PET detects pairs of gamma rays emitted indirectly by a positron-emitting radionuclide (tracer), which is introduced into the body on a biologically active molecule. Images of tracer concentration in three-dimensional (3D) space within the body are then reconstructed by computer analysis. Because of its accurate localization and non-invasive features, this technique is suitable for human subject studies.

3.6 Theory of Forgetting

Memory is an advanced mental process, which is influenced by lots of factors. Old association enables inference from results to reason, without any scientific demonstration. But Ebbinghaus broke through Wundt's assumption that memory and other advanced mental processes cannot be studied with experimental methods. After observing the result and strictly controlling the reason and carrying out quantitative analysis to the memory course, he specially created the pointless syllable and saved law for the study of memory.

Although there is much disputation among old association, they never analyzed association's own mechanism. Ebbinghaus spelled letter into pointless syllable as experimental material, which made associative content and structure unified and got rid of adults' interference of relating the association to the experiment. It is a great job to quantify memory experimental material. It is a very good means and tool. For instance, he spelled the letter into a pointless syllable in the form of a vowel and two consonants, such as zog, xot, gij, nov, etc. and about 2,300 syllables, then formatted a syllable group by several syllables, made up an experiment material by several syllable groups. Such a pointless syllable can only be remembered by repeatedly reading aloud. This created material unit for various memory experiments and made the memory effect identical and convenient for statistical comparison and analysis. For example, studying different length syllable groups (7, 12, 16, 32, 64 syllable groups of syllables, etc.) influences on knowing and remembering, retention effect and learning times (or over learning) related with memory.

In order to quantitatively measure the learning (memory) effects, Ebbinghaus created the saving method. He asked subjects to read the recognition material aloud again and again, until subjects could recite it out smoothly and errorless for the first time (or twice continuously). He wrote down number of times and time needed from reading aloud to reciting. After certain time (usually 24 hours), he asked the subjects to learn and recite the material again, compare the number of times and time of the second time with the first time, to see how many number of times and time in hours it will save. This is named saving method or relearning law. Saving method created a quantitatively statistical standard for the memory experiment. For instance, Ebbinghaus' experimental results proved that in the seven-syllable group, subjects were able to recite by reading aloud once. This was generally acknowledged as the memory span later. The 12-syllable group needed to read 16.6 times to recite, and the 16-syllable group took 30 times to recite. To memorize the same material, the more number of times one reads aloud, the deeper in the memory it is consolidated, then (the next day) the more one reads aloud the more the number of times the material is saved while relearning.

In order to make learning and memory hardly influenced by past and daily working experience, Ebbinghaus had employed the pointless syllable as the material of studying memory. He made, and tried with himself, learning the material until just being able to recite. After a certain time, he relearned the material, and made the time and number of times of reading aloud saved as the index of memory. He generally made a word form with 10–36 syllables. He successively learned thousands of word

Table 3.4. Memory performance affected by different time intervals

Time interval	Percentage of time saved in relearning
20 min	58.2
1 hour	44.2
8 hour	35.8
1 day	33.7
3 days	27.8
6 days	25.4
31 days	21.1

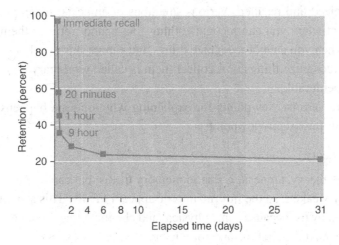

Fig. 3.17. Forgetting curve by Ebbinghaus

forms within seven or eight years. His research results were published in 1885 with the book title *Memory*. Table 3.4 is one example coming from his experimental results. By utilizing the table material, one can draw a curve which is generally called a forgetting curve (shown in Figure 3.17).

From Ebbinghaus's forgetting curve, it is obvious that the course of forgetting is unbalanced: within the first hour, the information kept in long-term memory reduces rapidly, then, the forgetting speed is slackened gradually. In Ebbinghaus' research, even after 31 days, there is still a certain intensity of saving; the information is still kept in some degree. Ebbinghaus' original work initiated two important discoveries. One is to describe the forgetting process as the forgetting curve. The psychologist replaced the pointless syllable with various materials such as word, sentence even story later on, finally found that, no matter what material had to be remembered, the developing trend of the forgetting curve was the same as Ebbinghaus' results. Ebbinghaus' second important discovery was how long the information in long-term memory can be kept. Research has found that information can be kept in long-term memory for decades. Therefore, things learned in childhood, which have not been used for many years, once they have an opportunity to be learned again, will resume original level shortly. If things had not been used any longer, which might be considered forgetfulness, but in fact it is not a complete forgetfulness.

Amnesia and retention are the two aspects of memory contradiction. Amnesia is that memory content which cannot be retained or is difficult to be retrieved. When trying to recollect things from remembrance, for example, they cannot be recognized and recalled in certain circumstance, or mistakes happen while things are being recognized and recalled. Various situations of amnesia: incomplete amnesia is the moment when you can recognize things but cannot retrieve them; complete amnesia is when you cannot recognize things and cannot retrieve them. Inability to temporarily recognize things or recollect them is called temporary amnesia, otherwise called perdurable.

There are various viewpoints for explaining why amnesia happens. Here, we introduce four important viewpoints:

(1) Decline theory

In the decline theory, amnesia is due to memory traces that cannot be strengthened but gradually weaken, so the information disappears finally. This statement is easy to be accepted by us, because some physical and chemical traces tend to decline and even disappear. At the circumstance of sensory memory and short-term memory, the learning material without paid attention or rehearsal may be forgotten because of declining in trace. But the decline theory is very difficult to verify with experiment, because of the decline of retention quantity within certain time, perhaps due to the interference of other materials, thus not due to the decline of memory traces. It has already been proved that even in case of short-term memory; interference is also an important cause of amnesia.

(2) Interference theory

Interference theory holds that long-term memory of the forgotten information is mainly due to learning and the memory is subject to interference by other stimuli. Once the disturbance was removed, the memory can be resumed. Interference can be divided into proactive and retroactive interferences. Proactive interference is that one has to learn new information on the inhibition of the old information. Basically, inhibition of memories of the old information. A series of studies showed that in long-term memory, the information was forgotten despite the spontaneous regression of factors, but mainly by the mutual interference between information caused. Generally speaking, two types of learning materials have become similar to the role of greater interference. Content for different learning on how to make reasonable arrangements to reduce the mutual interference effects in the consolidation of learning is worth considering.

(3) Suppression theory

According to suppression theory, forgetting is as a result of depressed mood or the role of motivation. If this suppression is lifted, memory will also be able to resume. First of all, Freud found this phenomenon in clinical practice. Through hypnosis among his patients, he found that many could recall the early years of life in many experiences, but some were usually not in their memories. In his view, these experiences could not be recalled because these memories were related to their unhappy and sad state, so he refused to enter their consciousness, its stored in the unconscious, which is suppressed by unconscious motives. Only when the mood weakens in Lenovo, which has been forgotten it can be recalled with the material. In daily life, emotional tension as a result of forgetfulness is often. For example, the examination may be perceived as the result of excessive emotional tension, with the result that some of the content learned may be forgotten. To suppress that, we take into account individual needs, desires, motivations, emotions, such as the role of memory, which are not in front of the two theories involved. Thus, while it does not have the support of experimental materials, it is still a theory worthy of attention.

(4) Retrieval failure

Some researchers believe that message stored in long-term memory is never lost. We cannot remember things because we extract the relevant information without the right clues. For example, we often have the experience that we are obviously aware of each other's names, but cannot remember what the name is. Extraction of the phenomenon of the failure suggests that long-term memory from the extracted information is a complex process, rather than a simple "all-or-none" issue. If there is nothing worthy in a memory or if we are unable to recollect information about the memory, it would be difficult to extract such a memory. It is like in a library to find a book, if we do not know its title, author and retrieval code, although the book is in the library, we can hardly find it. Likewise, a word in memory along with remembering the words of the other clues, such as word shape, word sound, phrase and the context and so on, will help us to make a word into a sentence.

In normal reading, the information extraction is very rapid, almost an automatic process. But sometimes, information is extracted through special clues. Extraction of clues enables us to recall what has been forgotten, or the re-identified is stored in the memory of things. When we cannot recall a thing, we should look for clues from various aspects. A clue to the effectiveness of extraction depends on the following conditions:

(a) The degree of tightness with encoding information

In the long-term memory, information is often organized by semantics and therefore closely linked with the information significance of the clues which are often more conducive to the extraction of information. For example, the sight stirs up one's feelings, the reason why we return to the imagination is because the ideas embedded are closely linked with the past, and they arouse our memories of the past.

(b) The degree of dependence on situations and status

Generally speaking, when the efforts of memories are paid in a learning environment, people tend to remember more things. In fact, we learn not only what will be coding in mind, but also what occurs in many of the environmental characteristics at the same time into a long-term memory. An environmental characteristic of these memories in the future is becoming an effective clue of retrieval. The similarity of the environment that facilitates or hinders the phenomenon of memory is called the context-dependent memory.

Just like the external environment, the study of the internal mental state will be incorporated into the long-term memory, as an extract clues memory is called a state of interdependence. For example, even when a person under the influence of alcohol is taught new material, he may be able to recall the learning later. When in a good mood, people often remember more beautiful memories of the past; when in bad mood, people often more remember their troubles.

(c) The effects of emotions

Emotional state and the match of the learning contents also affect memory. In one study, a group of subjects were told to read a variety of exciting and sad stories of the incident, and then let them recall under different conditions. The results showed that when people are happy then more memory is out of the story about the happy situations, and when in sorrow the opposite is true. Research has shown that the effect of the existing state of mind is consistency of coding of information also included in the extraction of information. Emotional intensity of the impact of memory depends on the type of mood, its intensity and has to bear in mind the information content. In general, positive mood than negative mood is more conducive to memory, a strong sense of emotional experience can lead to abnormal vivid, detailed, life lasting memory. In addition, when the material that has to be remembered does not have much contact with the information that is maintained in long-term memory, the effect of emotion on memory is most. In such circumstances, emotions are the only clues available to extract.

Ebbinghaus' study was the first time in the history of experimental research on memory; it is a pioneering work, opened up a new situation for experimental psychology, that is, if used experimental method with the so-called high-level psychological processes, such as learning, memory, thinking and so on. The study sought the methods of experimental conditions to control and measure the results, aroused psychologists' study of memory states boom, contributed greatly to the development of psychology and memory. Although Ebbinghaus' memory experiments made historic contributions to the field of psychology, they are not perfect. The main shortcomings are as follows: Ebbinghaus only carried on a quantitative analysis of memory developing process, the contents of memory were not included in the design and analysis; his meaningless syllables are used in artificial, divorced from reality, there are significant limitations; he treats memory as the result of mechanical repetition and does not take into account that memory is a complex active process.

3.7 Physiological Mechanism of Memory

"Where and how does the brain store memories? It is wonderful and mysterious." This sentence comes from a classical book written by Boring in 1950. Though more than 60 years have already passed from 1950 to now, it is still a question being solved so far. Conjecture at that time was all on the basis of the simpler electric fields or reflection circuits in the nerve tissue. But now, it is recognized that the physiological mechanism of memory is extremely complicated, the cooperation of researcher and theoretician in many scientific fields is demanded to explore this problem.

In neurophysiology, the general method to study memory is damaging the brain in part to observe the functional disorder. Mishkin removed monkey's bilateral hippocampus and amygdala simultaneously, which caused the memory disorder. O'keefe recorded the activity of a single neuron in rat's hippocampus and proposed spatial memory hypothesis. Olton *et al.* then provided another hypothesis about working memory related to hippocampus based on lesion results. Hence, there are closed relationships between memory and hippocampus.

Hippocampus body is a large neural tissue inside the brain, which is located in the joint between interior cortex of hemisphere and brainstem. It is composed of hippocampus, dentate gyrus and hippocampus flat. Hippocampus organized in layer structure has many branches without climbing fiber. There are two types of cells in hippocampus: pyramidal cells and blue cells. In hippocampus, the body of pyramidal cell constitutes the layered and paralleled pyramidal cellular layer whose

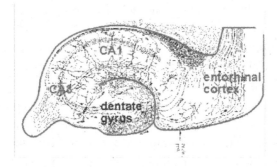

Fig. 3.18.   The structure of hippocampus

dendrite is extended to hippocampus sulcus. The blue cells are arranged in strict order. Figure 3.18 indicates the structure of hippocampus.

The hippocampus plays a vital role in the process of storing information. Short-term memory is stored in the hippocampus. If a memory segment, such as a phone number or a person's name is repeated in a short time, the hippocampus will transfer it into the brain cortex and become long-term memory. The information stored in the hippocampus is "deleted" if it is not used for a period of time. The information stored in the cerebral cortex is not entirely permanent, and when you do not use the information for a long time, the cerebral cortex might delete this information. After the injury of hippocampus, some people will appear to lose some or all of the memory. Memory in the transmission process between the hippocampus and the cerebral cortex will continue for a few weeks, and this transmission may be performed during sleep.

Some researchers use PET technology to research brain structure related with declarative or explicit memory. When the subjects completed the task of declarative memory, it was found that their cerebral blood flow in the right hippocampus was higher than complete procedural memory tasks. This finding supports the view that the hippocampus plays an important role in the declarative memory.

Amygdala, or exactly the almond complex, is composed of several nerve nucle-uses and is a center for the meeting of brain areas. Amygdala has direct connection with all the sensory systems in the cortex, which is along part of the memory system and also connected with the thalamus network. Finally, amygdala assembles sensory message into the same parts and its neural fibers are sent into the inferior thalamus in the brain, which is shown in Figure 3.19. Amygdala is thought to be served as a structure relevant to the memory. The nervous fiber from cortical sensory system goes to the amygdala, which initiated the sensory in this memory loop. This loop relies on the connection between the amygdala and the thalamus: the link between these two structures makes it possible to combine the experience and the emotion.

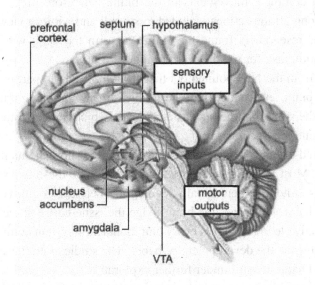

Fig. 3.19. Amygdala

These links connect the amygdala and the sensory path repeatedly, which make the learning being influenced by emotion and could provide an explanation that single stimuli evoke various memories. For example, when the smell of a familiar food is perceived, the memories of its appearance, quality and the taste are evoked naturally.

One is from the hippocampus and the other is from the amygdala in abovementioned two memory loops, which are responsible for various cognitive learning–recognition of familiar objects, recalling the unperceived character of sensory, memorizing the previous location and adding emotionality into the objects.

Besides the above memory loop, there is a second system used for learning, of which the key component is repeated stimulus. This kind of learning is called "habituation", which is the unconscious combination between stimuli and response. The behavioral psychologist confirmed this combination was the basis of all learning in early years. In their views, there are no terms such as "mind", "cognition" or even "memory". Learning relies on two different systems: one is from non-cognitive habituation; the other is the base of cognitive memory. So, this view could mediate the behaviorism and the cognitive approach. Behavior is possibly the combination between unconscious response to the stimuli and the action under the control of cognition and anticipation.

The structure contributed to the habit might be striatum, which is a complex structure in forebrain. Striatum receives many nervous fibers projected from cortical cortex (including the sensory system) and then sends the fibers to different regions which dominate movements in the brain. Therefore, it provides a more direct link among all the actions included in stimuli and habit in view of anatomy. Actually, some researchers found the ability to form the habit was weakened in object recognition task for monkeys with injured striatum.

MacLean from the NIH pointed out that striatum is an old part in the evolution of the human brain, even older than the limbic cortex. Simple animal learns how to respond to the stimuli at the unconscious level, which indicated that the habit is formed by primitive structure.

In a matured brain, it needs to be confirmed further how the memory interacts with the habit. Most learning behaviors seemingly utilize these two systems; however, it is easy to find that there are always conflicts between cognitive memory and non-cognitive habit. How does the brain judge the issue between the formation of habit and cognitive learning? Does every unit in memory system communicate with striatum to influence the development of habit? The studies into the areas involved in memory and habit are still under further exploration.

Prefrontal lobe seems to be important in working memory, during which the input message and the ongoing behavior are influenced by individual's view, perception or rule. These internal resources accumulated for a lifetime constitute human's inner world, which could offer some kind of weights to deter large number of sensory information into the brain.

3.8 Theory of Memory-Prediction

Hawkins believed that intelligence is the behavior of a large number of clusters of neurons, with a series of predictions of future events based on the world model of memory. In 2004, he put forward the memory-prediction theory, which is considered as a measure of the ability to remember and predict the world model; these models include language, mathematics, physical characteristics and social environment. The brain receives patterns from the outside world, stores them into memory and then predicts by their previous situation and what is happening presently [204].

Memory pattern of brain creates full conditions for the forecast. We can say that the intelligence is based on the memory. There are four attributes of neocortical memory:

(1) The neocortex stores sequences of patterns.
(2) The neocortex recalls patterns auto-associatively.
(3) The neocortex stores patterns in an invariant form.
(4) The neocortex stores patterns in a hierarchy.

3.8.1 Constant characterization

Figure 3.20 shows four visual cortical areas of the object, denoted as V1, V2, V4, IT. V1 indicates that the region of the striped visual cortex, which is rarely a pretreat image, but contains detailed information of the image. V2 indicates visual mapping and its visual mapping information is less than that of V1. Visual input with the upward arrow indicates, that it begins in the retina; therefore the transmission starts from the bottom to the V1 area. The input represents the time-varying model; visual neural transmission consists of about 1 million axons.

In the four different levels of regions from area VI to area IT, cells change from rapidly changing and spatial correlated ones which are capable of identifying subtle features, to stable and space independent ones which are capable of identifying objects. For example, in the case of the "Face cells" of IT cells, as long as there is a human face, the cell will be activated, regardless of whether the face is tilted, rotating or partially obscured, which is a constant representation of the face.

The feedback connection is very important when considering prediction, the brain needs to send the input information back to the original input area. Predictions need to compare what is real and what is expected to happen. Information about what really happens will flow from bottom to top, and the information that is expected to happen will flow from top to bottom.

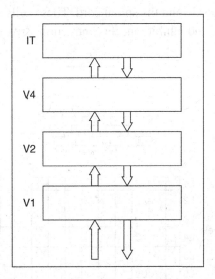

Fig. 3.20. Four visual cortexes in object recognition

3.8.2 Structure of cerebral cortex

The density and shape of cells in the cerebral cortex are different and this difference results in stratification. The first layer is the most unique one among all the six layers. It contains only a little number of cells, and is mainly composed of a layer of nerve axons which are parallel to the cortical surface. The second and third layers are similar mainly by many closed-up pyramidal cells. The fourth layer is composed of astrocytes. The fifth layer has pyramid-shaped cells in general and these pyramid-shaped cells are particularly large. The sixth layer also has several unique neuronal cells.

Figure 3.21 shows the level of the brain area, and the vertical column of the longitudinal cell unit that works together. Different layers of each vertical column are connected with each other by axons extending vertically and forming synapses. The vertical columns in the V1 region are some of the inclined line segments (/) in a direction, while others react to a line segment (\) in the direction of the other direction. Cells in each vertical column are closely interconnected, and they respond to the same stimulus as a whole. The activated cells in the fourth layer will activate the third and second layers. And then they will activate the fifth and sixth layers. Information is transmitted up and down in a cell of the same vertical column. Hawkins believes that the vertical column is a basic unit of prediction.

There is a direct link between the fifth layer of cells in the motor cortex (M1) and the movement in the muscle and the spinal cord. These cells are highly coordinated to continuously activate and inhibit muscle contraction, drive motion. In each region

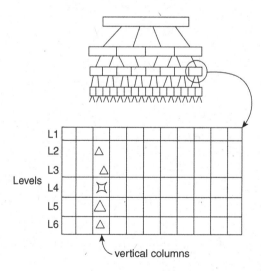

Fig. 3.21. Levels and vertical columns of the brain

of the cerebral cortex are spread all over fifth cells, which play an important role in all kinds of sports.

Axons of the fifth layer of cells get into the thalamus, and make connection with a class of nonspecific cells. These nonspecific cells will then project these axons back into the first layer of cerebral cortex in different regions. This loop is just like the delayed feedback sequence, which can learn from associative memory. The first layer carries a lot of information, including the name of the sequence and the position in the sequence. Using these two kinds of information of first layers, a cortical area is able to learn and recall patterns of sequence.

3.8.3 How does the cerebral cortex work

There are three kinds of circuits in the cerebral cortex: convergence along the cortical system with an approach from bottom to top, divergence along the cortical system with an approach from top to bottom, and the delayed feedback of the thalamus which is very important for the function of the cerebral cortex. These functions include:

(1) How does the brain cortex classify the input pattern?
(2) How does one learn the pattern sequence?
(3) How does one form a sequence's constant pattern or name?
(4) How does one make a concrete forecast?

In the vertical column of the cerebral cortex, the input information from the lower region activates the fourth layer of cells, leading to the cell's excitement. Then the fourth layer of cells activates third and second layer of cells, and then there is the fifth layer, which leads to the activation of the sixth layer of cells. So, the whole vertical column is activated by the input information of the low level area. When some of synapses are activated by second, third and fifth layers, they are enhanced. If this happens often enough, the first layer of these synapses will become strong enough to allow the second, third, fifth layers of cells to also get activated in case the fourth layer of cells was not activated. In this way, the second, third and fifth layers of the cell can predict when they should be activated by the first layer mode. After this study, the vertical column cells can be partly activated by memory. When the vertical column is activated by synapses of the first layer, it is predicting the input information from the lower region, and this is the forecast.

Some information received from the first layer is derived from the fifth layer cells of the adjacent vertical column and the adjacent area, which represents the event that has just occurred. Another part comes from the sixth cell, which are stable sequence names. As shown in Figure 3.22, second and third layers of cells

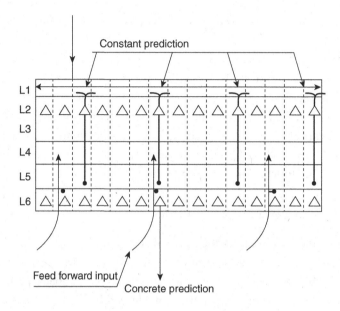

Fig. 3.22. Specific predictions based on constant memory of the cerebral cortex

of the axon usually form a synapse in the fifth layer, and the fourth layer of the axon forms a synapse in the sixth layer. The two synapses intersect the sixth layer receiving two kinds of input information, and then it will be activated, and make a specific forecast according to the constant memory.

As a general rule, the information flow along the cerebral cortex is transmitted through the synapses near the cell body. Thus, the upward flow of information is increasingly identified in the transmission process. Similarly, as a general rule, the feedback information flowing along the cerebral cortex is transmitted through the synapses away from the cell body. Synapses on the long range of thin dendrites can play an active and highly specific role in cell activation. In general, the axon fiber of the feedback is more than the feed forward; the feedback information can quickly and accurately activate many cells in the second layers of the cerebral cortex.

Chapter 4

Consciousness

The origin and essence of consciousness is one of the most important scientific problems. In intellectual science, the consciousness problems have special challenge meanings. Consciousness is not only the theme studied by philosophy, but is also the important subject of contemporary natural scientific research which studies how the existence determines consciousness and how the objective world reflects to the subjective world. Consciousness involves advanced cognitive processes such as the consciousness, attention, memory, signifying, thinking, language, etc., with its core being awareness. In recent years, because of the development of cognitive science, neural science and computer science, and specifically the appearance of the intact experimental technique, the research in consciousness has once again gained importance and has become the common focus of numerous subjects. In the 21st century, consciousness problems will be one of the forts which intellectual science will try hard to solve.

4.1 Overview

Consciousness is a complex biological phenomenon. Philosophers, physicians and psychologists have no common concept of consciousness. There is no final conclusion about consciousness so far. Famous contemporary thinker Dennett believes [113] that human consciousness is probably the last mystery which is difficult to resolve. Consciousness continues to be a puzzle to date. It is a unique topic which renders wise and farsighted thinkers at a loss for words and with a confused thinking.

In philosophy, consciousness is highly improving and a highly organized special material — the function of the human brain, and it is the reflection of the objective reality that is currently owned by mankind only. Consciousness is also the synonym of thinking, but the range of consciousness is relatively wide, including the cognition of emotional and rational stage, but thinking only means the cognition of rational stage. Dialectical materialism believes that consciousness is the result of high development of material, and it is the reflection of existence. There is also a huge activism role on existence.

In medical science, the understanding of consciousness of different disciplines has some difference too. In the field of clinical medicine, the consciousness refers to patient's understanding and reaction ability under surroundings and oneself. It is divided into different consciousness levels such as consciousness clearing, consciousness fuzzy, lethargy and coma. In spiritual medical science, consciousness differs between ego-consciousness and environmental awareness. Consciousness can become an obstacle in the form of clouding of consciousness, somnolence, stupor, coma, delirium, twilight state, dream-like state and confusion.

The view on consciousness in psychology is awareness or experience of objective things on the external environment and one's psychological activity, such as feeling, consciousness, attention, memory and thought. The evolutionary biologist and theoretical scientist Calvin lists some of the definitions of consciousness in the book *How Brains Think* [70].

From the view of intelligence science, consciousness is the experience integration with the external world, one's own body and mental process. Consciousness is "instinct" or "function" what is inherent in the brain, it is a "state", and it is many biological "combinations" of a lot of brain structure. Generalized consciousness is the life phenomenon that all higher and lower organisms have. With biological evolution, there has been continuous progress of consciousness. It is mainly the brain which is the organ of human consciousness activity. In order to reveal the scientific law of consciousness, and building the brain model of consciousness, it is not merely needed to study the conscious cognitive process, but one must also to study the unconscious cognitive process, i.e., the automatic information process of the brain, and the transformation mechanisms of two processes in the brain. The consciousness research is the indispensable content in cognitive neuroscience. The research of consciousness and brain mechanism is an important content in natural science. Philosophy involves the study of problems such as the origin of consciousness and the authenticity of existing consciousness etc., the key area of study in intellectual scientific research of consciousness includes the brain mechanism of how consciousness is produced — how consciousness helps one to be aware of external objects.

The first person in history to use the word "consciousness" is Bacon. His definition of consciousness is that consciousness is a person's understanding of what happens in his thoughts. So, the consciousness problem is a field of research in philosophy. German psychologist Wundt established the first psychology laboratory in 1879. He clearly proposed that consciousness research is a major area of study in psychology, where physiological methods are used to study consciousness, reporting the consciousness state under sitting quietly, working and sleeping. Psychology entered a new historical period with an identity of scientific experiment from then on, research on a series of psychological phenomena developed rapidly, but there was slow progress in the consciousness study, because it lacked the nonconscious aspect of direct objective indicators. James proposed the concept of the stream of consciousness in 1902, and pointed out that consciousness rises and falls, its origin is constant, just like flowing water. Freud believes that a person's feeling and behavior is influenced by consciousness need, hope and conflict. According to the view of Freud, the stream of consciousness has depth; it has different levels of understanding between the process of consciousness and the process of nonconscious. It is all or none phenomenon. However, because science was not developed enough at that time, introspection method was used, but it lacked the objective indicators, and only remained descriptive at the primary level, unable to advance. But since Watson declared psychology as a behavior science, the consciousness problem has been shelved. So for a very long time, no one studied neuroscience because it was found to be too complex, but psychology is unwilling to become a forgotten science in spite of its complexity.

In 1950s and 1960s, the scientists understood the neurophysiology foundation of the state of consciousness by anatomy, and physiologic experiment. For example, Moruzzi and Magoun found the reticular activation system of awareness in 1949; Aserinsky and Kleitman observed the consciousness state of rapid eye movement sleep in 1953; in 1960s and 1970s, they studied on the split-brain patient, which supports that there are independent consciousness systems in two hemispheres of the brain. The study led to the establishment of the foundation of cognitive neuroscience research of consciousness.

Modern cognitive psychology started in the 1960s. For cognitive psychologists, it is always a long-term challenge to expound the neural mechanism of objective consciousness. The direct research about consciousness of objective experience and neural activity relation is still very rare so far. In recent years, with the rapid development of science and technology, using modern electrophysiological techniques (electroencephalography (EEG), event-related potential (ERP)), and radiation imaging technology (positron emission tomography scan PET, functional magnetic resonance imaging (fMRI)), the consciousness study has already become the new born focus of life sciences and intelligence science.

The research on the brain mechanism of consciousness is very complex; the task is arduous, but the effect is of great significance. It has attracted the interest of scholars all over the world in many domains, such as cognitive science, neuro-science (neural physiology, neural imaging and neural biochemistry), social science and computer science. Association for the Scientific Studies of Consciousness was founded in 1997, and has already held the international academic conference of consciousness problem for five years in succession. The themes of the conference are: The relation of latent cognitive and consciousness (1997); Neural relevance of consciousness (1998); Consciousness and self-perception and self-representation (1999); Consciousness joint (2000); The content of consciousness: Consciousness, attention and phenomenon (2001); Consciousness and language (2002); The model and mechanism of consciousness (2003); Empirical and theoretical problems in consciousness research (2004).

Scientists who study the problem of consciousness have a wide variety of views. From the people's understanding of the ability to finally having the potential to solve the problem of consciousness, there is a sense of mystery and reductionism of the points. People hold the mystic view that we will never be able to understand. The famous contemporary philosopher Fodor in *Towards to Science of Consciousness* suspected publicly at the time of the meeting: How could any kind of physical system have consciousness state? In the study of consciousness, the very active American philosopher Chalmers thought that consciousness should be divided into the easy problem and the hard problem [73]. His total view of consciousness is: "without any rigorous theoretical physics (quantum mechanics or neural mechanisms) to understand the problem of consciousness."

Crick declared publicly his view that consciousness is reductionism in his book *The Astonishing Hypothesis* [105]. He and his young follower Koch stated this view in a lot of articles. They "reduced" the complex consciousness problem to the collective behavior of neural cells and related molecules. The view held by famous American neuroscientist Sejnowski and the American philosopher Dennett *et al.* was generally similar to Crick.

While studying consciousness from the philosophical point of view, there has always been two opposite points of view: one is monism, where spirit (including consciousness) is produced by the material (brain) and can study and explain the mind phenomena from the brain. Another kind is a dualism, which thinks the spiritual world is independent of the human body (human brain) and that there is no direct link between the two. Descartes is a typical dualist and he believes that everyone has a body and a soul (mind). Man's body and mind are usually held together, but the mind's activity is not bound by the laws of the machine. After the body dies, the soul will continue to exist and also play a role. The activities of a person's mind cannot be observed by others, so only I can directly perceive the state and process of my own heart. If the body is compared to the "machine", in accordance with the laws of physics to run, then the mind is "the soul of the machine". Descartes is a great mathematician, so he had to face the reality of the side in science explicitly. He proposed "people are machine" on science clearly. But he was influenced by ancient philosophy and the contemporary social environment deeply, so he put product of the brain (mind) as a completely separated thing from the human body.

Contemporary scientists were engaged in natural science research, in which many believed in dualism. Nobel laureate Eccles was keen to study the issue of consciousness. He himself is a scientist who studies the structure and function of synapses and has made great achievements in the structure and function of nerve cells. He does not deny his consciousness is dualism. He and his cooperators have published seven books on brain functions. The book written by him and philosopher Popper put forward the theory of "Three Worlds", in which the first in the world is the physical world, including the structure and function of the brain; the second world is all subjective spirit and experience; and the social, scientific and cultural activities as the third world. In his later works, according to the structure and function of the nervous system, he presented the hypothesis of the dendron. The dendron is the basic structure and the functional unit of the nervous system and is composed of about 100 top dendrites. It is estimated that there are 400,000 dendrons in the human brain. He then put forward the hypothesis of "psychon", the second world's psychon corresponds to the first world of the dendron. Quantum physics is likely to be used in the sense of consciousness because the microstructure of the dendrites is similar to that of the quantum scale.

The research of consciousness needs to rely on people, in particular, to use the human brain to study, which means the brain can understand the study of the human brain. Someone speaks in images; it is impossible that one's own hair is drawn up to break away from terrestrially with the handle. In fact, the study of consciousness is not completely clear between monism and dualism, between cognoscism and agnosticism and between materialism and idealism.

4.1.1 Base elements of consciousness

Farber and Churchland discussed consciousness concept from three levels in the article "Consciousness and the Neurosciences: Philosophical and Theoretical Issues" [142]. The first level is sense of awareness, including: feel awareness (by sensory channel with external stimulate), generality awareness (refers to a feeling without any connect to the channel, the internal state of the body is aware, such as fatigue, dizziness, anxiety, comfort, hunger, etc.), metacognitive consciousness (it refers to awareness of all things of one's cognitive range, including thinking activity in the present and the past), conscious remembrance (awareness of the thing that happened in the past), etc. Here, we can be aware of some signs of a thing and report this thing through language. This method is convenient to measure, at the same time can exclude the animal who cannot speak. The second level is the high-level ability; it is advanced functions that not only passively perceive and create awareness of information, but also have activity of function or control. These functions include attention, reasoning and self-control (for example, physiological impulse was inhibited by reason or morals). The third level is the consciousness state; it can be interpreted as a person's ongoing psychological activity, including linkage of the most difficult and the most common sense in the consciousness concept. This state can be divided into different levels: consciousness and unconsciousness, comprehensive regulation, rough feeling, etc. The definition for the first two levels of Farber for consciousness is an enlightening one, but the third level lacks the substantive content.

In 1977, Ornstein raised forward two modes where consciousness exists: active-verbal-rational mode and receptive-spatial-intuitive-holistic mode [344], referred as active mode and perception mode, respectively. He believes that the two modes are controlled on one side of the brain. Evaluation on the active mode is automatic and limits the human automation of awareness from not having associated experience, and incident and amazing direct in order to stop the viability of the system along with it. When people need to strengthen the induction and judgment, they increase the normal awareness through the perception mode. According to the view of Ornstein, sitting quietly, biofeedback, hypnosis and testing some specific drugs can also help in using the perceptual model to balance the active mode. The intellection activity is active and has an advantage in the left hemisphere, while receptivity with behavioral intuition, is dominant in the right hemisphere. The integration of the two modes is the basis of high-level functions of human beings.

Which key elements form the consciousness function? For this question, Crick thinks consciousness includes two basic functions [105]: one is attention and second is short-term memory. Attention has been the main function of consciousness, which has been recognized by everyone. Baars has the "theatre" metaphor, the metaphor of consciousness as a stage, where different scenes take turns in playing [35]. On the platform, the spotlight can be likened to the attention mechanism, which is a popular metaphor. Crick also recognized this metaphor. In people who have no memory, there is no "self-consciousness". Consciousness helps one to be aware of nonhuman objects (both seen and heard about) and remember them, similar to remembering interactions among humans. But the length of memory time can be discussed, long-term memory is important, Crick believes that short-term memory is more necessary.

American philosopher and psychologist James thought that the characteristics of consciousness are:

(a) Consciousness is personal and cannot be shared with others.
(b) Consciousness is always changing and will not stay in a state for a long time.
(c) Consciousness is continuous, one content contains another content.
(d) Consciousness is selective.

In short, James does not think consciousness is a thing, but a process, or a kind of "flow" and is a kind of process that can be changed in a fraction of a second. This concept of "stream of consciousness" vividly depicts some of his characteristics of consciousness, which is valued in psychology.

Edelman stressed the integration and differentiation of consciousness [126]. On the basis of the physiological pathology and anatomy of the brain, Edelman believes the thalamus-cortex system plays a key role in the production of consciousness.

Churchland, the American philosopher on mind, lists a characteristic table for the consciousness problem [142]:

• Working memory related;
• Do not rely on sensory input, i.e., we can think of something that does not exist and what is not true;
• Showed control of attention;
• Ability to interpret complex or ambiguous materials; disappears in deep sleep;
• Reemergence in a dream;
• A single unified experience can be inclusive of the contents of a number of sensory modalities.

In 2012, Baars and Edelman explained their natural view about consciousness in an article [42], and listed 17 characteristics of the state of consciousness:

(1) EEG signature of conscious states

The electrophysiological activities of the brain are irregular with low amplitude and fast electrical activity and the frequency is from 0.5 to 400 Hz. EEG of consciousness state and no consciousness state (similar to the sleeping condition) was significantly different. EEG of epilepsy and general anesthesia patients presents the state of consciousness with high amplitude, and slowly changing voltage.

(2) Cortex and thalamus

Consciousness is determined by the complexity of the hypothalamus, opened and closed by brainstem modulation and brain cortex area without interaction that does not directly support conscious experiences.

(3) Widespread brain activity

The report of the event is related to a wide range of specific brain activities. Unconscious stimulation only evokes local brain activity. Conscious moments also have a wide range of effects on the content of the outside attention, such as implicit learning, episodic memory, biofeedback training and so on.

(4) Wide range of reportable contents

Consciousness has a very wide range of different contents: the perception of a variety of sensations, the appearance of an endogenous image, emotional feelings, inner speech, concepts, action-related ideas and the experience of the familiar.

(5) Informativeness

Consciousness can disappear when the signal becomes superfluous; loss of information can lead to loss of consciousness. Selective attention studies also showed a strong preference for information on more abundant conscious stimuli.

(6) The adaptive and fleeting nature of conscious events

Experience sensory input can be immediately maintained for a few seconds. We have a brief knowledge of the duration of less than half a minute. On the contrary, the vast unconscious knowledge can reside in long-term memory.

(7) Internal consistency

Consciousness is characterized by uniform constraint. In general, the same time to stimulate the two is not consistent, only a sense of one can be. When a word is ambiguous, there is only one meaning at any time.

(8) Limited capacity and seriality

The ability of consciousness in any prescribed moment seems to be limited to only one consistent picture. The flow of such conscious scenes is serial in contrast to the massive parallel processing of the brain when it is observed directly at the same time.

(9) Sensory binding

The sensory brain is functionally divided into blocks, so that different cortical areas are specialized to respond to different features, such as shape, color or object motion.

One fundamental problem is how to coordinate the activities of the brain regions that are separated by their functional roles to generate the integrated gestalts of ordinary conscious perception.

(10) Self-attribution

Conscious experience is always characterized by self-experience, as William James called "observing ego". Self-function seems to be related to central brain areas, including the brainstem, precuneus and orbitofrontal cortex in humans.

(11) Accurate reportability

The most used behavioral index of consciousness is accurate reportability. The full range of conscious contents is reported by a wide range of voluntary responses, often with very high accuracy. The report does not require a complete explicit vocabulary because the subject can automatically compare, contrast, point to and play a role in the event of consciousness.

(12) Subjectivity

Consciousness is marked by a private flow of event available only to the experiencing subject. Such privacy is not in violation of legislation. This shows that self-object synthesis is the key to conscious cognition.

(13) Focus-fringe structure

Consciousness is thought to be inclined to focus on clear content, "fringe conscious" events, such as feelings of familiarity, the tip-of the tongue experience, intuition and so on, are equally important.

(14) Facilitation of learning

There is little evidence to show learning without consciousness. In contrast, the evidence for conscious experience to promote learning is overwhelming. Even implicit (indirect) learning requires conscious attention.

(15) Stability of contents

Conscious contents are impressively stable. Changes in input and task production are required, such as the eye movements that readers constantly use to scan sentences. Even as its own beliefs, concepts and topics of the same abstract content may be very stable over decades.

(16) Allocentric attribution

The scenes and objects of consciousness, in general, are concerned with external sources, although their formation is heavily dependent on the unconscious frameworks.

(17) Conscious knowing and decision-making

Consciousness is useful for us to know about the world around us as well as some of our internal processes. Conscious representation, including percepts, concepts, judgments and beliefs, may be particularly well suited to decision-making. However, not all conscious events involve a wide range of unconscious facilities. In this way, the content of the consciousness report is by no means the only feature that needs to be interpreted.

4.1.2 The attribute of consciousness

Johnson-Laird, a professor of the Psychology Department at the Princeton University, is a distinguished British cognitive psychologist. His main interest is to study the language, especially words, sentences and paragraphs. Johnson-Laird was convinced that any computer, especially a highly parallel computer, must have an operating system to control (even if not completely control) the rest of the work. He thought there exists a close relationship between the operating system and the consciousness in the brain's higher part [224].

Jackendoff, a professor of linguistics and cognition at the Brandeis University, is a famous American cognitive scientist. He has a special interest in language and music. Like most cognitive scientists, he thinks it's better to think of the brain as an information processing system [222]. But unlike most of the scientists, he regards "how to produce consciousness" as the most fundamental problem of psychology. His middle-level theory of consciousness believes that consciousness is neither from the processing of perceptual units nor from the top of the thoughts, but from the representative layers between the lowest surroundings (similar to feeling) and the highest central surrounding (similar to thought). He highlighted this very new point of view. He also believes that there is a close connection between consciousness and short-term memory. He said consciousness needs the content of short-term memory to support, which expresses such a point of view. But it should be added that short-term memory is involved in the rapid process and the slow change process has no direct phenomenological effect. When it comes to attention, he thinks, paying attention to the calculation effect is to make the attention of the material experience more in-depth and detailed processing. He thinks this can explain why the attention capacity is so limited.

Baars, a professor at the Wright's Institute, Berkeley, California, wrote the book *A Cognitive Theory of Consciousness* [34]. Although Baars is a cognitive scientist, he is more concerned about people's brain compared to Jackendoff or Johnson-Laird. He called his basic thought, the Global Working Space. He believes that information in this work space at any moment is the content of consciousness. As the working space of the central information exchange, it is connected with many of the unconscious receiving processors. These specialized processors have high efficiency only in their own areas. In addition, they can also get the working space through cooperation and competition. Baars improved the model in a number of ways. For example, the receive processor can reduce uncertainty by interacting until they conform to a unique valid explanation. In a broad sense, he thinks that consciousness is very active and that the attention control mechanism can enter the consciousness. We are aware of some of the projects in the short-term memory, but not all.

These three cognitive theoreticians have roughly reached three common understandings regarding the attribute of consciousness. They all agreed that the activities of the brain are not directly consciousness related and consciousness is an initiative course; they believe that the process of consciousness is involved in attention and some form of short-term memory; they may also agree that the information in consciousness can enter into long-term episodic memory, and can also enter the high-level planning level of the motor nervous system in order to control voluntary movement. In addition, their ideas are so different.

4.2 Theory of Consciousness

4.2.1 The theater of consciousness

The most classical assumption about the consciousness problem is a metaphor of "bright spot in dramaturgical". In this metaphor, we aggregate into a conscious experience from a lot of inputs of feelings, for example, a spotlight shows a light to somewhere in the dark theater, then spreads to a large number of unconscious audiences. In cognitive science, most of the assumption about consciousness and selective attention comes from this basic metaphor. Baars is the most important person to inherit and carry forward the "dramaturgical assumption" [35].

Baars closely combined psychology with brain science and cognitive neuroscience. The theater metaphor, which was used to understand consciousness from the time of Plato and Aristotle, was transformed into the theater model of consciousness and the use of a number of noticeable neuroimaging advanced research results describes the complexity of the human spiritual world (see Figure 4.1) [35].

The basic idea of this model is that man's consciousness is a limited stage, it needs a central cognitive working space, which is very similar to the stage of

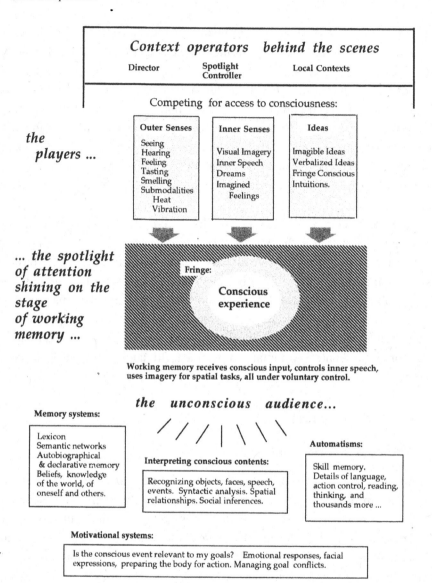

Fig. 4.1. Theater model of consciousness

the theater. Consciousness, as a kind of psychological state of great epistemological phenomenon, basically has five kinds of activities:

(1) Working memory is like a theater stage, mainly including two components: "inner language" and "visual imagination".

(2) The content of the conscious experience is like the onstage actor, showing the relationship between competition and cooperation in different contents of consciousness experience.

(3) Attention is like the spotlight, which shines on the actor on the stage of working memory, and the content of consciousness appears.

(4) The background operation of the backstage is carried out by the postern background operator's system of the setting, among them "oneself" similar to the director that operates behind the scenes in the background. A lot of ubiquitous unconscious activities form the stage-like background effect too, the background operator is the execution and control system on the cerebral cortex.

(5) The unconscious automatic activity procedure and the knowledge resources have formed the "audience" system in the theater.

According to his point of view, although people's consciousness is limited, the advantage is that it can access a lot of information and has a certain amount of computing power. These abilities include multi-sensory input, memory, innate and acquired skills, etc. According to Baars, consciousness in the brain work is widely distributed, like at the same time, there are many roles in theater with a total of four brain structure spatial dimensions, and four types of brain function module systems to support. They are also projected on the time axis, forming a super integration of three-dimensional (3D) space and time dimensions similar to the mind model of the theater stage. Four dimensions of the structure of the brain simultaneously project on the time axis: (a) Cortical dimensions from deep to cortex of the brain; (b) Front side development dimension from the back of the head forward to front head; (c) Two hemispheres of the brain function of left and right side development dimension; (d) Cerebral dorsal and ventral development dimension to form the space time dimension of a super cube.

Brain function system is composed of four modules: (a) Instinct related function modules with clear functional orientation; (b) Human species-specific instinct behavior module — the function orientation of automation; (c) Individual acquisition of habitual behavior module — positioning semi automation system; (d) High-level conscious activity — there is no clear positioning system. The contents of consciousness seems spread all over the brain's neural networks, so as to form a distributed structure of the system. Human consciousness experience is a unity, the self is the "director" of the unity.

Based on "the theater model of consciousness", Baars proposed "conscious and unconsciousness interaction model", a simple metaphor for the dynamic process of mutual transformation between the conscious and the unconscious, namely, diversified forms of consciousness activities with unconscious active reciprocal transformation consciously, form information processing of the whole job, consciousness content and rich and colorful experiencing the experience to restrain oneself subjectively in a kind of complicated brain. According to Baars' point of view, there is a special processor, which is either unified or modular. It needs to be specially emphasized that the move processor of unconsciousness is very effective and fast, it has few errors, at the same time, such a processor may be in operation with other systems, while a dedicated processor is separate and independent, and can deal with the main information dynamically. The characteristics of this special processor are very similar to those "modules" of cognitive psychology.

Is the formation of consciousness caused by a specific brain process? Can the complex system be used to establish a model for the formation of brain processes? These are the problems in consciousness research. The exploration of the active neural mechanism of consciousness finds that the sober state of consciousness is the primary condition that the psychological activity can carry on, and the sober states of consciousness are closely linked with net structure, thalamus of brain stem, etc., and neural pathways in the limbic system. Generally speaking, the excitability of the netted structural system of brain stem relates to the intensity of attention. Sensory input required a large amount of information in need through the network structure system for primary analysis and integration, many unrelated or secondary information is selectively filtered out, only to attract attention of relevant information in order to reach the network structure system. Therefore, some scholars have suggested that consciousness activity mainly reflects in attention mechanism based on the net structure as the neural basis, only pays attention to the stimulus to cause our consciousness, but a lot of non-attention to the stimulus fails to reach the level of consciousness and would not be realized, thus turning into a kind of definite spiritual function of activity reliance of consciousness — involvement that is paid attention to. Of course, consciousness and unconsciousness have different physiological basis and operating mechanisms. A large number of unconscious activities are part of parallel processing and the conscious activity is serial processing. Different states of consciousness can be converted fast within a very short time. Opening of consciousness refers to the unconscious transformation process of state to state consciousness [36].

The model accurately describes the relations and differences between the conscious and the unconscious, attention, working memory and self-consciousness, etc., also gets the support of many neurobiological evidence, and the influence is bigger and bigger in the academia. Famous scholar Simon said that Baars had offered an exciting explanation about consciousness to us, the philosophical question being whether to put it in a manner that studies the experiment firmly [36]. Some scholars think the consciousness theater model proposed by Baars has offered a kind of core assumption for the current consciousness studies. He compares the differences between the unconscious and the conscious mind, and the core idea is to say that there are two different processes of consciousness and non-consciousness. In this analysis foundation, Baars of conscious and unconscious events recognized that the nervous system has a variety of construction process. The research of Crick *et al.* shows that visual consciousness evolves from the cortex throwing area on the brain's occipital lobe, so if it is possible to offer "the theater stage" searchlight, it will be activated and lighted by attention, thus showing the coherent information of consciousness [107]. "Audience" means an unconscious brain area, such as the cortex, hippocampus, basal nucleus, amygdala, motor execution system and interpretation system. "Theater assumption" of consciousness implies that there are a lot of roles to perform on the stage at the same time, as the human brain accepts many kinds of stimuli of internal and external receptors at the same time. But only a small amount of role receives spotlights irradiation and the projector does not stay on a place, a role, but flows with time.

The theater metaphor of consciousness is also opposed by some scholars. Dennett believes that this assumption must have a "stage" to have a sense of "performance", that is, there is a special place in the brain as a stage of consciousness. This assumption easily falls into the Descartes philosophy about psychological soul of the 17th century "pineal body". Opponents believe that the brain does not have a special place to concentrate all of the input stimulus.

4.2.2 Reductionism

The Nobel laureate, the author of the DNA double helix structure, Crick, is a typical representative in this respect. He believes that the consciousness problem is a key problem in the whole advanced function of the nervous system, so he published an advanced popular science book in 1994, called *The Astonishing Hypothesis*. The book's subtitle is *The Scientific Search for the Soul* [105]. He boldly proposed "the astonishing hypothesis" based on "reductionism". He believes that "People's spiritual activity is completely determined by the behaviors of nerve cells and glial cells and the property of compositions and the effects of their atoms, ions and molecules". He firmly believes that consciousness is the difficult psychological problem and can be solved using the nerve scientific method. He believes that the consciousness problem relates to short-term memory and the shift of attention. He also believes that the consciousness problem involves feelings, but he would like to work from the visual sense because humans are vision animals, visual attention is easy to make psychophysical experiments and neural science has accumulated a lot of materials in the research of the visual system. At the end of the 1980s–early 1990s, there was a great discovery in visual physiological studies: The phenomenon of synchronous oscillations was recorded in shaking from different neurons. Around 40 Hz synchronous oscillations were considered to contact the neural signal between different picture characteristics. Crick proposed the 40 Hz oscillation model of visual attention and inferred that 40 Hz synchronous oscillations of neurons may be a form of "bundling" of different characteristic in visual attention. As for the "Free Will", Crick believes it relates to consciousness; it involves the execution of behavior and plan. Crick analyzed the situation of some persons who lose "Will", and believes that a part of the brain for deducting "Free Will" lies in anterior cingulate gyrus (ACG) close to Brodmanm area (area 24).

Crick and Koch think that the most difficult problem is to study the sense of the problem, i.e., how you feel the red color, the feeling of pain and so on. This is determined by the subjectivity and non-expression of consciousness and thus they turn to the study of the neural correlates of consciousness (NCC), i.e., to understand the general nature of neural activity in certain aspects of consciousness. Crick and Koch listed 10 frames of neural correlates in the study of consciousness [108].

(1) The (unconscious?) homunculus

First, consider the overall work of the brain, the front of the brain to look at the sensory system, the main task of the sensory system is in the back of the brain. And people do not know their thoughts directly, but only know the sense of image in the image. At this time, the neural activity in the forebrain is unconsciousness. There is a "hypothesis of homunculus" in the brain, and it is no longer fashionable now, but how can one imagine oneself?

(2) Zombie modes and consciousness

For sensory stimuli, many responses are rapid, transient, stereotyped and unintentional, while conscious processing is slower, more extensive, and requires more time to determine the right ideas and better responses. These two strategies evolved to complement each other, and the visual system of the dorsal channel (the large cell system) performs a rigid fast response to the ventral system (small cells).

(3) Coalitions of neurons

This alliance is the Hebb cluster plus the competition between them. The neurons in the coalition are not fixed, but dynamic. The alliance to gain an advantage in the competition will remain dominant for some time and that is when we realize something. This process is like a country's election, the election victory of the party that will be in power for a period of time and the impact of the next stage of the political situation. The role of attention mechanism is equivalent to public opinion and election forecasters trying to influence the election situation. Large pyramidal cells in layer V of the cortex seem to be on the ballot. But the time interval between each election is not regular. Of course, this is just a metaphor.

There are changes in the size and characteristics of the alliance. The consciousness of alliance and dreaming when awake implies that the imagination and what you see when you open the eyes to watch are not the same. Awareness of cerebral anterior part of the union may reflect the "pleasure", "rule", "free will" and posterior cerebral alliance may be produced in different ways, and before and after brain alliance may be more than one, which will influence and interact with each other.

(4) Explicit representations

An explicit representation of a part of the field of view implies that a group of neurons, which correspond to the properties of this part, can react as a detector without the need for a complex process. In some cases, the lack of some dominant neurons cause a loss, for example, color agnosia, prosopagnosia and movement agnosia. Other visual features of these patients remain normal.

In monkeys, a small portion of the motor cortex (MT/VS) is impaired, resulting in loss of motion perception. Less damaged parts can be recovered within a few days if the damage is caused by a large range of permanent loss. It must be noted that the dominant representation is a necessary condition for the neural correlates of consciousness, not a sufficient condition.

(5) The higher levels first

After coming to a new visual input, neural activity first quickly unconsciously uplinks to high-level visual system, maybe the forebrain. Then the signals are fed back to the low level, so they reach consciousness in the first stage at a high level, then the sense signal is sent to the frontal cortex, then into the lower level caused by the corresponding activities. Of course, this is a simple description. There are many cross-links in the whole system.

(6) Driving and modulating connections

It is important to understand the nature of neural connections and it cannot be considered to be the same type of excitatory connections. Cortical neurons can be roughly divided into two categories: one is the driving link and the other is the modulation. In cortical pyramidal cells, the driving links are mostly derived from the basal dendrites and modulated by the transmission of human derived from the dendrites, which include reverse projection, dispersion-like projection, especially the nucleus of the thalamus. The link from the side of the knee to the V1 region is the driving force. From the back of the brain to the front of the link is the driving force. And the reverse link is mostly modulated. The cells on the fifth layer of the cortex, which project to the thalamus, are driven, while the sixth layer is modulated.

(7) Snapshots

Neurons may in some ways be beyond the threshold of consciousness or to maintain a high firing rate or a type of synchronous oscillation or a cluster firing. These neurons may be pyramidal cells, which project to the forebrain. How to maintain a higher threshold of neural activity, which involves the internal dynamics of neurons, such as the accumulation of chemical substances Ca^{2+}, or the role of reentry circuits in the cortical system? It is also possible that the function of the positive and negative feedback loop can increase the activity of the neuron, reach the threshold and maintain a high activity for some time. There may also be some sort of complexity in the threshold problem, which may depend on the rate at which the threshold is reached, or how long it will be maintained.

The visual awareness process consists of a series of static snapshots, which is the perception that occurs in discrete time. The constant firing rate of the relevant neurons in the visual cortex representing a certain motion occurs. The motion occurs between a snapshot and another snapshot, and the duration of each snapshot is not fixed. As to the thing that the snapshot time of shape and color may happen to be the same, their dwell time relates to α rhythm or even δ rhythm. The dwell time of the snapshot depends on factors such as opening the signal, closing the signal, competition and adaptation.

(8) Attention and binding

It is useful to divide attention into two classes: a class that is fast, significant and bottom-up; the other is slow, self-controlled and top-down. The role of attention is around those active alliances in the competition. The attention is from bottom to top, the fifth layer of neurons in the cortex, projecting to the thalamus and the epitharamus. Attention from top to bottom proceeds from the forebrain, the dispersion of the back projection to the cortex I, II and III neurons in the apical dendrite, the possible pathway of the hypothalamic nucleus. It is commonly believed that the thalamus is the organ of attention. The function of the reticular nucleus of the thalamus is to make choices from a wide range of objects. The role of attention is to make a tendency in a group of competitive alliances, so as to feel the object and the event, but the object that has not been paid attention immediately disappears.

What is binding? It binds the different aspects of the object or the event, such as shape, color and motion, etc.. There may be several types of binding. If it is acquired or learned from experience, it may be embodied in one or several nodes and does not require a special binding mechanism. If the binding is new, the activities of the dispersed basic nodes need to be combined together.

(9) Styles of firing

Synchronous oscillation can increase the efficiency of a neuron without affecting the average firing rate. The significance and extent of synchronization is still controversial. Computational studies show that the effect is dependent on the degree of input. We no longer have sufficient conditions for the simultaneous oscillation (e.g., 40 Hz) as a neural correlate. The purpose of synchronous distribution may be to support a new alliance in the competition. If visual stimulation is very simple, such as a strip matters on the vacant auditoria, then there is no meaningful competition and synchronous firing may not occur. Similarly, a successful alliance is in a state of consciousness and this firing may not be necessary. As you get a permanent job, you may relax for a while. On a basic node, an earlier arrival of the spike may have greater advantage than the subsequent spike. In other words, the exact timing of the spike can affect the result of competition.

(10) Penumbra and meaning

Consider a small group of neurons, some of them have a reaction to certain aspects of the human face. The participants knew about the visual properties of the small group of cells, but how does the brain know what is represented by such firing? This is the question which addresses the meaning. Neural correlates are only directly related to the part of all pyramidal cells, but it can affect many other neurons, which is the penumbra. The penumbra is composed of two parts: one is the synaptic effect, and the other is the firing rate. The penumbra is not the sum of the basic nodal effects, but a result of the whole of the neural correlates. This penumbra includes neural correlates of past neurons, neural correlates of desired outcomes, and motor related neuronal correlates. By definition, the penumbra itself cannot be realized, and apparently part of it may be a part of the neural correlates. The penumbra of some members of the neuron may send feedback to the part of the members of the neural correlates, supporting the activities of the neural correlates. The penumbra neurons may be the site of unconscious priming.

The idea of Crick and Koch was that the framework of the consciousness weaves the idea of the neural correlates with the philosophical, psychological and neural perspectives, and the key idea is a competitive alliance. Guessing a node with minimum number of neurons may be a cortical function column. This bold hypothesis is no doubt that the study of consciousness pointed out a path, i.e., through the study of neural networks, cells, molecules and other levels of the material foundation, eventually the answer to consciousness will be found. But this hypothesis is faced with a central question: who has "consciousness" in the end? If it is the nerve cell, so then "I" who is it?

4.2.3 Theory of neuronal group selection

The Nobel laureate Edelman, according to the fact on physiological pathology and anatomy of the brain, emphasizes conformability and division of consciousness [127]. He believes that a thalamus-cortex system plays a key role in the generation of consciousness. The thalamus here refers in particular to the thalamus interlaminar nucleus, the bottom of the reticular nucleus and the forebrain, collectively referred to as "the reticular activating system". This part of neurons disseminate projection to the thalamus and the cerebral cortex, their function is to stimulate a thalamus–cortex system, and make the whole cortex in the waking state. In recent years, some no damage experiments show that multiple brain areas of the cortex simultaneously stimulate, rather than a single brain region alone being excited.

In 2003, Edelman published a paper [126] at the American Academy of Sciences (PNAs) series, in which he argued that we should abandon dualism. After analyzing the characteristics of consciousness, he pointed out that the study of consciousness must be considered:

(1) The contrast between the diversity and changeability of conscious states and the unitary appearance to the conscious individual of each conscious state. This unity requires the binding together of diverse sensory modalities that show constructive features such as those seen in Gestalt phenomena.
(2) The property of intentionality. This term refers to the fact that consciousness is generally, but not always, about objects or events. At the same time, consciousness is modulated by attention and has wide access to memory and imagery.
(3) Subjective feelings or qualia, for example, the experiencing of the redness of red, the warmness of warmth.

Neuroscience shows that consciousness is not the nature of a single brain region or some type of neuron, but the result of the dynamic interaction of a widely distributed group of neurons. A major system that is essential for conscious activity is the thalamocortical system. The integrative dynamics of conscious experience suggest that the thalamocortical system behaves as a functional cluster, i.e., it interacts mainly with itself. Of course, it also interacts with other brain systems. For example, interactions between the basal ganglia and the thalamocortical system are likely to influence the modulation of consciousness by attention as well as the development of automaticity through learning. The threshold of activity in these neural structures is governed by diffuse ascending value systems, such as the mesencephalic reticular activating system interacting with the intralaminar nuclei of the thalamus, as well as noradrenergic, serotonergic, cholinergic and dopaminergic nuclei.

Edelman believes that the brain is a selective system. In this selection system, the different road of the structure may carry out the same function or produce the same output. As the theory of neuronal group selection (TNGS) abandons the basic computational notions of logic and a clock, a means for spatiotemporal coordination must be put in place. This is provided by a process called reentry, the operation of which is central to the emergence of consciousness. Reentry is an ongoing process of recursive signaling among neuronal groups taking place across massively parallel reciprocal fibers that link mapped regions such as those found in the cortex. Reentry is a selectional process occurring in parallel; it differs from feedback, which is instructional and involves an error function that is serially transmitted over a single pathway. The interaction between competitive neuronal groups and reentry, in a wide range of synchronous activities in the brain areas, will be decided by the choice of the orientation of reentry. This provides a solution to the so-called binding problem: how do functionally segregated areas of the brain correlate their activities in the absence of an executive program or superordinate map? Binding of the activity of functionally segregated cortical areas for each sensory modality is essential for perceptual categorization. The selective discrimination of different objects or events is essential for adaptive purposes.

According to the theory of neuronal group selection, selectional events in the brain are necessarily constrained by the activity of diffuse ascending value systems. The activity of these systems affects the selectional process by modulating or altering synaptic thresholds. These systems, which include the locus coeruleus, the raphé nucleus, and the cholinergic, dopaminergic and histaminergic nuclei, are necessary to bias selective events and thereby favor certain species-specific behaviors during evolution. Value systems also affect systems of learning and memory. The dynamic synaptic changes in individual neuronal groups that are based on past perceptual categorizations are positively and negatively influenced by limbic and brainstem value systems. This system, based largely on the activity of frontal, parietal and temporal cortices, is critical to the emergence of consciousness.

Edelman proposed the theory of neuronal group selection (or neural Darwinism), which is the center of the theoretical framework of his consciousness, and is mainly reflected in the following two points: (a) By its nature, a selectional neural system has huge diversity, a property that is a necessary basis for the differentiated complexity of conscious brain events. (b) Reentry plays a key role to provide the critical means by which the activities of distributed multiple brain areas are linked, bound, and then dynamically altered in time during perceptual categorization. Both diversity and reentry are necessary to account for the fundamental properties of conscious experience. Therefore, both diversity and reentry are the basic properties of the conscious experience.

Edelman divides consciousness into two categories: one is primary consciousness, and the other is higher-order consciousness. Primary consciousness only considers the events of the present. Animals with primary consciousness can integrate perceptual and motor events together with memory to construct a multimodal scene in the present. Higher-order consciousness emerges later in evolution and is seen in animals with semantic capabilities such as chimpanzees. It is present in its richest form in the human species, which is unique in possessing true language made up of syntax and semantics. Edelman believes that the divergence of reptiles into mammals and then into birds, and the embryological development of large numbers of new reciprocal connections, allowed rich reentrant activity to take place between the more posterior brain systems carrying out perceptual categorization and the more frontally located systems responsible for value-category memory. At much later evolutionary epochs, further reentrant circuits appeared that linked semantic and linguistic performance to categorical and conceptual memory systems. This development enabled the emergence of higher-order consciousness.

On this basis, Edelman introduced the "reentry dynamic core" concept. In a complex system, it is composed of a number of small areas, which are semi-independent activities, and then they form a large cluster through interaction to produce the integrated functions. The critical reentrant events within an integrated circuit of this system are metastable and, in time periods of 500 MS or less, give way to a new set of integrated circuits. This process occurs in an ongoing manner over successive time periods within the thalamocortical system, which, as a functional cluster, interacts mainly with itself. This functional cluster has been called the reentrant dynamic core to emphasize its central properties as a complex system capable of yielding differentiated yet unitary states, which has much in common with Crick's "competitive alliance", and their coalitions correspond roughly to core states.

4.2.4 Quantum theories

Quantum theory reveals the basic laws of the microscopic physical world, which is the basis of all physical processes, biological processes and physiological processes. The quantum system goes beyond the particle and wave or the interaction with the material, which is integrated with the integral parallel and distributed processing. Non-local and long distance correlations are quantum properties, which may be closely related to consciousness.

Quantum wave function collapse is a change, which refers to the amount of wavelet function from numerous quantum eigenstates as a linear combination of the description state to the transition of an intrinsic pure state. Simply said, schema of many quantum superpositions of wave are transformed into a single quantum schema. The collapse of the wave function means selective projection from a subconscious memory to explicit memory awareness representation. Two possible memory and recall theories, the theory of quantum theory mentioned above, or the classic (nerve) memory theory might be a parallel distributed schema of synaptic connection systems, but may also be a fine structure, such as the quantum theory of parallel world and Bohm's hidden order, etc., proposed by Everett [139].

Philosopher Chalmers proposed a variety of quantum mechanics to explain consciousness [73]. He believes that the dynamic mechanism of the collapse provides an open space for the interpretation of the interaction. Chalmers thinks that the problem is the way we explain it. What we want to know is not just the association, we want to explain how consciousness emerges in the brain course, why will consciousness emerge? This is the mystery. The most likely explanation is that the state of consciousness is not likely to be superimposed on the state of consciousness and the overall quantum state of the system. The brain being a physical system of consciousness in the quantum state that is not superposed, physical state and spiritual phenomenon of this system are interrelated.

American mathematician and physicist Penrose developed his own theory from the Gödel theorem, that the human brain has the ability to exceed the axioms and the formal system. He proposed [353] in his first book about consciousness *The Emperor's New Mind*, that the brain has an additional feature which does not depend on the rules of calculation. It is a non-computational process, not driven by computational rule; and the basic properties of the algorithm is that most of the physics, and computer science must be driven by computation rules. For the non-computation process, the collapse of the quantum wave at a certain location determines the location of the random selection. The random nature of the collapse of the wave function is not restricted by the algorithm. The fundamental difference between the human brain and the computer may be caused by the uncertainty of quantum mechanics and the chaos of the complex nonlinear system. The human brain contains the non-deterministic nature of the neural network system. While the computer does not have the "intuition", it is the system having "fuzzy" processing ability and the efficiency of high performance. And conventional Turing machines are deterministic serial processing systems. Although it is possible to simulate such a fuzzy deal, efficiency is too low. The quantum computer and the neural network computer are in the study to solve such problems, to achieve the ability of the human brain.

Penrose also proposed a wave function collapse theory, which is suitable for the quantum system which does not interact with the environment. He believes that each quantum superposition has its own space–time curvature. When its away from more than Planck length (10^{-35} m) it will collapse, which is called the objective reduction. Penrose believes objective reduction represents neither a random, nor the majority of physics that depends on the algorithm process, but it represents non-computing, affected by the fundamental aspects of the geometry of space and time, and based on this the computation and consciousness will be produced.

In 1989, when Penrose wrote the first book on consciousness, it lacked a detailed description of the role of quantum processes in the brain. Hameroff who is engaged in cancer research and anesthesiology read Penrose's book, and presented the micro-tubule structure as support to the quantum of the brain.

Cooperation between Penrose and Hameroff, in the early 1990s, led them to jointly establish a controversial "harmonious and objective reduction model" (Orch-OR model). After operation in accordance with the Orch-OR provisions of quantum superposition state, Hameroff's team announced that the new quantum annealing coherent time scales required were greater by seven orders than those obtained by Tegmark. But this result is still less than the time required for the 25 ms. If you want to make the quantum process as described by Orch-OR, it should be associated with the 40 Hz gamma synchronization. In order to make up for this link, Hameroff's team made a series of assumptions and proposals. First, they assume that they can be converted to each other in the microtube between liquid and gel. In the gel state, they further assume that the water dipole along the periphery of the tubulin microtubules are arranged in the same direction. Hameroff thought that the orderly arrangement of water would shield any quantum annealing process in tubulin. Each tubulin also extends a negatively charged "tail" from the microtubule to attract the positively charged ions. This can further screen the quantum coherent process. In addition, there is speculation that the microtubule can be driven by biological energy into the coherent state.

Perus proposed an imagination of the combination of neural computing and quantum consciousness [358]. In the neural network theory, the state of the neuron system is described by a vector, which exactly reflects the activity distribution of the time of the neuron system. Particular neuron schemata represent certain information. In the quantum theory, the state of the quantum system can be described by the wave function changed over time. In this way, the neuron state is a kind of superposition of the neuron schema, which can be changed into a superposition of the quantum eigen wave function. The intrinsic wave function of quantum superposed usually has orthogonality and regularity. In the linear combination of the eigenstates, each of the eigenstates has a corresponding coefficient, which describes the probability of expression of a specific meaning in the actual state of the system. Integrated space–time neuronal signal can be described by the Schrodinger equation in the form of Feynman. The consciousness transformation from the subconscious in the nervous system corresponds to the "collapse of the wave function" with change from implicit order to explicit order [62].

The neural system model is to give the spatial information encoding of the nervous system in an explicit way, and for the time information encoding to be more indirect. However, through the Fourier transform, we can also easily establish a model with explicit time structure information. If we say that the neural activation pattern represents the description of the object of consciousness, then the Fourier transform of the neural activation spectrum, which represents the frequency distribution of the activation of neurons, is associated with the consciousness itself. There are the two aspects of the complementarity of the consciousness activities, with the globality space–time coding of consciousness coursing together.

4.2.5 Block model of consciousness

In 1988, Schacter proposed the block model of consciousness shown in Figure 4.2 [396]. Schacter has not given a specific reservation to the conscious awareness system, but he believes that there is a conscious awareness system. The activity is necessary for the conscious experience and is separated from the brain areas related to perception, cognition and action. Under this theoretical background, the unconscious vision can be explained by the separation of the visual system and the conscious awareness system. The awareness system plays a dominant role in the aspects of consciousness and performs other functions at the same time.

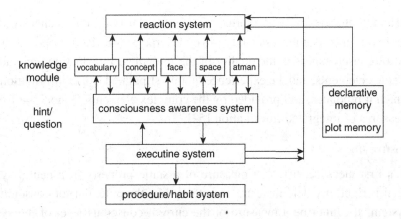

Fig. 4.2. Block model of consciousness

Philosopher and computer expert Burks put forward the theory of computer construction [67]:

(1) Consciousness must have the intention, namely, to be able to choose a goal, and to carry on the search in that direction.
(2) Consciousness must have direct experience, such as feeling the pain.
(3) Consciousness must have the function of correction and repair. When the local system of the computer fails, it can automatically go to another system, or automatically design new procedures in order to achieve its own perfection.
(4) Consciousness has to be awakened. People are equivalent to systematic inaction period during sleep, they have consciousness during awakening. Similarly, the computer has a protection system, in its inactive period, but can also be in a state of work.
(5) Consciousness can be carried out in short time control and the development of long time plan. From the construction point of view, consciousness is a specific computer control system, a relatively simple real-time control mechanism. When the system is in a state of arousal, it can guide the short-term activity and can carry out the plan.

According to the above conditions, a system should be able to make short-term and long-term plans, be able to input and output, recognize the results of their activities, to correct the error and then the system will be aware of consciousness. If this definition is feasible, then one day we can create a robot that can perform all the cognitive functions of a human being.

4.2.6 Information integration theory

Tononi and Edelman published a series of papers to clarify the comprehensive information theory in consciousness study [481]. Literature [48, 129] proposed that the amount of consciousness is the quality of the integrated information generated by the complex elements, and the experience quality stipulated by the information relation which it produces, and provided by the complex elements. Tononi put forward two measures of integrated information [52].

1. Measure Φ_1

Tononi's first measure, $\Phi 1$, is a measure of a static property of a neural system. If Tononi is right, it would measure something like the potential for consciousness in a system. It cannot be a measure of the current conscious level of the system, for it is a fixed value for a fixed neural architecture, regardless of the system's current firing rates. Tononi's first measure works by considering all the various bi-partitions of a neural system. The capacity to integrate information is called Φ, and is given by the minimum amount of effective information that can be exchanged across a bipartition of a subset. Tononi's approach requires examining every subset of the system under consideration. And then, for each subset, every bipartition is considered. Given a subset, S, and a bipartition into A and B, Tononi defines a measure called effective information (EI). Effective information uses the standard information theoretic measure of mutual information (MI):

$$MI(A : B) = H(A) + H(B) - H(AB),$$

where $H(\ldots)$ is a entropy, a measure of uncertainty. If there is no interaction between A and B, the mutual information is zero, otherwise it is positive.

But rather than the standard mutual information measure which quantifies the information gain from taking account of the connectedness between A and B, Tononi's EI is a measure of the information gain which would accrue if one considered the effect on B when the outputs of A vary randomly across all possible values.

2. Measure Φ_2

In a more recent work, Tononi and collaborators have proposed a revised measure of Φ, that is, Φ2. This revised measure has some advantages over the previous measure, in that it can deal with a time-varying system, providing a varying, moment to moment measure of Φ_2.

Φ2 is also defined in terms of effective information, though effective information is now defined quite differently from the version in Φ_1. In this case, effective information is defined by considering a system which evolves in discrete time steps, with a known causal architecture. Take the system at time t_1 and state x_1. Given the architecture of the system, only certain states could possibly lead to x_1. Tononi calls this set of states with their associated probabilities as *a posteriori repertoire*. Tononi also requires a measure of the possible states of the system (and their probabilities), in that situation where we do not know the state at time t_1. This he calls as the *a priori* repertoire. The *a priori* repertoire is calculated by treating the system as if we knew nothing at all about its causal architecture, in which case we must treat all possible activation values of each neuron as equally probable. The *a priori* and *a posteriori* repertoires will each have a corresponding entropy value, for instance, if the *a priori* repertoire consists of four equally probable states, and the *a posteriori* repertoire has two equally probable states, then the entropy values will be two bits and one bits, respectively. This means that, in finding out that the state of the system is x_1 at time t_1, we gain information about the state of the system one time step earlier.

Tononi argues that this is a measure of how much information the system generates in moving into state x_1. Having defined this measure of how much information the system generates, Tononi once again requires a measure of how integrated this information is. In the case where the system does not decompose into totally independent parts, we can once again look for the decomposition which gives the lowest additional information from the whole as opposed to the parts. Tononi calls this the minimum information partition. The effective information for the minimum information partition is then the Φ_2 value for the system.

We can do an exhaustive search across all subsystems and all partitions, and once again we can define complexes. A complex is a system with a given Φ_2 value, which is not contained within any larger system of higher Φ. Similarly, the main complex is the complex with highest Φ_2 in the whole system — and the true measure of Φ_2 (or consciousness) for the system is the Φ_2 of the main complex.

In examining Φ_2, we note that many of the problems with Φ_1 still apply. First, EI and Φ_2 itself are defined in ways which are closely tied to the particular type of system being examined. Although Φ_1, Φ_2 and EI are intended as general purpose concepts, the current mathematics has nothing like the broad range of applicability of standard information theoretic measures. For a further discussion of the shortcomings of information integration theories, we refer to Aleksander and Beaton [52].

Tononi recognizes that the integrated information theory is used to study the ability of maintenance state of the system, which can be termed as "intelligence". In literature [481], he described the state quality method and careful deliberation of qualia with Balduzzi. The qualia was originally used by philosophers to indicate the quality of the internal experience, such as the redness of the rose.

Tononi announced that it has found a sense information mechanism of qualia and faces the controversy around it with courage. Tononi adopts geometric manner, the introduction of shape, reflecting the system generated by the interaction of a set of information on the relationship as the concept of qualia. Literature [48] has proposed that the qualia involves the characteristic of the bottom layer system and essential feature of experience, offers geometric neurophysiology and geometrical original mathematics dictionary of phenomenology on qualia.

The qualia space (Q) is the axis space of each possible state (active mode). In Q, each submechanism provides a point of correspondence to the system state. The arrows within the Q project define the information relationship. In short, these arrows define the shape of qualia, reflecting the quality of the conscious experience with complete and clear features. The height W of the shape is the amount of consciousness associated with the experience.

4.3 Attention

The attention is mental state activity or consciousness in a certain moment for a certain object orientation and focus. Most of the time people can pay attention to the direction of their conscious control. Note that there are two obvious characteristics: direction and concentration. Direction means that people choose one object in every moment of mental activity or consciousness and ignore the rest of the objects. In the boundless universe, there is a lot of information for us. However, we are unable to respond to all the information and only point to consciousness for some of the things. For example, you go to the store to buy things, you only pay attention to the things you need and ignore other goods. So, attention point refers to mental activities or activities which our consciousness stores. Different people perceive information of the outside world differently. When mental activity or consciousness focuses on an object, they will completely concentrate and be absorbed in the excitability. This is the focus of attention. It can be said that the direction of attention is the object of mental activity or consciousness, then, concentration is the intensity or intensity of mental activity or consciousness in a certain direction. When people focus high degree of attention on an object, the attention to the point of the scope is narrow; point to a wide range of concentration, then the whole intensity is reduced. People's attention is highly concentrated, when targeting on the important matters, you will become blind and deaf to everything else around you.

4.3.1 Attention functions

Attention has the selection function, maintenance function, adjustment function and other functions. We are surrounded by the environment at any time that provides a lot of stimulations, but the information for us has different meanings. While some information is important and useful, some information on the task we are engaged is not. Even some harmful interference information, pay attention to the first function is from a large amount of information choice important information response are given, and excluding interference of harmful information, this is the choice of function. That can make the person's mental activity or consciousness remain relatively tense in a period of time, that is, it relies on the function of maintaining the attention. Only in a constant state of tension, one is able to carry out the processing depth to the selected information. Sustained attention function is also reflected in the continuation of time, and has important significance for complex activities to be carried out smoothly. Pay attention to the regulatory function not only in stable and sustainable activities, but also in the activity change. When people want to go to another activity from an existing activity, it reflects the important role in the regulation of attention. Paying attention to the adjustment function can help realize the transformation of activities and also to adapt to the changing environment.

1. Orientation control

Orientation control means that the brain leads the focus-of-attention to the place of interest and then realizes the ability of choosing space. There are two methods of choosing space information: first, attention mechanism involving the eyes. Urged by the outstanding goal in the visual field or personal will, the observer's eyes move to the place of interest to watch the corresponding goal. Eyes enable the goal representation in retina central concave through watching mechanism, thus obtaining more detailed goal information. This kind of orientation control and attention shift system which relies on eyes movement to realize is called explicit attention shift system. The second kind of attention shift mechanism occurs between two big beating eyes and turns attention to a certain place outside the watch point in an implicit way, which does not involve any whole move or head move. This kind of attention shift system is called implicit shift attention system. Posner holds that implicit attention may involve three kinds of attention operation: remove attention from the present focus-of-attention (involve the brain terminal leaf); Move the attention pointer to the area where the goal is (in the charge of midbrain district); Read the data in the place of attention point (the function of thalamus' pillow). Humans have the ability in implicit attention shift system. Through the experiment when turning attention to a certain place outside the watch point implicitly by attention clue, the person tested has not only improved the simulating response speed to this place, reduced threshold value of measuring, but also strengthened the corresponding electric activity of scalp. The directivity of attention explains that we cannot pay attention to many goals in the visual field at the same time, but move attention point sequentially one by one, that is to say that we can only adopt the serial way of moving. But we can choose corresponding input processing yardstick with the vision. Attention point can focus finely and it scatters in wider space range. In the attention cognitive model, the attention point as spotlight of the variable focus reflects this kind of characteristic vividly.

The directional alternative of attention is related to the limited information handling capacity of the attention system. The enhancement of the place information processing efficiency takes the non-attention information place being inhibited as cost.

Clinical observation proves that in the patient whose right terminal leaf of brain is injured, the attention clues appear in the right visual field, and the goal appears in the left visual field, when the directional control ability is damaged seriously; but in other situations, the harm is little. This indicates that the ability is damaged, when the attention is removed from the inducing clue place. From PET data obtained from a normal person, when attention moves from one place to another, whether this kind of movement is driven by will or stimulated by the external world, the terminal leaf area on left and right sides exhibits increased blood flow. This is the unique area activated by attention shift. The record from sober terminal leaf cell of monkey proves that terminal leaf neuron involves attention orientation control. P study reveals that the dissection network modulating the exodermis of other lines selectively crosses thalamus' pillow core; strain, loss, interference with or strengthening the operation of goal cause the obvious effect among thalamus pillow core too.

PET data and clinical observation indicate that the attention functions of two hemispheres of brain are asymmetric. The attention moves in two visual fields of left and right sides and can enhance the blood flow of the terminal leaf on the right side; and the enhancement of blood flow in the left terminal leaf only relates to the attention movement of the right visual field. This explains why right brain damage of hemisphere causes more attention damage than the left. But for a person with a normal brain, when equal amount disturbance targets distribution in the left and right visual fields, it cannot accomplish the task quickly when it has to concentrate with single vision. But to the patient resected callosum, when disturbance targets distribution in double visual fields, the speed of searching the targets is two times faster than disturbance targets concentrating on single vision. It means that when callosum is damaged, the attention mechanisms of left and right hemisphere are not connected with each other.

2. Guiding search

In the task of vision searching, the guidance function of attention is obvious. Generally speaking, the time taken by the tested target find to the goal increases with the disturbance targets' number with the linear increase. However, when we find out a certain goal, we will not need to search for all goals. There is conclusive evidence that the search can go on under the guidance of the characteristic of position in goal. These characteristics include color, form, sport, etc.

The experiment proves that when paying attention to the color, form or sport, the neural activity of the brain's frontal lobe district is obviously strengthened; but there is no enlarging effect in the brain terminal leaf district. It means that the guiding search is the duty of the attention system preceding.

In the preceding attention system, the anterior cingulate gyrus's function is called 'execution function'. "Execution" includes two meanings. First, the interior brain must notify "the executor" process course what is taking place; then, "the executor" implements the attention control to the whole system. The experiment finds that neural activity number in this area enhances with the increase of target number and the reduction of the training number. This is identical with attention's cognitive theory. In dissecting, the anterior cingulate gyrus has a pathway between the parietal and the prefrontal cortex. The prefrontal cortex plays a key role in keeping the representation of the past things. The anterior cingulate gyrus involves clear feel and control of the target. These findings indicate that the preceding attention system is the neural basis of the attention and at the center of issuing orders by the brain [106]. This kind of conjecture may be reasonable because the frontal lobe district of the human brain's cortex area is exactly the cortex, which is related to making plans. It is a psychologically supreme control center.

The experiment also found that it coincides to choose through the position or characteristics such as the color, form, etc., that interfere less with each other. So the preceding attention system and the after attention system may enable time share or time division.

3. Keeps vigilance

The function of the vigilance system is to make the brain ready and keep it vigilant in order to rapidly deal with the signal with supreme priority. Keeping vigilance is closely related to attention, and it involves a subnetwork of attention.

The positive electron fault scans reveal that when keeping the vigilance state, the blood flow of right frontal lobe district is strengthened; and when this area is damaged, mankind loses the ability to keep vigilance. It means that keeping the vigilance state involves an attention subsystem lying in the right side of the brain.

4. Inhibit–enhancement effect

A great activity can be inhibited or enhanced selectively through the regulation and control that is paid attention to. An enhancement effect of inhibition of noticing is the result of paying attention to cooperative effect of the subnetwork.

When having a large number of interference goals in the visual field, how does the brain find the correct place to finish the goal and measure? The experiment proves that there is enlarging or inhibiting the neural activity of every brain district selectively to finish the goal and measure. PET measurement reveals that when a person tries to instruct the brain to pay attention to an amazing attribute, the brain area that specially runs with this attribute is enhanced selectively. This kind of effect is especially obvious in the systematic line of exodermis of vision. The experiment finds that though the amazing picture in the visual field of person tried is all the same, but different one instructs the language to cause the activity of different brain districts to enhance. Let a person try to pay attention to a certain attribute with amazing vision through guiding languages (such as the movement pace). Observing physics with this attribute to stimulate directly (such as the movement goal) can cause the activity of the same brain district to enhance. Generally speaking, any brain area will be enhanced through the function of noticing.

One of the measures to pay attention with regard to the enhancement effect is the method to record electric potential of human brain scalp. In some search tasks, one cannot find the goal according to single characteristics such as the orientation or form, etc.; it must be a combination of two or more characteristics with a place to accomplish the task. One must try a serial process for moving from one place to another. If the brain does not allow the eyes to move at this moment, then one can only rely on obscure attention to shift. In the experiment, obscure attention shift driven by the induction clue appears in different places. Experiments find that when noticing the clue appearing in the position of goal, affording to conceal focus-of-attention will cause the enhancement of the electric potential of scalp of the carrying area after the person has tried. The place where this kind of enhancement effect takes place with positive electron fault scan studies the cortex area where the blood flow of midbrain enhances.

4.3.2 Selective attention

If you go to a cocktail party or talk in a noisy restaurant, there are three ways which can help you focus on people's word information (pay attention to the target): one is the discourse target different sensory characteristics (for example, high and low pitch, foot, rhythm); the second is the intensity (loudness); the third is the sound source position. After you pay attention to the physical characteristics of the target speaker, you can avoid the interference of the semantic content of the speaker's speech information. Obviously, the target volume can also help. In addition, you may intuitively use a strategy to localize sound, thus making the binaural listening task for dichotic listening task: in your ear to listen to the target speaker, while the other ear avoids the target speaker.

Selective attention mechanism is commonly used in the filter model, the attenuation model, the response selection model, the resource distribution model, etc.

1. Filter model

The model first proposed by the famous British psychologist Broadbent in 1958 was earlier a theoretical model of attention (see Figure 4.3). The model was called a single channel model later by Welford [513]. Filter model shows that the information from the outside world is a large number, but the high level of human nervous system processing capacity is very limited, so there is a bottleneck. In order to avoid overloading the system, the filter should be regulated, and some information into

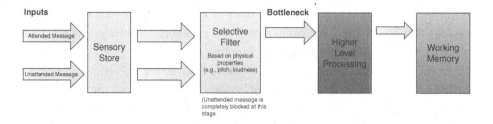

Fig. 4.3. Filter model

the stage of advanced analysis should be chosen. The rest of the information may be temporarily stored in a memory, which then declines rapidly.

Note that the attention function is like a filter, where some of the input channel information fillers through the internal capacity of limited access to the high central process, and other information is filtered out. Therefore, the attention of the work is carried out in a full way or no way.

You are talking to a few people at a cocktail party or some other party. At this time, your talk about other people cannot be identified, but if someone outside mentions your name, you may notice that the other people who are talking with you notice you but not the ones you do not pay attention to. Through the headset to the subjects in two ears and playback, each ear received stimulus information that is not the same. Through the experiment, the relationship between the response information and the information of the two ears was investigated. In order to understand the characteristics of attention, the experimental results show that the test in such an experiment will be based on the characteristics of the material to reproduce the stimulus information, such as 6, 2, 9.

There are two kinds of views on the results of this experiment:

(1) Filter channels can be quickly transferred.
(2) The working mechanism of the attention is not the single channel model the filter model is not correct.

2. Attenuation model

In 1960, American psychologist Treisman presented the attenuation model based on the revised filter model proposed by [485]. The theory suggests that the filter does not work in "all or nothing". The channel to receive information is not a single channel, but multiple channels. This model is based on the experimental results of processing the non-following ear's information in the following experiments, and the results of the improved filter model are further improved by Treisman.

Attenuation model is considered and the attention to the work of the way is not to all or none of the single channel, but to multi-channel mode. However, in

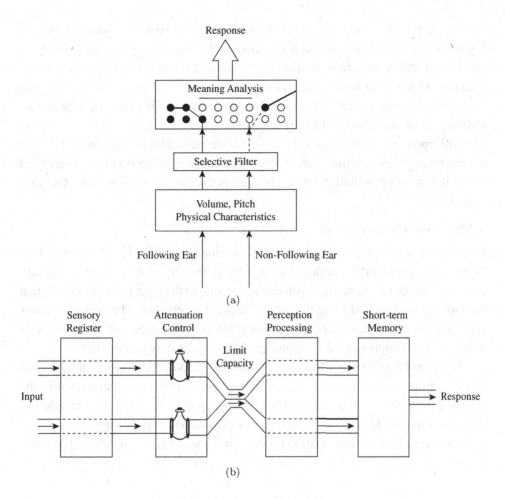

Fig. 4.4. Attenuation model

multi-channel information processing, each channel of information processing is different. As shown in Figure 4.4, the information processing mode of the following ear is like the filter model, and the non-following ear's information is also possible through the filter. Just follow the ear of the signal in which the filter signal is attenuated, so with dashed lines, in meaning analysis, they may be filtered out. Also, some other factors may be strengthened (such as their name).

According to Treisman's theory, selective attention involves three stages. In the first stage, we pay attention to the physical characteristics of the stimulus, such as volume (sound intensity), pitch ("frequency") and so on. This preattention processing is in parallel (simultaneous) processing on the sensory stimuli. We put the signal to the next stage for a target with a target stimulus, and the characteristic stimulus in having no goal, we only regard it as amazingly weakening. In the second phase, we need to analyze whether a given stimulus has a similar speech or musical pattern. For those with the target pattern of stimulation, we put the signal to the next stage, and there is no target mode of stimulation, as we also put it just as a weakening stimulus. In the third phase, we focus on the stimuli that are about to reach this stage, and the information that comes from the sequence is given the appropriate meaning of the selected stimulus information.

An important concept — threshold — was introduced into the attenuation model for top level of information. This is stored information in the brain in a high level of the threshold of excitation where they are not identical, thus affecting the filter selection.

3. Response selection model

In 1963, Deutsch proposed a response selection model [117]. The model (see Figure 4.5) argues that attention does not lie in the choice of perceptual stimuli, but in the choice of responses to stimuli. According to the theory, all the stimuli that sensory organs feel will enter the advanced analysis process. The central nervous system is processed according to certain rules, and the important information is made. Without important information, the new content may be flushed.

Different from Treisman's theory of attenuation, only the position of the signal blocking filter is to be placed on the perceptual processing needed to recognize the meaning of the stimulus. This post filter allows people to recognize the information that enters the ear, for example, to hear your own name or type of translation (for a bilingual person). If the information is not aware of a string, then people will throw it

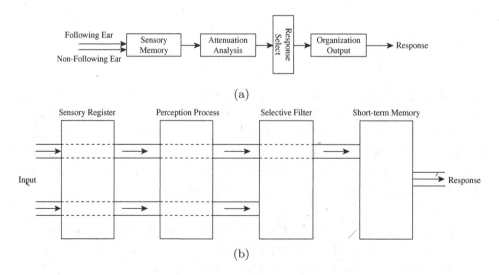

Fig. 4.5. Response selection model

away in the filtering mechanism. If there is, then, when you hear your name, you will pay attention to it. It needs to be pointed out that when the supporters for both after filtration mechanism and before filtration mechanism are put forward, the attention bottleneck exists and passes through only a single source of information. The model difference of these two theories only lies in the bottleneck assumption seat.

4. Resource distribution model

In 1973, Kahneman proposed the resource distribution model [229]. Resource distribution model suggests that attention is a limited amount of energy or resources that people can use to perform tasks. People in the activity can get resources for awakening linked together, such as the arousal level from emotions and drugs, muscle tension and other factors which influence generated resources through a distribution scheme and are assigned to different possible activities to finally form a variety of responses. Figure 4.6 shows a schematic diagram of the model of resource allocation.

5. Spotlight model

In the beginning of the 1980s, Treisman suggested that the feature integration model closely combined the internal process of attention and perceptual processing, and

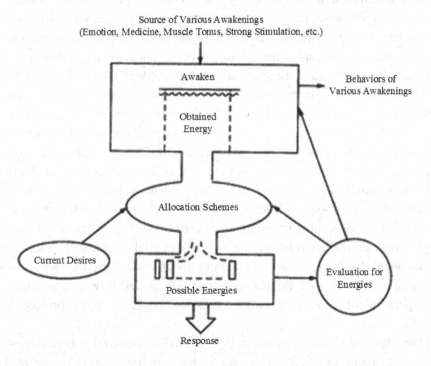

Fig. 4.6. Resource distribution model

the image of the "Spotlight" metaphor attention [486], which was acclaimed by cognitive psychologists, neurophysiologists and neural computing experts. According to this model, the visual processing process is divided into two interrelated stages, namely, preattention and focus attention stage. The former refers to the visual stimulation of color, orientation and movement and other simple features for rapid, automatic parallel processing. A variety of features in the brain encode to produce the corresponding "feature map". The various characteristics of the image features form representation. Preattention processing is a "bottom-up" information processing process, and does not need to focus attention. The position of each feature in the feature map is uncertain. To obtain the perceptual object requires reliance on focus, through the "Spotlight" for the location map scanning, to search the various characteristics that are organically integrated together, the feature of dynamic assembly. This is a slower serial process. Therefore, when the difference between the target and the interference target is only a single feature, the target can immediately be one from the perspective of "jump", target detection, or search time without any interference from the influence of the number of targets; and when the target and distractors performance give differences for the combination of multiple features, you need to use focused attention for each target location sequential scan. At this time, the search time increases linearly with the number of interference terms.

Recent experimental evidence shows that depending on the more complex properties, such as the 3D surface, it can also realize the attention distribution. Of particular interest, the concept of feature assembly in the feature integration model has been partially confirmed in the study of visual physiology. The brain's cortex does not have the neural unit of one-to-one correspondence with the objects we have seen, on the contrary, the vision system understands the object and the object's attributes are resolved into different features, such as color, orientation, motion, etc. These features are processed by different visual pathways and cortical regions, respectively. How to characterize all the properties of the same object with the firing of neurons in different regions, or find the common labeling of neurons that are related to the firing neurons, is the so-called "binding problem". Electrophysiological experiments showed that the concentration of attention could be related to the synchronously firing of neurons that are related to the event. This kind of synchronization is usually shown as the synchronous oscillation of about 40 Hz. This discovery provides physiological evidence for the feature integration model. However, how to move the "Spotlight" of attention from one location to another is still a problem to be solved.

The "Spotlight" model of attention is a model of cognitive psychology that has a wide range of effects. However, it has not been generally accepted by neurophysiologists. Even some theory on attention objective with the existence of "Spotlight" has also raised doubts. For example, the competition theory of attention believes that attention mechanism and field of vision is not a quick scan of the "Spotlight", but a variety of neural mechanisms of brain to solve object competition and behavior control of emergent properties.

Although there is no attention theory which has been widely recognized, a bottleneck problem of attention is recognized by everyone, this is the selective problem of attention. The basic idea is that primary information processing in general is quick and parallel; and the information processing of a certain stage requires a bottleneck to control information processing of the next stage. In a moment, only one thing is processed while the other which is located in the non-pay attention to the point of the event is temporarily suppressed. And then it moves on to the next thing and so on. This is a serial process that takes a long time to complete.

4.3.3 Attention distribution

Attention distribution is when people engage two or more activities and can pay attention to different objects at the same time. This phenomenon can be seen everywhere in life. For example, teachers while teaching also observe the situation of students listening; the car driver while driving makes a phone call, but also pays attention to changes in the surrounding environment, etc.

Theoretically, the brain has a limited capacity for information processing at the same time, and the attention is focused on the part of the information. When attention is focused on the processing requirements of all psychological activities to participate, there is a high tension, so attention cannot be pointed at the same time in two different directions. Having an awareness about both distribution and attention is contradictory. Since ancient times, there have been many experiments to prove that attention cannot be distributed or is difficult to distribute. In modern times, it was found that different kinds of stimuli were strictly in the same time, and the distribution of different kinds of stimuli was very difficult. The structure of the compound device is that it has a circular dial which is divided into 100 degrees and has a rapidly rotating pointer on the disk. The subject's task was to speak at the bell, a pointer. The results showed that the subjects usually cannot say when the bell rang for the exact degree of the pointer, what he says is always early to or later than the bell ringing degree. This shows that his attention is first directed to a stimulus (the location of the ring or pointer), and later to point to another stimulus. And research shows, that experiments were carried out wherein two ears were provided with different information at the same time, experiencing them at the same time, namely, carry on listening to distinguish one from another. It was difficult to accurately reflect the result of the experiments.

The study shows that there are different levels of attention distribution, which depend on the nature, complexity and the degree of familiarity or proficiency of a person's activities. When several kinds of activities are carried out at the same time, it is complicated or more difficult to pay attention. The efficiency of intellectual activity is reduced to a greater extent than the efficiency of motor activity at the same time when carrying out two activities including the intelligence and motion. At the same time, to carry out two kinds of intellectual activities, it is more difficult to distribute attention. Among the various factors that affect the attention distribution, the proficiency of the activity is most important. To perform attention distribution well, first, in two activities at the same time, there must be an activity that has reached a relative "automation", that needs more attention, so that people can put attention on unfamiliar activities. Secondly, to establish a certain link between the activities at the same time, or through the training of complex activities to form a certain reaction system, it is easier to carry out attention distribution.

The distribution and transformation of attention are closely linked. In the so-called attention transformation, a person according to a certain purpose takes the initiative to transfer attention from one object to another object. In order to successfully complete complex activities, attention is transferred to the center of the rapid transfer between different objects, it constitutes the phenomenon of attention distribution. If the speed of the transformation is too fast, more than the ability to pay attention to the transfer, the attention distribution is difficult to achieve. The results of composite experiment and binaural listen experiment illustrate this.

4.3.4 Attention system

According to the existing study results, Posner divides attention network into three subsystems: anterior attention system, posterior attention system, vigilance attention system [368]. The anterior attention system involves frontal cortex, anterior cingulate gyrus and basal ganglion. The posterior attention system includes frontal-parietal cortex, pulvinar and superior colliculus. The vigilance attention system then mainly involves the input from the locus coeruleus norepinephrine in the right hemisphere to the cerebral cortex. The functions of these three subsystems can be summarized as orientation control, guiding search and keeping vigilance, respectively. Anterior attention system is activated more and more in the task requiring consciousness. This system is also related to "action attention", which is tested in the selective course of action plan or choose an action. On the contrary, the posterior attention system is related to the cortical parietal lobe. The parietal lobe is a part of the thalamus, while some of the midbrain area is related to the eye movement. During the visual–spatial attention, the system is highly activated, and the subjects must be detached or converted to attention. Neural activity in the visual, auditory, motor or associative areas of the cortex during visual, auditory, motor or advanced tasks is also associated with attention. Anterior attention system and posterior attention system appear to be able to enhance the attention of different tasks. This indicates that they are used to regulate the activation of related cortical regions of specific tasks.

The activity of the attention system could be the result of the enhancement of the activity of the project, the inhibition activation to the non-attention item, or both. Posner etc., make a positive answer: to look at the situation and set. Specifically, as the specific tasks and the brain regions investigated are different, these three cases are possible. The task of the study is to determine what happens in the brain when performing tasks. To delineate the areas of the brain involved in a variety of tasks, cognitive psychologists often use positron emission tomography (PET), which can delineate regional cortical blood flow.

4.4 Metacognition

Metacognition is a very important concept in modern cognitive psychology; it was proposed by American cognitive psychologist Flavell in 1976 [146]. Flavell pointed out that metacognition is generally defined as any knowledge of the process and the results of the cognitive process, or any cognitive activity that regulates the cognitive process. The reason why it is called metacognition is that its core meaning is knowledge about cognition and control of cognition. That is to say, metacognition is the understanding of the cognitive subject to self-mentality, ability, objectives and tasks, cognitive strategies, and metacognitive and cognitive knowledge subject to their planning monitoring and adjustment of cognitive activities. The monitoring of cognitive activity is realized by the interaction between the four aspects, such as metacognitive knowledge, metacognitive experience, goal (or task) and action (or strategy).

4.4.1 Metacognitive knowledge

Metacognition knowledge is people's cognitive activities on the general knowledge that is accumulated through experience about cognition of declarative knowledge and procedural knowledge. Metacognitive knowledge is divided into three parts:

(1) Knowledge of person variables: General knowledge about how human beings learn and process information, as well as individual knowledge of one's own learning processes.

(2) Knowledge of task variables: Knowledge about the nature of the task as well as the type of processing demands that it will place upon the individual. First of all, it is the understanding of cognitive materials such as materials which provide useful information, and those that do not. First, what information is easy to obtain, what is obtained through reasoning; what information can be obtained on its own and what information is obtained by the will of the efforts to complete. Secondly, one should understand the nature of the task, including the task of the target, the type of the task, the way to complete the task.

(3) Knowledge of strategy variables: Knowledge about both cognitive and metacognitive strategies, as well as conditional knowledge about when and where it is appropriate to use such strategies. According to the nature and characteristics of cognitive tasks and objectives, to determine which is the preferred strategy, which is the chosen strategy, how to use these strategies.

4.4.2 Metacognitive experience

Metacognitive experience is the cognitive and emotional experience that people have when they engage in cognitive activities. A lot of cognitive experiences are related to the position of people in cognitive activities, the progress they are making and the possible progress. In the context of highly conscious and careful cognitive monitoring and regulation, the metacognitive experience is likely to be generated. In the difficult mathematical theorem or problem, each step forward is accompanied by success and failure, joy and confusion, excitement and anxiety.

4.4.3 Metacognitive monitoring

Metacognitive monitoring refers to the conscious monitoring, control and active regulation of the individual self-cognitive activities in the whole process of cognitive activity. Therefore, metacognitive monitoring is a kind of self-monitoring, which must be based on the individual's ability to have a certain metacognitive knowledge and metacognitive experience. The value of metacognitive knowledge and metacognitive experience in learning must be realized through metacognitive monitoring. Self-monitoring is the core problem of metacognition. It can be seen that the metacognitive process is actually a guide and adjusts our cognitive process. Its essence is people's self-consciousness and self-control of cognitive activity.

4.4.4 Metacognition training

Metacognitive training refers to the training on students' metacognitive monitoring ability of process, including teaching to the students' metacognitive monitoring strategy and the ongoing cognitive activities as the object of consciousness, the continued implementation of self-supervision and regulation. This process mainly includes four aspects: one is learning the activities on their own pertaining to prior planning and arrangements; the second is for their actual learning activities of supervision, evaluation and feedback; the third is on the basis of their learning activities, adjustment, modification and control; fourth is the summary and reflection of the cognitive activity. Metacognitive training has three training methods:

(1) Speech training method [123]: This is a student in the solution of problems themselves to their interpretation, (say) reason of speech activities, leading to activities, such as mobilizing students' metacognitive monitoring process, so as to improve problem-solving, and the efficiency of learning and thinking.

(2) Others questioning training method [53]: This divides the experimenters into five groups with traditional "Hanoi Tower" problem metacognitive tests, it presents the problem "why did you do that?" to students. It enables to draw people's attention from the information processing content to the actual process of information and raises an awareness on what to do and how to do, including better monitoring, evaluation, adjustment and correcting their cognitive activities, so as to improve their score.

(3) Oneself questioning training method [110]: Let the students in the computer solve the game "Roek's boots", and according to the difficulty of the problem, it is divided into three levels. The subjects are divided into three groups: the first stage: the first group and the second group will be given the general strategy of problem-solving (two classes) before teaching, the third group does not accept this kind of training. In the second stage, each student of the first group will be given oral answer question sheet training, these questions monitor the problem-solving process. The second and the third groups do not accept this kind of training. In the third stage, the result is tested. The test results show that the method used in the experiment is effective to solve the problem, especially for complex problems, and the effect is more obvious.

4.5 Motivation

4.5.1 Overview

Motivation is an internal motive force with subjective reasons, which directly drives the individual activities to achieve a certain purpose, and the psychological state is initiated and maintained by individual activities. Psychologists define motivation as the process that initiates, guides and maintains goal-oriented behaviors. In [327], Mook simply defined motivation as "the cause of action".

In 1943, Maslow put forward the demand theory of motivation [289]. Maslow's assumption is that people are in need of motivation, the sequence of human motivation includes the most basic physiological and safety needs through a series of love and respect, the complex needs of self-realization, where the need level has great intuitive appeal [291]. Over the years, people have proposed a lot of theories of motivation, and each theory has a certain degree of concern. These theories are very different in many ways, but they all come from a similar consideration, namely, behavioral arousal. They point to these three points that are the core of any kind of motivation.

Green and others advocated that the theory of motivation is divided into three categories of physiology, behavior and social [179]. Merrick proposed that the motivation theory is divided into four categories, namely, biological theory, cognitive theory, social theory and combined motivation theory [310]. The biological motivation theory tries to explain the motivation of the work process based on the biological level of natural system. The mechanisms of these theories are often explained by energy and motion, which directs the organism toward a certain behavior. The existing research on artificial system has been used to simulate the software agent and the natural system using the theory of biological motivation.

When one wakes up, hunger and thirst are felt in the body driven by motion or signs. This means eating or drinking or exploration is the physiological state of monitoring changes in the morning. However, in addition, improvements in response to physiological changes, such as feeding and drinking water, often occur to participate in such changes. Thus, cognitive motivation theory concentrates on how to determine the behavior, observe the effect of behavior and to what extent, according to the cost and benefit of different steps of action, to explain the individual behavior that will most likely result. Based on the concept of abstract machine learning and artificial intelligence, such as goal, planning or strategy, the cognitive theory of motivation can provide a starting point for the model.

The theory of social motivation refers to the behavior of individuals in their contact with other people. The social theory of motivation is the intersection of biology and cognitive theory. For example, the theory uses the fitness and cultural effects to describe the cognitive phenomenon, while the theory of evolution can be considered a biological social theory. Social motivation theory can be from the group situation of individuals to greater social, cultural and evolutionary systems. These theories provide an important initial state for the design of multi-agent systems.

Combined motivation theories include integrative biology, cognitive and social motivation theory, for example, Maslow's hierarchy of needs theory [292], Alderfer's ERG theory [7], and Stagner the steady-state model [468]. It is also the focus of the research on the synthetic model of the artificial system. This model provides a comprehensive algorithm to describe the behavior process in the aspects of hardware, abstract reasoning and multi-agent systems.

All kinds of behavior and activities of the people cannot be separated from motivation. Motivation has the following functions:

(a) Arouse the start function of the action. Personally, all the power of an individual's actions must be through his mind, must be changed to his desire for motivation, in order to make him act up.
(b) A directing function that focuses an individual's behavior towards or away from specific goals.
(c) An organizing function that influences the combination of behavioral components into coherent, goal-oriented behavioral sequences.
(d) Strengthen the function of motivation. One's experience of successes and failures on the activity has certain influence on his activity ambition. In other words, how does the behavioral result influence people's motivation? Therefore, motivation plays a regulation control appearing in the form of playing a positive or negative reinforcement role in people's behavior.

4.5.2 Theory of motivation

Motivation can be roughly divided into three stages: before the 1960s, it was mainly behaviorism and psychoanalysis theory, emphasizing the direct effects of instinct and impulse, drive, body balance and biological factors in the motivation and behavior of people. Since the 1960s, the cognitive view gradually involved motivation research which led to the attribution theory that emphasizes the cognitive factors of motivation theory, and is based on the traditional behavioral perspective theory of self-efficacy and learned helplessness theory. After the study of motivation in 1980s, it has been gradually moving toward integration, building a theory of motivation.

According to the need of our mind model CAM research, we focus on several kinds of motivation theories.

1. Hierarchy of needs theory

Humanistic psychologist Maslow attempts to unify a large number of human motivation research results and put forward the hierarchy of needs theory [292], as shown in Figure 4.7. He is committed to the study of human motivation and stated there are five basic needs. These have been arranged according to the level of satisfaction they bring to people. The most basic level includes physiological needs, namely, the need for food, water, air and other; once the physiological needs have been satisfied,

Fig. 4.7.   Maslow's hierarchy of needs theory

the needs of safety or protection follow; next, love, affection, belongingness needs follow; then, respect, value or esteem needs follow; the last is the need for self-actualization. The so-called self-realization is to make people more complete, more perfect, to more fully use their own ability and skills. Maslow believes that most of the time people use energy to achieve the most basic and unmet needs. When they need more or less to achieve, people will become more and more attentive to the needs of the higher level. He believes that in all the needs, the first four are due to lack of need and their physiological and psychological health is very important, that must give a certain degree of satisfaction, but once they are met, the resulting motivation is lost or disappears. The last need for the need for self-realization, which is the need for growth, and is seldom fully satisfied. For a healthy person, because the needs have been quite satisfied, their behavior is determined by the different types of growth needs. The theory of hierarchy of needs has influenced the clinical and counseling psychology and has become the basis of the theory of motivation.

On the basis of Maslow's needs theory of motivation, Bach proposed an expansion motivation framework of cognitive agent [43]. He describes a predefined finite set of drivers associated with the system requirements. The objective will be achieved through reinforcement learning with the environment interaction. Bach also pointed out all the behavior of the Psi agent directly to the target state. The target state meets all the needs of the consumer behavior. Bach put forward the theory of three layers of the agent's demand. The lowest level is for physiological needs, including fuel, water and integrity. The second layer is the cognitive needs, including the certainty, the integrity and the aesthetic. Third layer is for social needs, including the addition and request signal. Bach uses the Psi theory to the possible solution of a motivation-based, multi-agent motivation system. It can not only reflect the physiological needs, but also express the cognitive and social needs. It directly integrates the requirements and quickly adapt to different environments and agents. They developed a model that successfully evaluated the performance of a human being at the time of the game.

2. Curiosity growth theory

One of the basic concepts of growth theory is that human beings are not born with the ability to fully develop. In order to succeed in dealing with the environment, they are required to learn and develop their skills as much as possible. Based on Marsland's method [290], Saunders and Gero developed a curiosity and interest model in terms of novelty [392] [395]. They used real-time novelty detectors to discover novelty. Saunders and Gero also adopted the combined neural network to indicate the novelty using reinforcement learning to create a curious design agent.

In 1997, Schmidhuber developed a novel, creative explorer, with two co-evolution of the brain as an interest model [400]. Oudeyer and Kaplan developed the intelligent adaptive curiosity (IAC) system as the robot's motivational system [347,348], where encouraging scenarios concern can maximally improve the learning progress. Their model of IAC is maintenance driven, so that the abstract dynamic cognitive variables of learning progress are maintained at maximum. They call it a curious cognitive model and the robot agent can learn the abstract representation of the scene.

3. Achievement motivation theory

McClelland of Harvard University, USA, started on human needs and motivation research from 1940–1950s and put forward the famous "three needs theory". He believes that individuals have three important motives or needs in the work context: need for achievement, power, affinity [304]. McClelland believed that a person who has a strong need for achievement will be eager to do things more perfectly, improve work efficiency and achieve greater success. Their pursuit is fun as they strive for success to overcome difficulties and solve problems, and keep striving, after the success and personal sense of achievement, as they do not value the rewards success brings. Power demand is a kind of desire or driving force to influence and control others. Different people have different levels of desire for power. The person with higher power demand holds greater interest in influencing and controlling others, pays attention to strive for achieving status and influence. They often like to argue, are talkative, straightforward and possess a calm mind; they are good at asking questions and requirements; like to teach others, and are willing to talk. Affinity need is a desire to be loved and accepted by others. Highly motivated people tend to associate with others, at least for the sake of others, and this interaction will bring him a good time. High affinity needs to be compatible, like cooperation rather than competition in the work environment, where people hope to communicate with each other and are understanding, they are more sensitive to the environment of interpersonal relationships.

Atkinson's theory of achievement motivation is considered to be an expectancy value theory, because this theory dwells on the motivation level which is dependent on a person for the purpose of evaluation to reach the objective possibility assessment [29]. Atkinson pays attention to the function of the conflict, especially pays attention to achievement motive and conflicts while fearing to fail. The feature of this theory is that it can be described in a quantitative form. Atkinson believes that the initial high achievement motivation comes from the children's family or cultural groups, especially in early childhood education and training. Personal achievement motivation can be divided into two parts: one is to strive for success, and the other is to avoid failure. That is, achievement motivation involves emotional conflict between the expectations of success and the fear of failure.

4. Incentive theory

Incentive theory is a summary of the principles and methods of how to meet the needs of people and mobilize the enthusiasm of the people. The purpose of motivation is to stimulate people's correct behavior motivation, mobilize people's enthusiasm and creativity, in order to give full play to the human intelligence effect, make the greatest achievement. Since the 1920–1930s, many management experts, psychologists and sociologists have combined the practice of modern management, and put forward a lot of incentive theories. These theories can be divided into three categories: the theory of behavioral motivation, the cognitive motivation theory and the integrated motivation theory.

(1) The theory of behavioral motivation

In the 1920s, the United States of America popularized a kind of behavioral psychology theory, where substance of the management process is to encourage, through incentives, to induce people's behavior. Under the guidance of the theory of "stimulus–response", the task of the incentive is to choose a set of appropriate incentives, that is, the means of stimulation, in order to arouse the corresponding reaction standards and stereotypes.

Skinner, a behaviorist, then put forward the theory of operational conditioned reflex. According to this theory, the main means of stimulating people can not only rely on the stimulus variables, but also take into account the intermediate variables, that is, the existence of human subjective factors. In particular, in addition to the stimulus measures, it should take into account the needs of the subjective factors of workers. According to the new theory of behavior, the content of incentive measures should be based on the social and psychological point of view, in-depth analysis of the needs of people's physical and spiritual needs, and to meet the needs of individuals and organizations to achieve consistency.

The new behavioristic theory emphasizes that people's behavior is not only determined by the perception of the stimulus, but also depends on the outcome of the behavior. When the result of the behavior is conducive to the individual, this behavior will be repeated and play a role in strengthening the incentive. If the result of the behavior is negative to the individual, the behavior will weaken or disappear. Therefore, in the use of affirmation, praise, reward or denial, criticism, punishment and other means to strengthen the learner's behavior can be directed to control or change in order to guide the best state of the expected.

(2) Cognitive incentive theory

Behavior simply looks at the nervous system of the adult objective stimulation of the mechanical response, which does not conform to the objective laws of human psychological activities. The occurrence and development of human behavior should fully take into account the intrinsic factors, such as ideology, interest, value and need, etc. As a result, these theories focus on the content and structure of people's needs, and how to promote people's behavior.

Cognitive incentive theory also stressed that the purpose of motivation is to turn the negative into a positive behavior, in order to achieve the intended target of the organization to achieve better results. Therefore, in the process of motivation, we should also focus on how to transform and the transformation of human behavior. Skinner's theory of operating conditions, such as the theory of frustration also belongs to this type of theory. These theories believe that human behavior is the result of the interaction between external environmental stimuli and internal thought. Therefore, combining the change in the external environment to stimulate and the internal ideological understanding could achieve the purpose of changing the behavior of people.

(3) Comprehensive motivation theory

The behavioral motivation theory emphasizes the importance of extrinsic motivation, while the cognitive motivation theory emphasizes the importance of intrinsic motivation. Comprehensive incentive theory is the synthesis, generalization and development of these two kinds of theories. It points out a more effective way to solve the problem of mobilizing the enthusiasm of the people.

Psychologist Lewin put forward the theory of field dynamics which is the most early comprehensive motivation theory. This theory emphasizes that the development of human behavior is the result of interaction between individuals and the environment. Environmental stimulus is actually just a fuse, and people in need are an internal driving force, orientation of human behavior depends on the relationship between the strength of internal systems and the external lead wire. If the internal needs are not strong, then the strong lead wire also does not have much meaning.

In 1968, Porter and Lawler put forward a new comprehensive model of motivation combining the behavior of the external incentives and cognition of the intrinsic motivation [366]. This model contains effort, performance, individual quality and ability, individual perception, internal motivation, external motivation and satisfaction. Potter and Lawler regarded the incentive process as the unified process of the interaction of external stimulation, internal conditions, behavior and results. Most people think it has a satisfying performance. And they stressed that for the first performance to be satisfied, the reward is the premise of performance, people's satisfaction with the performance and incentives in turn affect the incentive value. The degree to which people work on a particular task is determined by the expected probability of obtaining a reward after the completion of the incentive value and personal feeling towards the job. Obviously, the higher the incentive value of the individual, the higher the expected probability, the greater the degree of effort to complete the work. At the same time, the result of people's activities is not only dependent on the individual's effort level, but also on the individual's quality, ability and the individual's perception of their work role.

5. Attribution theory

Attribution theory is the theory of description and theoretical analysis of the causal relations of people activities. People use it to explain, control and forecast the related environment, and with the environment and the behavior, through changing people's self-feeling, self-awareness to change and adjust human behavior. In 1958, Austrian social psychologist Heider proposed the attribution theory at first in his book *The Psychology of Interpersonal Relations* [207], from the perspective of naive psychology. The theory is mainly to solve how people identify events that are caused in daily life. Heider applied attribution theory to the development of naive analysis theory of action. Heider believes that people have a strong motivation: one is to form a consistent understanding of the need for the surrounding environment; the second is the need to control environment. There are two reasons for the event: one is internal, such as emotion, attitude, personality, ability and so on; the second is external, such as external pressure, weather, situation, etc. When explaining the behavior of others, most people tend to attribute their personality; in the interpretation of their behavior, they tend to display situational attribution.

Heider also pointed out that with attribution, people often use two principles: one is the principle of covariation, it refers to a particular reason in many different situations and a specific outcome. The reason does not exist, results also do not appear, we can see the results attributed to the reason. This is the principle of covariance. The second principle is the exclusion principle. If the internal and external reasons for a certain incident are good enough to explain the incident, we can rule out the other side of the attribution.

The guiding principle and basic hypothesis of attribution theory are: seeking understanding is the basic reason of behavior. Common attribution theories contain Weiner's attribution theory, Abramson's attribution theory, Kelly's attribution theory, attribution theory of Jones and Davis.

6. Intrinsic motivation

In 1960, Bruner emphasized the role of intrinsic motivation in the book *Process of Education*, and pointed out that intrinsic motivation is the real power to promote learning [66]. Since then, people began to pay attention to internal motivation of learning. American social psychologist Amabile proved that the internal motivation has a great effect on people's creativity through a large number of studies [10]. High level of intrinsic motivation is an important feature of the outstanding creative talents. Intrinsic motivation leads scientists to take professional studies as their own business, and to develop their own goals for the struggle. It is believed that "cognitive curiosity" is the core of the intrinsic motivation, which is a kind of internal driving force for the pursuit of external information and learning activities. It is shown as a curiosity, exploration, operation and mastery of behavior. People call it cognitive motivation.

Most intrinsic motivation models are task-oriented and experience-based models. Singh and others studied the agent with intrinsic motivation reinforcement learning [460], which can develop a variety of applications. In this model, the agent is programmed to determine the light changes and sound intensity of the significant interesting events. The reinforcement learning model of intrinsic motivation is very important in multi-task learning, and the key is not how to define the motivation. In contrast, the theory of intrinsic motivation in psychology provides a concise, field and task independent theory, which is based on the computation model of motivation.

4.6 Consciousness Subsystem in CAM

Figure 4.8 shows the architecture of the consciousness subsystem in CAM. It consists of global workspace, awareness, attention, motivation, metacognition and introspective learning modules.

4.6.1 Awareness module

Awareness begins with the input of external stimuli, and the primary features of the sensing system are activated. The output signal is sent to the sensory memory, where a higher level of functional detectors are used for more abstract entities, such as objects, categories, actions, events, etc. The resulting perception is sent to the workspace, where local connections with short episodic memory and declarative memory will mark a thread. These local associations are combined with perception to produce the current situation model, which is used to represent the understanding of the current events.

In CAM, awareness is basically a perception combination of detect sensation. Agents work effectively in complex environments, and a subset of these combinations must be selected as the value of perception. The awareness function is the sensed state of $S_{(t)}$ mapped to a subset of the $A_{S(t)}$.

Definition 4.1 (awareness function). Awareness function is defined as a perceptual combination of further processing of the sensory state that contains fewer sensory information that will affect the attention of the agent, and the subset of the state space

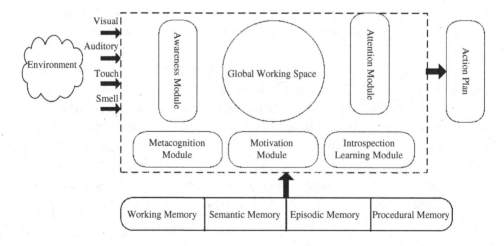

Fig. 4.8.   The architecture of consciousness subsystem in CAM

is limited. Among them, the typical awareness function $A_{S(t)}$ can be expressed as

$$A_{S(t)} = \{(a_{1(t)}, a_{2(t)}, \ldots, a_{L(t)}, \ldots) | a_{L(t)} = s_{L(t)}(\forall L)\}. \tag{4.1}$$

Equation (4.1) defines the awareness function $A_{S(t)}$, which means that each awareness is aware of the state of each element at the time t. L is the length of the element that is felt, which is variable.

Events are introduced to model the transitions between sensed states. Events differ from actions in that a single action may cause a number of different transitions, depending on the situation in which it is performed while an event describes a specific transition. Events enable attention focus on the actual transition that results from an action by modeling the difference between successive sensed states. Events are represented in terms of the difference between two sensed states. The difference between two sensed states, $S_{(t')} = (s_{1(t')}, s_{2(t')}, \ldots s_{L(t')} \ldots)$ and $S_{(t)} = (s_{1(t)}, s_{2(t)}, \ldots s_{L(t)} \ldots)$, where $t' < t$, as a vector of difference variables is calculated using a difference function Δ.

Definition 4.2 (difference function). Difference function is assigned a value that represents the difference between the two senses $S_{L(t)}$ and $S_{L(t)'}$ in the sense state $S_{(t)}$ and $S_{(t')}$ as follows:

$$\Delta(S_{L(t)}, S_{L(t')}) = \begin{cases} S_{L(t)} & \text{if } \neg \exists\, S_{L(t)}, \\ -S_{L(t')} & \text{if } \neg \exists\, S_{L(t)}, \\ S_{L(t)} - S_{L(t')} & \text{if } S_{L(t)} - S_{L(t')} \neq 0, \\ \text{null} & \text{otherwise.} \end{cases} \tag{4.2}$$

The information provided by the differential function reflects the change of the state of one after another.

Definition 4.3 (event function). Event function is defined as the combination of the different variables of the agent identification event, and each event contains only one non-zero difference variable. The event function can be defined as the following formula:

$$E_{S(t)} = \{E_{L(t)} = (e_{1(t)}, e_{2(t)}, \ldots, e_{L(t)}, \ldots) | e_{e(t)}\}, \tag{4.3}$$

where,

$$e_{e(t)} = \begin{cases} \Delta(s_{e(t)}, s_{e(t')}) & \text{if } e = L, \\ 0 & \text{otherwise.} \end{cases} \tag{4.4}$$

Events may be of varying length or even empty, depending on the number of sensations to change.

4.6.2 Attention module

Detection of new events is an important feature of any signal classification method. Because we are not able to train all the data that may be encountered in the machine learning system, it becomes very important to distinguish known and unknown object information in the test. Novelty detection is a very challenging task, which can be found in a complex, dynamic environment of novel, interesting events. Novelty detection is an essential requirement for a good classification or recognition system because sometimes the information contained in the test data is not known when the training model information is included. The novelty of awareness is related to cognition and the novelty of cognition is related to knowledge. Based on a fixed set of training samples from a fixed number of categories, novelty detection is a dual decision task for each test sample to determine whether it belongs to a known classification or not.

Definition 4.4 (Novelty detection function). Novelty detection function N uses the concept of the intelligent body state, $c \in C$, and is compared with the memory of a previous experience, $m \in M$, long-term memory construction produces a new state $n \in N$:

$$N: C \times M \to N. \tag{4.5}$$

In CAM, the detection of novelty is implemented by the self-organizing map (SOM) neural network proposed by Kohonen [241]. This neural network is an unsupervised and competitive learning clustering network. Kohonen thinks that for neural network to accept inputs from the outside world, it will be divided into different areas, where different regions of different modes will have different response characteristics, namely, different neurons may exhibit best response depending on the nature of the excitation signal, resulting in the formation of a topologically ordered map. The ordered map is also called feature map. It is actually a nonlinear mapping relation, where the topological relation of each mode in the signal space is almost invariably reflected in the picture, i.e., the output response of neurons. Since this kind of mapping is completed by the unsupervised adaptive process, it is also called self-organizing feature map.

Interestingness is defined as novelty and surprise, which depend on the awareness of the current knowledge and computing power. The degree of interestingness can be objective or subjective: the objective degree of interestingness in the use of relationships is completely considered to be interesting in the object, while the subjective interest is compared with the belief that the attributes of the object are determined by the interests of the user. The interestingness of a situation is the measure of the importance of the existing knowledge of the agent. It is interesting that the previous experience is not very similar, or very different.

Definition 4.5 (interestingness function). Interestingness function determines the interesting value of scenarios, $i \in \mathbf{I}$, based on novelty detection, $n \in \mathbf{N}$:

$$\mathbf{I} : \mathbf{N} \to \mathbf{I}. \tag{4.6}$$

Attention is to concentrate on a certain aspect of the environment and ignore other behavior and cognitive process of things selectively. According to the interestingness, the threshold selection mechanism (TSM) [274] is a threshold filtering algorithm. Assuming that we get a threshold value, T, if the interestingness is greater than T then the event is selected to create an incentive to attract attention; conversely, if the value is less than T the event is omitted.

Definition 4.6 (Attention selective). Attention is a complex cognitive function, which is the nature of human behavior. Attention is an external selection process (sound, image, smell ...) or internal (thought) events must be kept at a certain level of awareness. In the given context, the selective attention should be given priority in processing the information. Selective attention allows you to focus on a project, identify and distinguish the irrelevant information wisely. CAM uses the interestingness rate to realize the attention choice.

What we are discussing above is the awareness stage, or the attention to the context of the outside world, which plays an important role in the generation of consciousness. After the formation of consciousness, the other type of attention plays a role in arousing and coordinating all parts of brain functions, finishing the task in collaboration and reaching the desired goal.

4.6.3 Global workspace module

The global workspace module is in the working memory area, in which different systems can perform their activities. Global means that the symbols in this memory are distributed and passed through a large number of processors. Of course, each processor may have a number of local variables and run. But it is very sensitive to the symbol of the overall situation and the information can be made in a timely manner. When faced with new and different things that are different from the habit, our senses will produce an orienting reaction. At the same time, all kinds of intelligent processors will display their new things on the cognitive analysis scheme by way of cooperation or competition in the global workspace, until you get the best results. It is in this process that we have a sense of new things. The global working space can be seen as a blackboard system of information sharing. Through the use of the blackboard, each processor tries to spread the information of the global situation, the joint establishment of the problem-solving approach.

The internal structure of the work area is by a variety of input buffer and three main modules: current scenario mode, register and the queue of awareness contents. The current scenario model is a structure that stores the current internal and external events that represent the reality. The construction encoder is responsible for creating the structure of the elements in each seed model using the work area. By registering in the auxiliary space, the construction encoder can construct a possible structure, and then transfer it to the scenario mode. The queue of the consciousness content stores the contents of the continuous broadcast, which makes the CAM model understand and operate the concepts related to time.

When the competition of the global working space selects the most outstanding, the most relevant, the most important and the most urgent affair, their content becomes the content of consciousness. Then, the contents of the consciousness are broadcast to the whole space and the action selection phase is initiated.

4.6.4 Motivation module

1. Motivation model

Motivation could be represented as a three-tuple $\{N, G, I\}$, where N means needs, G is goal, I means the motivation intensity. A motivation is activated by motivational rules and their structure has the following format:

$$R = (P, D, \text{ Strength}(P|D)), \tag{4.7}$$

where P indicates the conditions of rule activation; D is a set of actions for the motivation; $\text{Strength}(P|D)$ is a value within interval $[0,1]$.

At present, CAM will be applied to animal robot which is a brain–computer integration system. All behaviors of brain–computer integration stem from a fixed and finite number of needs. According to characteristics and requirements of brain–computer integration, there are three types of needs, that is, perception, adaptation and cooperation:

(1) *Perception needs* Acquire environment information through vision, audition, touch, taste, smell.
(2) *Adaptation needs* Adapt environment condition and optimize impact of action.
(3) *Cooperation needs* Promise to reward a cooperation action between brain and machine.

2. Architecture of motivation module

The architecture of motivation system is shown in Figure 4.9. The architecture consists of seven components: environment, internal context, motivation, motivation base, goal, action selection and action composition. Their main functions are explained as follows:

(1) *Environment* provides the external information through sensory devices or other agents.

(2) *Internal context* represents the homeostatic internal state of the agent and evolves according to the effects of actions.

(3) *Motivation* is an abstraction corresponding to the tendency to behave in particular ways according to environmental information. Motivations set goals for the agent in order to satisfy internal context.

(4) *Motivation base* contains a set of motivations and motivation knowledge with defined format.

(5) *Goal* is a desired result for a person or an organization. It is used to define a sequence of actions to reach specific goals.

(6) *Action selection* is used to perform motivated action that can satisfy one or several motivations.

(7) *Action composition* is the process of constructing a complex composite action from atomic actions to achieve a specific task.

The action composition is composed of overlapping hierarchical decision loops running in parallel. The number of motivations is not limited. Action composition

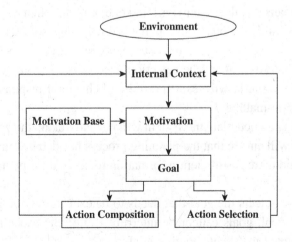

Fig. 4.9. Architecture of motivation system

of the most activated node is not carried out at each cycle, as in a classical hierarchy, but only at the end in the action layer, as in a free flow hierarchy. In the end, the selected action is activated.

3. Motivation execution flow

In the mind model CAM, the realization of the motivation system is through the short-time memory system. In the CAM system, the current belief of the belief memory storage contains the agent motivation knowledge. A desire is a goal or a desired final state. Intention is the need for the smart body to choose the current implementation of the goal. The goal/intention memory module stores the current goal and intention information. In CAM, the goal is a directed acyclic graph by the subgoal composition that is realized step by step. According to a directed acyclic graph a subgoal is represented by a path to complete, and the total goal will finish when all subgoals are completed.

For an execution system of motivation, the most critical is the internal planning part of the agent. Through planning, each subgoal will have to complete a series of actions, to achieve the task that we want to see. Planning mainly deals with the internal information and the new motivation generated by the system.

Motivation execution flow is shown in Figure 4.10. The receiver gets information from the environment and places it into the queue of motivation. The distributor selects events from the list of events, and provides the corresponding planning for the event. When the goal arrives, the conditions of the existing environment are detected to see whether they satisfy the goal. The distributor chooses the corresponding plan to accomplish the desired goal, which requires the cooperation of the reasoning machine. This means that the system will find one or more schemes which are made in the past. It is possible to find a solution that is not the only solution when it is used to reason about an existing object. At this time, the inference engine needs to select according to its internal rules. The selection criteria need to be specified before. Different selection criteria will lead to different behavioral responses in agents at the time of decision-making.

After choosing a good plan, the system will need to link up the goal and the plan in advance. This will ensure that the planning process has detailed understanding of the objectives, and there is sufficient information to be used for planning to achieve the goal.

The scheduler selects the goal that needs to be executed in the goal list. In the execution of the goal, goals cannot be interrupted, i.e., the execution of the goal cannot be interrupted to execute another goal.

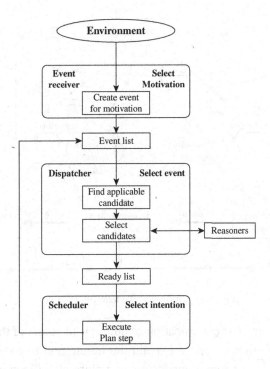

Fig. 4.10. Motivation execution flow

4.6.5 Metacognitive module

In the mind model CAM, metacognition provides the cognition and monitoring of thinking activity and learning activity of the agent, in which the core is cognition to cognition. Metacognitive module has the function of metacognitive knowledge, metacognitive self-regulation control and metacognitive experience. Metacognitive knowledge includes knowledge about the subject, the knowledge of the task, and the knowledge of the strategy. Metacognitive experience refers to the experience of their own cognitive process. In the cognitive process, through the metacognitive self-regulation control, the appropriate strategy is selected to realize the use of strategy, the comparison of process and goal, the adjustment of the strategy and so on.

4.6.6 Introspective learning module

Introspective learning module is shown in Figure 4.11, in which the knowledge base construction uses the ontology technology based on the general introspective learning model [124]. The classification problem of failure is an important problem in

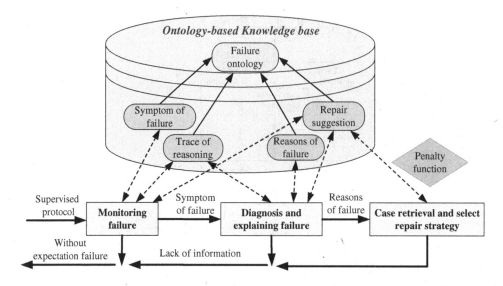

Fig. 4.11.　Introspective learning module

introspective learning. The classification of failure is the basis of the diagnostic task and it provides important clues to explain the failure and to construct the correct learning objectives. Two important factors of failure classification should be considered, one is the granularity of failure classification, the other is the relationship between failure classification, failure explanation and introspective learning goals. Ontology-based knowledge base is the combination of ontology-based knowledge representation and expert system knowledge base, which has the advantages of conceptual, formal, semantic and sharing. By using the method of ontology-based knowledge base to solve the failure classification problem of introspective learning, the failure classification will be clearer and the retrieval process will be more effective. On the key contents of introspective learning, please refer to Chapter 8.

Chapter 5

Visual Perception

Visual information processing is the process of finding what the objects are and where they are in the scenes from the images. From the input image to the description of the scene, there exists a huge gap. It needs a series of information processing and process understanding to bridge the gap. Understanding the nature of this process is the key to uncover the mystery of the vision. However, we are far from understanding these at present.

Vision mainly has two functions. The first is the perception of objects, i.e., what is it? The second is spatial perception, i.e., where is it? There are concrete facts that show that different brain systems are involved in the above two functions.

5.1 Visual Cortex Area

Visual cortex has two main kinds of nerve cells: stellate cells and cone cells. The axons of stellated cells contact with projecting fibers. A cone cell is triangular, with the tip moving towards surface layer emitting upwards a long dendrite and the fundus issuing several dendrites that contact breadthwise.

Visual cortex, like other cortex areas, includes six layers of cells, denoted by I–VI from the surface to the inner layer. The trunks of cortex cell's tubers (dendrites and axons) are all distributed in a vertical direction to the cortex surface; the branches of dendrites and axons are distributed breadthwise in different layers. The different cortex areas contact one another by axons through deep white matter, while the inner layers of cortexes contact through transverse branches of dendrites and axons in cortexes.

In recent years, the scope of visual cortexes has already extended to many new cortex areas, including the parietal lobe, the occipital lobe and part of amounting to 25 the frontal lobe [496]. Besides, it has seven visual association areas, which have visual and other sense or movement functions. All visual areas account for 55% of the area of the new brain cortex. Thus, the importance of visual information processing in the whole brain function can be seen. A present issue of visual cutting edge research is to research division function, grade relationship and reciprocity of the visual areas. The evidences of confirming an independent visual cortex area are: (1) the area has an independent visual field projecting map, (2) the area has the same input and output nerve connections as other cortex areas, (3) the area has similar cellular structure (4) and the area has different function characters from other visual cortex areas.

Wernicke and Geschwind believe that the information processing of the visual cortex is as shown in Figure 5.1. According to their model, visual information is transmitted from the retinas to the lateral geniculate body, passing from the lateral geniculate body to the primary visual cortex (V17), then reaching a more advanced visual nerve center (V18), and from here traveling to the angular gyrus, to arrive at Wernicke area [295]. In Wernicke area, visual information is then translated to speech (hearing) idea. After the sound patterns are formed, they pass on to Broca area.

The 17th area in the visual cortex is called as the first visual area (V1) or the stripe cortex. It receives the direct input of the lateral geniculate body, which is also known as the primary visual cortex. The functional studies of the visual cortex are mostly

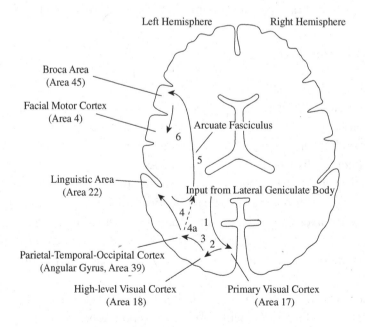

Fig. 5.1.   Information processing of the visual cortex

conducted on the cortex level. Except for the 17th area receiving direct projection from the lateral geniculate bodies, the vision related cortex also has stripe proparea (the 18th area) and stripe outskirt (the 19th area). According to morphological and physiological research, the 17th area does not project to the lateral cortex but to the 18th area and the 18th area projects forward to the 19th area and sends feedback to the 17th area. The 18th area includes three visual areas, called V2, V3 and V3A respectively, and their main input is from V1. Vl and V2 are the biggest visual areas. The 19th area buried deeply in the posterior parries of the superior temporal sulcus includes the fourth (V4) and the fifth visual area (V5). V5, also called as the middle temporal area, enters the scope of the temporal lobe. The other vision-related cortex areas in the temporal lobe are the inner upper frontal area and the inferior temporal area. There is the top occipital area, the ventral interparietal, the post abdominal area and the 7a area in the parietal lobe. The cerebral cortex area outside the occipital lobe possibly belongs to a higher level. Why are there so many representative areas? Do different representative areas detect different graphical characteristics (such as color, shape, brightness, movement, depth, etc.)? or not? Or do the different representative areas deal with information at different levels? Is there not a higher level representative area integrating the reparative graphical characteristics, thereby giving the biological meaning of graphics? Is there a special representative area which is responsible for the storage of images (visual learning and memory) or in charge of visual attention? These will be the issues to be resolved in visual research over a longer period of time.

5.2 Visual Computation Theory

The Center for Cognitive Science at the University of Minnesota held a "Millennium Project" event in 1999, the aim of which was to choose 100 outstanding works of the 20th century in the cognitive sciences. Among them, "Vision: A Computational Investigation into the Human Representation and Processing of Visual Information" [289] written by Marr came in second place, while "Two Cortical Visual Systems" [495] written by Ungerleider and Mishkin occupied in 73rd place.

5.2.1 Marr's visual computation theory

The professor of MIT Artificial Intelligence Laboratory, Marr, at the end of the 1970s up to the early 1980s, created the visual computation theory, which gave an impetus to visual research [289]. Marr's visual computation theory based on computer science, systematically summed up all the important results of psychological physics, neurophysiology and clinical neuropathology, and is by far the most systematic theory of vision. The emergence of Marr's theory has had a profound impact on the development of neuroscience and the research of artificial intelligence.

Marr believed that vision is an information processing process. This process generates descriptions useful to observers in accordance with the outside world's images. The descriptions are in turn composed of many different but fixed representations, each of which records certain characteristics of the outside world. The reason why a new representation is improved by a step is because it expresses certain information, and this information will facilitate further explanation of the existing information. According to this logic, a conclusion could be arrived at that before interpreting the data further, and we need some information of the observed objects, i.e., the so-called intrinsic images. However, the data entering our eyes needs light as the medium. Gray-scale images contain at least the information of the lighting situation and the observer's position relative to the objects. Therefore, according to the method of Marr, the first problem to be solved is how to decompose these factors. He believes that low-level vision (i.e., the first stage of visual processing) is to distinguish which changes are caused by which factors. Generally speaking, this process goes through two steps: The first step is to obtain representations representing changes and structures of images. This includes such processing as the detection of gray-scale changes, representation and analysis of local geometry, as well as detection of lighting effects. The results of the first step is known as the Primal Sketch appearance; the second step carries out a series of operations to the initial sketch to obtain representations which can reflect the geometric features of the surface appearance, and such representations are known as 2.5 D sketches or intrinsic images. These operations include extracting the depth of information from three-dimensional (3D) visual computing, restoring the surface direction in accordance with the gray shadow, texture and other information, obtaining surface shape and space relationship from the movement of visual computing. The results of these operations are integrated into intrinsic images, the level of intermediate representation. The intermediate representation is derived by removing many different meanings of the original image, purely representing the object's surface characteristics, including illumination, reflectance, direction, distance and so on. This information represented by intrinsic images can reliably divide images into clear-meaning regions (this is known as segmentation), obtaining more high-level descriptions than lines, regions and shapes etc. The processing level is known as the intermediate processing. The next representative level of Marr's theory is the 3D model, which applies to object recognition. This level's processing involves objects and relies on and applies prior field knowledge to constitute a description of scenes, called high-level visual processing.

Marr first researched strategies addressing the issue of visual understanding. He believed that vision is an information processing process. It requires three levels to understand and address:

(1) Computing theory level — researching what information and why it should be computed.
(2) Representation and algorithm level — the actual computation according to the computing theory, how to represent input and output? And the algorithm transforming the input to output.
(3) Hardware implementation — the implementation represented by representation and algorithm, implementing and executing algorithms, researching to complete a specific algorithm and specific institutions.

For example, the Fourier transform belongs to the first level of the theory, while the algorithms of the Fourier transform, such as the fast Fourier transform algorithm, belong to the second level. As for the array processors realizing fast Fourier algorithms, they belong to the hardware implementation level.

We can think that vision is a process that generates descriptions useful to observers in accordance with the outside world's images. The descriptions are in turn composed of many different but fixed representations, each of which records certain characteristics of the outside world. Therefore, choosing the representation method is of utmost importance to visual understanding. According to the assumption made by Marr, visual information processing process includes three main levels: the primal sketch, 2.5D sketch and 3D models. According to some evidence of psychology, human visual system representation is as shown in Figure 5.2.

1. The primal sketch

Gray-scale images include two important pieces of information: the gray-scale change and the local geometric characteristics in images. The primal sketch is a primitive expression method, which can fully and clearly express information. Most of the information in primal sketches focus on the rapid gray-scale changes relative to the actual edges and termination points of the edges. Each gray-scale change arising from the edges has a corresponding description. The description includes: the gray-scale change rate of edges, a total change of gray-scale, the edge length, curvature and direction. Roughly speaking, the primal sketches represent changes in gray-scale images in a draft form.

2. 2.5D sketch

Gray-scale images are influenced by many factors, which mainly include the lighting conditions, object geometry, surface reflectivity, etc., as well as the perspective of

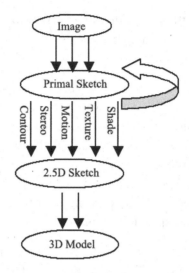

Fig. 5.2.   Visual system representation levels

the observer. Therefore, we must distinguish the effects of these factors, i.e., first describe in detail the surfaces of the objects in the scene in order to proceed with the establishment of 3D models of the objects. So it is needed to build an intermediate representative level, the 2.5D sketch. Local surface characteristics can be described by the so-called intrinsic properties. Typical intrinsic characteristics include surface orientations, distances from observers to the surfaces, reflecting and incident light, surface texture and material properties. Intrinsic images comprise single intrinsic property values of image points as well as where the intrinsic properties generate the discrete information. 2.5D sketch can be seen as a mixture of some intrinsic images. In short, the 2.5D sketch represents fully and clearly the information on the object's surface.

In primal sketches and 2.5D sketches, information is often represented by refer-ring to the coordinates linked to observers. Therefore, this representation is referred to as an observer-centered one.

3. 3D model

In 3D model representations, factoring based on standard axes of a shape is the most readily available. Each of these axes cone is relative to a rough spatial relationship; this relationship provides a natural combination of the main shape element axis in the scope of the spatial relationship. We call the module defined in this way as the 3D model. Therefore, every 3D model represents [289]:

(1) A model axis, refers to a single axis determining the scope of the spatial rela-tionship of the model. It is an element of representation that can tell us roughly

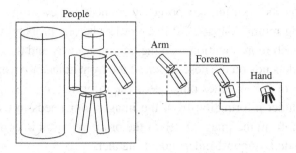

Fig. 5.3. The 3D model of a human

several characteristics of the overall shape described, for example, the size and directional information of the overall shape.

(2) In the spatial relationship determined by the model axis, either the relative spatial position or the size of the main element axis can be chosen. The number of element axes should not be too much, and they should also be roughly the same size.

(3) Once the 3D model of the spatial elements associated with the element axis is constructed, we are able to determine these element names (internal relations). The model axis of spatial elements corresponds to the element axes of the 3D model.

In Figure 5.3, each box represents a 3D model, with the model axis painted on the left side of the box and the element axis painted on the right side of the box. The model axis of the 3D model of the human body is an element, which describes clearly the general characteristics (size and direction) of the whole shape of the human body. The six element axes corresponding to the human body, head and limbs can be connected with a 3D model, which contains the additional configuration information, parsing further these element axes into smaller elements. Although the structure of a single 3D model is very simple, in accordance with the kind of hierarchical structure that combines several models, it is able to constitute two kinds of descriptions grasping the geometric nature of the shape at any accuracy. We call the hierarchical structure of the 3D model as the 3D model description of a shape.

The 3D representation represents fully and clearly the object's shape information. It is important to adopt the concept of generalized cylinders, as it is very simple. It can be regarded that an ordinary cylinder is generated by a circle moving along its center line. More generally, a generalized cylinder is generated by a 2D cross section moving along the axis. During the moving process, the angle between the cross-section and the axis is kept fixed. The cross-section can be of any shape. During the moving process, its size may be changed and the axis may not necessarily be a straight line.

Complex objects are often composed by connecting several generalized cylinders. Considering mutual impacts of different levels, one probability is that information flow to each representation is in the bottom-up way and the computation of each layer only depends on the description of the front adjacent layer. For example, the computation of 2.5 sketches only needs the information of primal sketches. It does not need direct information from the images, nor needs to use any clues of what can be seen from the image. Each of the processes used in computation carry on in an independent or quasi-independent manner.

Another possibility is that a wide variety of computing in the primary and 2.5D sketches is conducted by a mixed constraint spread. For example, the information from the 3D processing can be used to improve computing from a gray-scale shadow to the direction of the surface and vice versa. Information can flow in all directions.

It is also possible that information flows top-down, so the understanding of the image depends on controlled imagination to a large extent. In that case, early vision is guided by the fixed forecast of what should be seen.

5.2.2 Gestalt vision theory

Gestalt is a transliteration of the German Gestalt. It is often translated as "form" or "shape" in English. Based on studying apparent movement phenomena, the theory was created by German psychologist Wetheimer, Kohler and Koffka earlier in this century.

The psychologists' starting point of Gestalt psychologists' research is the "shape", which refers to the overall experience organized from the perceptive activities. In other words, the Gestalt psychologists believe that any "shape" is a result or function organized or constructed by perceptron, rather than what that the object itself has. In vision research, the Gestalt theory suggests that the gathering process that gathers point data into the overall characteristics is the basis of all other meaningful processes. The human visual system has the ability to obtain relative grouping and structure from the images of the scenes even in case of no knowledge of the objects. This capability is called perceptual organization. The basic principle of perceptual organization, according to the Gestalt theory, is known as the Pragnant, which means "simple expedient". Gestalt psychologists found that some "shape" has given people very pleasant feelings. These are the "shapes" in which the visual stimulation is best organized most regularly (symmetry, unity, harmony), with a maximum of simplexes and clearness under certain conditions. For such shapes, they invented a unique word, i.e., Pragnant and some people translate this word as "Gestalt". This word emphasizes the integrality of consciousness and that the whole is greater than the sum of the parts. Gestalt laws of the Gestalt theory include:

(1) Law of Proximity: Parts with proximate distance tend to form the whole.
(2) Law of Similarity: Parts similar in some aspects tend to form the whole.
(3) Law of Closure: Parts which belong to each other or constitute a closed entity tend to form the whole.
(4) Law of Good Continuation: Parts with simple graphical features of continuous, symmetric and smooth tend to form the whole.

5.2.3 Dual visual pathway

In 1982, based on the data of brain injury research on monkeys and humans, Ungerleider and Mishkin first proposed the double visual pathway theory of what pathway and where pathway [495]. They divided the mapping of the primary visual cortex (V1) into two different types of visual stream. A visual stream reaches the inferior temporal cortex along the ventro, while the other reaches the posterior parietal cortex along the dorso. Ventral stream processes object information for object recognition, while dorsal stream processes represent spatial information for spatial localization. These two pathways are called what pathway and where pathway, respectively.

As shown in Figure 5.4, the ventral stream begins from the retina, passes by the lateral geniculate nucleus (LGN), the primary visual cortex regions (V1, V2, V4), the inferior temporal (IT) along the ventro and eventually reaches the ventrolateral prefrontal cortex (VLPFC). It mainly processes shape and contour information of the object, which is mainly responsible for object recognition. Dorsal stream begins from the retina, passes by the lateral geniculate nucleus (LGN), the primary visual cortex regions (V1, V2), the medial temporal (MT) along the dorso and eventually reaches the dorsolateral prefrontal cortex (DLPFC). It mainly processes special and local information of the object, which is mainly responsible for object localization.

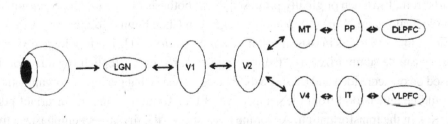

Fig. 5.4. What pathway and where pathway in the visual system

The research on information processing of the visual perception system mainly involves object recognition and localization perception. Its essence is to study the function of two visual pathways of what and where.

5.2.4 Topological vision theory

In 200 years of history, the study of visual perception has been full of disputation between the "part theory" and the "whole theory". In the view of the part theory, the perceptual process begins with the analysis of the specific features or the simple components of the object. The process is from the local features to the global features. However, the whole theory thinks that the perceptual process begins with the perception of the whole, and it is from the global features to the local features.

The overall computing framework of Marr's visual information processing is discussed above. In the primal sketch level, there are mainly two types of visual information, the intensity changes and the local geometric properties of images. The local geometric properties refer to parallel, relative position and direction and so on. The vision's initial process is computing the representation of the local features and characteristics, which are no more than some simple and small parts of images, such as line and column, and the partial relations between them. Then, based on the computing results of the local characteristics, visual information processing enters a higher level, such as 2.5D and 3D computing. "What is the roughest representation of visual information?" It is the central issue of visual study and is the issue that must be first answered to establish a visual image recognition model. From where do visual systems start to perceive the outside world's images? The answer to this question will determine the whole direction of the image recognition model. The answer to this question from Marr's primal sketches is simple graphical elements and their local features. Therefore, Marr's visual computing system starts from the local features, i.e., from computing the local detail features to the overall large-scale computing.

In 1982, in terms of the fundamental problem of where the perceptual process starts from, Lin Chen originally proposed the hypothesis of "the initial perception of topological nature" [80] in *Science*. In 2005, Lin Chen published the "major theme article" up to 88 pages in issue no. 4 of *Visual Cognition* [81]. The topological vision theory can be summarized as, "the topology research on perceptual organization is based on one core idea and two aspects. The core idea is that perceptual organization should be understood from the perspective of transformation and the invariant perception in the transformation. As for the two aspects, the first aspect emphasizes the topological structure of the shape perception. That is to say, the large-scale features of perceptual organization can be described by topological invariance. The second aspect further stresses the early topological properties of perception. That is to say, the topological properties of perception have priority to the local features. Here "priority" has two strict meanings. First, the global organization, which is determined by the topological properties, is the basis of the perception of local geometrical properties. Second, perception of topological properties based on physical connectivity has priority to that of local geometric properties".

5.3 Feature Binding

Feature binding problem, namely, how to form the expression of the whole object through binding the expression of the various separating characteristic properties, is the central and advanced problem in the field of cognitive science. It is known as one of the seven main problems in the field of cognitive science. A great amount of research on neuroanatomy and neurophysiology suggests that different perceptual information is processed in different areas of the human brain and representation of the same object is distributed in different parts of the brain. Take visual perception as an example. Color and shape features of the objects are represented in the ventral pathway from the occipital lobe to the temporal lobe, while spatial features are represented in the dorsal pathway from the occipital lobe to the parietal lobe. Therefore, in order to perceive objects of the external world as a whole, it is necessary to combine the dispersive information scattered in different cortex areas. This is the so-called feature binding. However, as the Nobel prize winner Kandel said: "it is amazing and very disappointing that despite the feature binding problem being so important to understand the function and mechanism of cognition and the massive resources put into research the feature binding problem in recent years, we are still not able to reach a consensus on the problem of feature binding." [5]

Combining the new development of the research on the problem of feature binding, Engel and Singer generalized the consensus on the feature binding problem defined by researchers in various fields [137], which can be ascribed to the following four points:

First, because the information processing is distributed in different brain areas or the neurons of subsystems, the neurons participating in the same cognitive process should be marked by the same label. This will require a mechanism to convey the specific relationship between the neural signals. This mechanism is the binding mechanism.

Second, to perceive and behave in a complex environment, it is usually necessary to process information of different objects or events parallely and the information must be distinguished in order to achieve the correct perception or accomplish the target behavior. Therefore, the neural activity associated with a particular object should be separated from the unrelated information area, so as to avoid confusion or mistake.

Third, in order to guarantee the generation of syntactic structure and certify the systematization and creativity of the cognitive process, the binding of the distributed activation model should be special and flexible.

Fourth, most cognitive functions require selecting related information from abundant alternative information. Binding takes highlighting partial information and combining this information with specific-related content as the precondition.

At present, the theory of the physiological study of feature binding mainly includes the temporal synchronization theory, the formal model and the feature integration theory.

5.3.1 Temporal synchronization theory

The temporal synchronization theory believes that feature binding is built on the basis of the neurons synchronously delivered. It is realized by the synchronous activation of neural activity [137, 459, 502]. The neurons representing the same object or event can synchronously activate their corresponding behavior in the time of a millisecond. And this synchronization cannot occur between cells responsible for different representations or cell mass. This instant context-dependent activation is the key mechanism of binding. Synchronous activation can mark selective labels for the response of neurons responsible for coding objects and can distinguish them from the response of neurons activated by other objects. This highly selective time structure allows multiple cell masses to be activated simultaneously in the same neural network and to be distinguished from each other. Furthermore, the binding based on temporal synchronization also acts as the mechanism for selecting the next processing object. Due to the precise synchronous activation, the specific content becomes a highlight event, which makes this kind of event to be detected by neurons of other brain areas, which is sensitive to time consistency. These selectively activated neurons can then accomplish the binding operation in different areas, so that the activation pattern can be transmitted in the neural network and further processed.

Evidence of the temporal synchronization theory mainly comes from the research on neurophysiology. The research on neurophysiology suggests that synchronous firing usually take the form of synchronous 40–70 Hz oscillation, and phase lock 40 Hz oscillation may be the best solution to the binding problem in the brain. The phase lock neural oscillations realize feature binding by marking the delivery neurons related to some visual stimulus.

The temporal synchronization theory is also supported by some studies on cognitive psychology. Black and Yang Yuede designed a new psychological physical task, which requires the temporal synchronization of composite features of testing complex visual graphics [220]. The results show that two features of complex graphics come from the same meaningful original graphics and are more easily detected than that of the mixed graphics coming from the temporal synchronization pattern. In addition, when features that are continuous in space vary in time, they can generate more strong neural signals. The research provided the psychological and physical basis for the temporal synchronization theory.

5.3.2 Formal model of feature binding

The model of feature binding was proposed by Ashby, Prinzmetalli and Ivry *et al.* [28]. The theory holds that the illusion combination occurs because the individual's perception of the visual features produces a position error. That is to say, the error of feature binding is caused by the perception error of the feature position. The model employs a multi-nomial model to eliminate the influence of its guess effect and uses the mathematical parameters (the probability of correct feature binding and object recognition) to evaluate the generating probability of true illusion precisely. In their partial experimental report, they found that when the distance between the target and the non-target is small, the occurrence rate of true (excluding the guess component) illusion combination is higher, i.e., the error of feature binding occurs frequently. At the same time, the probability of correct binding becomes high when the distance becomes large. This result cannot be explained by the feature integration theory, but it supports the view of the formal model that the distance of attention range affects the illusion combination.

The multi-nomial model proposed by binding formal theory can solve the problem of applying feature integration theory in data analysis in a better way. It can not only estimate the probability of true illusion combination by various parameters, but also model the other theories in the experiment of illusion combination using the same method. For example, the large number of connection responses of patients damaged in the parietal lobe may be caused by visual loss or failure of feature combination. By the formula of the multi-nomial model, the main reason behind how the patient's operation is done till end can be detected. Obviously, the method of the multi-nomial model of the location uncertainty theory has the advantages of generality and flexibility.

5.3.3 Feature integration theory

Treisman's feature integration theory [489] believes that it is realized by the spatial attention model that covers right from parallel processing of the early stages to integration of the late stage. The model consists of a location main map and a set of independent feature maps for each other. Location main map is used to register the location of the object, but does not reach the feature of the location. Feature map mainly contains two kinds of information: one is "marked flag" for marking whether a feature is somewhere in the visual field; the other is some implicit information about the arrangement of current feature space. The detector in each feature map is connected to the unit of the main map. In order to bind "what" and "where", the attentional window moves in the location main map, and selects any feature associated with the current attention location from the feature map. At the same time, features of all other objects are temporarily eliminated out of the perception level. As a result, feature of attention becomes representation of the current activating object and the structural relationship between them can be also analyzed, avoiding the binding error. After building the unified object representation, it can be matched with the stored template and recognized and related behavior can be accomplished. Thus, visual feature binding is realized by the attention of the spatial location. In addition, attention of the same location can bind the visual elements of the location.

The feature integration theory is supported by the research on illusion combination, parietal lobe damage and brain function imaging. According to this theory, when increasing the attention load or providing inaccurate spatial information, the feature binding will be disturbed. Treisman found that when subjects were temporarily presented different colors and then were asked to report the appearance of features of another letter at the same time, there existed significant illusion combination errors. (For example, if it presents a red X and blue O, the subjects sometimes very confidently reported that they see a red O or blue X.) The error report of subjects can be divided into two categories: one is the wrong combination among the unpresenting features, called the illusion combination; the other is the combination among unpresenting features. The results show that the ratio of the wrong combination among the presenting features is only 6%, and the ratio of the wrong combination among the unpresenting features is 18%. Consequently, presenting features are identified, but encounter problems in feature binding. The experimental results can be explained well by the feature integration theory. The reason why the ratio of illusion combination becomes higher lies in the fact that subjects cannot pay attention to the mutual location of object features on the condition that features are temporarily and vastly presented. Therefore, these features cannot be well bound.

5.3.4 Neural network model

The neural network model of feature binding was proposed by Watanabe *et al.* The model consists of a main map and two advanced modules. The two modules are responsible for two different features in the main map respectively. Each module is divided into three levels and each level is linked bidirectionally. The object of the outside world is represented by "the overall dynamic cell set" distributed in the main map and the two advanced modules. Detailed information that is confined to a certain position in space is encoded in the main map, while the complex feature information extracted in rough parallel space (or the overall integrated information) is represented in the two advanced modules. Feature binding is accomplished under the effect of "the overall dynamic cell set". The basis of the model is the "functional link" and the "bidirectional link" of the neural network. Functional link is a dynamic link between the neurons of the temporal spike of the neural network, which is encoded by the coupling detector. This link is different from the traditional synaptic connection, because its value can vary with the dynamic variation of the exciting level of the neural network and its intensity is determined by the time consistency level of the coupling action unit and each neuron. It is directly impacted by the temporal and spatial dynamic variation. The cell population linked by the functional link is called "dynamic cell set". The model uses the concept of functional bidirectional link to explain the neural release phenomenon of temporal synchronization, without introducing the neural oscillation unit of the temporal synchronization theory.

The model has been verified by computer simulation results. The theory uses neural network and a computer simulation paradigm to propose a more specific structural model for the binding mechanism. Since the model is proposed recently, it has not yet attracted wide attention.

From the point of view of literature, despite the research on binding cognition and neuroscience, although they have the same starting point, i.e., they are both binding problems, their theoretical perspectives differ greatly from each other and are even irrelevant. In order to have a more comprehensive understanding of the binding mechanism, the integration of these two studies is imperative. The way of this kind of integration may lie in the research on cognitive neuroscience. On the one hand, cognitive research should strengthen the neural mechanism of binding task through brain imaging technology; on the other hand, the research of neural physiology should be combined with the psychological and physical study. For example, if the theory of time synchronization can be widely verified by cognitive behavioral evidence or cognitive neuroscience data, its theoretical viewpoint will be more clear and specific. Although the two-stage binding theory tries to build an integration theory, it is unable to integrate the time synchronization theory into the binding theory because it still uses a cognitive research paradigm.

Visual feature binding is a special case which uses attention network to solve the general binding problem in various cognitive tasks. This general binding consists of cross-pathway binding, inter-concept binding, binding between high and low levels, or even binding of psychological processes (such as binding of emotion, motivation and cognitive activity). In order to build the theory of general binding mechanism, it is necessary to use the relation between binding mechanism and cognitive binding in the superior psychological process, such as the study of memory, language, problem-solving and decision-making.

5.4 Object Recognition

5.4.1 Visual representation

Representation is similar to perceptual experience, but occurs in the absence of appropriate external stimuli. Visual representation is to be presented in the brain system by means of a picture. The visual representation processing system proposed by Kosslyn [245] mainly consists of the visual buffer, the object attribute processing, the spatial attribute processing, the associative memory, the information distribution and the attention transfer, just as shown in Figure 5.5.

Inspired by Kosslyn's visual representation, Laird *et al.* add structure-related memory and processing in the Soar system, directly supporting representation based on perception [251]. SVI (spatial-visual imagery) focuses on the features simulating human mental imagery, while SVS (spatial visual system) combines the concrete spatial representation and abstract symbol representation. All these extensions enable the Soar system to have the ability of human reasoning.

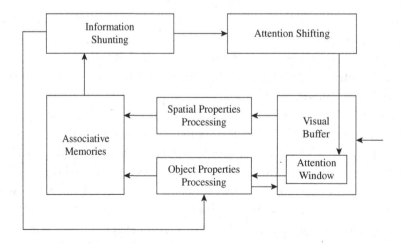

Fig. 5.5. Visual representation processing system

5.4.2 Object low-level feature extraction

The low-level feature extraction is the basis of object recognition and there is still no good method to get the contour of the numerous objects. In this case, the low-level visual information of image is extracted using the method of multi-range image feature. First, the image is divided into grids of similar size, using Texton filter to extract the Texton features of each pixel [223]. According to the process of Bag-of-feature, the visual word of each grid can be arrived at. The feature of the grid with the current size grid is called the local feature. Then increase the size of the grid, repeat the previous process and visual words of a bigger grid can be arrived at, called the regional feature. At last, the distribution of regional image feature is counted, and the global image feature vector is obtained and clustered. The cluster number is assigned to the corresponding image, and thus the global feature is obtained, just as shown in Figure 5.6 [448].

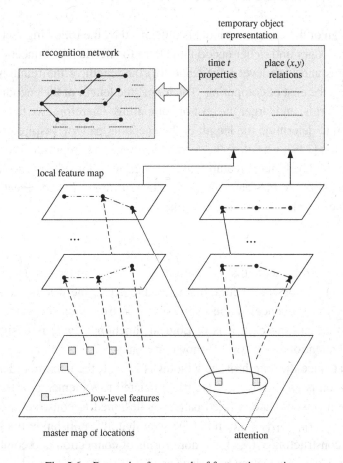

Fig. 5.6. Processing framework of feature integration

We propose a multi-range image feature which is based on the following considerations: First, the existing methods cannot accurately define the object contour, and thus we cannot extract the features of a single object. The multi-range image feature connects the local feature with regional and global features. It can make up for the loss of the features of independent objects to a certain degree. Second, multi-range image features enrich the correlative function of the relation encoding pattern, so that the relation encoding pattern has a better distinguishability.

5.4.3 Relation encoding

We design learning encoding pattern and reasoning encoding pattern respectively. In the learning encoding pattern, the low-level image features are connected to the corresponding object labels for learning; while the reasoning encoding pattern is just a specific low-level feature sequence, so the object category needs to be obtained by reasoning.

The design of the encoding model is influenced by the following factors: (a) we want to use a longer and richer encoding pattern to encode the connection between image features and high-level knowledge; (b) the length of the relation encoding pattern affects the cost of computing. The longer the length of the encoding pattern, the more the forms, and larger the cost of computing. Therefore, we take a compromise solution to determine the length of the encoding pattern. Inspired by the state feature function [249], we define the correlative function to represent the correlation between the low-level image features and the high-level knowledge. Assuming that o is the current observable feature, s_t is the state of time t, l is an object's category label, then the correlative function is defined as follows:

$$f_i(O, S_t) = \delta(x_i(O, t))\delta(s_t = l). \tag{5.1}$$

Here, $S_t = l$ represents that the current state S_t is corresponding to the object label l. $x_i(o, t)$ is a logical function that is used to determine whether it is a specific low-level feature sequence. If the expression e is true, then the value of $\delta(e)$ is 1, while in the opposite case it is 0. Logical function $x_i(o, t)$ is designed in the definition of attentional window, as shown in Figure 5.7.

Note that since the length of the window is $2n + 1$, the maximum length of the logical function is $2n + 1$, which can be associated to n elements of the sequence o and r. For a current state, a fixed pattern is designed to construct $x_i(o, t)$, such as o_0, $o_{-1}o_0$, $r_{-1}r_0$, $r_{-1}r_0o_0$ etc. It can be seen that all multi-range image features take part in constructing $x_i(o, t)$, so more forms of connection and combination of different low-level features can be arrived at, and the local features are related to the regional and global features.

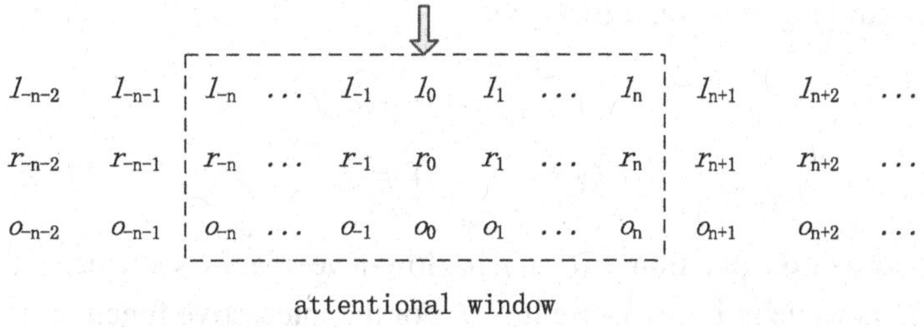

$$\Downarrow$$

l_{-n-2}	l_{-n-1}	l_{-n}	$\cdots$	l_{-1}	l_0	l_1	$\cdots$	l_n	l_{n+1}	l_{n+2}	$\cdots$
r_{-n-2}	r_{-n-1}	r_{-n}	$\cdots$	r_{-1}	r_0	r_1	$\cdots$	r_n	r_{n+1}	r_{n+2}	$\cdots$
o_{-n-2}	o_{-n-1}	o_{-n}	$\cdots$	o_{-1}	o_0	o_1	$\cdots$	o_n	o_{n+1}	o_{n+2}	$\cdots$

attentional window

Fig. 5.7.   Generative process of logical function $x_i(o, t)$

The used interaction function is similar to the boundary state function [249], which represents the transfer relationship between objects. The interactive function is defined as follows:

$$g_j(s_{t-1}, s_t) = \delta(s_{t-1} = l')\delta(s_t = l). \qquad (5.2)$$

Equation (5.2) shows that the interactive function represents the transition from the former state to the current state and the essence is the transfer mode of high-level knowledge. From the perspective of computer vision, we can also say that the interactive function provides context information. In addition, from the perspective of psychology, we can say that it is the expectation from top-down.

For 2D images, in order to construct the correlative function and interactive function, the horizontal and vertical adjacent features and the transfer relationship of current state should be taken into account. Then 2D image semantic concepts can be represented. Thus, the image semantic concepts are represented more accurately. This is also conducive to accomplish the binding process.

The correlative function and the interactive function form the learning encoding pattern. And the reasoning encoding pattern is much simpler. It is formed only by the function, $x_i(o, t)$, which is the encoding relation of the adjacent image features.

5.4.4 Learning recognition network

Learning encoding pattern provides a significant relationship between low-level feature and high-level knowledge. How to organize the correlative function and the interactive function and learn more information from the experience data? We hope to build a distribution to contain the maximum amount of information for these relation functions. That is to say, we need a distribution p, so that it can be as general as possible with the maximum entropy. We increase the corresponding constraints on the expectation of relational function:

$$E(f_i(o, s_t)) = \alpha_i, \tag{5.3}$$

$$E(g_j(s_{t-1}, s_t)) = \beta_j. \tag{5.4}$$

For the correlative function $f_i(o, s_t)$, if a low-level feature sequence is associated with a label, its value is 1, otherwise it is 0; For the interactive function $g_j(s_{t-1}, s_t)$, if a previous object class is transferred to the current object class, its value is 1, otherwise it is 0. In a large number of observations, we can set the expectation value as $\alpha_i = \propto, \beta_j = \propto$. Assuming that p_x is an element of vector P with finite length, we can transform the problem into a convex function optimization problem with linear constraints:

$$\max_p -\sum_x p_x \log p_x, \tag{5.5}$$

$$\text{subject to } \sum_x p_x f_i(o, s_t) = \alpha_i, \tag{5.6}$$

$$\sum_x p_x g_j(s_{t-1}, s_t) = \beta_j, \tag{5.7}$$

$$\sum_x p_x = 1. \tag{5.8}$$

Lagrange equation is obtained:

$$J = -\sum_x p_x \log p_x + \sum_i \lambda_i \left(\sum_x p_x f_i(o, s_t) - \alpha_i \right)$$
$$+ \sum_j \mu_j \left(\sum_x p_x g_j(s_{t-1}, s_t) - \beta_j \right) + \theta \left(\sum_x p_x - 1 \right). \tag{5.9}$$

Solve the partial derivative of p_x,

$$\frac{\partial J}{\partial p_x} = -1 - \log p_x + \sum_i \lambda_i f_i(o, s_t) + \sum_j \mu_j g_j(s_{t-1}, s_t) + \theta = 0. \tag{5.10}$$

Then

$$p_x = e^{\theta-1} \exp \left(\sum_i \lambda_i f_i(o, s_t) + \sum_j \mu_j g_j(s_{t-1}, s_t) \right). \tag{5.11}$$

As $\sum_x p_x = 1$, we can obtain

$$e^{1-\theta} = \sum_x \exp\left(\sum_i \lambda_i f_i(o, s_t) + \sum_j \mu_j g_j(s_{t-1}, s_t)\right) = Z. \quad (5.12)$$

So

$$p_x = \frac{1}{Z} \exp\left(\sum_i \lambda_i f_i(o, s_t) + \sum_j \mu_j g_j(s_{t-1}, s_t)\right). \quad (5.13)$$

This is the distribution required to solve. In the process of learning, we construct a discriminant model using posterior probability. In addition, we maximize the log-likelihood of objective function K by training image examples. Then we can estimate the value of each parameter [406].

$$\mathcal{L}(\lambda, \mu) = \sum_k \log p_x(s_k | o_k). \quad (5.14)$$

Define

$$F(s_k, o_k) = \sum_i \lambda_i f_i(o, s_t) + \sum_j \mu_j g_j(s_{t-1}, s_t). \quad (5.15)$$

Then solve the gradient of the objective function,

$$\nabla \mathcal{L}(\lambda, \mu) = \sum_k \left[F(s_k, o_k) - E_{p_x(S|o_k)} F(S, o_k)\right]. \quad (5.16)$$

Here, the expectation value $E_{p_x(S|o_k)} F(S, o_k)$ can be obtained using the forward–backward algorithm (249). As the relational function has a 2D structure, the transfer matrix can be derived as follows:

$$M_t(l', l) = \exp\left(\sum_m \lambda_m f_m(s_t, o) + \sum_n \mu_n g_n(s_{t-1}, s_t)\right). \quad (5.17)$$

Equation (5.17) indicates that the current matrix $M_t(l', l)$ will add the correlative function and the interactive function in a vertical and horizontal direction. To prevent data overfitting, the Gaussian prior item is employed to limit the likelihood function. Then the gradient of the log-likelihood function is iterated by inputting the L-BFGS algorithm. So the parameters $(\lambda_1, \lambda_2, \ldots \mu_1, \mu_2, \ldots)$ can be obtained.

We construct the identification network using weighted relational function. If objects of $|L|$ classes are learned, we can construct the knowledge transfer matrix of $|L| \times |L|$ by adding the interactive functions $g_j(s_{t-1}, s_t)$ that satisfy $s_{t-1} = l'$ and $s_t = l$:

$$M_i(l', l) = \exp\left(\sum_j \mu_j g_j(s_{t-1}, s_t)\right). \tag{5.18}$$

The transfer matrix represents the transfer probabilities among different classes of objects. At the same time, weighted correlative function, which represents the correlation degree between the low-level feature sequence and the category of an object, is also stored in the recognition network for query.

5.4.5 Link search

The process of object recognition is driven mutually by attention and some expectations. Note that scan image by attention window activates the corresponding feature to play a role. Then, the expectation forecasts the emergence of an object mainly through the constraints of context. Here, expectation is represented by the knowledge transfer matrix. After the previous preparation, we are here to explain the process of link search.

When observing an image, the image features are first extracted in the set $S = \{o_1, o_2, \ldots r_1, r_2 \ldots\}$. The main map records the location information of the feature. Each local feature o_i uniquely corresponds to position coordinates (x_i, y_i), namely $o_i \leftrightarrow (x_i, y_i)$. Then, the feature map is generated by the reasoning encoding pattern $x(o, t)$, and it correlates the adjacent features. Subsequently, at time t, the attention window with the maximum length of $2n + 1$ begins to scan the location main map. The features in the attention window are activated and other features are not considered for the time being. The activated feature constitutes the transient representation of an object, which contains the location of the current feature and the combination $\mathbf{x}(o, t)$ with its adjacent features. The searching and identifying network finds out which correlative functions contain the feature sequence $\mathbf{x}(o, t)$. The weighted correlative function corresponding to the same object label l is summed up. Through the query transfer matrix, we obtain the transfer probability from all other objects l' to l. Take these two factors and the maximal label l associated with the current state s_t

$$\max\left\{\underbrace{\exp\left(\sum_i \lambda_i f_i(s_t, o) + \sum_j u_j g_j(s_{t-1}, s_t)\right), \ldots}_{\text{total number } |L|}\right\}. \tag{5.19}$$

As the attention window moves forward step by step, the process will repeat. Considering the previous state, the recursive process is as follows:

$$\varphi_{t+1}(s_i) = \max_{s_j}(\varphi_t(s_j) \exp F(\mathbf{s}, \mathbf{o}, t+1)), \tag{5.20}$$

where $\varphi_t(s_i)$ represents the probability of state s_i associated with the object label l. When the attention window finishes scanning the whole image, we get the results of the link search which is as follows:

$$\mathbf{s}^* = \arg\max_{\mathbf{s}} \exp\left(\sum_t F(\mathbf{s}, \mathbf{o}, t)\right). \tag{5.21}$$

The Viterbi algorithm is employed to calculate the above process. When the link search is finished, we can get the whole understanding of the image. The link search process can be accelerated by feature suppression, i.e., active features suppress non-target features. In the low-level features, the feature map which is constructed by the adjacent and similar features is the same. We define these highly similar low-level features as non-target features. In the process of link search, if we encounter a non-target feature, we will skip it and continue to move the attention window. Through this process, we save the calculation amount and can get the same recognition results.

Link search corresponds all local features and object labels. Through querying the main location diagram and using correspondence $o_i \leftrightarrow (x_i, y_i)$, we can locate objects in the image, thus completing the process of object recognition.

5.5 Visual Space Cognition

In recent decades, researchers have carried out wide and profound research on reaction time, using strategy, representative content, mode and the structure features of visual space material itself when the individual solves the space problem. People analyze reasons which lead to differences in the cognitive ability of individual space, and establish corresponding machining model and the theory, similar to the model proposed by Just and Carpenter, the spatial cognition coordinate model [227], Gordon *et al.* proposed the differentiation theory of cognitive function [177] based on the side brain function lateralization theory proposed by Sperry. Furthermore, on the basis of previous theory, people work out cognitive test set CLB — a set of neuropsychological test tool to evaluate the side level and whole intelligence level of verbal and spatial cognitive functions. Kosslyn *et al.* understand and describe the specific visual–spatial cognitive function from the perspective of cognitive neuroscience, and propose a high level of visual processing subsystem theory [246].

The study of representation is an important research field of cognitive psychology, artificial intelligence, cognitive neuroscience and so on. It is involved in the neural basis, the nature and function of representation. Many scholars regard the visual–spatial representation as the core of spatial intelligence and think that the representation is an active cognitive way to realize the psychological content of consciousness. Its non-inference and perceptual characteristics are important in creative thinking [340].

The spatial cognition theory holds that the spatial cognitive ability of the individual can be decomposed into two aspects: spatial visualization and spatial orientation. Spatial visualization is a combination of a series of representation processing, which includes four procedures: the formation of distinct and high-resolution mental representation procedure, and the procedure of combining psychological representation with independent components, the procedure of checking psychological representation types and psychological representation rotation types. People's visual space is generally 2D and 3D. Spatial orientation is the ability to determine the location of objects in the visual space.

As a basic operation of the human visual–spatial cognition, psychological rotation has a good forecast effect on an individual's spatial ability. R. N. Shepard and his colleagues started to study the psychological rotation at the beginning of 1970s. They published experimental results in the *Science* magazine, opening a new page in the field of spatial cognition [410].

According to the theory of psychological rotation proposed by Shepard *et al.* the psychological rotation task can be divided into the information processing stages, which are independent of the function. These stages are: (a) perceptional encoding; (b) distinguish/describe graph and distinguish its location and orientation; (c) psychological rotation; (d) identical judgement; (e) selective response; (f) response execution [411]. These stages are understood to be a number of discrete information, organized from one stage to the next stage in order. However, some people have questioned the theory that these discrete, ordered stages are executed strictly in order and are parallely superimposed in a very small range.

Wintermute *et al.* add the SVS in the cognitive system Soar, which is the system chart shown in Figure 5.8. Blocks in the chart represent short-term memory. Circles represent information processing. Gray circles provide information access to long-term memory. The control association between working memory and other parts is not marked.

In SVS, the working memory plays the role of symbolic representation. SVS increases quantitative spatial representation in spatial scene short-term memory and increases the visual diagram representation in the visual buffer short-term memory. In addition to these two short-term memory components, there is also a long-term

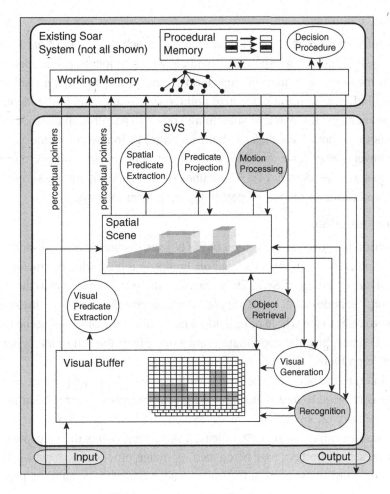

Fig. 5.8. Soar/SVS system chart

memory of visual, spatial and motional data, which are known as the perceptive long-term memory components. In order to simplify the diagram, these memory components are not clearly marked.

Theoretically, all the information in the SVS system can be derived from the sketch by adding a low-level perceptive system to the visual buffer. Conceptually, Soar/SVS uses 2D visual information to construct 3D spatial structure. In fact, SVS is used in virtual environment, and has no complete visual system. Many world structures represented by simulation environments can be directly input into the space scene. Although the vision from the bottom to the top is not used, the visual processing still plays an important role. Visual representation perception is useful, and it need not to be actually perceived.

1. Perceptive pointer

The perceptive pointer is similar to the identifier. Each item in the Soar long-term memory system has a corresponding symbol, which amounts to the identifier of long-term memory. Each item in short-term memory, whether it is a spatial scene or a visual buffer, also has a perceptive pointer, which amounts to the identifier of short-term memory. If the item is something known to perceive an instance of long-term memory, it should associate with the identifier of long-term memory. In SVS, naming convention attribute uses a long-time identifier *class-id*, while the correlative attribute has a short identifier *id*. The values of these identifiers are simply string symbols, and called as objects of perceiving long-term memory.

2. Memory encoding

In the interior, the space scene is a set of 3D objects in continuous coordinates. The perceptive pointers of an object's symbols compose a hierarchical structure in the working memory group of Soar. Only leaves of the tree correspond to the original polyhedron, but nodes at all levels are considered as objects; this allows the symbolic reasoning to refer to the whole or individual parts. Since the object of scene location is in the 3D space, how the coordinate framework affects the rest of the system may be a notable problem.

The internal encoding of the visual buffer is a set of bitmap. Each bitmap in the buffer is referred to as a sketch and there is a perceptive pointer pointing to the working memory. A single pixel in the sketch can be of a set color, or a special value indicating empty. In general, at least a sketch represents the perceptive scene centered on self and others may be created by image processing. A set of sketches allow multiple objects to exist in the same visual location; it can also be used as an attention mechanism, focusing on processing specific areas.

Internal representation of perceiving long-term memory is more heterogeneous than the rest of the SVS. It stores the quantitative relationship between the visual texture and motion model of the spatial object, for example, a specific vehicle's motion model. The long-time perceptive pointer is available to the construction of all the agents in the SVS. In current implementation, the knowledge engineer codes, based on the perception of long-term memory products in the field. For example, the spatial object can use external 3D modeling tools in the design and then import them to the perception of long-term memory. A useful research direction will be to try to understand the information, and then gradually add and modify the perceptive long-term memory of agents. In the other long-term memory of Soar, this learning mechanism will be combined with other learning mechanisms.

3. Predicate extraction

Predicate extraction provides a qualitative symbol processing of the Soar space scene and the content of the visual buffer. This processing framework has a set of fixed attributes that can be extracted and these attributes are not learned by agents. Different from the perceptive pointer, the qualitative predicate is created in working memory only, when the Soar requires. There is a large amount of qualitative information implicit in the SVS memory components, where each part can be derived by basic calculus. So this top-down control is necessary to make the system easy to calculate.

For the space system, there are three kinds of important relations: topology, distance and direction. Topological relation describes how the surfaces of the object are related to each other. In the current implementation of SVS, the only relation detected is whether the two objects are intersecting.

Distance query is also simple. In the current system, what can be used in distance query are any two objects along the nearest route in the scene. This kind of information is not qualitative. Of course, it is less than the quantitative content of the space scene, because it reduces the scalar scale of the 3D information. However, it is very useful in practice. The closest obstacle of agent can be determined by extracting and comparing the distance between the agent and all detected obstacles.

Direction query employs the method of Hernandez [209]. For each object, by defining a group of adjacent regions, they are respectively corresponding to a rough position, such as left and right. If an object is located in an adjacent area, it can be determined in a specific direction. Each object has an associated "forward" vector, which is used to define the reference eigen-frame based on the region on it. This can easily extend the query using a reference framework of other objects and also allow the use of a global coordinate system.

4. Image creation

For the Soar system, the agent is used to solve the problem of the general problem. It is usually insufficient to extract the provided information from the perceptive pointer and the predicate. Separate predicate extraction does not provide adequate information for the external world and it must use representation processing. Representation often proposes specific methods to solve the problem. Rarely, image creation mode of the irrelative problem is precisely seen.

5. Predict projection

Creating a new spatial image is often involved in translation of the scene from a qualitied description to a quantitative representation. In order to achieve this,

SVS combines predicate projection processing [503]. Predicates supported by SVS include geometric concepts, such as "shell" and "intersection". When there are two or more objects in the scene, hull image is a convex hull; and the cross point image is the cross region of two or more objects. In addition to this, SVS supports using predicates (such as "on") to prescribe the qualified spatial relations between objects, but it has nothing to do with image shape.

Similar to predicate extraction, predicate projection is a fixed process, but there is no strong commitment to explain the available operation in the current library. Further research is needed to determine which predicates are necessary for the function of the human level.

6. Memory retrieval

Different from the space described by the predicate projection and the qualitative attributes of visual images, memory retrieval extracts specific qualified information from the perceptive long-term memory by perceptive pointers, such as object, quantitative spatial relationship, motion model, visual texture, etc. SVS uses this information to construct or increase the space scene. For example, an agent can imagine a car, and there is no qualitative description of its shape or the relationship between the wheel and the body, but you can create an image with a combination of the two methods.

7. Movement representation

Despite the previous method of image creation which is very strong, it is not enough to solve non-trivial movement problems. For example, consider predicting whether a turning vehicle would hit obstacles. The agent must determine whether the vehicle can get to the target through a route that does not collide with obstacles.

In SVS, this kind of information uses the motion model for encoding [526]. By transforming the state of a continuous space to another state, the action model provides a more accurate quantitative analysis with small movement granulity. In the perceptive long-term memory, the motion model can be applied to any object in the space scene, thus generating motion simulation. This simulation is a sequence of steps controlled by Soar. Agents can use the predicate extraction one step at a time and the information obtained from the simulation, and such things as whether the vehicle intersects with obstacles. The motion model can be used to simulate a variety of movements, including the movement of the agent itself.

Movement model encoding is task knowledge rather than focus on the structure. In everyday life, the agent may encounter any number of different movement patterns. Assuming the agent first encounters the vehicle, it will learn the sports model of the vehicle. This learning process is the area of future research. At present, the knowledge engineer describes movement model by C++ language.

8. Visual generation

If SVS is a more comprehensive model of human processing, the perception in the visual buffer will directly create a structure. Spatial scene will be obtained from the internal processing of these structures. In the context of representation, the visual buffer will be modified in a top-down manner based on the working memory information of the spatial scene and symbol. This process is called visual generation. The process involves the conversion from 3D to 2D representation, so it can directly be used to solve the problem of shape. It can also be used to generate visual sketches to support further processing, such as predicate extraction or visual recognition.

9. Visual recognition

The characteristics of sketch representation will be used in the identification process of the visual system in SVS. Supporting visual recognition is generally a major challenge, but it is useful to allow a simple identification process in some areas. SVS realizes visual recognition by mathematical processing (for example, edge detection), or transforms encoding pixels to create new sketches by the "sketch operation" [255]. In Soar, pixel rewrite rules are prescribed and sent to SVS for processing. The form of the rule is that the left is the condition and the right is the action.

5.6 Visual Effective Coding

It is believed that the visual processing of the primary visual cortex is influenced by the statistical characteristics of the environment, but it is a difficult problem to establish an accurate digital connection between them. In 1954, under the influence and guidance of the information theory, Attneave proposed that the goal of visual perception is to produce an effective representation of an external input signal [31]. In the field of neural biology, Barlow proposed the "effective coding hypothesis" [50], which thinks that the main function of the primary visual cortex cell is to remove the statistical correlation of input stimulus. If this effective coding hypothesis is correct, as for the response characteristic of neural cells, what kind of behavior should we expect to observe? The neural system reflects this kind of characteristics of effective coding in two ways: the distribution curve of response of the single neural cell and the statistical independence of multiple neural cells.

In order to detect whether a single neuron has the maximum expression of the input signal information, when we investigate the distribution state of a single neuron's response to the natural environment, it is necessary to add some constraints to the response value of the neural cell. For example, if we assume that the maximum response value of the neural cell is R_{max}, it is easy to get when the neural cell response satisfies the average distribution in $[0, R_{max}]$, and information maximization can be achieved. That is to say, the neural cells must equally use each possible value in the intervals. The optimal distribution of neural cell response is closely dependent on the constraints of neural cell response. For example, if the variance of selecting constraints of neural cell response is constant, then the distribution of information maximization corresponds to Gaussian distribution; if the mean of constraints is constant, then the distribution of information maximization corresponds to exponential distribution.

In addition to the effective coding external stimulation of the individual neural cell, if a group of neural cells combine with an external stimulus pattern to code, the combined response of multiple neural cells must code as large as possible to input stimulus. Apparently, if certain information is coded by more than a neural cell, then the joint response efficiency of this group of neural cells will decline. In the mathematical sense, if the response of each neural cell satisfies the statistical independent condition, then the coding of this group of neural cells is most effective. Response of two neural cells meeting the independent condition means that the response of the other neural cell cannot be predicted by the response of a nerve cell. Compared to effective coding of multiple neural cells with that of the single nerve cell, the independence target does not require any additional constraints.

From the methodology, effective encoding research can be divided into two routes: the direct method is checking the response characteristics of nerve cells under the condition of natural images stimulus from the biological mechanism, which is called mechanism test; another alternative method is to establish a model to simulate the mechanism of the early visual processing system by using statistical properties of natural images, which is called model simulation.

Experiments can detect the response characteristics of the optic neural cell in the stimulus of natural images or image sequences. These studies use different methods to test the effectiveness of optic neural cell coding. The major experimental results verify the effective encoding hypothesis.

Baddeley *et al.* did experiments in V1 cells of the cat and IT zone cells of the monkey. They found that the distribution of firing rate of these neural cells follows the exponential distribution in natural images stimulus, which is consistent with the criterion of efficient coding of the individual neural cell. That is to say, under the conditions of fixed mean firing rate, exponential distribution can transmit most information [47]. In 2001, the results published in *Nature* by Nirenberg *et al.*

shows that, in the case of redundancy measures and natural stimulus, a group of retinal ganglion can code independent of the outside stimulus [341].

Neurophysiological studies have shown that each neural cell carries information components unrelated to statistics. Between the retina and lateral geniculate neurons, the visual system codes external information through optimized information transmission under the condition of the limited bandwidth of the neural tract; then, V1 neural cells transform the optimal stimulus to sparse coding and these neural cells represent the independent components in natural scenes. This sparse coding will not only promote the understanding of advanced visual areas of the visual system, but also increase the effectiveness of pattern recognition.

In model simulation, we first examine statistical characteristics of external environmental stimulus, building the response model according to specific statistical optimal criterion, which is called the efficient coding model. Then, we compare it with the response properties (neurophysiology) of neural cells in the primary visual cortex. The following focuses on how to build such a model, so as to form the association between statistical characteristics of external stimulus and the processing mechanism of the visual system.

Here the effective coding model is aimed at a number of neural cells and a single neural cell's coding is not within our research scope. The effective coding model can be described as: decomposing the input signal to form a set of independent responses. The basic model of the effective coding can be shown in Figure 5.9. Each small image block in Figure 5.9 corresponds to the receptive field of a neural cell. It should be arranged in columns forming a N-dimensional vector X. Assuming that

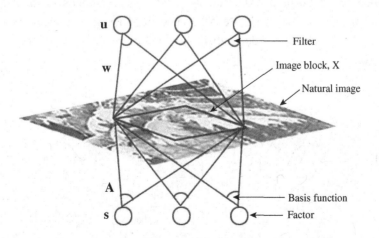

Fig. 5.9. Image linear superposition and effective coding model

X can be obtained by linear superposition of N basis functions, the N basis functions constitute columns of matrix A. At the same time, when linear superposition is conducted, weights of each basis function are represented by vector S, each component of which is usually called "factor". Linear superposition of images can be represented as

$$X = AS. \tag{5.22}$$

Effective coding model is to transform the image X (linear or nonlinear), to find the hidden "factor" S, and make S meet the effective coding criteria, such as statistical independent conditions. The simplified model can be represented as

$$S = F(WX). \tag{5.23}$$

This simplified model can be divided into two steps. The first step is linear filtering. The column vectors of W correspond to linear filters; then nonlinear transformation is conducted on the basis of the results of linear filtering. This step is optional.

With the increase of the dimension of input signal, the complexity of the joint distribution of the input signal will increase exponentially. Therefore, it is usual to simplify the problem for specific statistical properties, or to employ a specific decomposition algorithms. Commonly used effective encoding algorithms can be divided into three kinds. The first is based on the linear decorrelation method of the two order statistics, which corresponds to the region R2 marked by the dotted line in Figure 5.10. The second is the independent component analysis method based on high order statistics, which corresponds to the region R1 marked by the solid line in Figure 5.10. The third is the nonlinear decomposition method based on high order statistics, which corresponds to the region R3 in Figure 5.10.

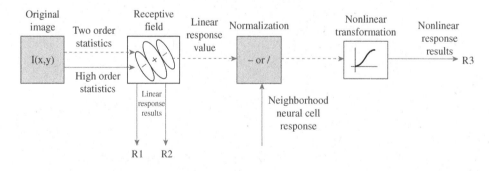

Fig. 5.10. Modeling diagram of effective coding

1. Linear filter model based on two order statistics

The simplest constraint is to consider the two order statistics of the input signal (covariance, correlation coefficient, etc.). Modeling with linear decomposition corresponds to Route R2 shown in Figure 5.10. Principal component analysis (PCA), which is widely used, can solve this problem. F corresponding to Equation (5.23) is the identity transformation, and S should satisfy:

$$Cov(S) = \text{Diagonal Matrix.} \tag{5.24}$$

The principal component corresponds to a number of such axes, which can eliminate the correlation of various data dimensions. We can rigorously prove that these axes must exist, though they may not have the unique direction. In particular, if the input signal satisfies the Gaussian distribution, various components generated by the PCA and the variables of each axis are independent of each other.

Although PCA can generate statistically independent components or axes for the signal to satisfy Gaussian distribution, it usually fails for the non-Gaussian distribution. The natural images meet the non-Gaussian distribution: so the "factors" obtained by the PCA decomposition satisfy the statistical irrelativity, but it cannot reach the requirement of statistical independence. The basis function response corresponding to the PCA method is the global spatial frequency of the image, as shown in Figure 5.11.

2. Linear filter model based on higher order statistics

The principal component obtained by the PCA corresponds to the image space frequency. This space frequency or two-order statistics is not sufficient to reflect the spatial local information of the image, such as boundary contour. So we must introduce additional constraints.

Field proposed method of sparse coding or minimizing information entropy coding, which corresponds to an input image stimulus and the number of activated neural cells should be as less as possible [145]. By optimizing the parameters of the Gabor filter, they found that the filter generated by these parameters is very similar to the response characteristics of simple cells in the visual cortex. They have the characteristics of location selectivity, direction selectivity and frequency selectivity.

Olshausen *et al.* studied the relationship between the receptive field property of simple cells and sparse coding by linear superposition method. They used the linear superposition of basis function shown in Equation (5.22) to represent input stimulus images. In the minimum mean square sense, they made the results of linear superposition similar to the original image as much as possible, i.e., they made the reconstruction error as small as possible. At the same time, they made the representative features as sparse as possible, or made the number that the corresponding weight

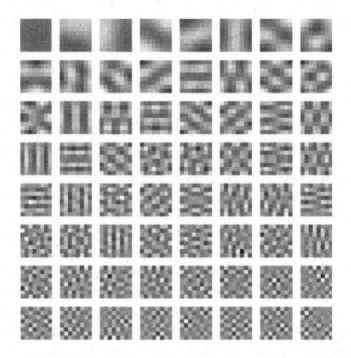

Fig. 5.11.   The basis functions obtained by PCA on a set of 8 × 8 image blocks

of basis function equal to zero as much as possible. This optimization criterion can be represented as

$$E(a, \Phi) = \sum_{x,y} \left[I(x, y) - \sum_{a_i \Phi_i(x,y)} \right] + \lambda_s \sum_i S\left(\frac{a_i}{\sigma_i}\right). \qquad (5.25)$$

Here, $a_i \Phi_i(x, y)$ corresponds to the column vector in Equation (5.22). The first item represents the complete degree of using the basis function set to reconstruct the original image and it is expressed by the square sum of the error. The second term represents the sparse features of coding, so that the original image can be represented by the basis function as small as possible. Image blocks arbitrarily selected from natural images constitute a training set. The basis functions obtained by initializing basis functions set randomly and training several 100 times have similar properties to the simple cells of the visual cortex.

3. Nonlinear model

Schwartz *et al.* eliminated the nonlinear relativity among "factors" in the linear coding results by a nonlinear transformation. The response values of each basis function were first adjusted, typically such as square operation. Then it was divided by the weighted sum of the adjusted neighborhood neural cell responses. The new response values could be treated as the final neural cell response. This adjustment was corresponding to the function F in Equation (5.23). This nonlinear process could be viewed as a hierarchical model consisting of two stages:

$$\{x_i\} \xrightarrow{T} \{s_i\} \xrightarrow{R} \{r_i\}. \tag{5.26}$$

The original image pixel x_i is first processed by a linear transformation T and the linear filter coefficient c_i is obtained. Then, the linear filter coefficients are transformed by a nonlinear transformation R. As mentioned above, the linear filter is a filter with position, direction and frequency selectivity. Nonlinear transformation R is a kind of control mechanism of information gain. It normalizes each linear filter coefficients through weighting on the energy of the neighborhood linear filter coefficients:

$$ri = \frac{\text{sgn}(s_i) * |s_i|^\gamma}{\beta_i + \sum_j h_{ij}|s_j|^\gamma}. \tag{5.27}$$

The results show that the statistical independence between the coefficients of the adjacent filter coefficients can be significantly improved by using the encoding coefficients of the nonlinear transformation, and the correlation between the response sparsity of the adjacent filter cannot be eliminated by linear transformation.

The nonlinear process can be found everywhere in the cerebral cortex, and the similar "dispersion normalization" model is widely used to explain the nonlinear behavior of neural cells. This nonlinear relationship can well adapt the non-Gauss statistical properties of natural images, and it can be used to minimize the statistical independence of the neural cell responses by optimizing the weights of the neighborhood in the process of normalization. The model's coding results are surprisingly consistent with most neurophysiological data.

Chapter 6

Motor Control

Movement is the fundamental of human and animal behavior, which is controlled by the central nervous system. The cerebellar and the basal ganglia are also involved in motor control. In this chapter, the nervous structure of motor control, the analysis of the brain's electrical signal, and neural encoding of movement are introduced in detail.

6.1 The Neural Structure of Motor Control

Movement is the fundamental of human and animal behavior, which is generated by muscle contraction force acting on the relevant parts of the body. Movement generally consists of three types, namely, reflex, voluntary movement and rhythmic movement. Reflex is the most simple and basic movement. It is usually caused by specific sensory stimuli and generates a motion which has a stereotype track. Voluntary movement is that of an object that moves itself by its own will. It can be a response to sensory stimuli, or can be generated by subjective intention. Rhythmic movement is another type of movement which combines reflex and voluntary movements, such as breathing, chewing, walking and so on.

Movement is controlled by the central nervous system, usually various neural structures that control movement together is called the brain motor system. The brain motor system is arranged as a hierarchy of three levels (Figure 6.1). The highest, middle and the lowest levels are respectively represented by the motor cortex, the descending pathway of the brainstem and the spinal cord.

The three hierarchical levels have their own tasks. For example, the spinal cord as the lowest level of the brain motor system can produce complex efferent impulse, and make the muscular tissue excited, thereby creating reflections. The senior motor system which is above the spinal cord is on this basis to give some general motion

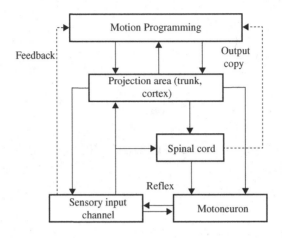

Fig. 6.1. The motor control hierarchy

commands, rather than solving the detailed problems such as how to coordinate the synergist muscle and the opposing muscle. On the other hand, in addition to the lower motor system, the senior motor system can also control lower-level neurons directly. For example, the motor cortex can excite the spinal cord neurons through the brain stem, and can also directly excite the spinal cord motor neurons and the interneurons through the corticospinal tract. From this viewpoint, the three levels are parallel. This kind of serial and parallel, direct and indirect repeating arrangement, provides flexible choices for the motor control realization, and has a great significance in the recovery and compensation of the damaged nervous system.

Many descending pathways which originate in the brain stem can affect the interneurons of the spinal cord, and a few of them can affect the motor neurons of the spinal cord. The descending pathway consists of two pathways, namely, the ventro-medial (medial) pathway and the lateral pathway [248]. The ventromedial pathways contain the vestibulospianl tract, the tectospinal tract and the reticulospinal tract, which originate in vestibular nuclei, the superior colliculus of the midbrain and the reticular formation of the pontine and medullary, respectively. These tracts descend in the ipsilateral ventral funiculus and terminate among the spinal interneurons controlling proximal and axial muscles. The tectospinal tract terminates in the neck part of the contralateral spinal cord. The lateral pathways mainly include the rubrospinal tract, which originates in the red nucleus of the midbrain, descends in the lateral part of the brainstem tegmentum and terminates in the lateral part of medial potions and the motor neurons of the ventral spinal cord.

The medial descending system is the basic system controlling the whole body movement. It mainly controls the trunk muscles and muscles of the proximal limbs.

Its functions include maintaining balance and vertical posture, integrating the movement of the body and the limb, coordinated movement of a single limb, etc. The lateral descending system mainly controls the muscles of the distal limbs. In higher primates and humans, the rubrospinal tract is underdeveloped, and most of its functions have been replaced by the corticospinal tract. It plays an important role in fine movement of the hands and fingers.

There are two pathways descending from the brainstem, i.e., the coeruleospinal system emanating from the locus coeruleus nucleus and the reticular formation of the brainstem, and the raphe-spinal system arising from the raphe nuclei group of the brainstem. The former is adrenergic, the latter is serotoniergic. Both of them end in the middle area of the spinal cord and motor neuron nuclei and they can adjust the excitability of the spinal cord neurons. The raphe-spinal system projects to the superficial layer of spinal dorsal horn and controls the transmission of nociceptive information. Lots of descending neurons of the brainstem are controlled by the somatosensory cortex neurons, so the cortex can indirectly command the spinal cord by the brainstem descending system.

6.2 Motor Cortex

The motor function of the brain is an important part of the brain function. The motor cortex consists of three parts, namely, primary motor cortex (M_1), premotor area (PMA) and supplementary motor area (SMA) (see Figure 6.2). The three parts directly project the spinal cord through the corticospinal tract, or indirectly affect the spinal cord by the brainstem descending system. PMA and SMA have fibers projecting to M_1, and they play important roles in the coordination and planning of complex movement. They all accept the fibers from the posterior parietal cortex and the prefrontal cortex. Recent studies found that a portion of the cingulate cortex located in the dorsal area of the cingulate sulcus is a part of the motor cortex, which is called the cingulate motor area.

In 1870, Fritsch and Hitzig first showed that the stimulation of some cortex of anesthetized dogs would elicit movement of the contralateral side of the body, and stimulation of different cortex areas would cause a twitch in the muscles in different regions of the body. These findings were also confirmed when stimulating the cortex of monkeys. Furthermore, it was found that stimulating the precentral gyrus of monkeys is most likely to cause movement. The precentral gyrus is equal to the area 4 of Brodmann, which is the primary motor cortex. In the primary motor cortex, there is a somatotopic map, which means that the excitement of some area in the primary motor cortex corresponds to the movement of certain regions of

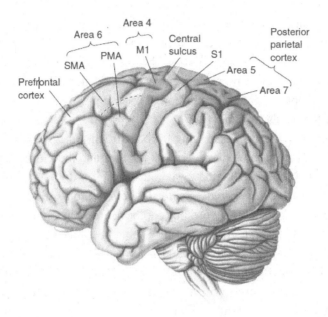

Fig. 6.2.   The motor cortex of the brain

the body, and this cortex area is called the representation area of the region of the body. When the hand moves, for example, the representation area of the hand in the motor cortex will be activated. However, some points in the motor cortex cannot accurately control the movement of the corresponding regions of the body, and also cannot control the movement of some muscles. In fact, the movements of the wrist and finger correspond to the activity of a group of the decentralized distribution of neurons, and one finger's movement representation area and another finger's movement representation area usually overlap largely.

The former sports area, or the secondary motor area, including the SMA, is located in area 6. In the implementation process of the exercise program, the prefrontal cortex, the anterior motor cortex and the supplementary motor cortex send out information to the primary motor cortex. Neurons in the prefrontal cortex respond to sensory signals that result in motion. The nerve activity of the anterior motor cortex was the most active during the preparation of the movement, but also showed a certain degree of activity in the implementation of the exercise. Some of the neurons in the cortex respond to sensory stimuli, especially those that are close to the hand or the face, which are most likely to respond to stimuli. Premotor cortex receives information related to the movement towards the target space, position and movement at the time of the body position and posture. These two kinds of information regarding a part of the body shift to a target motion is required. In order to organize the muscles in the different parts of the body to carry out movements, the primary motor cortex and the spinal cord output information are used. For example, in a person who wants to lift his arm, his muscle movements due to its palm move toward differently (up or down) and at this time the motor cortex of neurons will produce the corresponding functional activities.

The supplementary motor cortex is the most active in the preparation of rapid and continuous movement, where many of the neurons are excited only when they are ready for a particular order of motion. When people make fast-paced finger movements (such as playing the piano), the nervous activity of its cortex of auxiliary sport will be strengthened.

The nerve cells in the motor cortex can be divided into two categories: pyramidal and non-pyramidal cells. Axons of pyramidal cells leave the motor cortex to other cortical or subcortical structures, so it is a master efferent neuron. Non-pyramidal cells, including astrocytes, basket cells and granular cells have a considerable number of inhibitory neurons. Pyramidal cells in each layer of the cortex have different projections. Most of the cortex is under the projection origin in the layer V pyramidal cells, corticospinal neurons in the fifth layer of the deep, including the largest pyramidal cells, i.e., Betz cells.

6.3 The Basal Ganglia

The term 'basal ganglia' is the collective noun for a group of brain structures that are predominantly located in the forebrain. Cerebral basal ganglia exists in the agglomerate of gray matter from deep layer of brain to brain stem and consists of caudate nucleus (nucleus caudatus), putamen, globus pallidus, nucleus subthalamus and substantia nigra. Sometime, claustrum is also added here. Caudate nucleus, putamen and globus pallidus are collectively called striatum, where the globus pallidus is known to be the older in the striatum, while the caudate nucleus and putamen are newly evolved and hence are called as the neostriatum.

The basal ganglia are related to the stabilization of the voluntary movement, the control of the muscle tension and the processing of the sensory afferent impulse information. The afferent nerve fiber of the basal ganglia comes mainly from the brain cortex, the thalamus and the midbrain. They are mainly distributed in caudate nucleus, putamen and also have direct relationship with the pallidal fiber. There is the substantia nigra striatum pathway, which comes from the substantia nigra, reaching the new striatum (primarily caudate nucleus). There are some nerve fibers connected with caudate nucleus, putamen and globus pallidus in the basal ganglia. The spreading out of the basal ganglia is mainly from the inner and the substantia

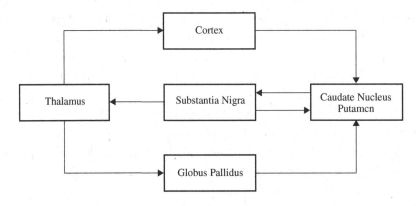

Fig. 6.3. Basal ganglia adjusting motion cycle

nigra neurons. These neurons last axons and terminate in the brainstem parts, including the anteroventral nucleus (VA), abdominal lateral nucleus (VL), ventromedial nucleus (VM), thalamus nucleus and superior colliculus and the midbrain-pons upper portion tegmental.

Basal ganglia play an important role in motor regulation [219]. Spreading of the connection of basal ganglion, and its regulation of the body movement function mainly relies on the cycle illustrated in Figure 6.3.

At present, researchers have proposed several kinds of different models, which are used to explain the behavior selection mechanism of the basal ganglia. The most influential model is the direct–indirect pathway model (DIPM), proposed by Albin [4]. The model can successfully explain the mechanism of Parkinson's disease. However, due to the DIPM being proposed earlier, it did not include the subsequent discovery of the interaction between the nuclear group pathway. Gurney and others reviewed the DIPM and proposed the selection-control pathway model (SCPM) [197]. The model incorporates a number of new neural information transfer pathways and considers the role and influence of dopamine neurons in the behavior selection process. The research results show that the control pathway model is more consistent with the physiological and anatomical test data, and it is better than the direct–indirect double pathway model.

The cerebral cortex is a parallel way to deal with a number of perceptual and cognitive information flow or information channels, and each channel may request the implementation of specific behavior [376]. But they are often conflicting or incompatible with each other between behaviors. In order to solve the conflict between them, the cerebral cortex will be at the center of all the behaviors of the request, through a series of topology parallel channels sent to the basal ganglia. The behavior requests flow through each nucleus of the basal ganglia, including the striatum, the

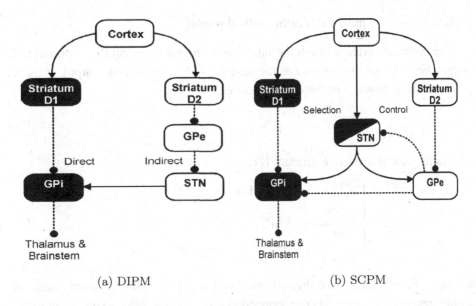

(a) DIPM   (b) SCPM

Fig. 6.4. The model of basal ganglia

globus pallidus outer nuclear GPe, the bottom thalamic nucleus STN and eventually reach the output nucleus of the GPi and substantia nigra pars SNr. GPi/SNr will maintain or increase the inhibition of the pathways which have not been selected and remove the inhibition of the selective pathway, thereby enabling the selected behavior to be performed by the thalamus. The interaction relations between the DIPMs of the basal ganglia and the selection of the control pathway models are shown in Figures 6.4(a) and 6.4(b).

In order to quantitatively study the behavioral selectivity characteristic of the basal ganglia, a mathematical model of behavior selection was established. Assumptions need to select a suitable behavior in the I pathway behavior. $I = 3$, for example, is the various nuclei of the basal ganglia also correspondingly divided into three pathways and each pathway with leaky integrator neurons represents the leakage integral neuron model. As shown in Equation (6.1), x is a neuronal state in the type, u is the neuronal input, y is a neuronal output, k, m, e is a model parameter respectively, H is a step function.

$$\begin{cases} \dfrac{dx}{dt} = -k(x - u), \\ y = m(x - \varepsilon)H(x - \varepsilon). \end{cases} \tag{6.1}$$

The mathematical descriptions of the two models of the basal ganglia are given respectively as follows.

1. Direct–indirect pathway mathematical model

(1) The cerebral cortex through the integration processing to get the importance S_i of each behavior pathway with i as the pathway index, and y as its output, y_i^C is the output of the pathway i of the cerebral cortex.

$$y_i^C = S_i. \tag{6.2}$$

(2) Mathematical model of striatum D1:

$$\begin{cases} u_i^{SD1} = w_{CSD1} y_1^C (1 + \lambda), \\ \dfrac{da_i^{SD1}}{dt} = -k(a_i^{SD1} - u_i^{SD1}), \\ y_i^{SD1} = m(a_i^{SD1} - \varepsilon_{SD1}) H(a_i^{SD1} - \varepsilon_{SD1}), \end{cases} \tag{6.3}$$

where u_i^{SD1}, a_i^{SD1}, y_i^{SD1} are the striatum D1 passway i neuronal input, state and output, respectively. w_{CSD1} is the connection weight from cortex to the striatum D1, $1 + \lambda$ is used for describing stimulation on striatal D1 of the dopamine neuron, ε_{SD1} is the output threshold for striatum D1, m and k are proportionality factors.

(3) Mathematical model of striatum D2:

$$\begin{cases} u_i^{SD2} = w_{CSD2} y_i^C (1 - \lambda), \\ \dfrac{da_i^{SD2}}{dt} = -k(a_i^{SD2} - u_i^{SD2}), \\ y_i^{SD2} = m(a_i^{SD2} - \varepsilon_{SD2}) H(a_i^{SD2} - \varepsilon_{SD2}), \end{cases} \tag{6.4}$$

where u_i^{SD2}, a_i^{SD2}, y_i^{SD2} are the striatum D2 passway i neuronal input, state and output respectively. w_{CSD2} is the connection weight from cortex to the striatum D2, $1 - \lambda$ is used for describing stimulation on striatal D2 of the dopamine neuron, it is the inhibitory function to striatal D2, ε_{SD2} is the output threshold for striatum D2.

(4) Mathematical model of the globus pallidus external nucleus GPe:

$$\begin{cases} u_i^{GPe} = w_{SD2GPe} y_i^{SD2}, \\ \dfrac{da_i^{GPe}}{dt} = -k(a_i^{GPe} - u_i^{GPe}), \\ y_i^{GPe} = m(a_i^{GPe} - \varepsilon_{GPe}) H(a_i^{GPe} - \varepsilon_{GPe}), \end{cases} \tag{6.5}$$

where u_i^{GPe}, a_i^{GPe}, y_i^{GPe} are the GP$_e$ passway i neuronal input, state and output respectively. w_{SD2GPe} is the connection weight from striatum D2 to GPe, ε_{GPe} is the output threshold value of GPe.

(5) Mathematical model of the subthalamus nucleus STN:

$$\begin{cases} u_i^{STN} = w_{GPeSTN} y_i^{GPe}, \\ \dfrac{da_i^{STN}}{dt} = -k(a_i^{STN} - u_i^{STN}), \\ y_t^{STN} = m(a_i^{STN} - \varepsilon_{STN}) H(a_i^{STN} - \varepsilon_{STN}), \end{cases} \qquad (6.6)$$

where u_i^{STN}, a_i^{STN}, y_i^{STN} are the STN passway i neuronal input, state and output, respectively. w_{GPeSTN} is the connection weight from striatum GPe to STN, ε_{STN} is the output threshold value of STN.

(6) Mathematical model of the globus pallidus inner nucleus GPi:

$$\begin{cases} u_i^{GPi} = w_{SD1GPi} y_i^{SD1} + w_{STNGPi} \sum_i y_i^{STN}, \\ \dfrac{da_i^{GPi}}{dt} = -k(a_i^{GPi} - u_i^{GPi}), \\ y_i^{GPi} = m(a_i^{GPi} - \varepsilon_{GPi}) H(a_i^{GPi} - \varepsilon_{GPi}), \end{cases} \qquad (6.7)$$

where u_i^{GPi}, a_i^{GPi}, y_i^{GPi} are the GPi passway i neuronal input, state and output, respectively. w_{SD1GPe}, w_{STNGPi} are the connection weights from striatum D1 and subthalamus nucleus STN to globus pallidus inner nucleus GPi separately, ε_{GPi} is the output threshold value of GPi. According to anatomical findings, the projection of the subthalamus nucleus STN to the globus pallidus inner nucleus GPi is very fragmented, and the u_i^{GPi} also includes inputs from all pathways of the STN.

Above the connection weights, w_{CSD1}, w_{CSD2}, w_{STNGPi} are positive, which shows they are excitability connected; w_{SD1GPi}, w_{SD2GPe}, w_{GPeSTN} are negative, which shows they are the inhibitory connections.

2. Selection-control pathway mathematical model

For the SCPM, the mathematical models of each nucleus in the basal ganglia are as follows [197, 198]:

(1) The output of the i pathway in the cerebral cortex is the same as the DIPM:

$$y_i^C = S_i. \qquad (6.8)$$

(2) Mathematical model of striatum D1:

$$\begin{cases} u_i^{SD1} = w_{CSD1} y_i^C (1 + \lambda), \\ \dfrac{da_i^{SD1}}{dt} = -k(a_i^{SD1} - u_i^{SD1}), \\ y_i^{SD1} = m(a_i^{SD1} - \varepsilon_{SD1}) H(a_i^{SD1} - \varepsilon_{SD1}), \end{cases} \tag{6.9}$$

where u_i^{SD1}, a_i^{SD1}, y_i^{SD1} are the striatum D1 pathway i neuronal input, state and output respectively. w_{CSD1} is the connection weight from the cortex to the striatum D1, $1 + \lambda$ is used for describing stimulation on striatal D1 of the dopamine neuron, ε_{SD1} is the output threshold for striatum D1, m and k are proportionality factors.

(3) Mathematical model of striatum D2:

$$\begin{cases} u_i^{SD2} = w_{CSD2} y_i^C (1 - \lambda), \\ \dfrac{da_i^{SD2}}{dt} = -k(a_i^{SD2} - u_i^{SD2}), \\ y_i^{SD2} = m(a_i^{SD2} - \varepsilon_{SD2}) H(a_i^{SD2} - \varepsilon_{SD2}), \end{cases} \tag{6.10}$$

where u_i^{SD2}, a_i^{SD2}, y_i^{SD2} are the striatum D2 pathway i neuronal input, state and output, respectively. w_{CSD2} is connection weight from the cortex to the striatum D2, $1 - \lambda$ is used for describing stimulation on striatal D2 of the dopamine neuron, it is the inhibitory function to striatal D2, ε_{SD2} is the output threshold for striatum D2. m and k are proportionality factors.

(4) Mathematical model of the globus pallidus external nucleus GPe:

$$\begin{cases} u_i^{GPe} = w_{SD2GPe} y_i^{SD2} + w_{STNGPe} \displaystyle\sum_i y_i^{STN}, \\ \dfrac{da_i^{GPe}}{dt} = -k(a_i^{GPe} - u_i^{GPe}), \\ y_i^{GPe} = m(a_i^{GPe} - \varepsilon_{GPe}) H(a_i^{GPe} - \varepsilon_{GPe}), \end{cases} \tag{6.11}$$

where u_i^{GPe}, a_i^{GPe}, y_i^{GPe} are the GPe passway i neuronal input, state and output respectively. w_{SD2GPe} and w_{STNGPe} are the connection weights from striatum D2 and subthalamus nucleus STN to globus pallidus external nucleus GPe, ε_{GPe} is the output threshold value of GPe. The projection of the subthalamus nucleus STN to the globus pallidus inner nucleus GPe is very fragmented, and the u_i^{GPe} also includes inputs from all pathways of the STN.

(5) Mathematical model of STN:

$$
\begin{cases}
u_i^{STN} = w_{CSTN} y_i^C + w_{GPeSTN} y_i^{GPe}, \\
\dfrac{da_i^{STN}}{dt} = -k(a_i^{STN} - u_i^{STN}), \\
y_i^{STN} = m(a_i^{STN} - \varepsilon_{STN}) H(a_i^{STN} - \varepsilon_{STN}),
\end{cases}
\tag{6.12}
$$

where u_i^{STN}, a_i^{STN}, y_i^{STN} are the STN passway i neuronal input, state and output, respectively. w_{CSTN} and w_{GPeSTN} are the connection weights from the cortex and GPe to STN, ε_{STN} is the output threshold value of STN.

(6) Mathematical model of the globus pallidus inner nucleus GPi:

$$
\begin{cases}
u_i^{GPi} = w_{SD1GPi} y_i^{SD1} + w_{STNGPi} \sum_i y_i^{STN} + w_{GPeGPi} y_i^{GPe}, \\
\dfrac{da_i^{GPi}}{dt} = -k(a_i^{GPi} - u_i^{GPi}), \\
y_i^{GPi} = m(a_i^{GPi} - \varepsilon_{GPi}) H(a_i^{GPi} - \varepsilon_{GPi}),
\end{cases}
\tag{6.13}
$$

where, u_i^{GPi}, a_i^{GPi}, y_i^{GPi} are the GPi passway i neuronal input, state and output, respectively. w_{SD1GPi}, w_{STNGPi} and w_{GPeGPi} are the connection weights from striatum D1, subthalamus nucleus STN, and globus pallidus external nucleus GPe to globus pallidus inner nucleus GPi separately, ε_{GPi} is the output threshold value of GPi. u_i^{GPi} includes the inputs of all STN pathways too.

But all of these models use leakage current integration neurons and are not in line with the biological characteristics of spiking neurons, and each nucleus only uses a neuron. Literature [204] adopts spiking neurons combining with the SCPM model to study the interactive relationship between the basal ganglia multiple pathways and multiple nuclei. Basal ganglia behavior selection of spiking neurons network model is proposed.

6.4 Motor Control Pathway

Motion is the foundation for sustaining life, completing tasks and transforming the objective world. All sports and activities that happen every moment in life have not stopped, but the brain stops momentarily in attention and commands all movements. While in motion at the same time, it is mainly engaged in all kinds of learning and thinking activity, while movement is set in the back of the head. Brain does not specifically control the movement of the organ. The basal ganglia are major organs to control and direct the movement.

The thalamus, the frontal lobe, the basal ganglia and the cerebellum all relate to sport. They cooperate in the division of the work respectively, plan, command, control, carry out and finish the kinematic purpose together. The thalamus mainly formats in releasing the sense of thalamus to think, which produces various movement consciousness. The brain spreads into information analysis and produces samples according to seeing and hearing, etc. This sample is about what kind of sport is carried on by people. It is the movement purpose of finishing the task, achieving the goal. Basal ganglion and the cerebellum analyze the sample produced controls, kinematic procedure, order. The striatum and be cerebellum are sport specific controls and commands. The execution of a movement is done by the body (such as the head, hands, feet) or effector.

The thalamus is the organ of the synthesis and release of the sense of thalamus. It is the main body of the "I". The brain association area is the activity place of the sense of thalamus. Consciousness in the brain association area is yet to be achieved. The outputs of motion samples, analyzed by the brain, the basal ganglia and the cerebellum activate the thalamus. According to the motion samples, the thalamus synthesizes and delivers to the brain association area, causes the brain to produce the awareness of motion and also produces the motion intention. Motion intention is consciousness and is divided into three categories: one is from the brain's motor intention, one is from the basal ganglia, the cerebellum's motor sensory and one kind is from sensory neurons after the motion sense.

The main function of the brain is to analyze the portion that produces samples. The frontal lobe is the most advanced and important organ, including the association area, the premotor and motor areas. Frontal, occipital and temporal association zones are the main areas of activity of consciousness. According to the needs of the external environment, they can produce motor intention, clear movement direction or a mode of behavior. The brain is not motor-specific control, command and does not analyze the program and instructions of motor, which are executed by the basal ganglia and cerebellum, so that people can concentrate on all kinds of thinking activity. The brain frontal lobe motor area administers the movement order and at the end of the procedure executes its release. The motor area will exercise the program, and the instruction is issued to produce the movement. The motor area obeys the association area and the consciousness. Consciousness may suspend the motor procedure, and the instruction release at any time, and thus the movement can be interrupted.

The basal ganglia are the main organs of motor control and command. Analysis of output samples of basal ganglia include control, campaign director, procedures and instructions. Motor sample analysis and production obey the motor intention. The basal ganglia and cerebellum analyze and produce motion samples according to the motor intention when brain association area forms the motor intention. Functions of the cerebellum are in many aspects, and there may participate in the consciousness, experiences and motor activities. In the process of movement, cerebellum analyzes output motion parameters, motion control details for motion accuracy and precision work.

When there is contact with external things, there is a need to take appropriate action to deal with it properly, and the brain analyzes and produces that with the real required sample. It produces the movement intention and arouses the basal ganglion, and the cerebellum is controlled, thereby commanding the body's involvement in sports. Brain produces samples according to the information analysis of afferent seeing and hearing, and this sample has two efferent pathways: the first pathway through associating fiber activation of the dorsomedial nucleus of the thalamus and the pulvinar. Dorsomedial nucleus of the thalamus, pillow and formats release the motion sense of thalamus to think, which enters consciousness, which is to carry on the kinematic intention; another pathway is through the projection fiber activation of the basal ganglia, cerebellum. According to the motion intention of basal ganglia and cerebellum, it analyzes and produces motion samples.

The main function of the basal ganglia and the cerebellum is to analyze and produce movement samples. There are three steps in the outgoing path of the moving sample. Through the three steps of the relay, the control and the command, the execution of the movement is completed. In the first step, basal ganglia, cerebellum with efferent fibers link to the ventral anterior nucleus of thalamus and ventral lateral nucleus. Basal ganglia and cerebellum analyze and produce the movement sample activated by the sense of thalamus of the ventral anterior nucleus of thalamus, ventral lateral nucleus through efferent fibers and then enter into the dorsal thalamus in the inner side of the nuclear after thalamic fiber contact, through the medial dorsal nucleus of the thalamus issued to the frontal association area into consciousness. The brain association area is the collection place of all consciousness. Samples of these sports have not been carried out before entering consciousness yet; it is sufficient to just tell the sports that the brain will carry on soon, and let brain know the upcoming movement before the start of the event. The brain can suspend sports at any time before the sports begin, and can adjust the movement purpose at any time according to the changing situation. Environmental changes to make basal ganglion and cerebellum to analyze and produce the new sport sample, thus achieving the goal of adjusting the movement; in the second step, the ventral anterior nucleus of thalamus, ventral lateral nucleus efferent fibers to the motor areas and the premotor cortex of the brain, ventral anterior nucleus and ventral lateral nucleus of thalamus will deliver motion samples to the motor areas, the premotor cortex of the brain by efferent fibers; in the third step, motor areas of the brain contact the low-grade motor neuron through the pyramidal tract, the motion sample is released to the motor neuron through the pyramidal tract. The front motor area is subject to the domination of the contacting area of the frontal lobe. In order to release, motion samples finally obey with the consciousness of the association area of the frontal lobe.

When the motion is executed, the motion sense will be introduced to the brain through the sensory neurons, the brain further analyzes the kinematic execution, performance and forms an intact loop. On analysis of the brain output samples and striatum, it was found that cerebellum analysis output motion samples are different. The brain analyzes and outputs samples which are mainly activated sense of thalamus to generate movement intention. These samples are produced by the frontal, temporal and occipital lobes according to changes in the external environment, objective behavior, need to complete the tasks of production that are analyzed, inability to command the movement. Motion samples are produced by striatal and cerebellar analysis that can control, direct the movement and activate the ventral anterior nucleus of thalamus, ventral lateral nucleus into consciousness. On the other hand, it controls, commands and directs the movement procedures and instructions. In the brain, the movement related consciousness has three aspects, namely, the movement intention, the feeling before movement and the feeling after the movement. The movement intention is the need for movement awareness in which the brain analyzes the output according to external environment. The feeling before motion is the upcoming motion consciousness, which is produced by the sense of thalamus activated by basal ganglia, cerebellum output analysis sample. The feeling after movement is after the effect of the motion is felt, which is produced by sensory neuron activated sense of thalamus.

According to the motor model, the basal ganglia analyze and output movement samples. The motion model is formed through learning and practice. People are born, with no technical skill, but they perform different things such as constant contact, various movements are constant and heuristic form the stationary movement mode progressively, set up motion model. The motion model in essence is still the motion sample, but the motion sample is stored in the basal ganglia. In the process of motor learning and action practice, the basal ganglia analyze and constantly output the motion sample, controlling and directing movement, while the motion samples are stored up, repeatedly forming the motion model many times. The formed motion model is the reference basis for the next motion sample analysis. When the motion model is established in the basal ganglia, the motion can exercise in accordance with the existing model automatically. It does not need the brain to participate in

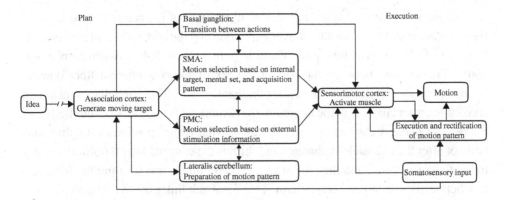

Fig. 6.5. Motor control pathway

the specifics and can automatically implement without consciousness. The habits which people often talk about and the various operative skills are like this.

The motor control path function can be roughly divided into motor planning, motor preparation and motor execution (Figure 6.5). Motor planning loop involves two parallel loops:

(1) Terminal leaf, outside motor front area and cerebellum pathway loop, is very important in the movement of the space direction. This movement is at the leading position in the early skill learning.
(2) When a skill has been acquired and driven by the internal representation, the SMA, the basal ganglia and the temporal lobe circuit become dominant.

These two loops converge in the motor cortex, where it is the connection between the cortex and the body. This connection makes it possible for autonomous movement.

The cerebellum participates in the regulation of body balance and muscle tension, as well as the coordination of free movement through the rich spread in and out the connections between it and the brain, brainstem and spinal cord. The cerebellum is a large regulator that regulates body balance. Body balance is a reflective process, and the flocculonodular lobe is the central unit of this reflex activity. The information that the body equilibrates the change is spread into the flocculonodular lobe of the cerebellum by the nerve and vestibule kernel of the vestibule and is carried out by the organ perception of the vestibule. According to this information, the cerebellum issues an impulse on body balance regulation, the vestibule spinal tract reaches the motor neurons in the anterior horn of the spinal cord, the spinal nerve reaches the muscle, coordinates the antagonistic muscles and tension of motion, so as to allow the body to maintain a balance.

Voluntary movement is the intentional movement of the cerebral cortex, while the coordination of the voluntary movement is done by the hemisphere of the cerebellum, namely, the new cerebellum. There is bidirectional link between cerebellum and cerebral cortex between the part of the cerebral cortex efferent fiber pontine neurons, and the projection to the cerebellar hemisphere. The cerebellar hemisphere spreads the fiber changes in the neuron in the dentate nucleus. The fiber emitted from the dentate nucleus can then project to the external lateral portion of the thalamus belly or after the red nucleus changes and throws the external lateral portion directly to the thalamus belly, and then throws to the cerebral cortex, forming the feedback link between the brain and cerebellum. This feedback link plays a regulatory role in the voluntary movement of the cerebral cortex and is the most advanced in mankind.

6.5 EEG Signal Analysis

6.5.1 EEG signal sorting

The electroencephalogram is divided for spontaneous electroencephalography (EEG) and evoked potentials (EP) too. Spontaneous EEG is the spontaneous generation of neural cells in the human brain without specific external stimuli. Here, the so-called spontaneous is relative, and does not refer to any particular outside environment to stimulate. The spontaneous electroencephalogram is non-stationary random signal, and not only does its rhythm, change with the changes in the mental state, but also in the background of the basic rhythm which occurs from time to time, such as rapid eye movement, etc. EP exerts and stimulates the sense organ (photic, acoustic or electric) and artificially changes the brain electric potential. Patterns evoked by stimulation can be divided into auditory evoked potential (AEP), visual evoked potential (VEP), somatosensory evoked potential (SEP) and the use of a variety of psychological factors such as the preparation of a variety of voluntary activity evoked event-related potentials (ERP). ERP fusion up the psychology of the cerebral cortex of neurophysiology and cognitive process. It includes P300 (reflecting the objective indicator of the cognitive function of the human brain), N400 (language comprehension and expression of related potentials) and endogenous components. ERP and a number of cognitive processes, such as psychological judgment, understanding, identification, attention, selection, making decisions, directional response and some language functions, etc. are closely related.

Spontaneous EEG signals reflect the electrical activity of the human brain and the functional state of the brain, and its essential features include cycle, amplitude, phase and so on. About EEG classification, according to the different frequency bands, the amplitude can be divided into the following EEG waves:

(1) δ wave: Frequency band range 0.5 $\sim$ 3 Hz, the amplitude is generally about 100 μV. In sober normal people's electroencephalogram, we cannot generally record δ wave. In the study of adult's lethargy, either on infant and preschool children and mature adult of intelligence development, we can record this kind of wave. When influenced by some medicines, the brain will cause δ wave while having organic disease.

(2) θ wave: Frequency band ranges 4 $\sim$ 7 Hz, the amplitude is generally 20–40 μV, it appears when the frontal lobe, terminal leaf are relatively obvious, generally sleepy. It is the manifestation of the inhibitory state of the central nervous system.

(3) α wave: Frequency band range 8 $\sim$ 13 Hz, the amplitude of the rhythm is generally 10 $\sim$ 0μV, with amplitude and space distribution of the normal person's α wave, also the individual difference exists. There are activities of the α wave, but the most prominent is by carrying the pillow department, and bilateral symmetry, that appear most when one is quiet and closes one's eyes. In this case, the amplitude is also the highest, but with open eyes, acceptance of others while being irritated at the question of thinking takes place and hence, the α wave disappears and presents the other fast wave.

(4) β wave: Frequency band range 14 $\sim$ 30 Hz, the amplitude is generally less than 30μV, distributes over the volume, central area and center front temple, it is easiest to present in the frontal lobe. α rhythm disappears, presents β rhythm at the time of physiological reaction. β rhythm relates to the fact nervously and excitedly. So, we usually think β rhythm is "activity" type or desynchronizing typologically.

(5) γ wave: Frequency band range 30 $\sim$ 45 Hz, the amplitude is generally less than 30 μV, frontal area and central authorities are the most affected, and β wave belongs to the fast wave, where the fast wave increases. It is the excitement-type manifestation increase of the nerve cell where the amplitude increases.

It is generally believed that normal brain wave frequency range in general is between 4 and 45 Hz, and cortex pathological change will cause the unusual frequency component in some brain waves.

ERP fusion up the psychology of the cerebral cortex of neurophysiology and cognitive process. Many cognitive processes, such as psychological judgment, understanding, recognition, attention, selection, making decisions, orienting response and some language functions, etc., are closely related associations. Typical ERP are as follows:

(1) P300: P300 is a kind of event-related potential, and its peak value is about 300 ms after the event occurs. The smaller the probability of occurrence of relevant events, the more prominent is the P300.
(2) VEP: the VEP changes in the brain specific parts of the brain, called VEP (EEG).
(3) Event-related synchronization (ERS) or desynchronization electric potential (ERD): In unilateral limb movements or imagined movements, the contralateral brain areas produce events related to the synchronous potential, the same side of the brain region generates ERS.
(4) Slow cortical electric potentials: slow cortical potential (SCP) refers to the changes of the cortical potentials, for the duration of a few hundred milliseconds to a few seconds. Through feedback training, it can autonomously control the positive or negative deviation in SCP amplitude.

The above-mentioned several kinds of brain electric signals are adopted as BCI input signal, having their own characteristics and limitations. P300 and VEP all belong to EP, they do not need training, their signal detection is simpler and has great accuracy rate. The weak point is that it needs extra amazing device to offer and stimulate, and depends on certain consciousness of people (such as the vision). Some other advantages are that the signal does not rely on outside stimulate and can produce, but requires a large number of special training.

6.5.2 EEG signal analytical method

In 1932, Dietch first used the Fourier transform for EEG feature analysis, and introduced classical methods such as frequency-domain analysis, time domain analysis, etc. in EEG research field. In recent years, methods such as wavelet analysis, nonlinear dynamics analysis, neural network analysis, chaos analysis, statistics, etc., and an organic combination of the analytical method effectively promoted the development of EEG signal analysis method. With the development of the research work, the analysis of EEG patterns with time and spatial information has also become an effective way to study EEG signals. EEG signal analysis technology is widely used at present:

1. Time domain analysis: the extraction of features directly from the time domain is the first developed method, because it has strong intuitive and clear physical meaning. Time domain analysis is mainly used to directly extract waveform features, such as zero crossing point analysis, histogram analysis, analysis of variance, correlation analysis, peak detection and waveform parameter analysis, coherent average, waveform recognition and so on. In addition, using the parameter model (such as AR model, etc.) is an important means to analyze the signal in time domain, and the feature parameters can be classified, identified and tracked by EEG. However, as the waveform of EEG signal is too complex, there is no particular effective method of EEG waveform analysis.

2. Frequency domain analysis: As many of the main features of the EEG signal are reflected in the frequency domain, power spectrum estimation is an important means of frequency domain analysis and spectrum analysis technology has special important position in EEG signal processing. Its significance lies in the change of amplitude with time of the brain wave transform to EEG power with frequency changes in the spectrum, which can be directly observed in the distribution and transformation of EEG frequency. Spectral estimation method can generally be divided into classical methods and modern methods. Classical spectrum estimation method is by definition with finite length data to directly estimate, namely, to short period data of the Fourier transform-based cycle method, mainly in two ways: indirect method to estimate the correlation function, after Fourier transform we obtain the power spectrum estimation (according to the Wiener Khintchine theorem); direct method and random data direct Fourier transform, where we take the amplitude square to get the corresponding power spectrum estimation, also known as periodogram. The common problem of the two methods is that the variance of the estimation is not good, and the estimated value along the frequency axis of the fluctuation is more severe, the longer the data, the more serious the phenomenon. In order to improve the resolution of spectral estimation, a set of modern spectral estimation theory is formed based on the parameter model. The parametric model estimation method can obtain high-resolution spectrum analysis result, which provides an effective method for the extraction of EEG signal in the frequency domain. However, the power spectrum estimation cannot reflect the time variability of the EEG spectrum. Therefore, the power spectrum of the time-varying non-stationary process of EEG can be lost when the power spectrum of the single frequency domain is lost.

3. Time–frequency analysis: The time–frequency analysis technology is different from traditional time domain or frequency domain analysis; it is a simultaneously in time and frequency domain of signal analysis technology, mainly divided into two types of linear and nonlinear transform. Linear transformation mainly includes:

short time Fourier transform, Gabor transform and wavelet transform technology. Nonlinear transformations mainly include: Wigner–Ville distribution, Cohen class distribution, etc. Time–frequency analysis of the main idea is spreading the time-domain signal in the frequency plane. It will be expressed in time as the independent variable signal expressed by two parameters: time and frequency as a function of the independent variables, thus showing the frequency components of the signal at different time points. Compared with the traditional Fourier transform, the time frequency analysis is more advantageous to the characteristic of non-stationary and time-varying signals. In the EEG signal analysis, the main application of time–frequency analysis technology is in EEG feature waveform recognition and feature extraction. At present, the most widely used method is the theory of wavelet transform. Wavelet analysis in high frequency uses short window, uses the window width at low frequencies, fully reflects the frequency analysis of the relative bandwidth and meets and turns into analytic thoughts of the definition, thus offers a possible route for real-time analysis of the signal. At present, the time–frequency analysis of EEG has made a lot of valuable research results.

4. Space–time analysis: Consider the space distribution of the EEG on the scalp, merged analytically with in the intersection of space–time and analytical method, you will find that this is helpful to reveal and enhance the implicit characteristics of the multi-signal. For example, motor, sensory and cognitive activities in space for performance parts have obvious difference, therefore, temporal and spatial information of identifying, analyzing and fusion may get more in-depth research results. The analysis methods of spatial and temporal patterns are more, such as the microstate, spatial spectrum estimation, classical statistical methods (correlation function), spatial filter and so on. These combined with multi-dimensional statistical analysis method of spatial filtering methods, such as principal component analysis (PCA), independent component analysis (ICA), public space model (common spatial pattern, CSP), in the EEG signal analysis processing fields have very important applications. Specifically, PCA is a linear transform and processing signal to do singular value decomposition, and then finds out the signals in the main composition as a basis for judgment. Based on the higher order statistics, the ICA represents the latest development theories of modern statistical signal analysis. Studies have shown that ICA is very suitable for multi-channel EEG signal analysis, and yields very good results in EEG elimination noise and feature extraction. Calculating the spatial filter to detect the event related to the phenomenon of CSP (ERD) algorithm is the most successful method in the EEG feature extraction algorithm, and has been widely used in BCI. Time and space analysis method can give people more information, and it is an important research direction in EEG signal analysis in recent years.

6.6 Encoding Motor

6.6.1 Overview

Brain information coding has been studied for a long time. In the 1920s, Adrian proposed the concept of nerve action potential, an experimental work in the 1930s. It provides some of the basic clues for exploring the information to the brain. In 1949, Hebb proposed the classical cell populations [206], to the 1972 Barlow's individual neurons coding assumptions [51], and in 1996, Fujii proposed dynamic neuron cluster space–time coding hypothesis [161]; the debate continues between different views. The important question is whether the single neurons or neuron clusters encoded stimulus information is neuronal action potentials of a clear time or potential pulse of the mean firing rate of carrying information? Due to the high complexity of the nervous system, using the existing experiment does not completely resolve neuron information coding principle. But more and more results suggest the coding of information in the nervous system and processing in the framework of specific firing rate and firing pattern, which is constituted by a large number of neuron encoding a cluster of activities. In the cluster of neurons, the activity of each neuron has its own characteristics, so there are some differences. However, through the short correlation with other neurons, they were coordinated, characterized by dynamic relationship between neuronal populations and the overall activity of the neurons, to achieve a variety of information parallel processing and transmission.

The population coding as a generic model of brain information processing is mainly due to the responses of single neurons to stimuli, which is full of noise and stimulates the value change and the lack of sensitivity of such experimental facts. Therefore, it is representative of a single neuron carrying information, which is very low. To overcome this limitation, the brain must allocate information to a large number of population of neurons to carry the precise information about the stimulus [381].

A key feature of population encoding is its robustness and plasticity, because information encoded on the basis of sharing by many neurons can be completed, so a single neuron injury can influence the coding process. Population encoding also has some other advantages, such as the noise level can be reduced, and contribution to the formation of short-range information storage, etc., while the encoding way also has the characteristics of complexity and nonlinearity.

A way of population encoding of neurons is the classical discharge rate model for the group of encoding. In the early stage of research, the response of the neuron to a given stimulus is described by the number of the action potential in the unit time. The measurement value for the discharge rate is generally induced by stimulation of the discharge rate of the average response, the typical case is bell-shaped distribution, and superimposed on the noise composition, where noise in each measurement changes. Early attention was focused on the discharge rate because the parameter is simple, easy to measure and easy to understand. Although not containing a wide variety of neural information, such as the size of the stimulus intensity, there is no complete understanding of the neural information on how the action potential is to be encoded, but the basic unit of action potential as neural information encoding is doubtful. Of course, the other aspects of the response characteristics, such as the precise timing of the action potential occurs, namely, the discharge sequence pattern is also important for the information encoding significance.

Considered under the influence of various noise levels and correlation of neurons through a given stimulus condition recorded neuronal activity, probability model was established to describe the relationship between external stimuli and neuronal response and has become a general method to the study of population coding. Based on a broad consensus, there has been lots of research on the population analysis of coding and decoding. Research has been performed on how to quantify population coding information. Rolls *et al.* used the information theory method for the quantification of neuron population coding information of the visual cortex in macaque temporal lobe. The study found that the coding information exists roughly in the linear growth with the number of neurons [38]; Franco *et al.* discovered that encoding information not only exists in the discharge times of single neurons; it is also affected by the neuronal activity of cross-correlation effects. It points out that the independent neuron stimulation of the cross-correlation effects generated based on the redundancy of discharge rate of the coded information is very small, and relies on the stimulation of the cross-correlation effects on the coding information in the inferior temporal visual cortex contribution, which is very small [158]. To explore the characteristics of population encoding and decoding from entropy and mutual information [350], Kang *et al.* adopted the statistical dynamics method to calculate the mutual information of population neurons. The results found mutual information exponent saturation with the population size in discrete stimuli, saturation exponent is different from acupuncture induced neuronal response probability of the Chernoff distance [231]; Paninski has canvassed and collected the non-parametric estimation problems of entropy and mutual information in population coding [350]. From the point of view of computing, Fisher information is a measure of encoding and the decoding accuracy of common means and effective indicators [374]. For example, Abbott *et al.* pointed out that under normal circumstances as long as the population size is large enough, correlation is not limited to finding coding accuracy for growth, and discussed some cases (for example, addition of noise and multiplicative noise) of correlation on how to improve coding accuracy [3], when they studied the neuronal influence on collecting the precision of population coding of discharge rate diversity of cross-correlation, through calculation of Fisher information volume of encoding course; Sompolinsky found that with positive correlation to reduce the prediction ability of neural network, information capacity increases with the cluster number of the neurons in the growth tend to be saturated, and negative correlation greatly improves the information capacity [466] through the calculation of the Fisher information, with respect to not being associated with neuronal population; Toyoizumi studied the loss of Fisher information estimation problem based on the spike potential of population decoding (without considering the occurrence time of spike potential) [483].

The inference rule of Bayesian is the key to studying the neuron and population coding and decoding; it is the quantization encoding and decodes the behavioral method. As far back as 1998, Zemel proposed the neuron population coding and decoding active probability interpretation under Bayesian's principle frame [535], compared the outside stimulation induced under the condition of neuronal firing activity in the Poisson model, kernel density estimation (KDE) model and the extended Poisson (extended Poisson) model of performance, including encoding, decoding, likelihood and error analysis. In recent years, the theoretical research showed that the brain including the coding and decoding of neural computation process is similar to Bayesian inference process [375]; the Bayesian approach has been successful for perception and sensory control of neural computation theory, and the emerging psychophysical evidence shows that the Ming brain perception computation is the optimal Bayesian, which also led to Knill *et al.* calling it as Bayesian coding hypothesis [238]. From the recording of the activity of neurons firing to reconstruct some of the characteristics of external stimuli, Bayesian inference provides the possibility to reveal the behavior of such decoding process [114]. Ge Yang *et al.* explored the consistency of Bayesian inference with the mixed model of logistic regression [172].

Population neuron coding and decoding is the key problem in the neural information processing, and is the theoretical framework to reveal the working mechanism of the brain and its development can promote the overall function of the brain, for studying more complex cognitive functions that can provide guidance to the basic theory and method. The encoding and decoding method based on Bayesian theory can reveal the characteristics of the information processing process of the nervous system in general, and make an objective and reasonable mathematical explanation for the working mechanism of the brain.

6.6.2 Entropy encoding theory

Information entropy is a measure of the random events of uncertainty, and the amount of information that can reflect by skewness and kurtosis represents the regularity, and is therefore suitable for expression of nonlinear neural firing coding. The coding method of entropy includes: binary string method, direct method, asymptotically unbiased estimation method, neuronal firing interval method, neuronal firing in logarithmic intervals and mutual information method and so on.

1. Two value string method

Mackay and McCulloch proposed two-value string entropy encoding in 1952, the entropy expression is used for neural coding for the first time. The principle of the method is that in time Δt contains r firing sequences that will be discrete in a plurality of narrowband with ΔT, where with and without firing in each band as represented by "1" and "0". The entropy expression of this "1" and "0" sequence is:

$$S[c] = \log_2(^nC_r), \tag{6.14}$$

where

$$^nC_r = \frac{n!}{r!(n-r)!} \tag{6.15}$$

n is the two-value string length, namely, the narrowband number of ΔT; r is the number of "1" value in two-value string.

The two-value string is very long, and it is difficult to calculate its length, so it is often used to approximate the equation. When $n, r, (n-r)$ are large, and the $r \ll n$, Equation (6.14) can be transformed into:

$$S[c|M, \Delta\tau] \approx \log_2 \frac{e}{M\Delta\tau}. \tag{6.16}$$

In Equation (6.16), M is the average firing frequency; ΔT is narrow bandwidth; e is the natural logarithm.

Binary string method can approximately calculate the entropy of the neuronal firing sequence, but this method exists for the problem of bandwidth limitation, namely for different firing sequence and discrete bandwidth where there are no clear standards to determine, thus leading to the calculation of entropy, which may be inconsistent with the actual.

2. Direct entropy encoding

In 1997, van Steveninck and others of Princeton University proposed a direct entropy encoding method [498]. The idea of the encoding method is based on the link between the time of the release of a specific time period before and after the stimulus. Expressions in coded form: will be issue discrete sequence into a plurality narrowband with bandwidth Δt, in each of the narrowband with and without firing were coded by "1" and "0". Under a certain set of constants L, by different combinations of L and adjacent narrowband coding expressions of different "word", and according to the different "word" in the firing sequence of probability distribution of firing sequence, entropy is calculated by:

$$S = -\frac{1}{L\Delta\tau} \sum_{i=1}^{n} p(w_i) \log_2 p(w_i), \qquad (6.17)$$

L is a constant presumed; n is the release of the sequence containing the number of words; w represents i one with length of L; $p(w_i)$ is the probability for the first i "words" in the firing sequence.

The advantage of the direct method is that the entropy has no relations with the narrowband distributing and stimulating the characteristic, but has it existing in a two-value string method to. "The bandwidth question" still exists. For the data sampling question", namely, in order to estimate accurately the appearing probability of "word", we need to gather a large number of data in the experiment; this is often difficult to realize.

In 1997, van Steveninck *et al.* applied constant stimulation and recorded the neuronal response to the fly visual central motor neurons, and used the direct method with quantitative entropy to calculate the repeatability and variability of neuronal firing sequence, in order to study the neural information encoding in a particular class of stimuli.

3. Asymptotic unbiased estimation of entropy encoding

In 2002, Victor proposed the asymptotic unbiased estimation method of entropy encoding. The basic principle of the method is that the neuronal firing sequence "embedded" in a vector space, from Euclidean space limited data set to estimate a continuous distribution entropy of firing sequence [500].

Specific expression of the coding method includes the neuronal firing sequences carrying information in two distributions: One is distribution about releasing the counting, namely, the distribution of the releasing number in time Δt; Another is about the releasing time distribution. Therefore, the discretization for the narrowband can be used to express the released count carry information encoding, a non-narrowband approach can be used to estimate the released time to carry the information encoding. The method makes the nonlinear firing sequence linear and there is continuous embedding space in the vector set, to avoid the "bandwidth".

But at present the method of coding results and the actual physiological mechanism differ and for practical applications, there is still some distance.

4. The neuron firing interval entropy coding

The main idea of releasing interval entropy coding is the application of inter-spike interval (ISI) to express the coding. Firstly, inter-spike interval histogram (ISIH) is used to represent the distribution of ISI, and then to find the appropriate interval probability density function $f_w(w|I)$ to fit the ISIH, and then using $f_w(w|I)$ we calculate the entropy of the ISI:

$$S[w] = -\int_{S_w} f_w(w|I) \log_e f_w(w|I) \mathrm{d}w. \tag{6.18}$$

In Equation (6.18), w is ISI sequence; $f_w(w|I)$ is a suitable conditional probability density function, for example, you can choose gamma function, normal function or Gauss probability density function and so on [293]; S_w is the definition of domain of $f_w(w|I)$.

ISI entropy encoding method can recognize the information which is neglected by the direct method. However, because the mean of ISI is the reciprocal of the release frequency, the ISI entropy method is essentially a encoding method based on the frequency. At present, the application of ISI entropy to express code has been applied in many neurons and cell firing sequence analysis, such as in 1996, Matthews analyzed releasing codes of motor neuron in humans in many kinds of different muscles by the ISI entropy coded method, in order to explain the influence on stimulating and responding to the synaptic noise; in 2001, Leng etc. applied it for explaining the inhibitory effect of neurons for sustained enhancement of synaptic inputs [261]; In 2004, Wetmore and Baker applied the ISI entropy coding method to monkey motor cortex cells firing code, and drew the conclusion that the probability increases gradually when the single neuron of monkey's motor cortex releases again after firing the action potential 30 ms [521] and so on. The problem of this method is that it is difficult to choose the fitting function of ISIH, and the fitting precision needs to be improved.

5. The entropy coding of neurons firing interval of logarithm

The entropy coding of neurons firing interval of logarithm is based on the ISI entropy. The logarithm value of ISI is instead that of ISI values as the x-axis of ISIH, where we construct logarithmic firing interval graphs again with the proper interval probability density function $f_w(w|I)$ to fit logarithmic firing interval graphs. Bhumbra *et al.* proposed to adopt bimodal Gauss function to fit the log interval of many kinds of neurons [54].

If x is $\log_e(ms)$, then a bimodal function $f(x)$ is the weighted coefficient c, two mean values are μ_1 and μ_2, two standard differences are σ_1 and σ_2, the fitting function containing more than five parameters is as follows:

$$f(x) = \frac{c}{\sigma_1\sqrt{2\pi}}e^{-(x-\mu_1)^2/2\sigma_1^2} + \frac{1-c}{\sigma_2\sqrt{2\pi}}e^{-(x-\mu_2)^2/2\sigma_2^2}. \qquad (6.19)$$

We use Levenberg–Marquardt iterative algorithm to optimize the above five parameters and then K–S test parameter D is used to measure the degree of compliance with the data and the bimodal function. In Equation (6.19), D is the largest gap between the expected cumulative density and the actual accumulation probability. The expression of expected cumulative density function $f(x_i \leq x)$ is as follows:

$$f(x_i \leq x) = \int_{-\infty}^{x_i} f(x)dx. \qquad (6.20)$$

Then $f(x)$ is substituted into Equation (6.18) to calculate the logarithm interval entropy.

There are limitations of the logarithm interval graph. It cannot express interval sequence information, since the information may be very important, so further with adjacent intervals of mutual information we measure the two interval information between a firing before and after. The procedure of calculating mutual information is as follows:

(1) With logarithmic interval Y and its precursor x, draw the logarithmic interval scatter plot.
(2) Smoothing the data by using convolution of standard deviation with one standard deviation for logarithm 1/6 2D gauss kernel and scatter plot.
(3) Construct the joint logarithmic plot.
(4) Obtain the joint probability mass distribution $P(x_i, y_i)$ of the adjacent intervals.
(5) By $P(x_i, y_i)$ to calculate the edge probability distribution of the precursor interval $P(x_i)$ and posterior displacement interval $P(y_i)$:

$$P(x_i) = \sum_{j=1}^{N_y} P(x_i, y_i), \qquad (6.21)$$

$$P(y_i) = \sum_{i=1}^{N_x} P(x_i, y_i). \qquad (6.22)$$

N_y and N_x in the above equations are the narrowband numbers of $P(y_i)$ and $P(x_i)$. The entropy $S(X)$ of $P(x_i)$ can be expressed as

$$S(X) = - \sum_{i=1}^{N_y} P(x_i) \log_2 P(x_i).$$ (6.23)

(6) The joint entropy of the joint probability mass distribution $P(x_i, y_i)$ is expressed as

$$S(X, Y) = \sum_{i=1}^{N_x} \sum_{j=1}^{N_y} P(x_i, y_i) \log_2 P(x_i, y_i).$$ (6.24)

The relative entropy $D(X, Y // XY)$ is expressed as

$$D(X, Y // XY) = S(X) + S(Y) - S(X, Y).$$ (6.25)

The relative entropy $D(X, Y // XY)$ is an approximate value of adjacent interval mutual information. However, this approximation is likely to be too high, so we need to introduce a randomized method to correct the random and heavy columns. The Monte-Carlo method can be used to verify whether mutual information is significantly greater than zero.

In 2001, Fairhall *et al.* applied the firing logarithm interval analysis method to the fly visual system to the rapidly changing stimulus response analysis to reveal the importance of short firing interval in neural information expression [140]. In 2004, Bhumbra applied the firing logarithm interval analysis method to compare the quantitative model of the upper kernel neuronal cells of the rat vision, the vasopressin and oxytocin cells [54]. The method also has the limitation of the difficulty of fitting the firing logarithm interval graph.

Compared with the previous four methods, the application of neuron firing series with logarithmically interval entropy and mutual information entropy coding, through the entropy's combination with mutual information can better express the firing neuron coding. One of the development trends of entropy encoding research is the combination of log interval entropy and mutual information entropy, to better reveal the mechanism of the neuron firing encoding.

6.6.3 Bayesian neuronal population encoding

A given stochastic model, connects encode and decode through Bayesian's rule. Here, r represents the response of single neuron or population neurons in stimulating. The stimulus is indicated by phase parameter θ. n neuronal responses are recorded as $r = (r_1, r_2, \ldots, r_n)$, where $r_i, i = 1, 2, \ldots, N$, shows the ith neuron firing rate by spiking count. Of course, in addition to the firing rate, there are the other neural response parameters. The probabilistic function describing the activity of N neurons is introduced as follows:

$P(\theta)$: represents stimulus probability with the parameter θ, it is often called *a priori* probability or prior knowledge.

$P(r)$: the probability of response r recorded in the experiment.

$P(r, \theta)$: the joint distribution probability of these records to the stimulus θ and response r.

$P(r|\theta)$: conditional probability of response r stimulated by stimulus θ.

$P(\theta|r)$: conditional probability of stimulus θ under responses r were recorded.

Note that $P(r|\theta)$ is the probability of observed firing rate r in the stimulus θ. $P(r)$ is the probability of firing rate for r, it does not rely on a particular stimulation value, thus $P(r)$ can be represented in sum of all stimulus weight probability using $P(r|\theta)$, namely,

$$P(r) = \sum_{\theta} P(r|\theta)P(\theta), \tag{6.26}$$

$$P(\theta) = \sum_{r} P(\theta|r)P(r). \tag{6.27}$$

By the definition of conditional probability, we know about the joint probability on stimulus θ and response r is expressed as

$$P(r, \theta) = P(r|\theta)P(\theta) = P(\theta|r)P(r). \tag{6.28}$$

Therefore, we have

$$P(\theta|r) = \frac{P(r|\theta)P(\theta)}{P(r)}. \tag{6.29}$$

It is assumed that $P(r) \neq 0$, which is Bayesian inference theory from $P(r|\theta)$ to $P(\theta|r)$. Coding is described by a set of the probability $P(r|\theta)$ of all stimuli and response, on the other hand, decoding a response is to obtain the probability $P(\theta|r)$. By Bayesian theory, $P(\theta|r)$ can be obtained by $P(r|\theta)$, but needs the stimulus probability $P(\theta)$. Thus, decoding requires the knowledge of the statistical properties of the stimulus that is in the experiment or is naturally occurring.

6.6.4 Bayesian neuronal population decoding

The advantage on decoding of Bayesian's method lies in impelling us to make the clear assumption, we can introduce some simple assumptions first when dealing with the likelihood ratio, then study how to make it more and more practical. Here, we give the joint likelihood $P(r_1, r_2, \ldots, r_n|\theta)$ of these n stimulus neuronal firing rate r_i in the stimulus θ. If we know the stimulus θ, and single neuron firing rate dependent on θ and independent from other neurons firing rate, it is assumed that the different neuronal firing rate is conditionally independent under the stimulus θ, that is,

$$P(r_1, r_2, \ldots, r_n|\theta) = \prod_{i=1}^{n} P(r_1|\theta). \qquad (6.30)$$

This assumption implies that the joint likelihood of all neuronal firing rates is equal to the product of their respective likelihood.

In the mathematical sense, encoding process is described by the conditional probability $P(r|\theta)$ available at a given stimulus θ, and decoding is an inferring process from the observed active population r. The literature [539] pointed out that most of the decoding method can be described systematically by maximum likelihood inference (MLI) or maximize *a posteriori* (MAP), specifically it is implemented by choosing an appropriate likelihood function and *a priori* distribution of the stimulus. They can be summarized as follows.

By Bayesian's rule, given the firing rate r *a posteriori* distribution $P(\theta|r)$ of the stimulus θ is

$$P(\theta|r) = \frac{P(r|\theta)P(\theta)}{P(r)}. \qquad (6.31)$$

Here, $P(r|\theta)$ is the likelihood function, $P(\theta)$ is the distribution of the stimulus θ representing the prior knowledge, $P(r)$ is the normalization factor. MAP estimates the stimulus based on maximizing *a posteriori* distribution logarithmic $\ln P(r|\theta)$, i.e.,

$$\widehat{\theta} = \arg \max_{\theta} \ln P(\theta|r) = \arg \max_{\theta}[\ln P(r|\theta) + \ln P(\theta)]. \qquad (6.32)$$

When the prior knowledge of $P(\theta)$ is unknown or straight, the reduction of MAP to MLI is

$$\widehat{\theta} = \arg \max_{\theta} \ln P(r|\theta). \qquad (6.33)$$

Note that in the decoding stage, by the estimation assumed that $P(r|\theta)$ is equal to the actual model $Q(r|\theta)$, it is said the estimation applied a credible model; when $P(r|\theta)$ is not equal to the $Q(r|\theta)$, it is called a non-credible model. Use of non-credible model is mainly based on two reasons, one is the decoding system where we often do not know the precise information of the coding system, so have to use the non-credible model, especially on the analysis of the experimental data; Second, the computational cost can be greatly reduced through proper simplification of the non-credible model without sacrificing too much decoding accuracy requirements.

The acquisition of the classification estimator $\hat{\theta}$ of maximal plausible reasoning can be obtained through maximizing the likelihood logarithm $\ln P(r|\theta)$, that is, to solve the equation $\nabla \ln P(r|\hat{\theta}) = 0$. Here, $\nabla P(s)$ shows as $dP(s)/ds$, $P(r|\theta)$ is called the decoding model. Three decoding models are considered here, all of these are based on the MLI, and are defined as follows:

(1) Faithful model, $P_F(r|\theta)$, uses all the coding information, and decoding model is the real coding model, that is, $P_F(r|\theta) = Q(r|\theta)$. This method is denoted as FMLI by abridging.
(2) Unfaithful model, $P_U(r|\theta)$, is based on describing neural response activities information of adjusting function, but ignores the interactions between neurons, denoted by UMLI.
(3) Vector model, $P_C(r|\theta)$, does not refer to using any information on the coding process, but makes the rough and simple assumption for the adjusting function, while ignoring the interactions between neurons, denoted by COM.

It needs to be pointed out that the use of the unfaithful model (such as $P_U(r|\theta)$ or $P_C(r|\theta)$ is of great significance. When the researchers reconstructed the stimuli from the recorded data, they were actually using an unfaithful model, because the real encoding process is not known. Further, the correlation between neurons is often complex and changes over time, the brain finds it hard to store and utilize all these information, so unfaithful model MLI (ignore the certain aspects of) is a key to solve such information "disaster".

6.7 Brain–Computer Interface

6.7.1 Overview

Brain–Computer interface (BCI) is the interface that connects the human brain or the animal brain with the outside world. However, this connection is not in a normal and regular way, but is in a special way to connect with the outside world, for example, stimulating the artificial cochlea, the external signal commanding the mice to walk in the maze, the monkey taking bananas with the machine hand and the brain wave controlling the computer. Someone thinks that the essence of the life is information. Since the essence of the artificial brain and the biological brain is to process information and they have the same mechanism in the information processing, they should be able to exchange with the help of the interface. Information is uniform in essence, which will enable great development in computer techniques, artificial brain, combination of human brain and computer.

In 1973, Vidal published the first paper related to BCI [501]. The BCI is not dependent on the brain normal output path, namely, nervous peripherals and muscular tissues, the system can realize human brain communication directly with the external world (computer or other peripheral devices). The failure of setting up the first brain machine interface system is due to its partial start in the program of IBM360/ 91 computer. This kind of machine is a batch processing machine, which cannot meet the needs of real-time processing of BCI system. The progress of recent computer and signal processing technology has opened up a new era of EEG signal analysis and BCI research, where the computer speed can meet the needs of BCI signal processing, so why is the detection of real-time thought still not achieved? Placed in neurons in the vicinity of the microelectrodes to record cell excitatory signals, the idea to control a BCI has many problems. First is to use a large number of brain electrodes to control the individual's thinking, because each individual has a million neurons. In addition, scientists do not understand the relationship between cell excitability and thinking.

The scientists of MIT, Bell Labs and Neural Information Science Research Institute have developed successfully a microcomputer chip which can simulate human nervous system, successfully implanted in the brain, and repair human nerve using the principle of bionics. It cooperates with brain and sends out the complicated order for the electronic device, monitoring the activity of the brain to achieve very good results. People will be able to put microchip in the brain to increase the memory, so that people have a spare brain in the near future.

American researchers in the field of biological computer bonded cells took the animal brain tissue with computer hardware, such developed machine is called biological electronic robot or cyborg. If the chip is in good agreement with the nerve endings, the chip can be connected to the nerve fibers and the body's brain nervous system. This will improve the human brain function through the computer.

In 1999, Liaw and Burger of the University of Southern California proposed a dynamic synapse neural circuit model [276], and in 2003 they developed a brain chip, which can replace the function of the hippocampus. The brain chip was successfully demonstrated *in vivo* mouse, which was consistent with the information processing in the brain of *in vivo* rat. This project is a part of the Mind-Machine Merger, which has made breakthrough progress, and has been ranked as one of the top 10 scientific and technological advances in the world in 2003 by the Chinese scientific community.

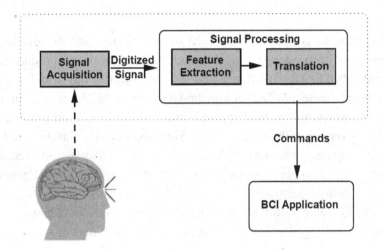

Fig. 6.6. Basic architecture of BCI system

BCI systems generally have three function modules containing signal acquisition, signal analysis and controller (see Figure 6.6).

(1) Signal acquisition: the experimenter header wears an electrode cap, gathers EEG signal and conveys to the amplifier, the signal generally needs to be amplified to about 10,000 times. Through the preprocessing, including signal filtering and A/D conversion, it is finally transformed into digital signals and stored in the computer.

(2) Signal analysis: utilizing algorithms such as FFT, wavelet analysis, etc., from the preprocessed EEG signals to draw the particular features correlated to experimenter's intention; after drawing the features, it will be classified by the classifier. The output of the classifier is regarded as the input of the controller.

(3) Controller: the classified signal is converted to the actual action, such as the cursor on the display movement, mechanical hand movement, the letter input, controlling the wheelchair, opening the television, etc. Some of the BCI systems are also provided with a feedback loop (as shown in Figure 6.6), which can not only let experimenters clear their thinking control results, but also help the experimenters to adjust the brain electric signal according to the result at the same time, in order to reach the desired objectives.

6.7.2 Brain–Computer interface technology

In the past 10 years, BCI technology has been developed rapidly in the following research directions of information technology.

1. VEP

A plurality of options is displayed on the display device, and the user looks at a desired option. By processing the display mode, it can make people produce different EEG signals when looking at different options. A more direct way to look at the target is to track people's attention. But this method requires the head to remain motionless, it is difficult to achieve practical applications. And the BCI based on EEG did not restrict the movement of the head. In 1992, Sutter developed a real-time BCI system called brain response system [474]. It displays $8*8$ matrix notation in accordance with a pseudo-random binary sequence (known as m-sequence) in red/green colors alternately. The user watches the symbol he/she wants to select. Comparing the measured EEG signal with the prerecorded template, you can determine whether the user watches the goal or not. User can use the system to operate word processing software.

2. ERP

(1) P300 potential

P300 is a kind of ERP, and its peak value appears about 300 ms after the dependent event. Event related probability is small, when caused by P300 it is significant and in the head of the parietal region (middle part in header or posterior) it is the most significant. When one exerts different kinds of constituent stimulus, by measuring the range of P300 that every kind of stimulus causes, one can find the P300 range in which those stimuli that seldom appear are large, and this kind of stimulus is required as they are counted by experimenters, or the stimulus that the user wants to choose. In 1988, Farwell *et al.* developed a virtual typewriter using P300 [143]. In A 6×6 character matrix by row or column flashing, the order is random, then "the user that wants to enter the character of the row or column flicker" is a related events. Seeking to cause the P300 amplitude of the largest row and column, the line and the column intersection on the character is to print the character.

(2) ERD

Pfunscheller and his colleagues developed a system [363], which is similar with the literature [530]. They adopted a concentrated approach in the central area of the scalp, namely, the multi-electrode on sensory motor cortex and observation with the produced μ rhythm (under awake state). When people do not process the sensory input to the process or generate the output motion, in the sensory and motor cortical areas often show EEG activity of 8–12 Hz. When the concentration is in the sensory or motor cortex, the slow wave is in μ rhythm. While the focus is on the visual cortex is called the amplitude change of visual μ rhythm and other rhythm. The amplitude of this particular frequency band is associated with increased and decreased motor activity, respectively, known as ERS and ERD.

Training a neural network helps to recognize the ERS/ERD patterns caused by particular sports (for example, right- or left-hand movement, or hold in one hand of the game card T to the right or left), and discern finally the pattern which is produced by the action that wants to achieve it. Then Hibert transform is adopted to extract the key features of these patterns, and learning vector quantization (LVQ) or Kohonen neural network is used to classify them. When the neural network is trained 100–200 times, the system will be able to identify the EEG pattern caused by specific movement with very high accuracy, which can control the cursor movement or other external devices. For example, when the EEG data for one second can be predicted with the left-hand or the right-hand movement, the accuracy rate is up to 89%. Now, researchers are studying the stability of the pattern that corresponds to the continuous motion and the method of improving the rate and accuracy of the pattern recognition.

3. Spontaneous EEG for action training

Wolpaw *et al.* found that people can learn to use the spontaneous EEG activity [529], which is not caused by the special evoked stimulation activities, to control the external instrument. They focus on the training the obtained μ rhythm and the related EEG component, the obtained μ rhythm is generated by the sensorimotor cortex, recorded at the center of the head of the electrical activity. Experimenters learn to use the selected μ rhythm and/or other EEG components. A cursor located in the center of the display screen is moved to the surrounding target. The cursor is moved as the output because it is objective, easy to implement and quantify. It can be used as a prototype of a variety of rehabilitation equipment, and can be used to operate the mouse driver. In a one-dimensional (1D) model, the target is located at the top or bottom of the screen edge, and the cursor moves vertically.

In a 2D mode, the target may be located anywhere (e.g., one of the four corners), and the cursor has both vertical and horizontal movements. The EEG in a specific frequency range is obtained by online spectral analysis, and is converted to the cursor movement. For example, in one dimension, high-amplitude rhythms recorded in the sensorimotor cortex of one cerebral hemisphere 8–12 Hz μ rhythm enable the cursor to move on. The low amplitude is used to move the cursor down. A function that transforms the magnitude to the cursor movement is a linear equation. The parameters are derived from the evaluation of the previous performance of the user. In a 2D model, an equation controls the vertical movement, another equation controls the level of movement. Most users can get obvious control ability after 5–10 stage. After more training, they will be able to reach the top or bottom of the target in 1–2 s with higher than or equal to 90% accuracy. For the 2D control, although it is very significant, it cannot achieve such a high accuracy rate. Now we try to improve the accuracy and speed of the cursor movement, depending on the definition of alternative and/or can increase the training of the EEG component, or rely on the improvement of the EEG control into the cursor moving algorithm. The ultimate goal of this work is like a mouse cursor movement, so as to make the EEG brain responsible for human–computer interface, which can be used to operate a commercial mouse driver.

4. Self-regulation of steady-state VEP

By movement training method, McMillan *et al.* trained some volunteers to control the steady-state VEP amplitude caused by fluorescent tubes with flash 13.25 Hz [307]. The electrode is placed in the occipital cortex to measure the change in the magnitude with a horizontal stripe and/or feedback auditory sound to the experimenter. The change in magnitude is transformed into the input of control through real-time analysis. If the VEPI amplitude is above or below the specified threshold, a discrete control output is generated. These outputs can be used to control many kinds of instruments. After training for about 6 hours, the experimenter can basically achieve an accuracy rate higher than 80% of the command of a flight simulator to the left or to the right turning. In-flight simulation training, the experimenter, after 3–5 stages of training, will be able to control a neuromuscular controller to execute the knee extension with 95% accuracy.

At present, in BCI area the leading laboratories in the world and their BCI research directions are as follows:

(1) Graz University of Technology, Austria
   Pfunscheller *et al.* apply ERS/ERD potential as BCI signal input. In this system, the experimenter can control the movement of the cursor.
(2) Wadsworth Center, USA
   Wolpaw *et al.* trained experimenters to adjust freely themselves to μ rhythm, and through changes of μ rhythms to achieve the cursor movement, letters' spelling and prosthetic control and other functions. Due to its flexible control owning the μ rhythm is more difficult, so not every experimenter can learn to use this device.
(3) Tübingen University, Germany
   Birbaumer *et al.* designed a thought translation device (TTD), through changes of the SCP to achieve control to the outside world, using visual feedback, to realize the function of letters' spelling.

(4) University of Illinois, USA

Farwell *et al.* adopted P300 EP as the BCI signal input. On a computer screen, 36 letters are shown in a 6 × 6 lattice. Experimenter is required to select a particular letter. Each line and each column flicker with a frequency of 10 Hz, for each row and each column the scintillation average reaction is calculated, measuring P300 amplitude. The greatest response to rows and columns that contain a particular letter' can be "found" in a specific letter from the P300 EP.

(5) Department of Biomedical Engineering, Tsinghua University, China

Gao *et al.* developed a non-invasive BCI system with high transmission rate based on steady-state VEP, which can be used for motion control, or environmental control equipment and other fields, after they studied in-depth the characteristics analysis and extraction method of steady-state visual evoked potential (SSVEP).

6.7.3 P300 Brain–computer interface system

P300-ERP is a kind of ERP which is induced by small probability event (visual, auditory, tactile and other sensory). It gained the name because a positive potential waveform in EEG after about 300 ms happens in the incident that corresponds to [475]. The P300 potential of BCI using a specific event stimulus sequence evoked the user's P300 potential through the occurrence of P300 to determine the user's awareness activities. This type of BCI is particularly suitable for selecting a target from multiple options. In recent years, there has been new P300-BCI systems; these systems have non-alphabetic symbols and objects as input options, and may combine EP P300 and virtual reality applications and so on.

1. Architecture

We take P300 Chinese input BCI system as an example to explain the architecture of the P300 BCI system. The system consists of user interface, EEG acquisition system and EEG analysis program, the composition of the system is shown in Figure 6.7 [531]. The user interface induces the P300 potentials of user by visual stimulation, and transmits the amplifier marking flashing moment event code. EEG acquisition system consists of P300 EEG signal, amplification, filtering, digitalization, merging with the event code and transfers to the EEG analysis program. The analysis program is responsible for the EEG online processing, converting the acquisition of P300 information into the selection of instructions, and then transmits real-time feedback to the user interface for the input of Chinese characters.

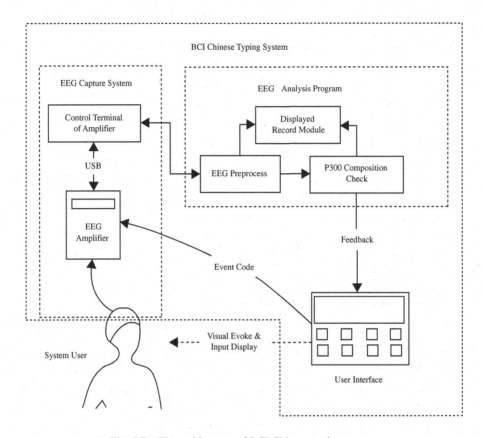

Fig. 6.7.   The architecture of BCI Chinese typing system

EEG analysis program and user interface program run on different PC machines. The user interface appears through the computer display. The EEG acquisition system uses a neuroscan with 40 EEG amplifier and multi-channel electrode cap. EEG analysis program processes EEG signal data and preserves intermediate data of EEG for later experimental analysis. As shown in Figure 6.7, if we regard the user as the constituent element of the system, then the flow of information of the overall system forms a closed loop.

In the course of typing, the user interface sends a flickering message to the EEG processing program to indicate the finish state and then enters the wait state, after the end of each selection phase. After receiving this message, the processing program reads the EEG data from the buffer, and sends the corresponding P300 command to the interface after analyzing and judging. If the program thinks that the P300 cannot be reliably identified, the command is sent out empty. An effective command is received by the interface and will be sent to the input of the Chinese character spelling module; if receiving an empty command the system does not carry out any action and restarts a new round of selection of flashing.

2. Visual elicitor subsystem

Visual-evoked signal is the core module of P300 BCI system. It is also the most flexible part in the entire system and has a certain decisive role to the configuration modes of other modules. The visual elicitor subsystem includes three parts: layout management, experimental parameter configuration and maintenance of experimental scheme. Layout management module supports different types of different control calls and location, distance and other parameters of the adjustment function, and has a very friendly operation and control. Parameter configuration interface involves a variety of experimental parameters and the configuration of the appearance parameters of the control. There is a very high configuration flexibility, which can almost meet the needs of the general P300 experiment parameters control. The final scheme maintenance module provides the maintenance of the experimental evoking design scheme, including the storage, reading and other functions of the experimental scheme.

3. EEG acquisition subsystem

EEG acquisition subsystem contains P300 EEG signal amalgamation with incident code after amplification, filtering, digitization and transferred to the EEG analysis program. It improves the reliability of P300 detection. The preprocessing program processes the EEG signal corresponding to each option as a unit.

(1) Removing the direct current drift of signals. We deduct the mean value of the original signal at first and remove the general direct component. This signal still contains the frequency of less than 0.5 Hz of the DC drift, the performance of the baseline of the ups and downs. We regard 1s as the sampling interval to fetch sample equally. The sampling points generate three spline curves, as the baseline of the signal. The signal is subtracted from the spline curve and the baseline drift is eliminated.

(2) Eliminating the electric disturbance of eyes. The blink movements of experimental subjects will align with the relevant electric potential of the eye in EEG. Because of its large peak amplitude, it will seriously interfere with the identification of P300 potential. Regression algorithm can be used to eliminate the interference of the eye. In addition to the EEG, the simultaneous acquisition of electrical signals of eye (EOG) is needed. By calculating we know whether the slope of the EOG baseline exceeds a certain threshold to judge the occurrence time of the blink. For this time period, the EEG signal is corrected.

(3) Filter. We signal to the cut-off frequency of low-pass filtering 15 Hz, eliminating the high-frequency interference. Five-order Butterworth filter is used as the filter algorithm.

(4) Signal segmentation. The selected signal is divided into n segments according to the corresponding round. Each round signal subdivides into seven flash sections. Each flash time spans 600 ms, begins to calculate appearance since incidents correspond to code constantly. The flash section contains possible P300 potential.

4. EEG analysis subsystem

EEG analysis subsystem is responsible for the EEG online processing, the P300 information is converted into the choice instruction followed by real-time feedback to the user interface for the input of Chinese characters. The system has the functions of superposition average, template matching, discriminant recognition and so on.

(1) Superimposed average. The different round flash data corresponding to the same event code is classified as one kind, so we get a total of seven categories, each class containing n flashing sections. The flashing sections of each class are superimposed on Equation (6.34):

$$mEEG_i = \frac{1}{n \sum_{k=1}^{n} EEG_{i,k}}, \qquad (6.34)$$

where $EEG_{i,k}$ is the value of the k flashing segment at the time point i, $mEEG_i$ is represented by the value of the superimposed signal at the time point i. After overlay, each choice gets the seven flash data segment search, respectively representing the EEG data after different option box flashing.

(2) Template matching. The template is a prepared P300 data in advance, which is a typical P300 potential waveform signal for each pathway of the user. The time span of the template signal is 400 ms, corresponding to the 200–600 ms of the scintillation (flash) segment.

Template matching is carried out by the degree of the difference between a metric that characterizes the measured scintillation (flash) signal segment and the template signal. Can the random signal correlation number s as the matching metric and pathway c and its template s value expressions as shown in Equation (6.35):

$$S_c = \frac{\sum x_{c,i} m_{c,i}}{\sqrt{\sum x_{c,i}^2 \sum m_{c,i}^2}}, \qquad (6.35)$$

where x_i and m_i are the flashing signal and template values in the moment i respectively, the subscript c indicates the c pathway. Because the flash and template mean is all set to 0, there is no need for each x_i or m_i minus mean value of the signal. The greater S value shows the signal is closer to the template.

(3) Discrimination. The EEG signal of M pathways is collected by the system. By template matching, every choice gets $7 \times m$ matching value. For each option, m matches the value of the average value s', which represents the electrodes to the acquisition of EEG and template similar to the average level, with maximum s' flash segment most likely as the place of P300 potentials. On the basis of improving reliability, the gap between maximum s' and other flash s' value should reach a certain level in order to assure the validity of results. For this reason, the system presumes that the discriminant procedure would send the corresponding option as the P300 command to the user interface only when the difference between maximum s' and the second largest s' is greater than 0.2; otherwise the program output will be an empty instruction.

6.8 Brain–Computer Integration

Brain–computer integration is a new intelligent system based on BCI technology, which is integrated with biological intelligence and machine intelligence. Brain–computer integration is an inevitable trend in the development of BCI technology. In the brain–computer integration system, the brain and the machine is not only the signal level of the brain machine interoperability, but also need to integrate the brain's cognitive ability with the computer's computing ability. But the cognitive unit of the brain has a different relationship with the intelligent unit of the machine. Therefore, one of the key scientific issues of brain–computer integration is how to establish the cognitive computing model of brain computer integration.

At present, brain–computer integration is an active research area in intelligent science. In 2009, DiGiovanna developed the mutually adaptive BCI system based on reinforcement learning [118], which regulates brain activity by the reward and punishment mechanism. The machine adopts the reinforcement learning algorithm to adapt motion controlled of mechanical arm, and has the optimized performance of the manipulator motion control. In 2010, Fukayarna *et al.* controlled a mechanical car by extraction and analysis of mouse motor nerve signals [162]. In 2011, Nicolelis's team developed a new brain–machine–brain information channel in the bidirectional closed-loop system [343], turn monkey's touch information into the electric stimulus signal to feedback the brain while decoding to the nerve information of monkey's brain, to realize the brain–computer cooperation.

Brain–machine integration system has three remarkable characteristics: (a) More comprehensive perception of organisms, including understanding the behavior and decoding of neural signals; (b) Organisms are also seen as a system of sensing, computing and executive body along with the information bidirectional exchange channel with the rest of the system; (c) Comprehensive utilization of organism and machine in multi-level and multi-granularity will greatly enhance system intelligence.

In 2013, Zhaohui Wu team of Zhejiang University developed a visually enhanced rat robot [509]. Compared with the general robot, the rat robot has the advantage in aspects of flexibility, stability and environmental adaptability. In this project, rats were the main carriers. Through the camera and combined with the computer vision technology, the visual recognition ability of the rat was strengthened. Visual enhancement of the rat robot system mainly consists of three parts: the implanted electrode, the rat pack and the calculation module. A pinhole camera is installed on the backpack and fixed to the mouse, which can real-time capture the video image of the rat, and analyze the video transmission on the computer through the wireless module of the backpack. According to the analysis results, the backpack on the stimulation circuit produces electrical stimulation signal which is transferred to the related brain regions of the rat and the rat robot will produce different (turn left, turn right and go) behavior and navigation as it explores unknown environments. In the computing system of brain computer integration, the spatial decision-making ability and execution ability of the rats are combined with the decision-making ability of the machine (closed loop control) and the perceptual ability (camera perception).

The core of brain computer integration is the cognitive computing model of brain computer collaboration. Cognitive process of brain machine collaboration is composed by environment perception, motivation analysis, intention understanding and action planning and so on, in support of the perception memory, episodic memory, semantic memory and working memory to complete brain machine group awareness and coordinated action. We mainly focus on four aspects, namely, environmental perception, cognitive modeling, joint intention and action plan, to carry out the research of cognitive computing model:

(1) The environmental perception of brain computer collaboration. For brain computer bidirectional information perception characteristics, integration of visual features of the Marr visual theory and Gestalt whole perception theory is needed as well as research on the environment group awareness model and method by combination of brain and computer. The discriminative, generative and other methods are applied to analyze the features of environment perception information, mine perception information patterns and knowledge, generate high-level

semantics, understand well the environment awareness, and build brain computer collaborative group awareness model.

(2) Cognitive modeling of brain computer collaboration. This involves combining the mutual cognitive characteristic of the brain computer, utilizing and studying the achievement made in intelligent science about consciousness, memory and studying the cognitive cycle in brain–computer collaborative information processing. According to the characteristic of the collaborative work of the brain computer, we utilize the research results of physiological mechanism of brain information processing, study the information representation method and reasoning mechanism in episodic memory and semantic memory of human brain, carry on cognitive modeling to information processing procedure in the brain computer collaboration.

(3) The joint intention driven by motivation. The essential characteristic of the brain–computer collaborative work is that the agents have common goals, commitments, intentions, etc. that are jointly restrained. In order to describe the characteristics that the brain–computer system should possess, one must study the joint intention theory to describe union restrictions of autonomous agents and reason balance of agent mental state; as required by brain–computer collaborative work, study the essence of the behavior motivation and generation mechanism, put forward the intention model driven by motivation; study the joint intention method for multi-agents, offer theory support for constructing the brain computer collaborative work of multi-agents.

(4) Action planning for brain computer collaboration. Under the support of the ontology knowledge system, study the action planning method of brain computer collaboration; using reinforcement learning and Markov decision theory, study the part of perception of the planning method, present the action planning theory with learnability and optimization methods.

We created a multi-level brain–computer collaboration cognitive model based on the motivation driven collaborative cognition, the agent model ABGP collaborative cognition and the information sharing collaborative cognition [449]. According to the need of the biological cognitive unit and the computer intelligent unit, we put forward the motivation model, which is expressed as the tri-tuple $\langle N, G, I \rangle$, where N represents the demand; G is the goal; I indicates the strength of the motivation. There are three kinds of needs in this project: perceived demand, adaptive demand and cooperative demand. In order to adapt to the environment changes, the brain computer integration system produces various motivations. Based on the motivations, the collaborative work will be realized.

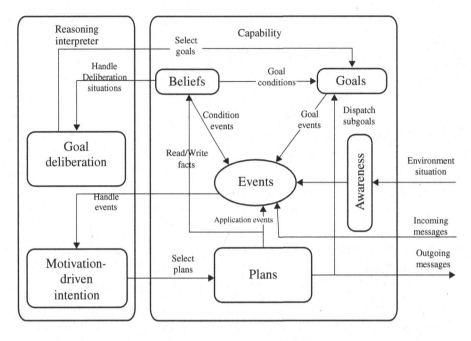

Fig. 6.8. Agent model ABGP

The biological unit and the computer unit can be abstracted as an agent and the multi-agent collaboration work, which greatly improves the whole performance of the brain computer intelligent system. We have proposed an agent model ABGP [449], in which A is the environmental awareness, B represents belief, G represents the goal, P represents the plan as shown in Figure 6.8. In the brain–computer integration system, based on the internal mind state and the BDI reasoning machine, each unit realizes multi-agent collaborative work; while going through, it interacts with the external environment, perceives the external environment objects and behaviors, adapts to the dynamic environment changes, achieves the better collaborative work.

Since the brain–computer integration system is a distributed and heterogeneous system, we have proposed a distributed dynamic description logic CD^3L. The CD^3L system consists of five basic components: the distributed dynamic description logic D^3L, the distributed TBox, the distributed ABox, the distributed ActBox, and the reasoning mechanism. CD^3L distributed dynamic description logic introduces the combination of consistency semantics, through the bridge rules for knowledge dissemination, provides a theoretical basis for the integration and sharing of heterogeneous information, and supports the collaborative cognition of distributed heterogeneous brain–computer integration.

Chapter 7

Language Cognition

The cerebral cortex, which is located on the surface of the human brain, lies in the highest level of the brain's nervous system. In addition to the perception and motor control of the external world, it also has the advanced cognitive function of language, learning, thinking and emotion. This book is only concerned with language cognition and learning. If you want to learn more about mind and emotion, you can refer to *Intelligence Science* [431]. This chapter describes language cognition while the next chapter discusses learning.

Language is the "material shell" of abstract thinking, which is the main driving force of human thought. Language cognition combines psychological language models and neural science together, to explain how the brain gets semantics through oral and written words and understands the neural model of the human language.

7.1 Mental Lexicon

Language is the most complex, the most systematic and the most widely used symbol system. Linguistic symbols not only express specific objects, state and actions, but also represent abstract concepts. A central concept of term representation is mental lexicon, which is concerned with semantics (meaning of term), grammar (how the terms are combined together to form one sentence) and morphology (their spelling and pronunciation model). Most language psychological theories admit the important role of psychological vocabulary in language processing. But some theories propose a mental lexicon with both language understanding and expression, while other models distinguish input and output. In addition, every model should consider visual-based orthography and representation of the verbal aspect based on sound. We know that there is a memory module (or some) in the brain, but how is the memory module organized as a concept?

Mental lexicon is different from the general college dictionary, which is organized in the form of a specific information network. Levitt [63] put forward the specific information network in the so-called lexeme level in the form of the word, while the lemma level is in the form of grammatical features. At the lemma level, the semantic features of words are also revealed. This kind of semantic information defines the concept level. Under this concept level, it is appropriate to use a specific word. For example, whether the word represents a living object or a non-living object. These features are expressed by the sense of the word in the lemma level and the concept level. The concept level exceeds the linguistic knowledge for a certain word. There is a big difference between word semantic knowledge and pure language knowledge. When we think of those words with a unique form of representation but with two or more semantic words (such as the word "bank"), the distinction becomes obvious. In order to extract the meaning of the word "bank",

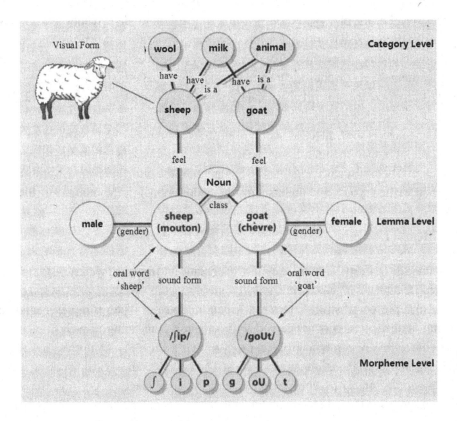

Fig. 7.1. An example of vocabulary network segment

you need to know about the context of the information. Figure 7.1 shows an example of the vocabulary network segment.

Semantic memory plays an important role in language comprehension and expression and therefore there is an obvious link with mental lexicon, which can be deduced from Figure 7.1. But semantic memory and mental lexicon are not necessarily the same. Our knowledge about the real world is reflected by concept or semantic representation. These representations can be activated through our thoughts and intentions or through our sense for words and sentences, images, photos and events in the real world. Although many studies are concerned with the characteristics of concept and semantic representation, "how and where" concept representations in the brain remain an open question.

In 1975, Collins and Loftus put forward an influential semantic network model in which the meaning for words can be represented [98]. In this network, the concept nodes represent words and they are connected with each other. Figure 7.2 shows an example of a semantic network. The connection strength and the distance between the nodes is determined by the semantic relations and the relationship between words. For example, a node that has a representation of the word "car" has a close and strong connection with the nodes of the word "truck".

In general, "how to represent the meaning of words" is a controversial issue. However, we all can agree that the psychological memory of lexical meaning is very important for understanding and expressing language. Evidence from brain damage and brain function imaging helps us to explain the organization of mental lexicon and conceptual knowledge.

7.2 Perceptual Analysis of Language Input

7.2.1 Spoken language input

The input signals for spoken language and written language are very different. For readers, the letters on the page are important physical signals, however, they will encounter a variety of sounds under a different environment. So, they need to identify and distinguish other "noise" related to the voice signal.

The important element of spoken language is the phoneme, which is the smallest unit to express different meanings. The brain of the listener should have the ability to deal with the difficulties caused by the speech signal and some of the difficulties are associated with the signal variability. The phoneme is usually not in the form of

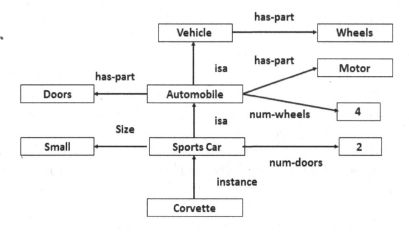

Fig. 7.2.   An example of a semantic network

a separate piece of information, which usually causes additional difficulties for the listener. In other words, they lack segmentation. In written language, however, the physical boundaries will separate words and sentence. When you read an English article, you will find the space between each word and each sentence ends with a full stop. These physical tips help you distinguish between words and sentences. On the other hand, the boundaries of the spoken word are ambiguous. In addition to a pause, an oral sentence always lacks a clear gap.

There are a lot of changes in the listener's auditory input. In spoken language, it is impossible to get a 1–1 contact for physical signal and memory representation and so the human perception of the auditory transmission should be taken into account. In the face of such variance in the extracted the physical signals, how is the meaning of the speech for the brain and what is the abstract unit of speech input representation?

Some researchers propose that these statements are based on the spectral characteristics of the input signal. These spectral features vary with the sounds. These features may form a speech representation, while the speech representation may be encodings extracted from the phoneme. But other researchers present different representations of the unit, such as the phoneme, syllable and the way the speech is planned. Other theorists refuse to accept that sound signal can be represented by discrete units.

Sound information from a speech rhythm and a speaker's voice can help us to break down the speech stream into meaningful parts. The rhythm of speech comes from the duration of the word and the change of the position of the pause. Rhyme is obvious in all the spoken languages and it can be detected when the narrator puts forward a question or emphasizes something. The narrator will increase the frequency of the sound at the end of a story while raising the volume of the sound and adding a pause, if he is willing to emphasize.

7.2.2 Speech coding

Digital speech coding technology can be divided into two categories: one is to follow the premise of the waveform, encoding the analog waveform into digital format; while another is to deal with the analog waveform and only encoding speech that can be received. Three kinds of speech coding technology are most commonly used: pulse code modulation (PCM), differential pulse code modulation (DPCM) and delta modulation (DM). Under normal circumstances, public telephone network takes advantage of these three technologies in the digital telephone. The second method is mainly applied to narrow band transmission system or related to a speech coder for digital devices with limited capacity. Digital technology of the device is often referred to as a voice coder, which is now beginning to expand the application, especially for frame relay and voice.

In addition to the compression coding technology, people also use a lot of bandwidth saving technologies to reduce voice bandwidth and to optimize network resources. The mute suppression technology in the ATM and the frame relay network can eliminate mute data while not affecting the transmission of other information. Voice activity detection (VAD) technology can be used to dynamically track the noise level, as well as set a voice detection threshold level, so that the speech mute detector can dynamically match the user's background noise environment and the suppression of silence can be reduced to the minimum. In order to replace the audio signal in the network so that the signal is no longer transmitted through the network, the comfortable sound of the background can be integrated into the network at any end of the network to ensure that the voice quality and the natural sound of the voice are connected to the ends of the network. Speech coding method can be divided into three categories: waveform coding, source coding and hybrid coding.

1. Waveform coding

Waveform coding is relatively simple. Speech signal is quantized to be analog first based on sampling theorem and then amplitude quantization is adopted to perform binary encoding. The decoding operation is conducted to perform digit/analog conversion which can restore the initial analog signal. This is the simplest pulse coding modulation (PCM), also known as linear PCM. Data compression can be achieved by nonlinear quantization, the difference between the source sample and the target sample, adaptive prediction method, etc. The objective of waveform coding is to recover the analog signal by the decoder, which is in line with the original waveform with minimum distortion. The method is simple, and the digital rate is relatively high, the quality of the 32–64 kbit/s is excellent and the quality of the 32 kbit/s is lower than that of 16 kbit/s.

2. Source encoding

Source encoding is also known as sound code. The voice signal analysis is conducted on the encoding side to decompose speech into sound and soundless signal. Source encoding analyzes speech signals from time to time and transmits sound/soundless filtering parameters. In the decoding end, the speech is then synthesized via the received parameters. Encoding rate can be very low, such as 1.2 kbit/s or 2.4 kbit/s, but it also has its drawbacks. One of the drawbacks is that the synthetic speech quality is poor. To be more specific, it may be clear but not natural enough. It is also difficult to determine the speaker; and the other problem is its relatively high degree of complexity.

3. Hybrid coding

Hybrid coding is a combination of waveform coding and source coding, having 4–16 kbit/s digital speed and sound quality that is always good. But recently some algorithms have achieved comparable quality to that of waveform coding and the complexity is almost the same as the waveform coder and source coding.

The above coding mechanism can be further divided into many different encoding solutions. The properties of speech encoding can be classified into four categories, namely, bit rate, delay, complexity and quality. Bit rate is a very important aspect of speech encoding. The range of bit rates can be from secure telephone communications (2.4–64 kbit/s) to a broadband (7 kHz) speech coder.

7.2.3 Rhythm perception

Rhythm is a common feature of all natural languages. It plays a very important role in verbal communication. By comparing the combination of voice information, rhythm can denote the speaker's intention and understanding better. The perfection of rhythm control model determines the natural property of synthetic language. Rhythm perception attracts increasing attention in the field of linguistics and language engineering. It is vital to understand the rhythm of natural language for research of speech coding and development of speech synthetics. Speech stream information is composed of speech information and rhythm information. The former is revealed by timbre while the latter is revealed by the prosodic features.

The earlier research focused on the processing of grammar and semantics, leaving rhythm aside. Until the 1960s researchers did not begin to systematically study rhythm.

1. Prosodic features

Prosodic features comprise of three aspects: stress, intonation and prosodic structure (boundary structure of prosodic components). Since it can cover two or more sound segments, it is also called supra segmental features. Prosodic structure is a hierarchical structure, which owns a variety of classification methods. It is generally recognized as having three levels: rhythm of the word, prosodic phrase and intonation phrase [556].

(1) Chinese Stress

(1) Word stress and sentence stress.
(2) The type of sentence stress.
(3) The location and level of stress of the sentence.

Chinese prosodic stress is complex. In the announcer language, a large number of contrast methods, including the contrast of the distance and the time of the contrast are adopted. Figure 7.3 shows the pitch of the following statements:

'If there are four seasons in musical instruments,

Spring should be trumpet, summer is timpani,

Autumn is the cello, winter is the flute.'

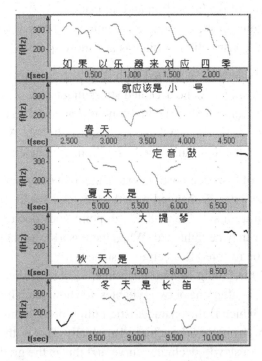

Fig. 7.3. An example of a Chinese pitch

Note that in the four parallel clauses, the stress will be emphasized at the end of the sentence while the start of the sentence has a lower stress. Four seasons in four sentences are spoken with high and low stresses alternatively, followed by the corresponding instruments. At the end of the sentence, there is a very low voice, which is the so-called broadcast accent. Contrastive stress often has the characteristics of syllable lengthening. It is normal to increase a high-pitched voice on the stress of the sentence. There is no "low stress" for sentence stress. In Figure 7.3, the falling-rising tone of small drum is not complete enough, while the low voice segment is not detected. The range of pitch is 140–400 Hz in the logarithm scale. For instance, Dong 220, Tian 240, Shi 235, Chang 290 and Di 270 (ms).

(2) Chinese intonation

The intonation structure is composed of a combination of linguistic accents. It is a language form, which shows the functional semantics of grammar by information focus. Rhythm can be obtained from tree-type relations. Multihierarchy rhythm units are constructed via finite decomposition of the acoustic form. The language stress and rhythm stress can regulate the high and low audio line of the pitch. The combination of all audio range features can distinguish the different tone types. Therefore, the tone is the important element for readjustment of pitch, while pitch range forms the basis of pitch function and intonation.

The basic elements of pitch Chinese are composed of pre-head, head, nucleus and tail. The typical construction of pitch is as follows [525]:

(1) The head and nucleus are accented with strong stress, while the pre-head only has tone syllables, there is no accented stress in the tail.
(2) A distinct gap is formed after the high line is down in the nucleus.
(3) In the nucleus of the voice, a syllable is obviously lighter. After the syllable has a significant rise, the high line appears to fall in the nucleus pitch.

A large number of facts demonstrate that in the light of syllable combination, the level of high and low pitch is changed with the language itself. In the former strong and weak groups, after a syllable of the high point goes down, with the potential difference, the latter may be lightened. When there is a strong language at the back, the high notes can be restored to a certain distance.

In a statement, the falling of high pitch line is soon finished. Therefore, at the beginning of the tail or after one or two syllables, the high pitch line has already been to the lowest level, which is the characteristic falling of high pitch. Under question type, the falling of high pitch can be achieved gradually. That is, the first few syllables in the tail will show a slowly declining curve and this is the gradually falling type. The high and low pitch line are two independent factors, so the statement tone is a combination of sudden falling and low pitch falling and is not the adjustment type of range factor that is of a single degree of freedom. Similarly, the question tone is a combination of gradual falling of high-pitch and low-pitch folding, which is composed of two freedoms, forming four basic combinations. The matter of fact of voice shows that the sudden falling and low-pitch folding is the normal imperative tone besides statement and questions. The gradual falling of high pitch and delay of low pitch are very important intonations of exclamation. These four functional tones have different variations. Different intonations and other pitches have a lot to do with the whole or a part of the adjustment of voice range.

(3) Intonation marking

(1) High note without marks denotes a sudden drop of tone. High pitch line suddenly drops after the nuclear and the light syllable will show up.
(2) High note with marks denotes a gradual drop of tone. High pitch line gradually drops after the nuclear and the light syllable will show up. Some researches show that the sudden rise and falling will appear after the four tones in Chinese pronunciation.
(3) Low note without marks denotes decurrence tone. The low note has a large rise and fall.
(4) Low note with marks denotes the folding of intonation. The low note will get smaller and smaller and the convergence is most obvious in the nuclear and the tail.

Generally speaking, the intonation of the interrogative sentence is strongly convergent and the imperative tone is of weak convergence. There may be other unknown features. The classification of function tone and intonation are consistent, which includes similar acoustic characteristics, and the increase of bandwidth characteristics. They have least adjustment of high and low pitch line. The meaning of "intonation" is related to the basic function of the functional intonation (semantic).

(4) Prosodic structure

(1) Prosodic word: Chinese rhythm is reflected by double syllables or triple syllables and the inner rhythm cannot be stopped, while a pause can appear at the boundary of prosodic word.
(2) Prosodic word group: It is generally composed of two or three more closely linked prosodic words. There is usually no obvious pause between the prosodic words in one prosodic word group and there is a pause at the end of each prosodic word group but not necessarily. It can be observed from a clear silence segment in the language point of view.

(3) Prosodic phrase: A prosodic phrase consists of one or several prosodic word groups and there is usually a distinct pause between the word groups, which can be observed clearly as a silence segment. The important feature of the prosodic phrase is the gradual decline of the low-voice line.

(4) Intonation phrase: It is composed of one or several prosodic phrases. Intonation phrases can be simple sentences, complex sentences or clauses, isolated by punctuation marks. After the intonation phrase, there is usually a long pause.

As seen from the above definition, there is inclusion relation among four prosodic units, i.e., the boundary of the intonation phrase must be the boundary of prosodic phrase, while the boundary of the prosodic phrase must be the boundary of the prosodic word group. But the boundary of the prosodic word group is not necessarily the boundary of the dictionary and vice versa.

2. Prosodic modeling

The characteristics of context and rhythm have a strong correlation under different contexts. The distribution of prosodic features is influenced by contextual information and this distribution satisfies a certain probability rather than a simple function. From a probabilistic point of view, given a sentence as a parameter, the corresponding rhythm feature is a parameter which is the largest of all prosodic features. It is denoted as follows:

$$Y = \underset{n}{\arg \max} \, P(Y_n|A). \tag{7.1}$$

Based on the Bayesian formula,

$$Y = \underset{n}{\arg \max} \, P(Y_n|A) = \underset{n}{\arg \max} \, \frac{P(A|Y_n)P(Y_n)}{P(A)}. \tag{7.2}$$

The statistical distribution of the context information can be considered as a constant and then Equation (7.2) will be further converted to:

$$Y = \underset{n}{\arg \max} \, P(Y_n|A) = \underset{n}{\arg \max} \, P(A|Y_n)P(Y_n). \tag{7.3}$$

Equation (7.3) shows that the $P(Y_n|A)$ can be converted to $P(A|Y_n)$ and $P(Y_n)$ is the distribution of the prosodic features, which is reflected by the probability of occurrence and interaction between the prosodic features. $P(A|Y_n)$ is *a priori* probability. In theory, it can be used as the basis for its implementation.

3. Prosodic labeling

Prosodic labeling is a qualitative description of the prosodic features with language function in speech signals. The labeling sentence has the functional linguistics, like intonation patterns, stress patterns and tonal changes in the prosodic structure. The changes of the pitch under the influence of different tones are a part of prosodic labeling, while the inherent variations of tones for vowel and collaborative pronunciation for different syllables do not belong to prosodic labeling. Prosodic labeling is often of hierarchy, in which the segment of sound becomes the basis for prosodic labeling and therefore, it becomes an essential hierarchy. The labeling for different levels is based on practical application and characteristics of speech. Chinese prosodic labeling system should have the following characteristics:

(1) Reliability: Different labeling should be consistent with human annotation;
(2) Comprehensiveness: the most important prosodic phenomena should be revealed;
(3) Learnability: labeling can be learnt in a short period of time;
(4) Compatibility: the labeling system should be combined with the latest methods of speech synthesis, speech recognition and the current syntax, semantics and pragmatics;
(5) Operability: the labeling symbol should be simple;
(6) Open: the uncertainty of the label item is allowed to exist;
(7) Readability: the labeled symbol can be identified by machines.

From the viewpoint of engineering application, the prosodic labeling is a description of the phonological system, which is related to the linguistics and speech. It is easy to model the correlation between linguistics and speech information based on the labeled information. Therefore, prosodic labeling plays an increasingly important role in oral speech recognition and speech synthesis system.

The prosodic labeling is of hierarchy, where each level marks different prosodic or related phenomena. Generally speaking, users can choose a certain labeling level based on their needs. The system is divided into three points in the C-TOBI's prosodic labeling system:

(1) Syllable level: labeling syllable of Mandarin in the form of pinyin, for instance, Chinese takes four tones 1,2,3 and 4 which is represented by four tones in a neutral tone.
(2) The actual pronunciation level: it involves labeling the actual pronunciation of consonants, vowels and tones. International phonogram symbol (IPA) system SAMPA-C is adopted.
(3) Tone level: the construction of tone is determined by the prosodic structure and stress. That is, if the stress structure and the prosodic structure are decided, the tone curve can be decided as well. Research shows that the change of tone is mainly demonstrated in tone range and order, which is based on the change of the tone. The tone range will change based on the psychological status, mood

and prosodic structure. Therefore the label for tones should reflect the expansion and narrowing of tone range. Besides, it should reveal the trend of the whole curve of the tone.

The segmentation is performed on each speech unit (including a syllable, tone, or even a smaller voice unit) and then gives a detailed description of the characteristics of the sound. The Chinese audio segment labeling should be performed on different levels. The label expansion for speech segment is mainly focused on labelling the actual pronunciation based on regular pronunciation and labeling the phenomenon of sound change on segments and suprasegments. Therefore, the Chinese phonetic system corresponding to the use of SAMPA-C is adopted. For the spoken language corpus, we should also label the language and nonlanguage phenomenon.

SAMPA is a universal and internationally recognized reading and speech keyboard symbol system, which is widely used in segment labelling system. A practical SAMPA-C symbol system is already formulated in the Mandarin pronunciation part. We hope that this system can be extended to include Chinese dialects. Therefore, we must first determine the establishment of the SAMPA-C Principle:

(1) The Chinese language symbol is formulated based on the symbol system of SAMPA (http://www.phon.ucl.ac.uk/home/sampa/).
(2) An additional symbol should be appended for the special speech phenomenon of the Chinese language.
(3) As an open system, new symbols can be added and those not applicable can be amended.

SAMPA-C mainly focuses on labeling Chinese audio segment, designing Chinese label system for consonants, vowels and tones. The symbol systems of Mandarin are listed. Besides, a specific voice symbol system is designed for Guangzhou dialect, Shanghai dialect and Fuzhou dialect. Other dialects can be expanded based on this mode.

4. Prosodic generation

Prosodic generation has attracted attention as words can be considered as part of phonological encoding at the beginning. With the development of research methods, the prosodic generation for the phrases and sentences are also studied. These studies are mainly conducted from the perspective of information processing. Some representative prosodic generation models are Shattuck-Hufnagel scanned copy model and Dell connectionism model. These two models do not specifically discussing the prosodic generation. So far, the most comprehensive prosodic encoding and processing model has been presented by Levelt *et al.* [262].

Levelt believes that during the generation of spoken sentences, all the sentence processing stages are parallel and gradual. There are different prosodic encoding processes (i.e., some on the word level while others on the sentence level). During the expansion of a sentence based on grammar structure, the audio plan for vocabulary occurs at the same time. The vocabulary is generally divided into two parts: characters (including the semantic and syntactic features) and morpheme extraction (including morphology and phonology). The latter is performed on the morpheme-prosody stage, which needs characters as input to extract corresponding terms and prosodic structure. Thus, the generated prosodic features do not need to know the audio segment of the information. This morphological and prosodic information is used to extract the audio segments of the word (including the location of the phoneme and syllable) during the extraction phase and the prosody and sound segments are combined together.

In the final stage, the prosody generator executes the language planning, resulting in the sentence prosody and intonation patterns. There are two main steps for the generation of prosody: firstly, prosody units, such as prosodic words, prosodic phrases and intonation phrases are generated; and then rhythm grid of the prosody structure is generated; lastly, the rhythm can denote stress and time pattern. Specifically, the generation of prosody units is as follows: the results of morphology-prosody extraction is combined with connection components to form a prosodic word. A prosodic phrase can be constructed based on the grammar structure of the sentence, with other information. Intonation phrase is obtained via the pause at some point during the audio stream. The generation of rhythm grid is based on the prosody structure of the sentence and rhythm grid for a single word.

Levelt presented a new point of prosody generation for word generation in 1999 [264], claiming that there is a word prosody pattern in a stress language such as Dutch, English and German. In these, the stress is on the first syllable. Therefore, stress of regular words is not extracted but automatically generated based on this rule. Stress of irregular words cannot be generated automatically. Thus, only irregular words of the prosodic structure are stored as a part of the speech code. The prosodic structure of irregular words is used to guide the prosody of irregular words. The prosody of the result is the generation of a larger prosodic unit.

These models are constructed based on the study of English, Dutch and German. Compared with these languages, Chinese pronunciation has two significant features: the number of syllables is small and only 1/10 of the English language and Chinese is a tonal language, while English and other languages are stress languages without tone. Thus, the mechanism of the prosody generation in Chinese is different from these models [532]. However, there are a few studies of the Chinese prosody generation.

5. Cognitive neuroscience of prosody generation

Levelt *et al.* analyzed research results of 58 brain function images using the meta-analysis method [266], and came to the conclusion that during the generation of vocabulary, the left part of the brain that includes the frontal gyrus (Broca's area), the middle temporal gyrus, the superior temporal gyrus, the temporal back (Wernicke's area) and the left thalamus can be easily activated. The introduction of visual concept involves the occipital and ventral temporal lobe and the frontal zone. The activation comes to the Wernicke area, where the phonological code is stored. This information then spreads to the Broca area, with post-phonological coding (275–400 ms), followed by speech encoding. It has a lot to do with the sensory motor area and the cerebellum, activating the sensory motor area to pronounce.

In 2002, Mayer *et al.* took advantage of fMRI to study the normal prosody produced by brain activity [294], finding that the front cover at the bottom of the left and right hemisphere of the skull is relatively small and the nonoverlap region has correlation with the prosody. The prosody of the language is activated only in the left hemisphere, while the prosody of the emotion is activated only in the right hemisphere.

7.2.4 Written input

In writing, there are three different ways to symbolize text: Letters, syllables and knowing. Many Western languages (such as English) use the alphabet system and the symbol is similar to the phoneme. However, some languages using alphabet system differ from each other in terms of close correspondence of letter and pronunciation. Some languages, such as Finnish and Spanish, have a close relationship, i.e., the simple text. Relatively speaking, English often lacks correspondence between letters and pronunciation, which means that English has a deep orthography.

Japanese have a different writing system. Japanese writing system uses the Katakana syllable system, where each symbol represents a syllable. There are only 100 different syllables in Japanese and so a syllable system is possible for Japanese. Chinese is an ideographic system where each word or morpheme refers to unique symbols and Chinese characters can represent morpheme. However, the Chinese character also corresponds to the phoneme, so Chinese is not a pure understanding system. The existence of this representing system is because Chinese is a tonal language. The same word can express different meanings depending on the pitch or tone. It is difficult to represent this pitch change in a system that only represents a sound or a phoneme.

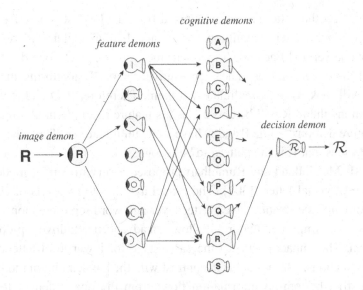

Fig. 7.4. Structure of the pandemonium model

The three writing systems stand for different perspectives of language (phoneme, syllable morpheme or word), but they all use the mandatory symbol. Regardless of the writing system, the reader must be able to analyze the original function or shape of the symbol. For the Pinyin text system, the processing is visual analysis for horizontal, vertical, closed curves, open curves and other basic shapes.

In 1959, Selfridge proposed the Pandemonium model [404]. Based on feature analysis, the model was divided into four levels for pattern recognition, where each level had a number of "demons" to perform specific tasks. These levels worked in a certain sequence and the ultimate realization was for pattern recognition. The structure of the model is shown in Figure 7.4.

As seen in Figure 7.4, the first level is the "image demon", which encodes the external stimulus to which form a stimulating image. Then, the second level is the "feature demon", which mainly focuses on analyzing the image and decomposes into various features. In the process of analysis, each function demo is specific, which is only to find the feature he is responsible for, such as the letter of the vertical line, horizontal line, right angle, etc. Besides, a clear report should be given on the amount of features and whether there is a specific feature. The third level is the "cognitive demons", who are always monitoring the responses of the "feature demons". Each of the "cognitive demons" is responsible for one pattern (letter), where they are looking for some of the features related to the specific pattern from the response of the "feature demon". When the relevant functions are found, they will shout. The more features they find, the louder they will shout. Finally, the "decision demon", (fourth level) will select the pattern to be recognized from the loudest "cognitive demon". For example, in the letter recognition, the "image demon" will first report there are altogether one vertical line, two horizontal lines, one diagonal, one discontinuous curve and three right angles. These "cognitive demons" monitoring the "feature demons" will look for features related to them. Therefore, P, D and R will shout loudly. Among them, R will be chosen, as his feature is totally in accordance with all the feature demons' while P and D have some unfit features. Thus, the "decision demon" decides that R is the pattern to be recognized.

In 1981, McClelland and Rumelhart proposed a very important model for the recognition of visual letters [301]. The model assumes three levels of characterization: word alphabet feature layer, letter layer and word representation layer. The model has a very important feature: it allows an advanced cognitive top-down word information. The impact occurs at the early stage for lower level letters and feature representations. This model is in contrast with the Pandemonium model, which follows a strict bottom-up information flow: from the image demon to the feature demon, to the cognitive demon and finally the decision demon. The difference between these models is actually a significant difference between the modular and the interaction theory.

In 1983, Fodor published a book entitled *The Mental Module* [149], formally proposing module theory. He believed that the modular structure of the input system should have the following characteristics:

(1) Specific areas: The input system receives different information from different sensory systems and a specific encoding system is adopted to deal with this information. For example, the language input system converts the visual input to a voice or oral speech representation.
(2) Information encapsulation: The process follows a strict direction, and so incomplete information cannot be sent. There is no top-down effect in language processing.
(3) Functional positioning: Each module is implemented in a specific area of the brain.

The interactive view challenges all of these assumptions. However, the most important objection to the modular structure theory is that higher levels of cognitive processing can be influenced by the feedback of the system, while the module theory claims that different subsystems can only communicate with each other in a bottom-up mechanism.

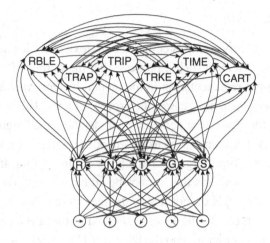

Fig. 7.5. The network of the letter recognition

Another important distinction between these two models is that in the McClelland and Rumelhart model, processing can be parallel, so a few letters can be processed simultaneously. However, in the Pandemonium model, only one letter can be processed in a sequence each time. Figure 7.5 shows the network segment of letter recognition. Three different levels of nodes are represented by features of letters, letters and words. Each layer node can be connected to each other by the external display (arrow) or implicit (line), which will affect the level of activation of other nodes. The McClelland and Rumelhart model allows the excitement and inhibited contact between two layers [301]. For example, if you read the word "tip", and then all the letters and functions matching the word "tip", together with the word "trip" itself will be activated. But when the word node "tip" is activated, it sends an inhibitory signal to the lower layer, namely nodes with the letters and features not matching the word node "tip". The McClelland and Rumelhart model shows its superior performance when it is applied to a simulation word. When three kinds of visual stimuli were briefly presented to the subjects, we observed this effect in experiments. The stimulation can be a word (trip), non-word (Pirt) or a letter (T). The task to be tested is to decide whether what they saw contains letter "t" or "k". When this letter appears in a real word, the subjects can do a better job. Interestingly, the letters in a certain word seem to be better than when they are in a single letter. This result suggests that word is not perceived on the basis of the alphabet. The McClelland and Rumelhart model explains the "best word effect". Based on their model, top-down information can be activated and inhibited, which will be helpful for letter recognition.

7.2.5 Word recognition

The process of lexical processing is composed of, lexical choice and lexical integration. Lexical access refers to such a process, that the output of the visual analysis activates orthographic representation in the mental lexicon, including the semantic and syntactic properties. In most cases, the process of lexical access is different from the visual and auditory form. For people who understand the language, unique challenges exist under two circumstances as the encoding signal connected to the mental lexicon has different morphological characteristics. In writing, there is a question of how we can read the words that cannot be converted directly into sounds, and also read "false words" that do not match the real words. Reading the false words cannot be mapped directly to the form of the text output because there is no such mapping. Therefore, in order to read the false word "lonocel", we need to convert it to its corresponding phoneme letters. On the other hand, if we want to read the word "Colonel", if we convert it to the corresponding phoneme, we'll read the wrong word. In order to prevent such mistakes, a direct orthogonal representation should be used for orthographic units. This observation makes researchers present the dual pathway reading model: a direct pathway from the morphology to the orthography and an indirect pathway or synthesis pathway which will convert the text input speech to form a mapping.

In 1993, Coltheart presented a direct path from reading the character to word representation. However, the input of the Chinese character to word representation in the mental lexicon can be accomplished in two ways: morphological pattern of speech, i.e., the so-called indirect path and the direct written input to mental lexicon, i.e., a direct access [100].

In 1989, Seidenberg and McClelland proposed a single access computer model that uses only speech information [402]. In this model, the written unit and the speech unit will continue to interact with each other and the information feedback is allowed to learn the correct pronunciation. This model is very successful for real words, but it is not very good at reading false words, which in turn is not very difficult for ordinary people.

7.2.6 Speech generation

Speech generation (spoken language) is the process of organizing the communication intention, activating the concept, extracting the word meaning, syntax and pronunciation information and controlling the sound of the vocal organs. It is an important part of the human language ability and it is an important way for expression of human consciousness.

The speech generation process can be divided into three levels [111]: The highest level is conceptualization, which is the process of establishing the concept of intention and expression. The intermediate process is language organization, which is converting the concepts to the form of language. The last level is articulation, which involves a more specific pronunciation and pronunciation program, i.e., converting the voice encoding into a vocal muscle exercise program and executing the program. Speech organization includes vocabulary generation and grammar encoding. The latter deals with the choice of words and sorts these words, i.e., a syntactic framework of a sentence is produced via the meaning of words and the grammatical nature of the correct words. The former is one of the core issues in the study of speech generation. This process can be divided into five parts [265]. They are concept preparation, vocabulary selection, voice encoding, encoding and articulation.

Concept preparation refers to the process of conceptualizing thoughts and ideas in the brain, which is the initial stage of speech generation. Lexicalization and lexical selection is performed after concept preparation. The prepared concept will activate the corresponding semantic representation in the mental lexicon and the activated semantic representation will be converted into the lexical representation of a word. It is generally believed that there is an abstract representation between the semantic and phonological representation, lemma, which covers the grammatical features of the word. Lexicalization consists of two stages: the first stage is transferring the activation of semantic representations into the specific lemmas of the input level, i.e., lemmas will be activated by the concept. After a period of time, the lemma with the highest ratio of activation is activated and the lemma is used to provide the syntax of the sentence for grammar encoding. The second stage is phonological form. To be more specific, the activation of the intermediate layer is further transmitted to a phonetic representation for a specific lemma, thus allowing the speaker to extract the pronunciation of the lemma. The activated or extracted phonetic representation will perform the so-called morpho-phonological encoding. In this stage, the structure of the word, the prosodic feature and the phoneme segment will be expanded and the phonological information of the morpheme unit is combined to conform to the actual pronunciation of the syllable. It is generally believed that this syllabification is performed from left to right and the phoneme segment and prosodic structure are extracted respectively. The phoneme segment will be inserted into the prosodic structures from left to right to form a syllable of a word. The extraction of a syllable pronunciation may occur between speech encoding and phonate. The abstract pronunciation program that is frequently used is stored in a "warehouse", which is extracted from left to right. Activation of these procedures is also attributed to the activation of the spread of the speech encoding. Once the syllable pronunciation program is extracted, the pronunciation of a word starts immediately. The pronunciation system calculates the best scheme for performing the abstract pronunciation program, thus guiding the respiratory system and the throat system to make a sound.

At present, the theoretical model of language generation is symbolic and concrete, but not distributed and abstract. There are two important models that need to be noticed: a two-stage interactive activation model presented by Dell [111] and a two-stage independent model (or serial processing model) presented by Levelt [265] and Roelofs [383]. The two-stage interactive activation model can be divided into three levels in terms of the extraction process from semantic representation to speech. Each level has a large number of nodes. The top layer is the semantic layer, whose nodes represent semantic features; the middle layer is the lemma layer while the bottom layer is the morpheme layer, which is composed of the onset phoneme, the nucleus phoneme and the coda phoneme. The main contribution of this model is to propose the idea of interactive activation in language generation. The activation of the transmission mode is the waterfall, i.e., the activation can be transmitted between any node in the network. The "interaction" means that all nodes are connected in a way that they can only promote the connection between them and the connections cannot be inhibited, while the activation of the transmission is also bidirectional, which means that they can be transmitted from the top level to the bottom level and vice versa. Words and lemma nodes with the highest activation ratio will be chosen and this is determined by the structure of the external syntax. The selected word nodes will transfer the activation to their corresponding speech encoding. In this model, the high-frequency words with bidirectional coupling and feedback structures are more easily activated, which suggests that it can explain the words' frequency effect and syllable frequency effect.

The two-stage interactive activation model can also be divided into three levels. Nodes in the top layer represent the entire lexicon concept, which denotes the semantic features; the middle layer is the syntactic layer representing grammar and features, including grammar structure, change in features and parts of speech. The bottom layer is the phonological or lexeme level, containing a large number of lemma nodes, or phonological and phoneme nodes. In the whole model, there is no inhibition relationship between the nodes. Levelt *et al.* assumed that the concept layer and the lemma layer share language generation and recognition while the lexeme level only exists in the language generation system [272]. The connection between the concept layer and the lemma layer is bidirectional, where the activated information can be transmitted. The lemma level and the lexeme level are independent from each other, which means there is a one-way transmission of information without any feedback. Thus it is called as the two-stage interactive activation model. In 1997, Roloff *et al.* summarized the research and proposed Word-form Encoding by Activation and Verification (WEAVER) [383].

Almost all language generation theories admit the five-stage process for lemma generation, but there are serious differences in the specific details of each stage and real-time processing at different stages. In the concept selection and word semantic activation stage, a controversial question is how the meaning of a word is stored in the mental lexicon. Another important issue in the process of speech information conversion is how to deal with the prosodic structure of a word, such as the combination of light and stress, vowel and consonant.

7.3 Chomsky's Formal Grammar

In computer science, a formal language is a set of strings of symbols that may be constrained by rules that are specific to it, while formal grammar is a method to depict the set. The reason to name formal grammar is because it is similar to the grammar in the natural language of human beings. The most common grammatical classification systems were presented by Chomsky in 1950, and all of the grammatical categories were classified into four types: phrase structure grammar, context free grammar (CFG) and regular grammar. Any language can be expressed by unrestricted grammar and the remaining three categories of grammar and the corresponding language classes are enumerate language, context-free language (CFL) and formal language [83]. According to the arrangement, these four types of grammar have increasingly strict rules and the language they can express becomes severe. Although the expression ability is weaker than that of phrase structure grammar and context sensitive grammar, CFG and regular grammar are the most important types of grammar.

7.3.1 Phrase structure grammar

Phrase structure grammar is a kind of non-restricted grammar, also known as 0-type grammar, is a kind of important grammar in the formal language theory. A four-tuple $G = (\Sigma, V, S, P)$, where Σ is terminal symbols over a finite alphabet, V is the non-terminal symbols over a finite alphabet, $S \in V$ is the start symbol, P is a finite non-empty set of generation rules. The generation rules are defined as $\alpha \rightarrow \beta$, where $\alpha \in (\Sigma \cup V)^* V (\Sigma \cup V)^*$ and $\beta \in (\Sigma \cup V)^*$. Phrase structure grammar is also called 0-type grammar as there are no restrictions on α and β and hence it is also called unrestricted grammar. Zero-type grammar can generate the exact same

Table 7.1. Closure properties of algebraic operation for L_0 and L_1

Algebra Operation	Language L_0	L_1
and	✓	✓
link	✓	✓
closure	✓	✓
complement	×	?
intersection	✓	✓
regular language	✓	✓
inversion	✓	✓
replacement	✓	×

Note: ✓ closed × not closed ? unsolved.

language which the Turing machine accepts and it is called L_0 language or recursive enumerable language (commonly used LRE for short).

For example, let G = G = ({a}, {[,], A, D, S}, S, P), where, P = {S → [A], [→ [D, D] →], DA → AAD, [→ ∧,] → ∧, A → a}. Apparently, G is a phrase structure grammar, which can generate a 0-type language $L(G) = \{a^{2^n} | n \geq 0\}$.

Some closure properties of algebraic operations of 0-type language are shown in Table 7.1 while some results about decision problems are demonstrated in Table 7.2. In the table, D stands for determining while U stands for non-determining and L denotes language.

The standard form of phrase structure grammar is A → ξ, A → BC, A → ∧, AB → CD, where ξ ∈ (Σ ∪ V), A, B, C, D ∈ V, ∧ are empty words.

Context sensitive grammar, CFG and regular grammar can be obtained when some restrictions are applied on the generation rules in phrase structure grammar.

7.3.2 Context-sensitive grammar

Context-sensitive grammar is an important type of grammar in the formal language theory, in which the left-hand sides and right-hand sides of any production rule may be surrounded by a context of terminal and non-terminal symbols.

A formal grammar $G = (\Sigma, V, S, P)$ where V is a set of non-terminal symbols, Σ is a set of terminal symbols, P is a set of production rules and S is the start symbol, is context-sensitive if all rules in P are of the form $\alpha A \beta \to \alpha \gamma \beta$, where $A \in V, \alpha, \beta \in (\Sigma \cup V)^*, \gamma \in (\Sigma \cup V)^+$. Context-sensitive grammar is also called one-type grammar, with an intuitive meaning that A can be replaced by γ under the context

Table 7.2. Determining problems for L_0 and L_1

Decision Problem	Language L_0	L_1
$x \in L(G)$?	U	D
$L(G_1) \subset L(G_2)$?	U	U
$L(G_1) = L(G_2)$?	U	U
$L(G) = \emptyset$?	U	U
$L(G) =$ unlimited set?	U	U
$L(G) = \Sigma^*$?	U	U

of α in the left and β in the right. The language generated by one-type grammar is called context-sensitive language or one-type language. L_1 is used for denoting one-type language class.

Monotonous grammar: if all of the production rules of grammar $G = (\Sigma, V, S, P)$ is of the form $\alpha \rightarrow \beta$ and $|\alpha| \leq |\beta|$, where $\alpha \in (\Sigma \cup V)^* V (\Sigma \cup V)^*$, $\beta \in (\Sigma \cup V)^+$, then G is called monotonous grammar. Monotonous grammar can be simplified where the length of the right hand of all production rules is at most 2, i.e., if $\alpha \rightarrow \beta \in P$, then $\beta| \leq 2$. It is already proved that the language class generated by monotonous grammar is the same as one-type language class. Therefore the definition of monotonous grammar can also be used for context sensitive grammar.

For example: $G = (\{a, b, c\}, \{S, A, B\}, S, P)$, where $P = \{S \rightarrow aSAB/aAB, it BA \rightarrow AB, aA \rightarrow ab, bA \rightarrow bb, bB \rightarrow bc, CB \rightarrow cc\}$, obviously, G is monotonous grammar, which is also the context sensitive grammar. The language that it generates is $L(G) = \{a^n b^n c^n | n \geq 1\}$, which is context-sensitive language.

The standard form of context-sensitive grammar is as follows: $A \rightarrow \xi, A \rightarrow BC, AB \rightarrow CD$, where $\xi \in (\Sigma \cup V)$, $A, B, C, D \in V$. Context-sensitive language classes have the same language class as that of what a linear bounded automaton can accept. The one-type language of the operation of the closure and some results on the determination of the results of the structure of the syntax are shown in Tables 7.1 and 7.2. In particular, it is pointed out that this one-type of language is a problem when it is not closed to the latest of the operation.

7.3.3 Context-free grammar (CFG)

CFG is a kind of important transformational grammar in the formal language theory. In the formal language theory, CFG is a formal grammar in which every production rule is of the form $V \to w$, where V is a single non-terminal symbol and w is a string of terminals and/or non-terminals (w can be empty). A formal grammar is considered "context free" when its production rules can be applied regardless of the context of a non-terminal.

CFGs can be simplified as one of the two simple paradigms, i.e., any CFL can be generated by two kinds of standard CFG: one is the Chomsky model, where the production rules are of the form $A \to BC$ or $A \to a$ while the other is the Grey Bach paradigm, which is of the form generative $A \to aBC$ or $A \to a$, where A, B, $C \in V$ (non-terminal); $a \in \Sigma$ or terminator; $\alpha \in \Sigma^*$.

There are a lot of methods of inference to generate language via grammar. For instance, there are two inferences for grammar $\{S \to AB, A \to a, B \to b\}$: $S \Rightarrow AB \Rightarrow aB \Rightarrow ab$ and $S \Rightarrow AB \Rightarrow Ab \Rightarrow ab$. If the non-terminal on the left hand of the left is taken from the rule each time for inference, like the former in the example, it is call left inference. If there are two different left inferences for the same result, this grammar is ambiguous and is called an ambiguous grammar. Otherwise it is called an unambiguous grammar. For some ambiguous grammars, there is an equivalent unambiguous grammar to generate the same language. Language without ambiguous grammar is called as essence ambiguous language. For instance, $\{S \to A, S \to a, A \to a\}$ is an ambiguous grammar. $L = \{a^m b^n c^n | m, n \geq 1\} \cup \{a^m b^m c^n | m, n \geq 1\}$ is an essence ambiguous language. Pushdown automaton can accept CFL. Determined pushdown automaton and undetermined pushdown automaton can accept determined CFL and undetermined CFL respectively. The former is the proper subset of the latter. For example, $L = \{a^n b^n | n \geq 1\} \cup \{a^n b^{2n} | n \geq 1\}$ is an undetermined CFL.

For any positive integer n, let $\Sigma_n = \{a_1, \ldots, a_n\}$, $\Sigma'_n = \{a'_1, \ldots, a'_n\} G = (\Sigma, V, S, P)$ is defined for $(\Sigma_n \cup \Sigma'_n, \{S\}, S, \{S \to, Sa_i Sa'_i S | 1 \leq i \leq n\})$. The generated grammar is called Dyck set. If a_i is considered as an open bracket and a_i' is considered as a closed bracket, then the n-dimension Dyck set is a matched sequence composed of n kinds of different brackets. For example, $a_1 a_2 a_2 a'_2 a'_2 a'_1$ and $a_1 a'_1 a_2 a'_2 a_1 a'_1$ all belong to D_2.

Dyck set is a tool to expand regular language to CFL. For any CFL L, there are two homomorphic mappings H1 and H2 and a regular language R, making $L = h_2[h_1^{-1}(D_2) \cap R]$ where $D2$ is two-dimensional (2D) Dyck set- and vice versa.

In addition, the family of CFLs is a minimal language family, which contains D_2, and three kinds of algebraic operations which are closed, namely, homomorphism, inverse homomorphism and the intersection of regular language.

As CFGs are widely applied to depict grammar of programming language, it is vital to obtain subgrammar of CFG that automatically performs grammar decomposition. The most important one is unambiguous CFG, as unambiguity is very important for grammar analysis of computer language. A subclass of unambiguous CFG is *LR* (*k*) grammar, which only needs to look for *k* symbols to perform grammar decomposition correctly from left to right. *LR*(*k*) grammar can describe all of the deterministic CFLs. For arbitrary $k > 1$, the language generated by *LR*(*k*) grammars can be generated by an equivalent *LR*(1) grammar. Language generated by *LR*(0) grammar is the subclass of language generated by *LR*(1) grammar.

7.3.4 Regular grammar

Regular grammars come from the study of the natural language in the middle of the and 1950s and it is the three-type grammar in the Chomsky grammar structure. Regular grammar is proper subclass of CFGs (two-type), and has been applied to the lexical analysis of computer programming language compiler, switch circuit design, syntactic pattern recognition and so on. It is one of the topics for information science, physics, chemistry, biology, medicine, applied mathematics, etc.

There are a variety of equivalent definitions for regular grammar and so we can use "left linear grammar" or "right linear grammar" to define regular grammar. The production rule of "left linear grammar" can only contain one non-terminal symbol, while the right hand of the rule can be an empty string, a terminal symbol or a non-terminal symbol followed by a terminal symbol. While "right linear grammar" requires the left hand of the production rule to contain only one non-terminal symbol, the right hand of the rule can be an empty string, a terminal symbol or a terminal symbol followed by a non-terminal symbol.

A "left linear grammar" is defined as $G = (V, \Sigma, P, S)$, where V is a set of nonterminal symbols, Σ is a set of terminal symbols, P is a set of production rules and S is the start symbol, $w \in \Sigma^*$. It is a regular grammar if all rules in P are of the form $A \rightarrow w$ and $A \rightarrow wB(A \rightarrow Bw)$. The "right linear grammar" is equivalent to "left linear grammar" which means they can generate the same language.

The structure and complexity of a regular grammar is determined by the number of variables, the number of production rules, the height of the directed graph of the grammar and the number of nodes of each layer. $S \underset{G}{\overset{*}{\vdash}} w$ denotes inference of w with finite number of production rules used in P. The regular grammar G can be used for a generator to produce and depict regular language $L(G) = \{w \in \Sigma^* | S \underset{G}{\overset{*}{\vdash}} w\}$. For instance, $G = (\{S, A, B\}, \{0, 1\}P, S)$, $P = \{S \rightarrow 0A|0, A \rightarrow 1B, B \rightarrow 0A|0\}$, where G is a regular (right linear) grammar (G) and contains terminal 0, ($S \rightarrow 0$), $01010(S \rightarrow 0A \rightarrow 01B \rightarrow 010A \rightarrow 0101B \rightarrow 01010)$. The regular language is also called a regular set, which can be expressed as a regular expression. For any regular expression, non-deterministic finite automata (NFA) with ε actions can be constructed to accept it in linear time and a deterministic finite automata (DFA) without ε actions can also be constructed to accept it in the time square. The regular language can also be accepted by two-way deterministic finite automaton (2DFA), NFA, DFA and a2DFA as they are equivalent, i.e., the class of languages that can be accepted are the same.

Regular expressions are recursively defined as follows: let Σ be a finite set,

(1) $\emptyset$, ε and $a(\forall a \in \Sigma)$ are regular expressions on Σ respectively and they denote empty set, empty word set $\{\varepsilon\}$ and set $\{a\}$;

(2) If α and β are regular expressions on Σ, then $\alpha \cup \beta$, $\alpha \bullet \beta = \alpha\beta$ and α^* are regular expressions on Σ. They represent the $\{\alpha\}$, $\{\beta\}$, $\{\alpha\} \cup \{\beta\}$, $\{\alpha\}\{\beta\}$ and $\{\alpha\}^*$, (operator $\cup$, $\bullet$, $*$ denote the union, connection and the star (the power of closure $\{\alpha\}^* = \{\cup_{i=0}^{\infty} \alpha^i\}$) and the priority orders are $*$, $\bullet$, $\cup$ respectively;

(3) The expressions obtained by the limited use of (1) and (2) are regular expressions on Σ and the regular set is defined as the regular expression on Σ.

In order to simplify the regular expression, the following formulae are usually used:

(a) $\alpha \cup \alpha = \alpha$ (Idempotent law),
(b) $\alpha \cup \beta = \beta \cup \alpha$ (Exchange law),
(c) $(\alpha \cup \beta) \cup \gamma = \alpha \cup (\beta \cup \gamma)$ (Binding law),
(d) $\alpha \cup \emptyset = \alpha, \alpha\emptyset = \emptyset\alpha = \emptyset, \alpha\varepsilon = \varepsilon\alpha = \alpha$ (Zero or one law),
(e) $(\alpha\beta)\gamma = \alpha(\beta\gamma)$ (Binding law),
(f) $(\alpha \cup \beta)\gamma = \alpha\gamma \cup \beta\gamma$ (Distributive law),
(g) $\varepsilon \cup \alpha^* = \alpha^*$,
(h) $(\varepsilon \cup \alpha)^* = \alpha^*$.

When α is changed to β using (a) and (b), α is said to be similar to β.

It is convenient to use the regular expression equation $X_i = a_{i0} + a_{i1}X_1 + \cdots + a_{in}X_n$ to deal with language, as in such equations, the union of $\Delta = \{X_1, \ldots, X_n\}$ with Σ is $\emptyset$. a_{ij} is the regular expression on Σ. If a_{ij} is $\emptyset$ or ε, it is just the same as the coefficient of the ordinary linear differential equation as 0 and 1 respectively, which can be solved, based on the Gauss elimination method. Of course, the solution is a set, which suggests that the solution is not unique, but the algorithm can correctly determine a minimal fixed point solution. Suppose R is a regular language and there is a constant n, making all words w, whose length is not less than n can be written as $xyz(y \neq \varepsilon$ and $|xy| \leq n)$ and for all non-negative integers i, $xy^i z \in R$, which is called the pumping lemma. It is a powerful tool to prove that certain languages are not regular and it helps to establish an algorithm to determine whether a given language is finite or infinite, generated by a certain regular grammar. We can use arithmetic operations of language to determine whether a certain language is regular or not. It is known to all that, regular language is closed on Boolean operations (and, union, complementary), connection, * (Krini closure), left and right business, replacement, inverse INIT (prefix), FIN (), MAX, CYCLE, Reversal, MIN, etc. When $p(x)$ is a non-negative integer coefficient polynomial, R is a regular language, $L_1 = \{w|$ for some $|y| = p(|w|), wy \in R\}$, $L_2 = \{w|$ for some $|y| = p(|w|), wy \in R\}$ is also a regular language. When R, R_1 and R_2 are regular languages, the following problems are determinable: $w \in R? R = \emptyset? R = \Sigma^*? R_1 = R_2? R_1 \subseteq R_2? R_1 \cap R_2 = \emptyset?$

7.4 Augmented Transition Networks

In 1970, artificial intelligence expert Woods presented an automatic language analysis method, known as the augmented transition networks (ATN) [530]. ATN is an extension of finite state grammar. A finite state grammar can be represented by a state graph, but the function of this grammar is generation. If we start from the point of view of the sentence analysis, we can also use the state graph to express the analysis of a sentence and such a state graph is called finite state transition diagram (FSTD). A FSTD consists of many finite states and arcs from one state to another. The arc can be marked with a terminal symbol (that is, the specific word) and lexical category symbols such as <Verb>, <Adj>, <Noun>, etc. The analysis starts at the beginning state and following the direction of the arrow in a finite state transition graph, the input word is scanned one by one and the input is checked to see if it matches the label on the arc. If the end of an input statement is scanned, the FSTD enters to the final state, which suggests that the FSTD accepts an input sentence and the analysis is successfully finished (see Figure 7.6).

ATN can only recognize limited state language. We know that the rewritten rules of finite state grammars are A→aQ or A→a, which is relatively simple and the FSTD is sufficient to identify the languages generated by finite state grammars.

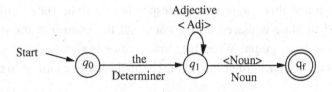

Fig. 7.6. ATN

For example, we can put forward a noun phrase, which is analyzed by the FSTD. It starts with a <Noun> in the beginning and ending and there are arbitrary <Adj> at the beginning and ending. Such as:

the pretty picture(Beautiful picture),
the old man(The elderly),
the good idea(Good idea).

The FSTD is shown in Figure 7.6. If the noun phrase entered is "the pretty picture," the analysis starts from the state q and follows the arc that is marked with 'the'. As 'the' is the word toward the left for the input string, these two are matched and then entered into the state q1 and the rest of the input string to be dealt is 'pretty picture'. Following the arc of the circle marked with <Adj>, we enter the state q1 again and the rest of the input string is 'picture'. Since the word is a noun and the arc of the label <Noun> is therefore matched, the final state qf is reached. At this time, the input string of all the words are checked and the results of the analysis are arrived at and the FSTD accepts this symbol string.

Finite state grammars are not suitable for dealing with complex natural languages. Therefore, it is necessary to extend the FSTD to provide a recursive mechanism to increase the recognition ability, so as to deal with CFL. For this purpose, the recursive transition networks (RTNs) was proposed. RTN is also a finite state transition graph. However, the marking on the arc not only contains terminal symbols (i.e., the specific word) and lexical category symbols, but also phrase type symbols (such as NP, S, PP, etc.). Since each phrase type symbol can be represented by a finite state transfer graph, the RTN is capable of recursion. This means that when it scans the phrase type, RTN can temporarily transfer to another finite state transition graph corresponding to the phrase type, so that the analysis process can be temporarily controlled. In this way, RTN can not only recognize the finite state language, but also recognize the CFL, which expands the FSTD recognition ability (see Figure 7.7).

The operation mode of RTN is similar to the operation mode of the FSTD. If the mark on the arc is a terminal symbol or a lexical category symbol, then you can deal with this arc like the FSTD. For example, the word "ball" can be matched with the arc of <Noun>, but not with <Adj> as a marker. If the symbol on the mark is of phrase type and this phrase type corresponds to a finite state transition graph, then the current state is placed into a stack and the control is transferred to the finite state transition graph. When the performance is successful or when it fails, the control will turn back, returning to the original state to continue to deal with the phrase.

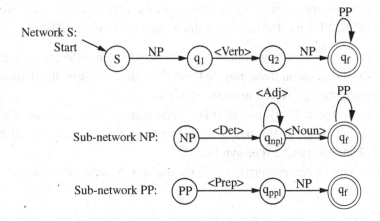

Fig. 7.7. RTN networks

For example, a RTN is made up of a network named S and two subnetworks NP and PP. Here, NP stands for noun phrases, while PP represents a prepositional phrase. <Det> is a 'determiner', <Prep> is a preposition, <Adj> is an adjective, <Noun> is a noun and q_f represents the final state. If the input string is "the little boy in the swimsuit kicked the red ball", the above RTN will be analyzed in the following order:

  NP: the little boy in the swimsuit
  PP: in the swimsuit
  NP: the swimsuit
Verb: kicked
  NP: the red ball

In the network S, the scanning process starts from S, then it scans to the subnetwork NP where 'the little boy in the Swimsuit' will be dealt with and when 'the little boy' is scanned, in PP 'in the swimsuit' will be scanned and the control comes into the subnetwork PP and continues continuing processing. In this subnetwork, after scanning the <Prep> that is 'in', NP 'the swimsuit' should be scanned. Therefore, Control enters subnetwork NP and deals with 'the swimsuit' and enters the final state of the NP. After, 'the little boy in the swimsuit' has been successfully dealt with, we go back to network S. Enter into q_1 and 'kicked' is scanned, enter into q_2, scanning NP, 'the red ball' is finally dealt with and the sentence analysis is then finished.

RTN can handle CFL. However, we know that CFGs, which can generate CFLs, are still not perfect in processing natural languages. Therefore, further expansion of the RTN is necessary to own a stronger recognition ability. In this way, Woods has proposed ATN. ATN has the following three aspects to expand RTN:

(1) Add a register for storing information. For example, in different subnetworks, a number of derivation trees may be formed locally, such that the derivation tree can be temporarily stored in these registers.
(2) The arc in the network can also be checked from the condition of the entry besides marking the symbols like the terminal symbol, the lexical category symbol and the phrase type symbol.
(3) Certain actions can be performed in the arc and the structure of a sentence can be reorganized.

In addition, as the register, condition and operation are expanded, the function of ATN can be increased to the level of the Turing machine. In theory, ATN can recognize any language that a computer can recognize.

The operation mode of ATN is similar to RTN. The difference lies in the following. If the arc is marked with a check, you must first perform this check and only when the check is successful, you can continue to scan the arc. In addition, if the arc is to perform the action associated with it, then, after the scan is done, these actions must be performed. At present, the research of ATN has been successfully applied to the man–machine conversation and generation of articles.

ATN also has some limitations it such as being excessively dependent on grammar parsing, which limits its ability to deal with some of the sentences which are semantically correct but do not completely conform to grammar.

7.5   Conceptual Dependency Theory

In 1972, Schank proposed the conceptual dependency theory [397], serving as a representation of the meaning of phrases and sentences. It also provides a common reasoning knowledge for computers and the automatic understanding of language can thus be understood. Basic principles of the conceptual dependence theory are as follows:

(1) For any two sentences with identical meaning, regardless of language, there is only one conceptual dependence representation.
(2) The meaning of this conceptual dependence representation is composed of a very small semantic meaning, which includes the meta-motion and the original state (the value of the property).
(3) Any information in the implicit sentence must be represented by an explicit representation of the meaning of the sentence.

The conceptual dependence theory has three aspects:

(1) The concept dependence→action elements, including:

   (a) The basic physical action world={GRASP, MOVE, TRANS, GO, PROPEL, INGEST, HIT}.

   (b) The basic movement of the spirit world={MTRANS, CONCEPTUALIZE, MBUILD}.

   (c) Basic movements of the means or tools={SMELL, LOOK-AT, LISTEN-TO, SPEAK}.

(2) The script → description of common scenes in a number of basic fixed set of movements (by the action of the basic elements).

(3) Plan → each step is composed by the script.

Here, we introduce the conceptual dependence theory and it is divided into the following categories:

(1) PP: A concept term that is used only for physical objects and is also called the image generator. For example, people, objects, etc. are PP. It also includes the natural wind, rain, lightning and thinking of the human brain (the brain as a generative system).

(2) PA: Physical objects' properties, together with its values can be used to describe the physical objects.

(3) ACT: It is the action performed by a physical object in relation to another physical object and it may be a physical object of its own actions, including physical action and mental action (such as criticism).

(4) LOC: An absolute position (determined by the cosmic coordinates), or a relative position (relative to a physical object).

(5) TIME: A time point or time slice, also divided into two kinds, namely absolute or relative time.

(6) AA: An action (ACT) attribute.

(7) VAL: Value of various attributes.

Schank formed a new concept by the following method (conceptualization):

(1) An actor (active physical object), plus an action (ACT).

(2) The following is the modification of the above concept:

   (a) An object (if ACT is a physical action, then it is a physical object and if ACT is a mental action, then it is another concept).

   (b) A place or a receiver (if ACT occurs between two physical objects, it indicates that a physical object or concept is passed to another physical object. If ACT occurs between two sites, it denotes the new location of the object).

(c) A means (which in itself is a concept).

(3) An object with a value of a property that is added to the object.
(4) A combination of concepts in some way, forming new concepts, for example, in combination with a causal relationship.

Originally, the goal of Schank was to make all the concepts atomic, but in fact, he only made the atomic action (ACT). He divided ACT into 11 kinds:

(1) PROPEL: Application of physical forces for an object, including push, pull, play, kick, etc.
(2) GRASP: An actor grabs a physical object.
(3) MOVE: The body part of the actor transforms space position, such as lifting, kicking, standing up, sitting down, etc.
(4) PTRANS: Transformation of the physical objects, such as entering, going out, going upstairs, diving, etc.
(5) ATRANS: Changes in abstract relationships, such as (holding and relationship changes), to give up (all of the relationship changes), the revolution (rule of change), etc.
(6) ATTEND: Use a sense organ to obtain information, such as the use of eye to search, ears to hear and so on.
(7) INGEST: The actor wants to bring a thing in, such as eating, drinking, taking medicine, etc.
(8) EXPEL: The actor puts something out, such as vomiting, crying, urinating, spitting, etc.
(9) SPEAK: A voice, including singing, music, screaming, wailing crying, etc.
(10) MTRANS: The transfer of information, such as conversation, discussion, calls, etc.
(11) MBUILD: The formation of new information from old information, such as anger from the heart.

Based on the definition of the 11 kinds of atomic action, Schank had a basic idea. These atomic concepts are not designed mainly for representing the action itself, but the result of that action is of the essence. Therefore it can be considered as concept reasoning. For example: 'X transfer Y from W go to Z by ATRANS' indicates the conclusions of the following reasoning:

(1) Y is in W at first;
(2) Y is now in Z (no longer in W);
(3) A certain purpose of X is achieved by ATRANS;

(4) If Y is a good thing, it means that things are going to be in favor of Z, which is not conducive to the direction of W and otherwise it is not.

(5) If Y is a good thing, it means that X does this action for the benefit of Z and otherwise it is the opposite.

One of the important sentences is the causal chain. Schank and some of his colleagues have designed a set of rules based on the conceptual dependency theory. The following are the five important rules:

(1) The action may cause a change in the state.

(2) The state can start actions.

(3) The state can eliminate actions.

(4) State (or action) can activate the mental event.

(5) Mental events may be the cause of the action.

This is the basic part of the world knowledge. Concept dependency includes each (and the combination) shorthand for causal connection. In the conceptual dependency theory, any information in the implicit sentence must be a clear representation of its explicit meaning. For example, the concept dependency of the sentence, "John eats the ice cream with a spoon" is explained in Figure 7.8. Vectors D and I that are expressed are used to explain the direction and the dependence respectively. Note that in this case, the mouth is a part of the concept, even though it does not appear in the original sentence. This is the basic difference between concept dependency and parse tree.

7.6 Language Understanding

7.6.1 Overview

The research of natural language information processing began with the advent of electronic computers and in the beginning of the 1950s, machine translation tests

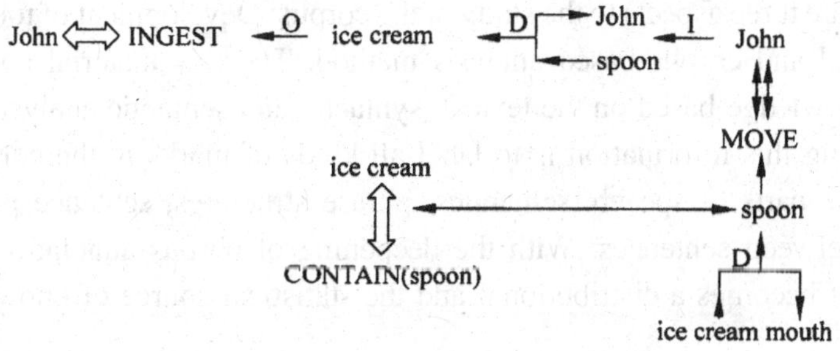

Fig. 7.8. Concept of the dependence of implicit information

were conducted. The research method of that time cannot be called "intelligent". Chomsky's transformational generative grammar was widely recognized. The core of generative grammar is the phrase structure rules. The process of the analysis of the sentence structure is the process of using rules from the top to the bottom or from the bottom to the top.

Realizing that grammar generation always lacks semantic knowledge, in the 1970s, the development of cognition science took place with semantic representation methods such as the semantic web, the conceptual dependency theory, the framework etc. These grammatical and semantic theories were developed quickly and they gradually integrated with each other. In the 1980s, a number of new grammar theories were presented, including the lexical functional grammar (LFG), the functional grammar (FUG) and the generalized phrase structure grammar (GPSG), etc. These rule-based analysis methods can be called "rationalism" in natural language processing. The basic starting point of rationalism is the pursuit of perfection, in an attempt to solve the problem one hundred percent perfectly. Chomsky proposed the standard theory in the 1960s and in the 1970s, the extension of standard theory was presented. Government and binding theory was proposed in the 1980s and the Minimalist Program was introduced in the 1990s. The goal of rationalism is abstract. On the basis of the study of language cognition or pure language theory, it looks for a kind of cross language similarity element periodic table. Although the existing analysis method can understand single sentences, it is difficult to cover the comprehensive phenomenon of language, especially for the whole paragraph or text.

The research of "empiricism" is the main research direction based on the large-scale corpus. Corpus is a collection of a large number of texts. After the emergence of the computer, the data can be easily stored and it is easy for the computer to retrieve relevant information. With the emergence of electronic publications, data collection is no longer difficult. Brown and LOB were two computer corpora, which were compiled in the 1960s, with a vocabulary size of 1,000,000. In the 1990s, it is easy to list a number of corpora, such as DCI, ICAME, ECI, BNC, LDC, CLR and so on, with a scale up to 10^9.

There are three aspects to the study of the corpus: Development of tool software, corpus label and corpus based analysis method. The raw material collected can provide knowledge based on the lexical, syntactic and semantic analysis. The way of processing this information is to label all kinds of marks in the corpus, which includes the parts of speech, semantics, phrase structures, sentence patterns and relations between sentences. With the deepening of corpus annotation gradually maturing, it becomes a distributional and the statistical source of knowledge. The use of this knowledge source can be used for many linguistic analyses, such as the frequency of the new text can be annotated by the frequency of the data from the annotated corpus.

The knowledge provided by the corpus is represented by statistical intensity, rather than certainty. With the expansion of the corpus scale, it is designed to cover the full linguistic phenomenon. However, the basic rule of language is still used to judge the size of statistical strength, which is contrary to people's common sense. The problem in "empiricism" can be made up with the "rationalism" method. The fusion of the two kinds of methods is also the trend of the development of natural language processing.

Olson, an American cognitive psychologist, proposed the standard of language comprehension as follows:

(1) The ability to answer questions about language materials, i.e., the ability to answer questions is a standard to understand language.
(2) After giving a large amount of material, the ability to summarize.
(3) Can use their own language, i.e., to use different words to repeat the material.
(4) Translate from one language to another.

If the above four abilities are present, language comprehension can be used in the following aspects:

(1) Machine translation: multi-lingual translation consisting of 10,000 words as vocabulary, 90% of accuracy of machine translation and 10% of artificial intervention. In the comprehensive system, computer serves as a translator for the participation from editing to printing at all levels. Translation of total spending in artificial translation is 30% or less than in human translation.
(2) The understanding of the document: machine reading, digesting the contents of the document to make a summary of the document or to answer specific questions on this basis.
(3) File generation: the machine can be stored in the computer in the form of information stored in the computer, thus generating a natural language.
(4) Other applications: for natural language interface, so as to place natural language interface for big systems. For example, for a large database using natural language retrieval, under the support of the United States Department of Defense and Naval Research, the LADDiR system was developed. This system stores more than 100 waters and 40,000 ships in a considerable number of computers. It can be used to talk to the staff or the decision maker and ask questions.

7.6.2 Development stage

The development of the natural language understanding system can be divided into two stages: the first generation system and the second generation system. The first generation system is established on the basis of the analysis part of the speech and word order and the statistical methods are used frequently. The second generation system begins to introduce the semantics and even pragmatic and contextual factors. Statistical techniques are rarely used.

The first generation of the natural language understanding system can be divided into four types:

1. Special format system

Early natural language understanding systems were always of special format, as they usually took advantage of special formats to carry out human dialogue based on the characteristics of the content of human nature. In 1963, Lindsay developed SAD–SAM system in the Carnegie Institute of Technology with IPL-V list processing language, using a special format on kinship man–machine dialogue. The system established a database about kinship, which could receive kinship questions in English. In 1968, Bobrow designed "STUDENT" system in the Massachusetts Institute of Technology. This system summarized high-school math problems to some patterns and the computer could be used to understand the problems in English. In early 1960s, Green established the BASEBALL system in the Lincoln Laboratory in the United States, which also used the V-IPL table processing language. The database stored federal baseball score records in the United States in 1959, which could also answer some questions about the baseball game. The system's syntactic parsing ability was poor, it as could only handle very simple input sentences. Besides, there was no connection word and no comparison between the form of adjectives and adverbs. It mainly relied on a machine dictionary to identify the word and used 14 lexical categories. All of the questions were represented as a specially specified expression answer.

2. Text-based systems

Some researchers were not satisfied with the format restrictions in the special format system. Since there were special fields, the most convenient way to use a system was not to use a special format for the human machine dialogue, which limited the structure of the system. This became the basis of the text system. In 1966, Simmons, Burger and Long designed the PROTOSYNTHEX-I system, which was based on text storage and retrieval.

3. Finite logic system

The finite logic system further improved the system based on text. In this system, natural language sentences were replaced by a more formal notation, which could form a finite logical system. In 1968, Rafael used LISP language to establish the SIR system in MIT, which proposed 24 matching patterns in English. The input of English sentences and the matching of these patterns could be used to determine the structure of the sentence. In the process of answering the question from the database to the storage knowledge, we could deal with some concepts, such as inclusion relations, spatial relations and so on. Besides, simple logical reasoning could be carried out and the machine could learn from the dialogue, remember learnt knowledge and engage in some of the initial intellectual activity. In 1965, Slagle established the DEDUCOM system, which could perform deductive reasoning in information retrieval. In 1966, Thompson established the DEACON system, which could manage a fictional military database in English. The design used the concept of ring structure and approximate English concepts to carry out reasoning. In 1968, Kellog designed the CONVERSE system on the IBM360/67 computer, which could carry out the reasoning based on 1,000 facts about 120 cities in the United States.

4. General deduction system

The general deductive system takes advantage of some standard mathematical notations (such as the predicate calculus notation) to express information. Achievement of theorem proving for logicians can be considered as the basis for the establishment of the valid deductive system, and thus the system is able to express any questions from the perspective of the theorem to prove. Also, the information can be deducted and expressed as natural language. The general deductive system can express complex information which is not easy to be expressed in a logical system and thus it further improves the ability of the natural language understanding system. From 1968 to 1969, QA2 and QA3 use predicate calculus and format data to carry on deductive reasoning and solve problems in English, which became a typical representation of the general deductive system.

Since 1970, there have been a certain number of second generation natural language understanding systems. These systems are mostly procedural deduction systems, using a large number of semantic, context and pragmatic factors for analysis. Some of the more famous systems are the LUNAR system, the SHRDLU system, the MARGIE system, the SAM system and the PAM system.

The LUNAR system is a natural language information retrieval system designed by Woods in 1972. This system used the formal question language to express the meaning of the question, and thus made a semantic interpretation of the question. It also retrieved from the database, resulting in finding the answer to the question.

The SHRDLU is a system with natural language command for robot movement designed by Winograd in 1972 at the Massachusetts Institute of Technology. The system combines syntactic parsing, semantic analysis and logical reasoning together, which greatly enhances the function of the system in language analysis. The object for the dialogue system is a toy robot with a simple "hand" and "eye". The toy robot is able to handle toy building blocks, such as cubes, pyramids and boxes, etc., which was placed on the table with different colors, sizes and shapes. The robot is able to pick up these building blocks, move them to build a new brick structure, based on the command of the operator. In the process of man–machine conversation, operators can get visual feedback sent to the robot and observe the ability of the robot in understanding the language and executing commands real-time. The TV screen can also show the simulated image of the robot as well as the vivid scenes of the same in real time on the computer.

The MARGIE system was developed by Schank in 1975 in the Stanford Artificial Intelligence Laboratory in America. The purpose of this system was to provide a visual model for natural language understanding. The system first converts the English sentence into the concept-dependent expression and then starts to reason according to the relevant information of the system. In the end, a large number of facts can be deduced from the concept of dependency expression. When a human being starts to understand a sentence, more content involving the sentence will be extended. Therefore, the system provides 16 types of reasoning, such as the reasons, effects, instructions, functions and so on. Finally, the results of the inference are converted into English output.

The SAM system was established in Yale University in the United States by Abelson in 1975. This system uses the script to understand the story written in natural language. The so-called script is used to describe people's activities (such as going to restaurants, seeing a doctor) as a standardized series of events.

The PAM system is a system for the understanding of the story, which was designed by Wilensky in 1978 in Yale University in the United States. The PAM system can also explain the story, answer questions and make a summary. In addition to the sequence of events in the script, it also presents a plan as a basis for understanding the story. The so-called plan, is the method adopted by the characters of the story in order to achieve their purpose. If you want to understand the story through the "plan", you need to find out the purpose of the characters and the actions taken to accomplish this goal. The system is equipped with a "plan box", which stores information about various purposes and various methods. In this way, when the system needs to understand the story, as long as the plot of the story matched with the plan are stored in the plan box it can understand the purpose of this story. If a barrier occurs when matching with a story and script, the failure of the story to be understood will not appear as the "plan" but it can provide the general purpose information. For example, in rescuing a man snatched by the mob, there are some objectives under the "rescue" catalogue, including arrival of mob lair and various methods of killing mobs, which becomes the basis for the next step behavior. Simultaneously, the purpose can be inferred from the subject. For example, entering a story: "John is in love with Mary. Mary was robbed by the mob." The PAM system can expect actions John will take to rescue Mary. Although there is no such content in the story, according to the "love theme" in the plan box, it can infer the plots that "John will take actions to save Mary".

The above systems are all written natural language understanding systems, whose input and output are written. The oral natural language understanding system, which involves complex techniques such as speech recognition, speech synthesis and so on, is clearly more difficult. In recent years, the research of oral natural language understanding systems are also in progress.

7.6.3 Rule-based analysis method

From the perspective of linguistics and cognition, a set of linguistic rules are set up so that the machine can understand the natural language. The rule-based approach is a theoretical approach. Under ideal conditions, the rules can form a complete system, which covers all the language phenomena. The rule-based method can be used to explain and understand all the language problems.

The natural language understanding system involves syntax, semantics and pragmatics to some extent. Syntax is the rule that links words to phrases, clauses and sentences, while syntactic parsing is one of the best options for the three areas. Most natural language understanding systems contain a syntactic parsing program that generates syntactic trees (see Figure 7.10) to reflect the syntactic structure of an input sentence, in order to prepare for further analysis. Figure 7.9 shows syntactic tree of "the fact that Zhang San is right".

Considering the existence of multiple syntactic ambiguities, many different words can be considered as different lexical categories in different contexts, so the correct syntactic structure information can only be obtained by syntactic parsing. So it is necessary to rely on some form of semantic analysis. Semantics is given to the meaning of words, phrases, clauses and sentences. For example:

(a) He is at home. ("zai" is a verb).

Example: Facts proved that Zhang San was right.

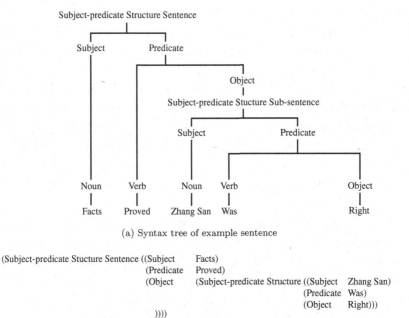

(a) Syntax tree of example sentence

(Subject-predicate Stucture Sentence ((Subject   Facts)
                                  (Predicate   Proved)
                                  (Object   (Subject-predicate Structure ((Subject   Zhang San)
                                                                (Predicate Was)
                                                              (Object   Right)))
                                ))))

(b) Express for syntax tree of example sentence

Fig. 7.9. Two kinds of syntactic representation

(b) He sleeps at home. ("zai" is a preposition).

(c) He was eating. ("zai" is an adverb).

The same "zai" word in different contexts can not only act as different lexical category, but also have different meanings. These examples show that even in the course of syntactic parsing, in order to get the correct analysis as soon as possible, certain semantic information is often needed and even the intervention of knowledge from the external world is also needed. There are two different approaches for the analysis of syntax and semantics:

(1) Serial processing of syntactic parsing and semantic analysis are separate separately (as shown in Figure 7.10(a)). The traditional linguists claim that the analysis of syntactic parsing and semantic analysis should be completely separated. But many famous natural language understanding systems, such as the SHRDLU systems, allowed calling the functions of semantic interpretation of the input statements in the course of processing to assist the analysis (as shown in Figure 7.10(a)). However, these two methods will generate some form of syntax tree as a result of syntactic parsing.

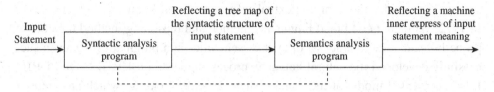

(a) Analyze separation process scheme of syntactic and semantics

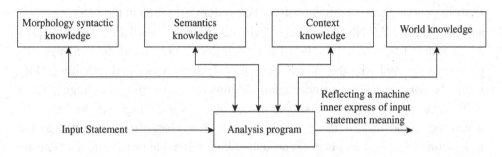

(b) An integration process method of syntactic and semantics

Fig. 7.10. Solutions to the natural language analysis system

(2) Integration of syntax and semantics, as shown in Figure 7.10(b). This kind of treatment plan can be considered as the mode whose representative is Shank, a professor in artificial intelligence of Yale University. The feature of this scheme is to cancel the relative independence of the syntactic parsing module and thus no longer produce the intermediate results of the syntactic structure of the input sentence. Their guiding ideology is to make comprehensive references in the analysis as early as possible. They are not completely without syntactic knowledge in the analysis; but do not rely on the syntactic parsing excessively. Many psychologists have argued that this integrated approach is more close to the understanding of language. The representative of this scheme is the CA and the ELI.

Semantic knowledge engineering, which is a part of natural language processing, has been studied since the 1980s. The semantic knowledge base has mainly focused on semantic relationship with the characteristics of relativity. The semantic knowledge is mainly used as the constraint condition and it plays an important role for computers to transform languages. Emphasis is attached to the semantic category and the semantic constraint condition can be extracted. The resulting semantic knowledge can serve natural language processing more directly and in a better way.

One of the tasks of pragmatics is considering factors such as who writes the sentence and where (place) and when (time) this happens in order to make a more comprehensive interpretation of the sentence. This analysis clearly requires that the system has a wider range of contextual information and knowledge of the world. In 1972, Winograd combined linguistics method and reasoning method together to properly handle the interaction of syntax, semantics and pragmatics. He even successfully developed the natural language processing system SHRDLU On PDP10. It is a theoretical model of the human language understanding, which has aroused many researchers' interests [527].

This system includes an analytical procedure, English grammar, a semantic analysis program and a problem solver. The system is written in the LISP language and the MICROPLANNER language, which is based on the LISP. The design of the system is based on such a belief that, in order to understand the language, the program must deal with the overall view of syntax, semantics and reasoning. Only when the computer system understands its subject, it can study the language and system reasonably. There is a simple model of its own intelligence, for example, it can recall and discuss its plans and actions. Knowledge is represented as the process in the system and is not represented by a rule table or pattern. The knowledge is exhibited by syntax, semantics and reasoning, as each knowledge can be a process. It will be able to directly call any other knowledge in the system and therefore the SHRDLU system has the ability to achieve unprecedented level of performance.

Yixin Zhong put forward a concept of full information. The information expressed in natural language is a variety of information, which obviously belongs to the category of epistemology. The main body of knowledge, generally speaking, is a person, or it can be a variety of creatures, or even a man-made machine system. However, the most meaningful subject is the person himself. From the perspective of epistemology, there are three basic characteristics of the normal subjects for cognition. They are observation, understanding and purpose. Therefore, the main body of the perception or the expression of the "thing's movement state and its mode of change" must include:

(1) The grammatical information of things, concerned with the form of the movement of things and the way of its change;
(2) The semantic information of the object, concerned with the meaning of the movement of things and the way of its change;
(3) The pragmatic information of things, concerned with the movement of things and its change in the way of understanding the purpose of the subject. Organic whole information is formed by the combination of grammatical information, semantic information and pragmatic information, which is called full information [540]. Figure 7.11 gives a full illustration of the concept.

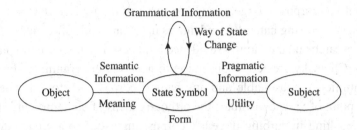

Fig. 7.11. Full information concept diagram

In Figure 7.11, the movement of things and states change (the central part of the figure), which is the grammatical information of things. It is the form of performance of movement of things and how it is changing. Once the form of this state and its change is associated with its corresponding real object, it has a concrete practical meaning (the central and left part of the figure), which is the semantic information. It is no longer abstract but very concrete thing. Furthermore, if the form of the state, its changing way and its meaning are associated with a particular subject, it will show the effectiveness as the main purpose for the subject, which is the pragmatic information.

Thus, grammatical information is an abstract information level, while semantic information is the result of the correlation between grammatical information and its corresponding objects. Pragmatic information is the result of the mutual relationship between grammatical information, semantic information and the subject and therefore it is the most concrete level. Grammatical information and semantic information are only related to objects while pragmatic information has the relationship with the subject. It can be seen that the concept of full information is an organic system.

7.6.4 Statistical model based on Corpus

Research on Corpus Linguistics focuses on the acquisition, storage, labeling, retrieval and statistics of natural language. The aim is to quantitatively analyze the linguistic facts of large-scale real texts and support the development of the natural language processing system. Its application areas include measurement and analysis of language, language knowledge acquisition, work style analysis, dictionary compilation, full text retrieval system, natural language understanding system and machine translation system.

The origin of modern corpus linguistics can be traced back to the structural linguistics era of the late 1950s in the United States. At that time, the linguists thought that the corpus is large enough to serve as a language database. This linguistic data is occurring naturally, and thus is necessary and sufficient for the task of linguistic research and the intuitive evidence is, at best, in a poor second place. In the late 1950s, Chomsky created a conversion to generate the grammar. He advocated that the intuition is reasonable and any natural corpus is distorted. The rationalism of his point of view constitutes the orthodox ideas of contemporary theoretical linguists, resulting in curbing the early corpus linguistics to a great extent. However, practice has proved that it is impossible to cover all kinds of linguistic facts that appear in real large-scale texts. With the rapid development of computer and computing technology, the size of the corpus has extended from 100,000 words in the 1960s to 1–10 billion times in 1990s, thus expanding thousands of times in 30 years. This was not foreseen by the experts who rejected the intuition method in the 1950s and the corpus-based methods in the 1960s. This fact makes a language of vocabulary. Syntax phenomenon can rely on the corpus to conduct an open survey.

In 1959, some scholars put forward the idea of establishing a corpus of modern English Usage Survey. In the beginning of the 1960s the Brown Corpus of modern American English was established in the United States, which marks the beginning of the second period of corpus linguistics. To create the keyboard input mode of the brown corpus in the 1970s, the modern British English LOB corpus was known as the first generation of corpus and their storage capacity was 100,000 words. In the 1980s, optical character recognition (OCR) technology replaced the corpus based on artificial keyboard entry mode, so the corpus size started growing rapidly. During this period, the establishment of the corpus included COBUILD corpus, with 200 million words and Longman/Lancaster English corpus with 300 million words. They belong to the second generation corpus. Since the 1990s, due to popularity of word processing and editing software and desktop publishing, a huge number of machine readable texts have become corpus as inexhaustible resources, following (1–10) billion words corpus, that is the third generation corpus, such as the American Institute of Computational Linguistics' ACL/DCI corpus, Oxford text archive in the United Kingdom, and so on. Based on the growth of the corpus in the past 30 years, Leech predicted there will be super large-scale corpus with 1 trillion words in the year 2021.

The size of the corpus and the principle of material selection are important, as they will directly affect the reliability and applicability of the statistical data. However, the supporting environment of corpus linguistics and the processing depth of corpus are more important for the corpus. Taking Chinese for example, the original "raw" data can only be used for word frequency (including several adjacent word co-occurrence frequency) and sentence length statistics, providing a simple keyword search (KWIC). In order to achieve the word level count and retrieval, we must segment the original corpus using marking signs. In the process of subsequent processing, it is also able to label the corpus with parts of speech, syntactic relations and semantic items and so, the inventory data is gradually converted from "raw" to "mature". All kinds of information carried by the data is full, the corpus will eventually become the corpus of the language knowledge base.

The main contents of corpus linguistics include:

(1) The construction of the basic corpus;
(2) Corpus processing tools, including automatic word segmentation, parts of speech tagging system, syntactic analysis system, meaning tagging system discourse analysis system, etc.;
(3) A "mature" corpus with labeled information is established, which is based on data processing;
(4) Technology and method acquired from linguistics knowledge is in the corpus.

At present, the world has already established hundreds of corpora, including a variety of languages, which is an important resource for researchers in the linguistic research and development of natural language processing system. At the same time, the construction and use of the corpus has become an important part of international academic journals and conferences. Held in July 1993, the Fourth Machine Translation High-level Conference in Britain had scholars who made a special report that pointed out that since 1989, the world has entered the third generation machine translation system research. The main sign being the corpus-based method introduced to the classical rules-based method, including statistical methods, instance-based methods and linguistic knowledge base obtained from the data processing of the corpus.

In order to make the Chinese corpus universal, practical and popular, as well as become the basic facility to provide the important resources of natural language processing, we should build a multi-level corpus of Chinese corpus, which is composed of the fine processed corpus, the basic corpus and the Web corpus. Then the research focus on the construction of the corpus will turn to how to get the resources of the three levels of corpus and to use them effectively. The fine processing corpus can provide an excellent and large amount of language processing specifications and examples for various language studies. The basic corpus is a broad and large-scale raw corpus, which can provide more accurate data for language analysis. The Web corpus is a language resource that can realize the dynamic updating, including many new words, new collocation and new usage. It can be used to track the Web language, new words and popular words and can also be used to observe the changes in time. It can overcome the problem of sparse data and corpus update in the traditional corpus based on multi-level Chinese corpus. On the corpus scale, the scale of the corpus is gradually reduced, but the quality of the processing depth is gradually improved. Fine corpus is maintained on the scale of 10 million words and it is more reasonable to maintain more than 1 billion words for basic corpus. The underlying Web corpus is the opening of online resources.

7.6.5 Machine learning method

Machine learning is based on the understanding of the mechanism of human learning, such as physiology and cognitive science, to develop various learning theories and methods. It can study the general learning algorithm and carry on theoretical analysis. Finally, a learning system based on task-oriented learning is established. These studies' targets will be promoted with a mutual influence. At present, machine learning methods are widely used in language information.

1. Text Classification

The purpose of classification is to learn a classification function or classification model (also often referred to as the classifier). The model can map the data in the database to a given class. Classification and regression can be used for prediction. The purpose of the prediction is to automatically derive from the historical data records for the promotion of a given data description, so as to predict future data. Unlike the regression method, the output of the classification is a discrete category value and the output of the regression is a continuous value. Here, we will not discuss the regression method.

To construct a classifier, a training sample data set is required as input. The training set consists of a set of database records, or a tuple. Each tuple is a feature vector, which is composed of the value of the field (also called the attribute or feature). The form of a specific sample can be: $(v_1, v_2, \ldots, v_n; c)$; where v_i represents a field value and c represents a class.

The construction method of the classifier includes the statistical method, the machine learning method, the neural network method, etc. The statistical methods include the Bayesian method and the non-parametric method (nearest neighbor learning or case-based learning) and the corresponding knowledge representation is the discriminant function and the prototype case. Machine learning methods include decision tree and rule induction, where the former corresponds to the decision tree, while the latter is generally related to production rules. The representative neural network method is the BP algorithm, which is a forward feedback neural network model (composed of the nodes of the neural network and the edge of the connection weight). The BP algorithm is in fact, a nonlinear discriminant function. In addition, a new method of the rough set has recently emerged, whose knowledge representation is of the production rules.

2. Text Clustering

According to the different characteristics of the data, it can be divided into different data clusters. Its purpose is to make the distance between individuals belonging to the same category as small as possible, while the distance between individuals in different categories is as large as possible. Clustering methods include the statistical method, the machine learning method, the neural network method and the database oriented method.

In statistical methods, cluster analysis is one of the three methods of multi-variate data analysis (the other two are regression analysis and discriminant analysis). It is mainly focused on clustering based on geometric distance, such as the Euclidean distance, the Ming Kowski distance, etc. The traditional statistical clustering analysis methods include the system clustering method, the decomposition method, the adding method, the dynamic clustering method, the ordered sample clustering, the overlapping clustering and the fuzzy clustering. The clustering method is based on global comparison and it needs to investigate all the individuals to decide the final cluster. Therefore, it requires all the data which must be given in advance, but it cannot dynamically add new data objects. The clustering analysis method does not have linear complexity, as it is difficult to apply to the database when it is very large.

In machine learning, clustering is called unsupervised or non-teacher induction when compared to the classification. Examples or data objects are labeled, while the clustering is with unlabeled data, which need to be determined by the clustering algorithm. In most artificial intelligence literature, clustering is also called concept clustering. Since the distance is no longer the geometric distance in the statistical method, it is determined by the description of the concept. When clustering objects can be dynamically added, the concept cluster is called the concept formation.

In neural networks, there is a kind of unsupervised learning method, the self-organizing neural network method, such as the Kohonen self-organizing feature map network, the competitive learning network, etc. In the field of data mining, the neural network clustering method, which is reported in the field of data mining, is a self-organizing feature mapping method, and IBM takes advantage to cluster the database.

3. Case-based machine translation

The case-based machine translation was first proposed in the 1990s by Japanese scholars. This method is based on case-based reasoning (CBR). In CBR, the problem or situation that is faced by the current situation is referred to as the target case, while the memory of the problem or situation is called the source case. In a simple way, the CBR is a solving strategy based on the hint of the target case to acquire the source case and solve the problem under the guidance of the source case. Therefore, the general idea of translation is as follows: a corpus consisting of a bilingual translation unit is created in advance. Then, the search unit chooses a searching and matching algorithm and the optimal matching unit is searched in the corpus.

If we want to translate the source language text 'S', the translation examples S' that need to be found in the bilingual corpus is similar to S. According to the S', T is the translation case. The translation result T is finally acquired. In general, the case-based machine translation system includes several steps, such as the pattern retrieval of candidate instances, sentence similarity computation, bilingual word alignment and analogical translation. The finding of the most similar translation examples from the source language text is the key problem of the case-based translation method. So far, researchers have not found a simple way to calculate the similarity between sentences. In addition, the evaluation of sentence similarity problem still requires a lot of human engineering, language psychology and other knowledge.

The case-based machine translation method is almost not needed to analyze and understand the source language. It only needs a relatively large sentence aligned bilingual corpus, so it is easy to get the knowledge acquisition. If there are similar sentences in the corpus, the case-based method can get a good translation and the more similar the sentence is, the translation effect is better and the quality of the translation will be higher.

There is one more advantage for the case-based translation method. The knowledge representation of an instance pattern can be expressed in a concise and convenient way to express a large amount of human language.

However, shortcomings of case-based machine translation are also obvious. When a similar sentence is not found, the translation will declare a failure. This requires the corpus to cover a wide range of linguistic phenomena. For example, like the PanEBMT system of the Carnegie Mellon University [65], which contains about 2,800,000 English and French bilingual sentence pairs. Although the researcher of the PanEBMT system thinks in a lot of other ways, if not for the open text test, the coverage of translation of the PanEBMT is only 70%. In addition, it is not easy to establish a large high-quality bilingual sentence aligned corpus, especially for those with minority language.

Trados is a desktop computer auxiliary translation software, which is based on translation memory (TM) base and term base and provides a complete set of tools for creating, editing and checking high-quality translation [463]. The company of Trados GmbH was founded in 1984 by Hummel and Knyphausen in Germany. The company began to develop translation software in the late 1980s and released the first batch of windows software in the early 1990s. They developed Multi-Term and Workbench Translator's in 1992 and 1994 respectively. In 1997, thanks to Microsoft using Trados software for localization translation, the company became the desktop TM software industry leader in the late 1990s. Trados was acquired by SDL in June 2005.

SDL Trados Studio 2014 worked in a team to collect their translation, in order to establish a language database (TM). In this database, the software is determined to be reused. When translators translate new content and correlate the translated sentences that are similar to or in the same sentence, the software automatically puts forward suggestions of reusable content. The features of SDL Trados Studio are as follows:

(1) Based on the principle of TM, it is currently the world's most famous professional translation software and has become the standard for professional translation.
(2) Supports two-way translation of 57 languages.
(3) Greatly improves work efficiency, reduces costs and improves quality.
(4) Its background is a very powerful neural network database to ensure security of the system and information.
(5) Supports all popular document formats, which users do not need to layout. (DOC, RTF, HTML, SGML, XML, FrameMaker, RC, AutoCAD, DXF, etc.)
(6) Improves the auxiliary functions, such as time, measurement, form, automatic replacement and other fixed format, that can help customers greatly improve work efficiency.
(7) The interface is clear. Both the original and the translated work are clearly displayed on both sides. It is able to customize the environment in a variety of ways: Keyboard shortcuts, layout, color and text size can be customized, so as to maximize the comfort and work efficiency.
(8) Provides the most extensive file format support, from the Office2013 Microsoft file to the complex XML file.

If the study of cased-based machine translation, one of the main aspects of the research is to focus on how to improve the translation of the translation system under the relatively small size of the cases, or how to reduce the size of the case model to maintain the effectiveness of the translation. In order to achieve this goal, we need to extract as much linguistic knowledge as possible from the database of case patterns, including syntax, lexical knowledge and semantic knowledge.

7.7 Functional Area of Brain

Language is concerned as a high-level human brain function. Since Broca found Broca's area in 1861, neuro-linguistic research has been the hottest areas in brain science research. For more than a century, two basic conclusions have been drawn in terms of scientific research of language: One is that the different parts of the brain perform different functions in language while the other is different damages in the different brain regions cause different speech disorders. With the development of functional imaging and electrophysiological monitoring, the functional area of brain language has made great progress.

7.7.1 Classical function area

The functional areas of the brain can be divided into the motor speech center and the sensory center of speech. The former is located in the posterior inferior frontal gyrus (Brodmann 44, 45, abbreviated as BA44, 45), namely Broca area. This area is also known as the speaking area, often described as inferior frontal gyrus after 1/3. For planning and implementation of speech, the lesion of the area will lead to motor aphasia, which is the main performance for oral expression. The auxiliary motor area (SMA), also known as the language area, is located in the front of the rear area of the central front back to the lower limbs. The medial boundary of the cingulate sulcus, which is the lateral extension to the adjacent convex hemisphere, has no obvious boundary between the front and the side. The SMA and the primary motor area, the anterior cingulate cortex and the prefrontal cortex, the cerebellum, the basal ganglia and the parietal lobe are all associated with each other. This complex anatomical function system is used to launch and control motor function and language expression. Further, SMA is divided into the SMA prop-area and the SMA inherent area, respectively, to participate in the preparation and execution of complex movements.

The dominant hemisphere motor cortex PMC is described as the primary motor cortex (Brodmann 4) and the anterior frontal cortex (Brodmann 6). The area is divided into two subregions: PMC (ventral part of the PMC region of the central front of the Brodmann6 area) and the side of the front of the central sulcus (Brodmann6). The study found that the PMC involved in the ventral side of the pronunciation and was involved in the naming of the PMC. Neuroimaging studies further support the dominant hemisphere PMC to participate in different linguistic components, such as reading tasks, repeating words, naming tools, etc.

There is a writing center (BA8) located behind the back forehead. Sensory center of speech can be divided into auditory language center and the visual language center. There are no clear boundaries between them, namely, the Wernicke's area. The Wernicke's area is also known as postspeech area and generally refers to the dominant hemisphere superior temporal gyrus, but there are also scholars who believe that the area including Brodmann 41 and 42 rear zone of the superior temporal gyrus, middle temporal gyrus belongs to the top of the inferior parietal lobule supramarginal and angular back (BA22, 39). The Wernicke's area, Brodmann 5 area, the seven regions (Brodman 41, 42) and the visual area (Brodmann, 18, 19) are closely related for regional language sense stimulation. The area of the lesion had a sensory aphasia, while the patient's voice is normal, but the person who speaks cannot understand what others say. The answer is not coherent, or not relevant and thus it is difficult for the audience to understand.

Middle part and inside portion of temporal lobe is a complex, multifunctional area, with a wide range of visual and auditory functions. Electrical stimulation study found that the left temporal lobe, which is the medial part plays an important role in auditory language. The stimulus in the region can cause abnormal changes in language. Lesions can cause a slight disorder of language, including the difficulty of finding the word, the name of the defect, etc.

The time zone is located in the language-dominant hemisphere and the distance from the temporal pole is 3–7 cm, serving as an independent regional out of the Wernicke's area. There is a direct link between the white matter tracts and the white matter tracts below the Wernicke area. Study of electrical stimulation shows that the language function of the temporal lobe cortex is a lack of feeling and expression. After electrical stimulation for the temporal lobe, 80% of patients show difficulty in naming and understanding.

Along with further research, some other brain regions have been discovered. The temporal lobe of the left is not easy to form a model of ischemia reperfusion injury, since its dual blood supply comes from the anterior and posterior arteries. Later it was found that this region is related to the retrieval of words, which is known as the basal temporal lobe language area.

The basal ganglia has the function of the central nervous system, which not only regulates the movement and coordination of the cone system, but also supports the simple cognitive and memory functions, such as conditional reflex, spatial deduction and attention conversion. Studies have found that the basal ganglia may participate in complex cognition and memory functions such as priming effect related to language, logical inference, language processing, language memory, grammar memory, etc. It has the abilities of language processing, sorting and coordination. Other studies have found, that in addition to the classical language functional areas, the left superior parietal lobule, the bilateral fusiform gyrus, the left inferior occipital gyrus, on both sides of the occipital gyrus, the auxiliary motor area and the inferior frontal gyrus and other are involved in the processing of language.

From a psychological point of view, there are three main types of language memorization, namely, phonological, grammar and semantic, i.e., the language in the brain consists of the sound, form and meaning of processing. Language sense is introduced through audio visual and touch (Braille) and the way of the language to be expressed can be pronunciation, writing and drawing. Different stimuli can activate different functional areas, such as visual, auditory and tactile functional areas and the different responses of the subjects can activate a number of brain regions, such as the motor area, the cerebellum, etc. The activation of these regions can sometimes interfere with the accurate positioning of language function area. At present, finer division is given to language semantics, phonology and spelling of the language in the brain's functional areas.

7.7.2 Semantic-related functional area

Semantic processing of words is one of the basic activities of human brain language processing. The study of Mummery found that semantic tasks can activate a wide range of areas, including the left superior temporal middle part and the lower part of the superior temporal cortex.

Binder studied stimulation of sound afferent the stimuli were used in the name of the animal. The control task was used to stimulate the sound and the rest state. The subjects used the mouse to indicate whether the animal is native or not for human use. The study found that awareness of lexical semantic activates some brain areas and the left hemisphere showed its obvious advantages, including most of the bilateral superior temporal gyrus, extending to the left hemisphere temporal gyrus and the active region ventral temporal gyrus, the fusiform gyrus, the parahippocampal gyrus, the middle frontal gyrus, a large part of the inferior frontal gyrus, abdominal and cingulate gyrus of the frontal gyrus, former corner back and around the corpus callosum pressure region.

More in-depth research shows that phonological activation is of left inferior frontal gyrus (BA44, 45), while semantic processing activated the left inferior frontal gyrus ventricular surface (BA45, 47).

7.7.3 Phonological-related functional area

In terms of language processing, it is difficult to completely rule out the influence of language processing, such as semantic or phonological factors. The research also shows that it is inevitable to perform phoneme processing in terms of behavior of semantic processing of Chinese characters and English words. Thus, there is a number of semantic overlaps between activation of the brain regions and phonology.

Heim took advantage of event-related methods to study and found that the upper and the left frontal lobe of Broca's area (BA44) and (BA 45, 46) and the temporal lobe (PSTC) have been significantly activated in phonological tasks and this activation shows itself in phonological understanding and generation. Recent studies have found that the left superior temporal gyrus and the middle temporal gyrus were significantly activated in the recognition of language and non-language phonology.

Further study of the two basic components of the syllable and phoneme in the phonological structure found that they activated the left inferior frontal gyrus and the anterior part of the left middle frontal gyrus, respectively.

7.7.4 Spelling-related functional area

Booth observed the normal language function area based on the visual input of vocabulary spelling task and auditory input of lexical phonological task. It was found that the BA19, 37 was activated in the spelling of a word. The superior temporal gyrus (BA22, 42) is activated in sound processing. Using different task types between cross stimulation, the supramarginal and the angular back (BA 40, 39) is responsible for conversion between orthography and phonology.

Compared with English or other Western languages, the unique structure of the Chinese characters need more processing for the spelling of Chinese characters. According to this theory, studies have found that the left superior temporal gyrus (BA9) shows more activation properties in the recognition of Chinese characters, which suggests that the brain regions may be responsible for the coordination of Chinese characters and their integration.

7.7.5 Bilingual brain functional areas

Do different regions of the human brain represent different languages? The study of this problem is a hot topic in language functional imaging. Many scholars have bilingual or multilingual individuals as subjects, to observe the different language activation performance. Although the results vary from person to person, most scholars believe that the bilingual language and the second language have a lot of overlap in the brain activation area, including Wernicke and Broca areas. For example, the visual stimuli in the brain regions activated by both Chinese and English bilingual brain regions is located in the left frontal lobe and the left temporal regions. When Spanish and Catalan bilinguals are listening to the stories, the left temporal lobe and hippocampus will overlap. A wide range of overlap between the left temporal lobe and the parietal lobe were also found in Spanish and English.

There is a large amount of overlapping brain activation areas between the native language and the second language area. The second language area is often found to be activated with broad extension and intensity compared with the mother tongue. This phenomenon usually occurs in less fluent bilingual subjects and rarely appears in bilingual subjects. It is not related to when the second language is learnt but is associated with the frequency of usage of the second language.

7.8 Neural Model of Language Understanding

7.8.1 Aphasia

Brain injury may lead to language barrier of aphasia. Aphasia is common after stroke, where about 40% will experience severe aphasia at least in the first several months. However, many patients will find it difficult to understand and write the spoken language and the written language for a long time. Primary and secondary aphasia are different. Primary aphasia is caused by the problem of speech processing system while secondary aphasia is caused by cognitive damage, memory disorders or problems of attention. Some researchers only confirmed aphasia caused by damage to the language system. In the 19th century, researchers believed that brain damage in a particular location would result in the loss of a specific function.

Broca made a conclusion that the generation of the oral speech is located in the left hemisphere based on the study of the aphasia and this region was later called the Broca area. In the 1870s, Wernicke treated two patients speaking fluently, but uttering meaningless sounds, words and sentences who had serious difficulties in the interpretation of utterances. Wernicke's examination revealed damage was found in the superior temporal gyrus region. As auditory processing occurs in the vicinity, i.e., in the front of the temporal back on the transverse temporal gyrus, Wernicke speculated that more regions from the back involved in word auditory memory. The area was later known as the Wernicke area. Wernicke believes that since this region has lost the memory associated with words, the damage of the region leads to the difficulty of understanding language. He pointed out that there is no meaningful discourse of the patient because they cannot monitor their own word output. It has established a mainstream view that has affected the relationship between the brain and the language for 100 years. Damage to Broca's area of the left hemisphere frontal side causes language difficulties, i.e., expression of aphasia. The left hemisphere parietal lobe posterior and lateral temporal cortex, including the supramarginal gyrus, the angular gyrus and the superior temporal gyrus region's injury will hinder language understanding, i.e., acceptance of aphasia. Figure 7.12 shows the distribution of the language area of the human brain.

Figure 7.12 shows the major groove of the left hemisphere and the area associated with the language function. Wernicke area is located near the posterior superior temporal cortex, i.e., the auditory cortex. The Broca language area is near the motor cortex of the facial representation area. The linking region between the Wernicke and the Broca region is called the arcuate fasciculus. In model B, The Brodmann partition of the left hemisphere is given. The 41 area is the primary auditory cortex,

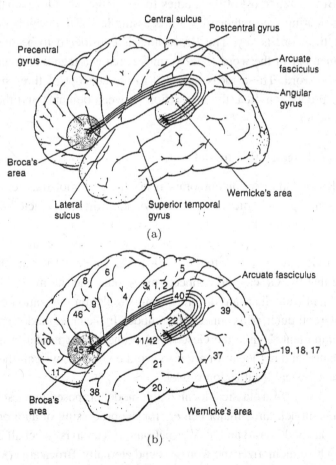

Fig. 7.12. Language area distribution of the brain

22 area is the Wernicke language area, the 45 region is the Broca language area and 4 is the primary motor cortex. In accordance with the original model, people hear a word, by listening to the nerve of the medial geniculate body information from the basilar membrane of the cochlea, which is then transmitted to the primary auditory cortex (Brodmann area 41) to higher cortical areas (42) behind the angle (39). The angular gyrus is a specific area of the parietal, temporal and occipital cortex, which is believed to be related to the integration of afferent auditory, visual and tactile information. Therefore, the information is sent to the Wernicke district (District 22) and the Broca area of the arcuate fasciculus (zone 45). In the area of Broca, the perception of language is translated into phrases of grammatical structure and stores the sounds of memory. Then the information of the phrase's sound pattern is transmitted to the facial motor cortex to control the area of pronunciation, so that the word can be uttered clearly.

In the Broca area, most of the studies focus on the word level analysis, almost without considering the sentence-level processing loss. This view believes that the memory of the word is key. The Broca area is considered to be the position of the action memory of the word. The Wernicke area is a region associated with the feeling of the word. These ideas have led to the concept of three brain centers, namely, the production area, the interaction between domains and the concept of language function.

7.8.2 Classical localization model

Wernicke, Broca and their contemporary researchers promoted a view that the language positioned on the structure of anatomy and further constructed the formation of the brain. Sometimes this is called as a classical localization model or a linguistic model of the language. In the 1960s, the idea was to develop after the American psychologist Geschwind [174], to the 1970s in the whole of the dominant position. Please note that the Geschwind connectionist model and the model developed by McClelland and Rumelhart are different from simulation realization of interaction by means of a computer, or a connectionist model. In the latter model, the interaction process is important. Unlike the Geschwind connectionist model, it is considered to be distributed and not local. In order to avoid confusion, we call the Geschwind model as the classical localization model.

Figure 7.13 shows a classical localization model proposed by Geschwind in the 1880s. In this model, three major centers for the processing of auditory or spoken language are labeled as A, B and M. Wernicke area (A area) is on behalf of the speech dictionary, which memorizes the words' sound eternally. Broca area (M area) is the area of planning and organizing the spoken language. Concept memory is located

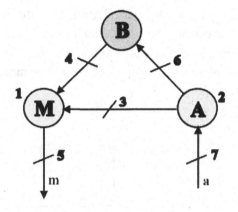

Fig. 7.13. Geschwind model for language processing

in B area. The concept is widely distributed in the brain of the language model in the 19th century, but the new Wernicke–Lichtheim–Geschwind model is more discrete. For example, in this model, the supramarginal gyrus and the angular back is considered as the processing of sensory input characteristics (auditory, visual, tactile) and regional characteristics.

The classical localization model of this language suggests that the linguistic information is local, in which the individual brain regions are interconnected by the white matter area. Language processing is considered to be active in these language representations and involves transmission of the representations of language. The idea is very simple. According to the classical localization model, the information flow of the auditory language is as follows: auditory input is converted in the auditory system and the information is transmitted to the center of the occipital cortex and then transmitted to the Wernicke area, which can be extracted the from the speech information. Information flow will be transferred from the Wernicke's area to the Broca area and this is the place where grammar features are stored and the and phrase structure can be arranged here. Then, the concept representation will activate the relevant center concept. In this way, the auditory comprehension occurs. As for oral language, in addition to the activation of the concept area to generate concept pronunciation in the Wernicke's area and its transmission to the Broca's area to organize oral English pronunciation, the other processes are similar.

In Figure 7.13, there is a cross-link between A, B and M. These connections represent the white matter fibers between the Wernicke area, the Broca area and the concept center, which are connected to each other in the brain. These fibers are considered to be separated from these regions. Damage to the A, B and M center itself will cause specific language barriers. Therefore, if the Wernicke–Lichtheim–Geschwind model is correct, we can predict the form of the language defect from the form of brain damage. In fact, all kinds of aphasia are in line with the prediction model, so this model is quite nice. Figure 7.14 is an ideal model for the processing of linguistic information. [295].

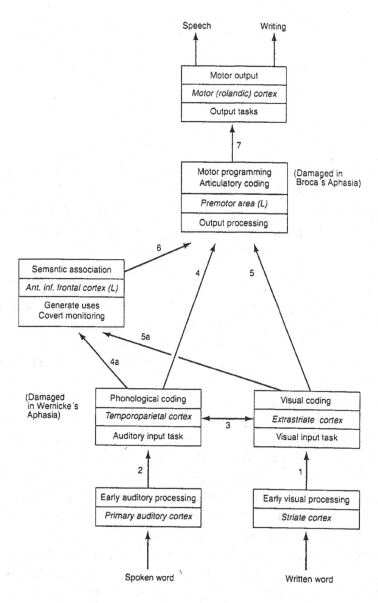

Fig. 7.14.   Language information processing model

Some of the existing evidence supports the basic ideas of the Wernicke–Lichtheim–Geschwind model, but cognitive and brain imaging studies show that the model is too simple. Language function involves a complex interaction between multiple brain regions and these regions, not by the Wernicke area to the Broca area and the links that can be summarized. There are still some obvious defects in the model. They are:

(1) Prior to the advent of computer tomography (CT) and magnetic resonance imaging (MRI), neural imaging technology, damage localization was very rough and sometimes we had to rely on autopsy information which was difficult to obtain or based on other better definition of concurrent symptoms;
(2) Determining the differences in the site of injury from autopsy studies and neuroimaging data;
(3) The damage itself is also a great difference, for example, brain damage can sometimes lead to Wernicke aphasia;
(4) The patient is often classified in more than one diagnostic category in the classification. For example, there are a number of components of Broca aphasia.

7.8.3 Memory-integration-control model

Neural network model of the new generation is different from the classical Wernicke–Geschwind model. The new model will be connected to a variety of psychological language findings and neural circuits in the brain. In these models, neural circuits of language are still considered to be determined by Broca and Wernicke's traditional language processing areas, but these areas no longer were considered as the classical model that is language specific and they not only appear in language processing. In addition, some other areas of the brain have become a part of the language processing circuit, but not necessarily a part of specific language processing.

In 2005, Hagoort proposed a new language model [199], which is the result of brain and language research. He points out the three functional components of language processing and the possible representation of them in the brain (Figure 7.15):

(1) Memory. Storage and extraction of lexical information in the mental lexicon or long-term memory.
(2) Integration. The extracted speech, semantic and syntactic information are integrated into a global output characterization. In language understanding, the processing of speech, semantic and syntactic information can be performed parallely and it can also be carried out simultaneously. Besides, all kinds of information can be interactive. The integration process allows the Hagoort model

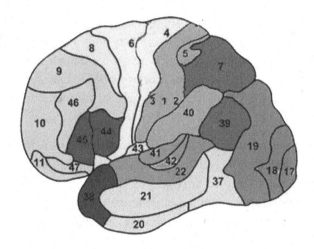

Fig. 7.15. Memory consolidation control model

to become a model of interaction based on constraints. Friedrich gives a more modular language processing neural model instance [160].

(3) Control. Language associates with actions, as in a bilingual translation.

As shown in Figure 7.15, the temporal lobe is particularly important for the characterization of memory and word extraction. The three parts of the model are marked with a color, which is covered in the left hemisphere with a Brodmann partition. There is a yellow marker in the left temporal lobe; the integration part is marked with blue and the left superior frontal gyrus is marked with gray. Voice and memory of phonetic features are in the superior temporal gyrus (Wernicke's area) center, with expansion to the superior temporal sulcus (STS). Semantic information is distributed in different areas of the left superior temporal gyrus and the superior temporal gyrus.

The processing of speech, lexical semantics and syntactic information happens in many areas, including the Broca area or the left inferior frontal gyrus. But, as the Hagoort neural model has revealed, Broca is certainly neither a language generating module, nor is the location of syntactic parsing. Moreover, the Broca area is not likely to perform a certain function as defined in the first place.

When people carry out the actual exchange such as alternative talking during the conversation, the model of control is particularly important. There are few studies of cognitive control in language understanding, but in other tasks involving cognitive control of the brain, such as the cingulate gyrus and the back of the prefrontal cortex, (i.e., 46/9 Brodmann area) language understanding of the cognitive control also play a role.

The human language system is too complex and how can such a wealth of language and language understanding in the biological mechanism of the brain be achieved? There are too many problems that need to be studied. The combination of mental language model, neural science and psychological calculation can clarify the language of the human spirit of encoding. Future language research is full of hope.

Chapter 8

Learning

The learning ability is a fundamental characteristic of the human intelligence. People learn from the objective environment and self-experience constantly their whole life. A person's cognitive ability and wisdom to their lifelong learning is the gradual formation, development and improvement. This chapter mainly discusses reinforcement learning, deep learning, introspection learning and the brain's cognitive data analysis.

8.1 Introduction

The learning ability is a fundamental characteristic of the human intelligence. People learn from objective environment constantly in the whole life. A person's cognitive ability and wisdom to lifelong learning is the gradual formation, development and improvement. The learning system model is shown in Figure 8.1 [431]. In 1983, Simon gave a better definition of learning: "A certain long-term change that the system produces in order to adapt to the environment, that can make the system finish the same or similar work more effectively next time." Learning is the change taking place in a system; it can either be the permanent improvement of the systematic work or the permanent change in the behavior of the organism. On December 12, 2015, *Science* magazine published a paper to show human-level concept learning through probabilistic program induction [252]. In a complicated system, the change of learning is due to many aspects of reasons; that is to say, there are many forms of learning processes in the same system.

AlphaGo is a computer program developed by Google DeepMind in London to play the board game Go. In October 2015, it had beaten a professional named Fan Hui, the European champion. In March 2016, it had beaten Lee Sedol, who is the strongest Go player in the world, in a five-game match of 4 to 1. AlphaGo's victories

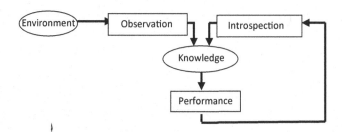

Fig. 8.1. The Learning system model

are a major milestone in artificial intelligence research. AlphaGo's algorithm uses a Monte Carlo tree search to find its moves based on knowledge previously "learned" by machine learning, specifically by a deep neural network and reinforcement learning [455].

Learning theory is about learning the essence of the learning process, learning the rules and constraints to study the various conditions to explore the theory and the explanation. Learning theory must provide knowledge in the field, analyze and explore learning methods and means,make clear which aspects of learning are the most worthy of learning, which independent variables should be controlled and which dependent variable should be analyzed, which methods and techniques can be used and what kind of terms should be used to describe the results of the learning, so as to provide educators with a framework for research and learning. From this sense, learning theory refers to the guidelines and resources that people learn, to conduct scientific research and thinking. It also means to summarize a large amount of knowledge about learning the rules and systematizing and standardizing them. However, any theory in abstract and generally a large number of specific knowledge of the process will result inevitably in losing a certain degree of specificity and accuracy and precisely because of this, theories a general guide. Learning theory should explain how learning works, why some learning methods are effective and some invalid. The learning rules tell us "how to learn" and the learning theory then tells us "why to learn like this".

Learning is a kind of process, where individuals can produce lasting changes on their behavior by training. What does the change denote on earth? How does an individual's behavior change? Psychologists have not come to an agreement with these problems so far. Therefore there are various learning theories. For over 100 years, psychologists have provided all kinds of learning theory schools due to differences in their own philosophical foundation, theory background and research means. These theory schools mainly include the behavioral school, the cognitive school and the humanism school. Some psychologists interpret learning as the formation of habit, by using the relationship between stimulus and response by training. In their opinion, an unprecedented relation can be established between a certain stimulus and related response, and such an establishing process is so-called learning. This kind of learning theory is called the stimulate–response theory, or the behavioral school. The learning theory of the behavioral school emphasizes the behavior that can be observed. According to this theory, numerous happy or painful consequences can change the individual's behavior. Pavlov's classical conditioned reflex theory, Watson's behaviorism view, Thorndike's connection doctrine, Skinner's operation conditioned reflex theory, etc., classically belong to the behavioral school.

Some other psychologists do not agree with the concept that learning is the process of the formation of habits. In their opinion, learning is a cognitive process of the individual's cognizing relation with the things in its environment. So, this kind of theory belongs to the cognitive school. Gestalt school's learning theory, Tolman's cognitive purpose theory, Piaget's schema theory, Vygotsky's theory of internalization, Bruner's cognitive development theory, Ausubel's meaningful learning theory, Gagné's information processing learning theory and the learning theory of constructivism are all considered as representative theories of the cognitive school. This school's representative persons are Piaget, Newell, etc.

Humanistic psychology is a psychological thought that rose in the 1950s or 1960s in the United States. Its main representatives are Maslow and Rogers. Humanistic psychologists thought that to understand human behavior, one must understand the sense behind the behavior of the person. When understanding human behavior, an important aspect is not the external fact, but the meaning of the behavior. If we want to change a person's behavior, we should change his faith and perception first. When the way in which he looks at a problem is different, his behavior is also different. In other words, the humanism psychologists attempt to explain and understand the behavior from the behavior of the person himself instead of the observer.

The introductions about the behavioral school, the cognitive school and the humanism school can be understood from literature [431]. The methods and algorithms about machine learning can also be understood from literature [420]. This chapter mainly focuses on the methods and algorithms of the mental model CAM.

8.2 Reinforcement Learning

8.2.1 RL model

Reinforcement learning (RL) is defined by the action in the environment and the responding environment instead of the special learning methods. Whatever methods are used to implement interactive learning, they can be viewed as an acceptable reinforcement learning method. RL is not supervised learning, which can be received from chapter machine learning. In supervised learning, the "teacher" directly or trains conducts a learning program by the instance. In RL, the learning agent learns the optimal strategy of the objective achieved in the environment through training error and feedback by itself.

Reinforcement learning (RL) technology was developed from control theory, statistics, psychology and other related fields and can even be traced back to the Pavlov conditioning experiment. Until the late 1980s and the early 1990s, RL technology was widely researched and applied in artificial intelligence, machine learning and automatic control, etc., and was considered as one of the core technologies designing intelligent systems. Especially with the breakthrough of the mathematical foundation research in RL, the research and application of RL is gradually developing and has become a focal point of research in machine learning.

The model of RL in Figure 8.2 is learned by the interactions between the agent and the environment. The interactions between the agent and the environment include action, reward and state. The interactions can be represented as, in each step, the agent selects and executes an action according to strategy selection, then perceives the state and the real-time reward in the next step and amends the strategy by its experiences. The objective of the agent is to maximize the long-time reward.

The RL system accepts the state input s from the environment and the corresponding actions a in terms of the internal reasoning mechanism are given as output. The environment changes to a new state s' under the system action a. The system accepts the new state input from the environment and meanwhile gets the instantaneous rewards and punishments feedback r that the environment responds to the system. The aim of the RL system is to learn a behavioral strategy $\pi : S \rightarrow A$, which makes the system's action obtain the largest cumulative value of environment

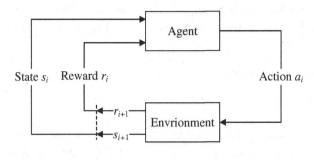

Fig. 8.2.   The RL model

reward. In other words, the system maximizes Equation (8.1), where γ is a discount factor. In the process of learning, the fundamental of RL technology is the tendency of the system in having an increased chance of producing an action if an action of the system results in a positive reward, whereas the tendency of the system to produce the will be decreased. This is similar to the conditional reflex principle in physiology.

$$\sum_{i=0}^{\infty} \gamma^i r_{t+i} \quad 0 < \gamma \leq 1. \tag{8.1}$$

If the environment is a Markov model, the order type of RL problems can be modeled through the Markov decision process. The formal definition of the Markov decision process is described in the following.

Markov decision process is defined by a four-tuple $< S, A, R, P >$, which includes the environment state set S, the system action set A, the reward function $R : S \times A \rightarrow R$ and the state transition function $P : S \times A \rightarrow PD(S)$. $R(s, a, s')$ indicates the instantaneous reward, and that the system adopts the action a to change the environment state from s to s'. $P(s, a, s')$ denotes the probability that the system adopts the action a to change the environment state from s to s'.

The essence of the Markov decision process is that the probability and reward of the state transition from the current moment to the next moment is decided by the current state and selected action and has nothing to do with the history of the state and action. Therefore dynamics programming technology can be used to solve the optimal strategy when the state transition function P and reward function R are known. However, the research of RL focuses on how to learn an optimal strategy when P and R are not known.

To solve the above problem, Figure 8.3 shows the relation between four essential factors of RL namely the strategy π, the state value mapping V, the reward function r and the environment model (common cases). The relationship between four essential factors is the pyramid structure from the bottom to the top. Strategy is defined as the agent's selection and the method of action at any given time. Thus the strategy can be represented through a group of production rules or a simple query. As said just now, the strategy under the special situation may be widely search and query, a result of a model or planning process. The strategy is stochastic and is an important component of learning, because it can produce the actions whenever.

The reward function R_t defines the relation of the state/object of the problem at time t. It maps each action or elaborate state-response pair into reward value to indicate the magnitude of success that the state accomplishes, as desired by the

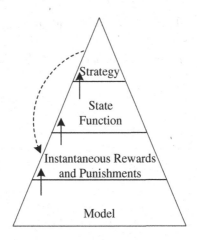

Fig. 8.3.   Four essential factors of RL

objective. The agent in RL has the task of maximizing the total reward that it gets after accomplishing the task.

The assignment function V is an attribute of each state in the environment, which indicates the expected reward of the system when the state continues. The reward function evaluates the instant expected value of a state–response pair, while the assignment indicates the long-time expected value of a state in the environment. The value of a state is computed through its inner quality and the following quality, that is to say the value is the reward under these states. For example, a state/action maybe has a small instant reward and later a bigger reward, because a bigger reward is usually produced after its state. A small reward means maybe that the state is not related to a successful solution path.

There is not reward value if there is not reward function and the only aim of evaluation value is to obtain more reward. But we are most interested in the value when we make the decision, because the value indicates the highest reward state and state fusion. The determined value is more difficult to get than the determined reward. The reward can be received from the environment, while the value is arrived at by evaluating and it needs to constantly evaluate according to success and failure as time goes by. In fact, it is most difficult and important to build an effective method to evaluate the value in RL.

The model of RL is a mechanism obtaining the environment's behavior. We need to evaluate future actions without any practical experiments. The plan based on the model is a new supplement of the RL case, because the early system tends to a pure agent's example and error to reward and value parameters.

The environment the system faces is defined by the environment model. Because of the unknown P and R in the model, the system can only select the strategy in terms of the instantaneous reward obtained in each experiment. In the process of selecting behavioral strategy, the uncertainty of the environment model and the chronicity of the objective ought to be considered. So the value function (the utility function of state) constructed by the strategy and the instantaneous reward will be used to select strategy.

$$R_t = r_{t+1} + \gamma r_{t+2} + \gamma^2 r_{t+3} + \cdots = r_{t+1} + \gamma R_{t+1}, \tag{8.2}$$

$$V^\pi(s) = E_\pi\{R_t | s_t = s\} = E_\pi\{r_{t+1} + \gamma V(s_{t+1}) | s_t = s\}$$
$$= \sum_a \pi(s, a) \sum_{s'} P_{ss'}^a [R_{ss'}^a + \gamma V^\pi(s')]. \tag{8.3}$$

A reward function R_t is constructed through Equation (8.2), which denotes the accumulative discount of all rewards of the system after the state s_t in a learning cycle conducted by a strategy π. Due to the uncertainty of the system, R_t obtained by the system in each learning cycle conducted by a strategy π may be different. The value function under the state s ought to consider the expected value of all reward functions in different learning cycles. So under the strategy π, the value function of the system with the state s is defined by Equation (8.3), which can give the expected accumulative reward discount if the system adopts the strategy π.

According to the Bellman optimal strategy formula, under the optimal strategy π^*, the value function of the system with the state s is defined by Equation (8.4).

$$V^*(s) = \max_{a \in A(s)} E\{r_{t+1} + \gamma V^*(s_{t+1}) | s_t = s, a_t = a\}$$

$$= \max_{a \in A(s)} \sum_{s'} P_{ss'}^a [R_{ss'}^a + \gamma V^*(s')]. \tag{8.4}$$

In the dynamic programming technique, when the environment model knowledge, the state transition probability function P and the reward function R, are known, the system starting from the strategy π_0 can adopt the strategy iteration to approximate the optimal V^* and π^*. k in Equations (8.5) and (8.6) indicate the number of iterations.

$$\pi_k(s) = \arg\max_a \sum_{s'} P_{ss'}^a [R_{ss'}^a + \gamma V^{\pi_{k-1}}(s')], \tag{8.5}$$

$$V_k^\pi(s) \leftarrow \sum_a \pi_{k-1}(s, a) \sum_{s'} P_{ss'}^a [R_{ss'}^a + \gamma V_{k-1}^\pi(s')]. \tag{8.6}$$

Due to the unknown P and R functions in RL, the system cannot directly compute the value function through Equations (8.5) and (8.6). So the approximation is usually used to evaluate the value function and Monte Carlo sampling is one of the main methods. In Equation (8.7), R_t denotes the actual accumulative discount reward value that the system obtains by adopting the strategy π in the state s_t. Keeping the strategy π invariant, Equation (8.7) is repeatedly used in each learning cycle. Equation (8.7) will approximate to Equation (8.3).

$$V(s_t) \leftarrow V(s_t) + \alpha \left[R_t - V(s_t) \right]. \tag{8.7}$$

Combining the Monte Carlo method and the dynamic programming technique, Equation (8.8) shows the value function iteration formula of temporal difference (TD) learning in RL.

$$V(s_t) \leftarrow V(s_t) + \alpha [r_{t+1} + \gamma V(s_{t+1}) - V(s_t)]. \tag{8.8}$$

8.2.2 Q learning

In Q learning, Q is a function that the state-action pair maps to a learned value. For all states and actions:

$$Q : (\text{state x action}) \rightarrow \text{value}.$$

The first step of Q learning is:

$$Q(s_t, a_t) \leftarrow (1 - c) \times Q(s_t, a_t) + c \times [r_{t+1} + \gamma \underset{a}{\text{MAX}}\, Q(s_{t+1}, a) - Q(s_t, a_t)], \tag{8.9}$$

where $c, \gamma \leq 1, r_{t+1}$ is the reward of the state s_{t+1}. We can get the Q learning method from Figure 8.4(a). It is different from Figure 8.4(a) in the sense that its root node is a state–action pair. The backtracking rule updates each state–action pair to the top state as shown in Figure 8.4(b). Hence, the root node of backtracking becomes a pair built by an action node and a state that produces the action node.

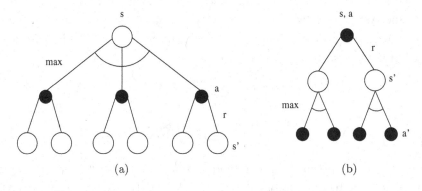

(a)   (b)

Fig. 8.4.   Backtracking of (a) V^* and (b) Q^*

In Q learning, backtracking starts from the action node and maximizes all possible actions and rewards of the next state. In a completely recursive definition of Q learning, the bottom node of the backtracking tree starts from the action of the root node and the sequence of reward of following actions of the root node can reach all the end nodes. Online Q learning extends forward according to the possible actions and does not need to build a complete world model. Q learning can work offline. We can know that Q learning is a TD method.

The Monte Carlo method approximates the actual value function through the entire reward functions that are obtained in a learning cycle. RL evaluates the current state value function through the next state value function (bootstrapping method) and the current instant rewards. Obviously, RL needs repeated learning cycles to approximate the actual value function. Therefore we can make a new λ-reward function $R_{t'}$ as Equation (8.10) by modifying Equation (8.8), where the system reaches the terminal state after T steps in a learning cycle. The physical interpretation of the λ-reward function R'_t is shown in Figure 8.5. The value function iteration obeys Equation (8.11).

$$R'_t = r_{t+1} + \lambda r_{t+2} + \lambda^2 r_{t+3} + \cdots + \lambda^{T-1} r_{t+T} \tag{8.10}$$

$$V(s_t) \leftarrow V(s_t) + \alpha [R'_t - V(s_t)]. \tag{8.11}$$

The value function update of RL performs in each learning step (namely updating operation occurs after obtaining $<s, a, r, s'>$ experience). The new TD(λ) algorithm needs to be designed so that the value function of the learning algorithm in a learning cycle can satisfy Equation (8.11). In the TD(λ) algorithm, the $e(s)$ function is constructed to support the value function updates in terms of Equation (8.11).

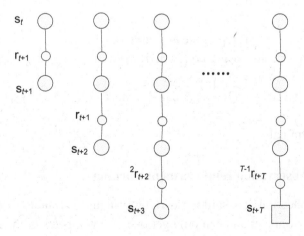

Fig. 8.5. The λ-reward function

Algorithm 8.1. TD(λ) algorithm

    Initialize $V(s)$ arbitrarily and $e(s) = 0$ for all $s \in S$

    Repeat (for each episode)

        Initialize s

        Repeat (for each step of the episode)

        $a \leftarrow$ action given by π for s (e.g., ε-greedy)

        Take action a, observer r, s'

            $\delta \leftarrow r + \gamma V(s') - V(s)$

            $e(s) \leftarrow e(s) + 1$

        for all s

          $V(s) \leftarrow V(s) + \alpha \delta e(s)$

          $e(s) \leftarrow \gamma \lambda e(s)$

        $s \leftarrow s'$

    Until s is terminal

The evaluation of the value function and the strategy evaluation can be merged into one operation step. The state–action pair value function, the Q function, is constructed in the algorithm. The definition of the Q function is shown in Equation (8.18). Theory suggests that the Q learning algorithm will converge to the optimal state–action pair value function when learning rate α satisfies a definite condition. The Q learning algorithm is one of the most popular RL algorithms.

$$Q^\pi(s, a) = \sum_{s'} P_{ss'}^a [R_{ss'}^a + \gamma V^\pi(s'). \tag{8.12}$$

Algorithm 8.2. Q-learning algorithm

    Initialize $Q(s, a)$ arbitrarily

    Repeat (for each episode)

        Initialize s

        Repeat (for each step of the episode)

        Choose a from s using policy derived from Q (e.g., ε-greedy)

           Take action a, observer r,s'

             $Q(s, a) \leftarrow Q(s, a) + \alpha[r + \gamma \max_{a'} Q(s', a') - Q(s, a)]$

             $s \leftarrow s'$

    Until s is terminal

8.2.3 Partial observation reinforcement learning

In practical application, it is hard for learning systems to accurately observe the true state of the environment and can only get one or few aspects of the true state. The uncertainty of the state observation brings more uncertainty to the action evaluation,

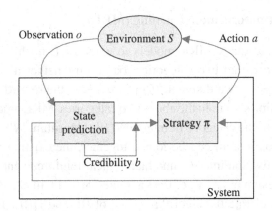

Fig. 8.6. The Partial observation Markov model

thereby directly affecting the quality of the selected action. Figure 8.6 shows the partial observation state Markov model. This model adds a state prediction based on the classical Markov model and sets credibility b for each state to indicate the confidence level of the state. The system decides the action based on b and makes the state prediction in terms of the observed value. This can solve some non-Markov model problems.

The core of the partial observation problem is the uncertainty of the observation state. So the core of partial observation RL research is to eliminate the uncertainty. In theory, the uncertainty can be represented by the probability (credibility) and then we construct a Markov decision process based on credibility. But the method presented above does not work well, because the credibility in practice is a continuous value and the function estimate RL technique will be adopted to solve the large-scale decision-making task [228]. The actual solution is as follows:

(1) A series of historical observations is used to construct states satisfying the Markov attribute, such as the K-history window method [277].
(2) Analyze the observation, such as the ability to predict the next observation and the reward of prediction behaviors, then split the actual observation into some expected actual states. The representative methods are the NSM and the USM methods [296].

In the prediction state representation model, it is unnecessary to hide the actual state. The action–observation value sequence is used to construct the system model [279]. The planning and learning based on the prediction state representation model has more advantages than the partial observation Markov decision model.

8.2.4 Motivated reinforcement learning (MRL)

At present, there are many MRL models to extend RL in different ways. MRL model can be divided into two categories: based on whether it (1) introduces the motivation signal as a reward signal; (2) and whether the reward signal is used to replace the motivation signal. In the above two categories, MRL model can be further divided according to the category of integrated RL algorithm. While the motivation and function approximation can be joined together, the existing work focuses on integrating the motivation into RL and hierarchical reinforcement learning (HRL). Furthermore the design objective of the integrated model will change. Some models are intended to accelerate the algorithm speed of RL and HRL. The other models implement more self-adaptive and multi-task learning through viewing motivation as an automatic attention mechanism.

The term "motivation signal" is used to distinguish the reward signal. This signal views the motivation computing model as an agent experience function to compute online, rather than as a set of predefined rules mapping the value of the known environment state and the state transition. The model I in Figure 8.7 considers the motivation signal $R_{m(t)}$ as reward signal $R_{(t)}$ and emphasizes on applying motivation in RL and HRL. These models are designed to use the motivation signal to speed up the existing RL algorithm and also to implement more self-adaptive and multi-task learning through viewing the motivation as an automatic attention mechanism. Motivated hierarchical reinforcement learning (MHRL) converts the process of recognizing the subtask into a motivation process. This process produces a motivation signal to supplement the standard signal from the environment. The main objective of the motivation signal is to conduct learning by recognizing the subtask defined by the reward signal. The model I strictly obeys the objectives of RL and HRL and basically speeds up the learning of the reward task.

In Figure 8.7, the type II MRL model directly replaces the reward signal $R_{(t)}$ with the motivation signal $R_{m(t)}$. This method is mainly used for the integration of the RL algorithm. Though there are a lot of HRL and MHRL (I) models, claim that they can be extended as MHRL (II) models, have been made. However, there hardly exists results describing these kinds of models.

1. Motivation signal is used to supplement reward signal

In Figure 8.7, the MRL (I) model integrates the reward signal and the motivation signal into RL. A motivation process will reason the current observation state $S_{(t)}$ and all observed state set S so far and produce a motivation signal $R_{m(t)}$. This motivation signal and the reward signal are integrated as the input of the RL process (Q-learning) according to certain rules or weight.

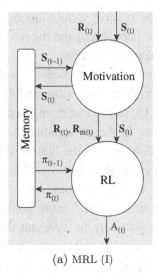
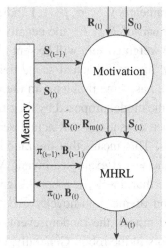

(a) MRL (I)

(b) MHRL (I) extends RL and MHRL
by introducing the motivation signal

Fig. 8.7. Type I MRL model

Literature [218] implemented a MRL (I) model, the aim of which was to develop a robot evaluation system to support the simple machine vision system. In this model, the motivation signal is defined by a novelty computation model. The novelty is computed by the consistency level between the expected observation and the actual observation. When each state $S_{(t)} = (s_{1(t)}, s_{2(t)}, \ldots, s_{|S|(t)})$ is observed, the novelty of this state will be used to compute the difference between primed sensations $s_i'(t)$ and the actual sensations $s_{i(t+1)}$, as given in Equation (8.13).

$$N_{(t)} = \sqrt{\frac{1}{|S|} \sum_{i=1}^{|S|} \frac{(s_{i(t)}' - s_{i(t+1)})^2}{\sigma_i^2}}. \tag{8.13}$$

Primed sensation predicts the state that will be perceived after adopting an action. Primed sensation computes the most discriminative features based on sensation state set S through an incremental hierarchical discriminant regression (IHDR) tree [516]. The expectation deviation σ_i^2 is a time discount average of $(s_{i(t)}' - s_{i(t+1)})^2$. The more accurate the robot's prediction is, the lower the novelty.

Besides the motivation signal, literature [218] also uses the human teacher reward signal from the environment. The reward signal is fed back to the agent through the teacher who controls the two keys, "good" and "bad". The reward signal and the motivation signal are merged to a weighted sum.

$$\{R_{m(t)}, R_{(t)}\} = \alpha F^+ + \beta F^- + (1 - \alpha - \beta)N_{(t)}, \tag{8.14}$$

where the parameters $0 < \alpha, \beta < 1$ indicate the relative weight among F^+, the positive value part of $R_{(t)}$, F^- the negative value part of $R_{(t)}$ and the novelty $N_{(t)}$. Afterward the weighted sum will be sent to the learning process.

Generally, like many actual scene fields, the motivation model based on the novelty maybe has some problems in the environment containing random events. For example, the model proposed by literature [218] shows that there is a difference between primed sensations and actual sensations in the environment containing random events. This means that the random events tend to the high novelty. In a simple machine visual example, Juyang Weng *et al.* used fast switching images to demonstrate that the SAIL robot designed by their model was able to keep the visual attention of the high-novelty events. If there exists a more complex and realistic world model, the random events are most likely to represent the noises from the sensors in the robot. Generally, there is nothing that can be learned from the random events in a situation such as this. Moreover, this model assumes that human teachers exist in the outside world to guide the robot learning through "good" and "bad" reward signals. The motivation function based on the novelty is viewed as an additional search function to supplement the learning. Literature [308] extends the function of motivation as the primary attention focus mechanism of RL, which gets rid of the need for human teachers.

The other motivation models of MRL(I) focus on more complex cognitive phenomenon, such as interest, curiosity, boredom, etc., which avoid the problem of the model based on the novelty. Schmidhuber, one of the early researchers on the MRL model, proposed some cognitive models of motivation. In his "curious neural controller framework", he used a predictability model of the learned environment to describe "curiosity" and "boredom" as the reinforcement and inhibition cells [401]. The predictability is described as a state set S that is represented by a self-supervised neural network. The classification result of the sequence sensations $S_{i(t)}$ and $S_{i(t+1)}$ is:

$$p_{i(t+1)} = s_{i(t+1)}(1 - s_{i(t+1)}) \left(\sum w_{in} p_{i(t)} + \delta_i s_{i(t)} \right). \qquad (8.15)$$

Schmidhuber's "curious neural controller" is defined as the following: the state that the predictability of the network model is not optimal is viewed as the strongest motivation to stimulate the agent to amend these states and improve the network model. The motivation $R_{m(t)}$ given at the highest predictability and the lowest predictability is used to simulate the "boredom" under this state. The highest motivation given at the medium predictability is used to describe the "curiosity" level of the state when prediction and reality do not match with the ideality. This motivation process expresses a theory that a system cannot learn some incomprehensible things.

Introducing "curiosity" and "boredom" into the Schmidhuber model, the direct purpose is to improve the capability that the self-supervised neural network describes as the environment model. The indirect purpose is to simplify task learning defined by the reward signal. In Schmidhuber's following work, two coevolution brains are used as detectors of curiosity and creativity in the motivation model. This shows that the application of motivation signal can accelerate the RL speed of the reward task. He claims that his model can be applied to the scene without the reward signal and cannot give an evaluation for the result agent. For the MRL agent that the motivation is used as the primary focus mechanism, the literature [310] proposes a new evaluation method designed to evaluate its behavior.

Literature [458] proposes a different MRL(I) framework in Figure 8.9, which learns how to cumulate rewards in the most efficient way, rather than just cumulating rewards. They call this framework as "optimal search", which learns a necessary strategy in the following usage. In their framework, the agent maintains two value functions: one is used to describe the learned strategy for the reward task; the other one is used to select the motions. The above two value functions are called as the task value function and the behavior value function respectively. According to the observation on the immediate reward and the succeeding environment state, the task value function produces the motivation signal to guide the behavior value function.

$$R_{m(t)} = p + \sum_{S \in S} (v_{(t)}^{\max}(S) \cdot v_{(t-1)}^{\max}(S)). \tag{8.16}$$

In Equation (8.16), $V_{(t)}^{\max}(S) = \max_{T < t} V_{(t-1)}^{\max}(S)$ and $\rho < 0$ is a small motion penalty constant. In this model, there is a hypothesis that the reward signal describes the single task by the state or the state transition mapping and learns the single solution strategy for the single task. Literature [310] considers that the learning task will become complex with the multi-task appearing over time. In the huge or dynamic state space environment, a learning agent can distinguish and focus on the self-adaptive, multi-task learning by introducing the corresponding structure and process.

The MHRL(I) model extends to the MRL(I) model through adding the callback and reuse. This method can further improve the learning rate compared with the MRL(I) model and the RL model. The MHRL(I) model integrates the reward signal and the motivation signal into HRL (Figure 8.10(b)). Literature [460] models MHRL by dividing the HRL located in the internal environment and the external environment. The critics understand the external stimulations and produce the external reward signal. The external reward signal can be integrated with the intrinsic reward (motivation) computed by the internal environment.

Each new salient event will initialize this event selection and the learning of a selection model. Furthermore, each event will produce a motivation signal. The motivation signal is proportional to the prediction error of the selection model. The updated "motion-value" function will repeatedly try to implement this event after the agent encounters an unexpected salient event a certain number of times. The agent interacts with the environment in terms of e-greedy strategy, which is a "motion-value" function learned by combining Q-learning and the SMDP plan. When the agent moves in the environment, all initialized selections and models will be updated according to the internal selection learning algorithm. As time goes on, the agent recognizes and learns the behaviors selected and described by the model. These behaviors will become the motion selection library and lead to construct the behavior set of the layer structure. When the agent repeatedly tries to implement the salient event, the strategy executing this motion and the selection predicting this event will be improved in the learning. As there is improvement in the selection strategy and the model, the motivation signal disappears and agent becomes "bored" to continue.

Literature [460] builds a proportional relationship (in Equation (8.17)) between the motivation signal and the prediction error according to the learned salient event. Otherwise the motivation will be 0. The motivation signal and the reward signal exist as a weighted sum in the Q-learning iteration update of the behavior "motion-value" function.

$$
R_{m(t)} = \begin{cases} \phi[1 - p^{ts}(S_{(t+1)}|S_{(t)}) & \text{if } S_{(t)} \text{ is a salient event,} \\ 0 & \text{otherwise.} \end{cases} \tag{8.17}
$$

Therefore, the motivation signal indicates the intensity value of the salient event in the MHRL(I) model. But literature [460] does not focus on how to recognize the salient event. Though they believe the model has been generalized to integrate all aspects of the motivation, such as internal state, memory and accumulated knowledge, in practice they just use a simple rule-based model, where the intensity change for the light and the sound will be viewed as the salient event. This is adopted to combine the reward signal of the usage state and the state transformation rule and then to do the reward learning of the single task in the simple game room scene. In literature [310], the motivation, rather than the rule-based reward signal, is used for the primary attention focus mechanism. Through designing an algorithm, the psychological motivation theory is modeled as an experience-based reward signal and these models are used for the performance evaluation of the different MRL models. Thus, the existing work is extended.

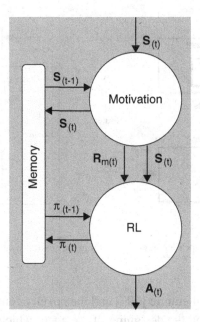

Fig. 8.8. The type II MRL model: Extend RL by replacing the reward signal with the motivation signal

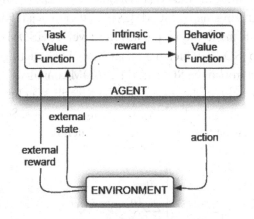

Fig. 8.9. Task value function and behavior value function are used to model MHRL(I)

2. Motivation signal replaces reward signal

In Figure 8.8, the MRL(II) model replaces the reward signal with the motivation signal. The motivation process makes the reasoning about the current state $S_{(t)}$ and all perceived state set S to produce the motivation signal $R_{m(t)}$ served as the input of the RL algorithm.

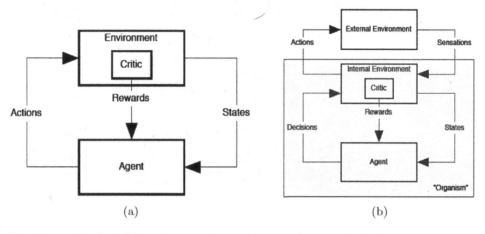

Fig. 8.10. (a) RL; (b) Build type I RL agent by dividing the environment into the internal environment and the external environment

The experiments in literature [393] and the novelty computing models are integrated into RL to develop the designing of the agent which can find problems and solve problems in the complex designing space. Finding problems is the process of recognizing the novel designing task. Solving problems is to search novel solutions for these problems. Unlike the methods in literature [218], literature [393] employs a habituated self-organizing map (HSOM) [290], rather than an IHDR tree, to describe the sensed state set S and to model the novelty level. A HSOM contains a standard self-organizing map (SOM), which has an additional habituating neuron connecting to each clustering neuron in the SOM [242]. A SOM contains a group of topological structures of neuron set U, where each neuron describes a cluster of sensed states. Whenever a stimulation $S_{(t)} = (s_{1(t)}, s_{2(t)}, \ldots, s_{|S|(t)})$ arrives, SOM will select a best matched "winner" neuron, namely the neuron which is closed to the stimulation at distance d

$$d = \sqrt{\sum_{i=1}^{|S|} (u_{i(t)} - s_{i(t)})^2}. \qquad (8.18)$$

The weights between the "winner" neuron and the eight topological neighbors are adjusted by Equation (8.25). Then, the "winner" neuron will close the input stimulation, where $0 \leq \eta \leq 1$ is the learning rate of the SOM. The size of the neighbor circles and the learning rate remains a constant to ensure that SOM can constantly learn.

$$u_{i(t+1)} = u_{i(i+1)} + \eta(s_{i(t)} - u_{i(t)}). \qquad (8.19)$$

The activities of the "winner" neuron and its neighbors as the synaptic value $\zeta(t) = 1$, are propagated to the habituated layer along the synapse. For the neurons, that are beyond the neighbor scope of the "winner" neuron, $\zeta_{(t)} = 0$. The effectiveness $N_{(t)}$, of the synapse is computed by the habituated model in literature [449]:

$$\tau \frac{dN_{(t)}}{dt} = \alpha[N_{(0)} - N_{(t)}] - \zeta(t). \tag{8.20}$$

In Equation (8.20), $N_{(1)} = 1$ is the initial novelty level, τ is a habituated rate constant and α is a restoring rate constant. Equation (8.20) is employed to compute the derivative of the value of $N_{(t)}$ at time t according to $N_{(t-1)}$ stored in the habituated neurons. Then the derivative is approximated as the following:

$$N_{(t)} = N_{(t-1)} + \frac{dN_{(t-1)}}{dt}. \tag{8.21}$$

Though the novelty-based model is propitious to design the agent, it also faces the problem that the model in literature [218] is applied in the environment containing random events. In this environment, we need to search for a method that replaces the techniques based on the novelty level to model the motivation.

Some replaceable models in literature [232] are designed to solve the problems presented above. They design a method to stimulate the search for the scene that shows the biggest learning potential. In this model, three stimulation variables are employed to define the scene: predictability, familiarity and stability in the robot sensory-motor scene. Sensory-motion vector at time t is defined as all possible sensory and motor vectors: $SM(t) = (S_{1(t1)}, S_{2(t2)}, \ldots S_{|S|(t)} \ldots, A_{1(t)}, A_{2(t)}, \ldots)$. The predictability $P(t)$ is defined as the current error e that the sensory-motor vector $SM_{(t-1)}$ predicts at the sensory state $S_{(t)}$:

$$p_{(t)} = 1 - e(SM_{(t-1)}, S_{(t)}). \tag{8.22}$$

The familiarity $\Gamma(t)$ is used to measure the inversion frequency between the sensory motion $SM_{(t-1)}$ and the sensory state $S_{(t)}$ in recent period $t - T$:

$$\tau_{(t)} = f_T(SM_{(t-1)}, S_{(t)}). \tag{8.23}$$

The stability is adopted to measure the distance between the observed value $S_{i(t)}$ of the sensory state $S(t)$ and the average observed value $S_{i(T)}$ in the recent period $t - T$. Each robot agent is stimulated by multiple stability variables, where each stability variable needs to keep stable for a specific joint and function of the robot. For example, four stability variables in literature [232] respectively correspond to the joints of the robot's head and neck: the pan position of the head, the tilt position of the head, the pan position of the relative light, the tilt position of the relative light.

The robot agent keeps the stability of the head relative to the light using the four parameters.

$$\sigma_{i(t)} = 1 - \sqrt{(S_{i(t)} - S_{i(T)})^2}. \tag{8.24}$$

The motivation signal is employed to construct the formula based on the following intuition: the reward should be highest when the stability reaches maximum value and the predictability and the familiarity are improving. With the improvement of the predictability and the familiarity, the stimulations of the high novelty events such as the random events, will be excluded from the high stimulations, only if they become more predictable and familiarity.

$$R_{m(t)} = \sigma_{1(t)} + \sigma_{2(t)} + \cdots + \begin{cases} \tau_{(t)} - \tau_{(t-1)} : \tau_{(t)} > \tau_{(t-1)} \\ 0 : \tau_{(t)} \leq \tau(t-1) \end{cases}$$
$$+ \begin{cases} p_{(t)} - p_{(t+1)} : p_{(t)} > p_{(t+1)} \\ 0 : p_{(t)} \leq p_{(t-1)} \end{cases}. \tag{8.25}$$

The MRL(II) model has greater potential for incentive self-adaption and multi-task learning than the MRL(I) model, because the MRL(II) model does not depend on the reward signal based on a set of fixed states or the state transition rules. These reward signals are defined before learning and employed to the final focus objective of learning. However, the MRL(II) motivation model based on the novelty and the stability does not solve the problem in the complex and dynamic environment. The novelty-based model maybe encounters some problems in the environment containing the random events, because the random events, such as the sensory noise, do not always have learning value. For generalization, the motivation signal variables, such as predictability, familiarity and stability, can be applied to a series of joint control problems as well. However the stable variables make the model especially applicable to the problems which always need to keep the stable properties. Though literature [348] improves their model by introducing intelligent self-adaptive curiosity as the motivation model of the robot, the improved model is not applied to the RL scene.

Though so many researchers claim that the HRL and MHRL(I) technique can be applied to the MHRL(II) model without the reward signal [457], there are not results like what this system gives whether in theory or in experience. Moreover, the existing standard measures and benchmarks are not applicable to the MHRL(II) scene, because the goal has not been to accelerate the learning speed, but to focus on self-adaptive and multi-task learning.

8.2.5 Reinforcement learning of Soar system

One simple model of Soar RL given in Figure 8.11 [251], shows the interaction between the agent and the environment. The agent tries to adopt the action to obtain the future maximum reward which is expected. The reward is a signal from the external environment. The internal states of the agent are decided by the environment awareness. The agent maintains a value function, called Q function, which provides the expected reward and the state mapping from the environment for each action applied to the state.

Soar maintains the reward structure of each state and provides the reward support produced in the internal and the external environment. The reward value is set by the agent's knowledge (rules) in order to get the maximum flexibility. This agent can be based on the reward input from the external environment. The simplest case is to copy the specific sensory reward value. The agent can help create the appropriate values of the internal reward structure.

Here building blocks are used to demonstrate the basic concept of RL. Suppose the agent repeatedly attempts to solve the stack issues about building blocks A, B and C. The simplest method is to revise rule P12 to increase the reward computing. This means that the agent detects that the expected states have been reached and it will produce a reward.

```
P12*halt* all-blocks-in-desired-position
If block A is in its desired position and
    block B is in its desired position and
    block C is in its desired position
then
    create a reward of 1 and
    halt
```

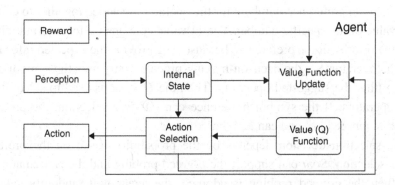

Fig. 8.11. RL agent in Soar

The value function of Soar is represented by the operator-evaluation rules and it builds the preference number. These rules are viewed as RL rules. If the RL rule matches with the state structure and the specified operator, the preference number is built for the operator. The preference number of the operator is assembled into a single value, which is used to select the operator. The assembled value is the operator's expected value of the current state. This is called as the Q value in RL.

In RL, the simplest value function form is the tabular form. Each different state-operator respectively has the Q value. The table is indexed and advised by the operator of the current state. The associated Q value is used to select the next operator. In order to reach the same function in Soar, the RL rule is created as the state-operator pair. The following is an example of the RL rule:

```
P13*evaluate* move-block*RL*stack-A-B-C*A-Table*
    B-Table*C-Table*moveA-B
If the state has problem space move-single-unit-block
        and
    the desired is (on A B) (on B C ) (on C Table) and
    the state is (on A Table) (on B Table ) (on C Table)
        and
        an operator is proposed to move A on B
then
create a numeric preference for the operator with
    value 0.0
```

In the building blocks world, each expected state needs 29 rules. As 13 different expected states exist, it means that $13 \times 29 = 277$ rules need to be satisfied, to overcome all the problems in the building blocks world.

In Soar, all preference numbers for the operator are added together to construct the Q value of the specific number. The Q value contains useful information indicating the priority of the preference, because they provide the expected information about the operator. So, the decision-making process firstly uses the symbol preferences to filter the suggested operators. Then the Q value is used to select the rest of the operators. If the symbol preference can satisfy a selection, the preference number is unnecessary and can be ignored.

The selection decision depends on the probability based on the preference number selection. Soar can support the ε-greed probing and the Boltzmann probing. When the ε-greed probing is adopted, the agent will randomly select the action (uniform probability). Otherwise, the agent will adopt the highly expected

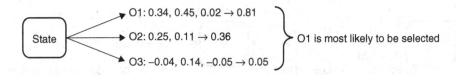

Fig. 8.12. An example of selecting the operator

action. When the Boltzmann probing is adopted, if the agent's suggested operators $O_1, \dots O_n$ correspond respectively to the expected values $Q(S, O_1), \dots, Q(S, O_n)$, the probability of the operator O_i is

$$\frac{e^{Q(s,O_i)/\tau}}{\sum_{j=1}^{n} e^{Q(s,O_j)/\tau}}, \tag{8.26}$$

where τ is the temperature. The lower temperature will result in an operator with high Q value having a strong preference value when the selection is done. This means that the best item is always selected when $\tau = 0$. The higher temperate will lead to a more random selection. The selection is completely random when $\tau = \infty$. If $\tau = 1$, the operator selection is a uniform distribution based on the Q value.

Figure 8.12 shows three operators of the given states: O_1, O_2, O_3. The preference numbers of the operators are summed to get the Q value ($O_1 : 0.81, O_2 : 0.36, O_3 : 0.05$). The schemes ($\varepsilon$-greed or Boltzmann) of handling selection, select handlers. Under this circumstance, O_1 is most likely to be selected as the operator because of it's highest value.

The learning part of RL refers to the update value function, which means that the preference value of RL rules will be amended in Soar. Soar support Q-learning [511] and the SARSA algorithm learning of and TD [388]. In the two processes, the value function is updated based on the received reward of adopting the action and the expected future reward discount.

In TD, the value function is updated by the current value and the amended value. The amended value is the difference between discounting the expected future reward and the current reward. Thus, the value update function of TD is:

$$Q(s, O) \leftarrow Q(s, O) + a[r + \gamma Q(s', Q') - Q(s, O)], \tag{8.27}$$

where s is the current state, s' is the next state, O is the current operator and O' is the operator added to s'. The current value $Q(s, O)$ is amended by adding $a[r + \gamma Q(s', Q') - Q(s, O)]$. The received reward is r and discounting the future reward we get $\gamma Q(s', Q')$. γ is a parameter of the future reward discount. There exists a non-determinacy as to whether the future reward is accepted. The learning

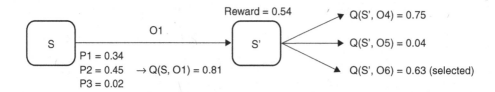

Fig. 8.13.   Modification evaluation rules in RL

rate parameter α modifies the changed effect of amending the future reward. The discount and the learning rate are assigned with a value between 0 and 1.

Figure 8.13 shows that the agent in the beginning state, selects the operator O1.The integrated Q value based on P1, P2 and P3 is 0.81. The following operator is applied and receives the reward 0.54, then it gives the three operators, O4, O5 and O6. If the operator O6 is selected, the amending process is like the following.

In SARSA, the expected future reward is used for the next selected operator as the Q value. In this case, the value of O6 is 0.63. In the above example, we can fill in a new update value: $\alpha[0.54 + \gamma\,^*0.63 - 0.81]$. If $\gamma = 0.9$ and $\alpha = 0.1$, the updated value is changed as:

$$0.1 * [0.54 + 0.9 * 0.63 - 0.81] = 0.1 * [0.54 + 0.567 - 0.81]$$
$$= 0.1 * [0.297] = 0.0297.$$

In Q learning, the expected future reward is the maximum value of the suggested operator. Like in this example, the value of O4 is 0.75. So, in Q learning the updated value is:

$$0.1 * [0.54 + 0.9 * 0.75 - 0.81] = 0.1 * [0.54 + 0.675 - 0.81] = 0.1 * [0.405]$$
$$= 0.0405.$$

8.3 Deep Learning

8.3.1 Introduction

In June 2012, Google's Brain project in the *New York Times* gained public attention. This project was led by Andrew Ng and Jeff Dean at the Stanford University. The parallel computation platform with 16,000 CPU cores was served to train the deep neural networks with 10 billion nodes. The mass data was directly loaded into the algorithm, and the system automatically learnt from the data.

In November 2012, Microsoft publicly demonstrated a fully automatic simultaneous interpretation system in Tianjin, China. The speaker made a speech in English and the backend computer automatically accomplished the speech recognition, the machine translation from English to Chinese and the Chinese speech synthesis. The key technology used backstage is also deep learning.

On April 24, 2014, Baidu held the fourth technology Open Day in Beijing. During the Open Day, Baidu announced that they were officially launching a large data engine, which included the big core data capability with the three major components Open Cloud, Data Factory, Baidu Brain. Baidu provided big data storage, analysis and mining techniques to the public through the large data engine. This was the first big open data engine in the world. Andrew Ng was part of the Baidu Institute and carried out the deep learning research.

Deep learning is a new field in machine learning. It's core idea is to simulate the hierarchy abstraction structure of the human brain, analyze the large-scale data using unsupervised methods and reveal the valuable information contained in big data. Deep learning was designed to research big data, which provides a deep thinking brain.

Suppose that there exists a system S with n layers $(S1, \ldots, Sn)$. The system with the input I and the output O can be visually represented as $I \Rightarrow S1 \Rightarrow S2 \Rightarrow \cdots \Rightarrow S_n \Rightarrow O$. If the output O is equal to the input I, then the information of the input I is not lost after the system transformation. To maintain the same, the input I after each layer S_i does not have any loss of information, that is, in any layer S_i, it is the other kind of representation of original information (that is, input I).

The idea of Deep Learning is to stack multiple layers and the output in the current layer serves as the input of the next layer. In this way, the layer-wise representation of the input information can be realized.

In addition, the hypothesis presented above that the input is equal to the output is too strict. This limitation can be slightly loose in a way that the difference between the input and the output is little, as far as possible. This loose principle can result in other deep learning methods. The above presentation is the basic idea of deep Learning.

8.3.2 Human brain visual mechanism

The human brain visual mechanism is shown in Figure 8.14. For a long time, people researched the human brain visual system.

In 1981, the Nobel Prize in medicine was awarded to David Hubel, Torsten Wiesel and Roger Sperry. The main contribution of the first two people was in finding the information processing of the vision system: like the visual cortex graded in Figure 8.15. The low-level V1 extracts the edge features. V2 extracts the shape

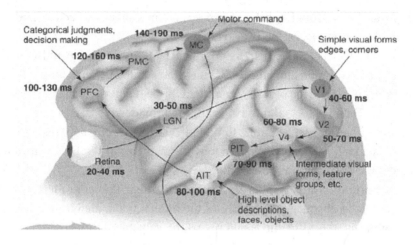

Fig. 8.14.   The human brain visual system

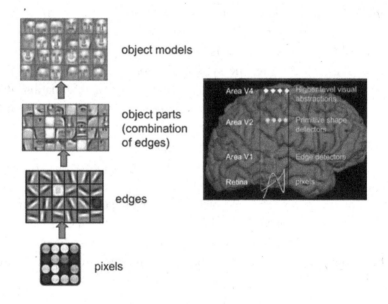

Fig. 8.15.   Visual cortex grading handling

or object parts, etc. The higher level regions extract the entire object, the behavior of the object, etc.

8.3.3 Autoencoder

The autoencoder is a hidden single layer neural network with the same number of nodes in the input layer and the output layer as given in Figure 8.16. The aim of

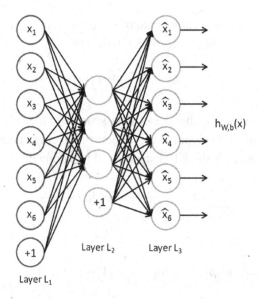

Fig. 8.16.   Autoencoder

designing the Autoencoder is to reconstruct the input signal of the neural network as far as possible. This means that we need to solve the function $h_{W,b}(X) \approx x$, namely the output of the neural network is equal to the input as expected.

Suppose that there exists a sample set $\{(x^{(1)}, y^{(1)}), \ldots, (x^{(m)}, y^{(m)})\}$ containing 'm' samples. The batch gradient descent method can be used to solve the neural networks. In particular, for a single sample (x, y), the cost function is

$$J(W, b; , x, y) = \frac{1}{2}||h_{W,b}(x) - y||^2. \tag{8.28}$$

Equation (8.28) is a variance cost function. Given a dataset containing 'm' samples, we can define the entire cost function as following:

$$J(W, b) = \left[\frac{1}{m}\sum_{i=1}^{m} J(W, b; x^{(i)}, y^{(i)})\right] + \frac{\lambda}{2}\sum_{l=1}^{n_l-1}\sum_{i=1}^{s_l}\sum_{j=1}^{s_l+1}(W_{ji}^{(l)})^2$$

$$= \left[\frac{1}{m}\sum_{i=1}^{m}\left(\frac{1}{2}||h_{W,b}(x^{(i)}) - y^{(i)}||^2\right)\right] + \frac{\lambda}{2}\sum_{l=1}^{n_l-1}\sum_{i=1}^{s_l}\sum_{j=1}^{s_l+1}(W_{ji}^{(l)})^2. \tag{8.29}$$

The first item $J(W, b)$ in Equation (8.29) is a mean square error. The second item is a weight decay. Its aim is to reduce the scope of weight to prevent the overfitting.

$a_j^{(2)}(x)$ indicates the activation value of the input vector x on the hidden unit j. The average activation value of the hidden unit j is

$$\hat{\rho}_j = \frac{1}{m} \sum_{i=1}^{m} [a_j^{(2)}(x^{(i)})].$$

(8.30)

In order to reach a sparsity, the least (most sparse) hidden units will be used to represent the feature of the input layer. When the average activation value of all hidden units is closed to 0, the KL distance will be adopted:

$$\sum_{j=1}^{s_2} \rho \log \frac{\rho}{\hat{\rho}_j} + (1 - \rho) \log \frac{1 - \rho}{1 - \hat{\rho}_j}.$$

(8.31)

For ease in writing,

$$\text{KL}(\rho || \hat{\rho}_j) = \rho \log \frac{\rho}{\hat{\rho}_j} + (1 - \rho) \log \frac{1 - \rho}{1 - \hat{\rho}_j}.$$

(8.32)

So, the entire cost function of neural networks can be represented as

$$J_{\text{sparse}}(W, b) = J(W, b) + \beta \sum_{j=1}^{s_2} \text{KL}(\rho || \hat{\rho}_j).$$

(8.33)

The error computation formula $\delta_i^{(2)} = (\sum_{j=1} W_{ji}^{(2)} \delta_j^{(3)}) f'(z_i^{(2)})$, BP is modified as

$$\delta_i^{(2)} = \left(\left(\sum_{j=1}^{s_2} W_{ji}^{(2)} \delta_j^{(3)} \right) + \beta \left(-\frac{\rho}{\hat{\rho}_i} + \frac{1 - \rho}{1 - \hat{\rho}_i} \right) \right) f'(z_i^{(2)}).$$

(8.34)

Therefore, the dimension of data can be reduced greatly. Only a few useful hidden units can represent the original data.

8.3.4 Restricted Boltzmann machine

In 2002, Hinton of the University of Toronto proposed a machine learning algorithm called as contrastive divergence (CD) [210]. CD could efficiently train some random Markov model with simple architecture, including the restricted Boltzmann machine (RBM) [464]. This laid the foundation for the birth of deep learning afterward.

The RBM is a random single layer neural network (generally the input layer is not included in the layer number of neural networks) as given in Figure 8.17. The RBM is essentially a probability graph model. The input layer is fully connected to the output layer, while there are not connections between the neurons in the same layer. Each neuron is either activated (the value is 1) or is not activated (the value

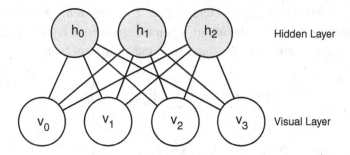

Fig. 8.17. Architecture of the RBM

is 0). The activation probability satisfies the sigmoid function. The advantage of the RBM is that a given layer is independent from the other layer. So it is convenient to randomly sample a layer when the other layer is fixed. Then this process is carried out alternately. Each update of the weights in theory needs all neurons to be sampled infinitely. This is called as CD. Since CD works too slowly, Hinton proposed an approximation method called as the CD-n algorithm in which the weights are updated once after sampling n times [210].

If the RBM has n visual units and m hidden units, the vector **v** and **h** are respectively used to represent the states of the visual layer and the hidden layer. Here v_i indicates the state of the ith visual unit and h_j indicates the state of the jth hidden unit. So given a set of states **v, h**, the system energy of the RBM can be defined as

$$E(v, h) = -\sum_{i=1}^{n}\sum_{j=1}^{m} v_i W_{ij} h_j - \sum_{i=1}^{n} v_i b_i - \sum_{j=1}^{m} h_j c_j. \tag{8.35}$$

In Equation (8.35), W_{ij}, b_i, and c_j are the parameters of the RBM. They are real numbers. W_{ij} indicates the connection intension between the visual unit i and the hidden layer j. b_i indicates the bias of the visual unit i. c_j indicates the bias of the hidden unit j. The task of the RBM is to solve the value of the parameters to fit the given training data.

The states of the RBM satisfy the form of the canonical distribution. This means that, when the parameter is confirmed, the probability of the state v, h is

$$P(v, h) = \frac{1}{z} \exp(-E(v, h)),$$

$$Z = \sum_{v,h} \exp(-E(v, h)). \tag{8.36}$$

Suppose RBM is in the normal temperature $T = 1$, the temperature variable T is omitted. Based on the above definition, when the states for a layer of units is given, the conditional distribution of the states for another layer of units is

$$P(v_i|\boldsymbol{h}) = \sigma \left(\sum_{j=1}^{m} W_{ij} h_j + b_i \right),$$

$$P(h_j|\boldsymbol{v}) = \sigma \left(\sum_{i=1}^{n} W_{ij} h_j + c_j \right). \tag{8.37}$$

In Equation (8.37), $\sigma(\cdot)$ is the sigmoid function and $\sigma(x) = 1/(1+\exp(-x))$. Since the units in the same layer in the RBM are not connected to each other, when the states for a layer of units is given, the conditional distribution of the state for another layer of units is independent, namely,

$$P(v_i|\boldsymbol{h}) = \prod_{i=1}^{n} P(v_i|\boldsymbol{h}),$$

$$P(h_j|\boldsymbol{v}) = \prod_{j=1}^{m} P(h_j|\boldsymbol{v}). \tag{8.38}$$

This means that if we make a Markov chain Monte-Carlo (MCMC) sampling on the distribution of the RBM [25], the block Gibbs sampling can be adopted. The block Gibbs sampling starts with an initial sate v, h, then $P(\cdot|h)$ and $P(.|v)$ are alternatively used to compute the state transformation of all visual units and hidden units. This shows the efficiency advantage of the RBM in the sampling.

The unsupervised learning method can be served to the RBM through the maximum likelihood principle [211]. Suppose there is training data $v^{(1)}, v^{(2)}, \ldots, v^{(d)}$, then training the RBM is equal to maximizing the following objective function, where the biases b and c are omitted:

$$L(\boldsymbol{W}) = \sum_{k=1}^{d} \log P(v^{(k)}; \boldsymbol{W}) \equiv \sum_{k=1}^{d} \log \sum_{h} P(v^{(k)}, \boldsymbol{h}; \boldsymbol{W}). \tag{8.39}$$

In order to use the gradient ascent algorithm in the training process, we need to solve the partial derivatives of the objective function with regard to all parameters. After the algebraic transformation, the final results are

$$\frac{\partial L(\boldsymbol{W})}{\partial W_{ij}} \propto \frac{1}{d} \sum_{k=1}^{d} P(h_j|v^{(k)}) - (v_j h_j)_{P(v,h,W)}. \tag{8.40}$$

Equation (8.40) can be split into two parts: the positive phase and the negative phase. The positive phase can be computed by Equation (8.37) based on the entire training dataset. For the negative phase, $\langle f(x) \rangle_{P(x)}$ is defined as the average value of the function $f(x)$ on the distribution $P(.)$. In the RBM, this average value cannot be directly represented as a mathematic expression. That is the reason why training the RBM is very difficult.

Obviously, the simplest method, i.e., the MCMC, is used to solve the average value of the negative phase. In each MCMC sampling, a large number of samples are made to ensure that the samples conform to objective distribution. So we need to get a large number of samples to accurately approximate the average value. These requirements greatly increase the computational complexity of training the RBM. Therefore, MCMC sampling is feasible in theory, but it is not a good choice in efficiency.

Hinton proposed the CD algorithm by considering that the state of the MCMC starts with the training data [210]. In the CD algorithm, the computing process of the average value in the negative phase can be represented as the following. Firstly, each training data is respectively used in the initial states. After a few times of Gibbs sampling on the state transformations, the transformed state is served as the sample to evaluate the average value. Hinton found that just a few times of state transformation can ensure the good learning effect in practical application.

The CD algorithm greatly improves the training process of the RBM and makes a great contribution to the application of the RBM and the rise of deep neural network. The general maximum likelihood learning is similar to minimizing the KL-divergence between the RBM distribution and training data distribution. In the CD algorithm, this principle is inadmissible. Therefore, the essentially the CD algorithm is not a maximum likelihood learning [473] as the model learned by the CD algorithm has a bad model generation capability.

8.3.5 Deep belief networks

In 2006, Hinton proposed deep belief networks (DBN) in his paper [214] as shown in Figure 8.18. A deep neural network can be viewed as a stack of multiple RBMs. The training process can be carried out by the layer-wise training from the lower layer to the higher layers. Since the CD algorithm can be served to quickly train the RBM. So, DBN can avoid the high complexity of directly training neural networks through splitting the entire networks into multiple RBMs. Hinton suggested that the traditional global training algorithm can be used to fine-tune the whole network in the above training way. Then the model will converge to a local optimal point. This training algorithm is similar to the method that involves initializing the model

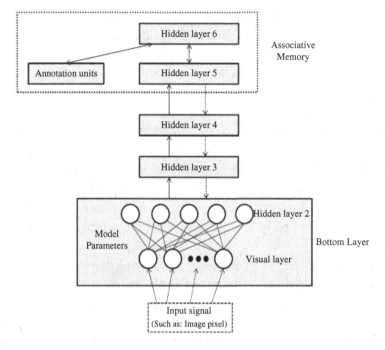

Fig. 8.18. DBN architecture

parameters to a better value using the layer-wise training way and further training the model through the traditional algorithm. Thus, the problem that the speed of the training model is slow can be solved. On the other hand, a lot of experiments have proven that this method can produce very good parameters with initialization values and improve the quality of the final parameters.

In 2008, Tieleman proposed a training algorithm called as the persistent contrastive divergence (PCD) [479], which improves the imperfection of the CD algorithm that was unable to maximize the likelihood degree. The efficiency of the PCD is similar to the CD and it does not destroy the training algorithm of the original objective function (maximum likelihood learning). In Tieleman's paper, a lot of experiments prove that the RBM trained by the PCD has a stronger model generation capability compared with the CD. In 2009, Tieleman further improved the PCD and proposed a method employing additional parameters to increase the effect of training the PCD [480]. He revealed the effect of MCMC sampling on training the RBM. This laid the foundation for improving the subsequent learning algorithms about the RBM. From 2009 to 2010, there existed a series of tempered Markov chain Monte-Carlo (Tempered MCMC) RBM training algorithms based on Tieleman's research results [116, 390].

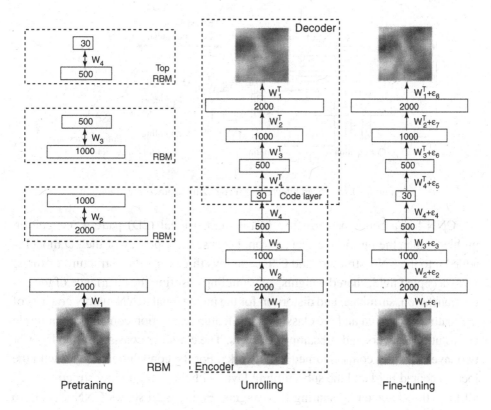

Fig. 8.19. An example of DBN

The figure to the left in Figure 8.19 is a typical DBN with four layers. It compresses a high dimensional image into a single representation with 30 dimensions corresponding to the top layer of size 30. We can also use the symmetry architecture of this network to map the 30 dimensions of compressed signal to the original high-dimensional signal (the middle figure in Figure 8.19). If this network is employed to compress the signal, we can see that the output of the network is equal to the input of the network. Then the BP algorithm is used to fine-tune the weights of the network (the right figure in Figure 8.19).

8.3.6 Convolutional neural networks

Convolutional neural networks (CNN) is a multiple-stage of globally trainable artificial neural networks [258]. CNN can learn the abstract, essential and advanced features from the data with a little preprocessing or even the original data. CNN has been widely applied in license plate detection [82], face detection [345], handwriting recognition [259], target tracking [141] and other fields.

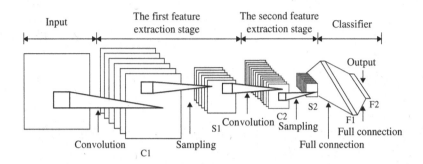

Fig. 8.20.   CNN architecture of recognizing handwriting digits

CNN has a better performance in two-dimensional (2D) pattern recognition problems than the multi-layer perceptron, because the topology of the 2D model is added into the CNN structure and CNN employs three important structure features: local accepted field, shared weights, subsampling ensuring the invariance of the target translation, shrinkage and distortion for the input signal. CNN mainly consists of the feature extraction and the classifier. The feature extraction contains the multiple convolutional layers and subsampling layers. The classifier consists of one layer or two layers of fully connected neural networks. For the convolutional layer with the local accepted field and the subsampling layer with the subsampling structure, they all have the character of sharing the weights. Figure 8.20 shows CNN serving to recognize handwriting digits.

In Figure 8.20, CNN has seven layers: one input layer, two convolutional layers, two subsampling layers and two fully connected layers. Each input sample in the input layer has $32 \times 32 = 1,024$ pixels. C1 is a convolutional layer with six feature maps and each feature map contains $28 \times 28 = 784$ neurons. Each neuron in C1 is connected with the corresponding local accepted field of size 5×5 in the input layer through the convolutional core of size 5×5 and the convolutional step of length 1. So C1 has $6 \times 784 \times (5 \times 5 + 1) = 122,304$ connections. Each feature map contains 5×5 weights and biases. Therefore, C1 has $6 \times (5 \times 5 + 1) = 156$ trainable parameters.

S1 is the subsampling layer containing six feature maps and each feature map consists of $14 \times 14 = 196$ neurons. There is a one-to-one correspondence between the feature maps in S1 and the feature maps in C1. The window of subsampling S1 is a matrix of size 2×2 and the step size of the subsampling defaults to 1. So there are $6 \times 196 \times (2 \times 2 + 1) = 5,880$ connections in the S2 layer. Each feature map in S1 contains a weight and a bias. This means that there are 12 trainable parameters.

C2 is the convolutional layer containing 16 feature maps and each feature map consists of $10 \times 10 = 100$ neurons. Each neuron in C2 is connected to the local accepted field of size 5×5 in the k feature maps in S1 through the k convolutional core of size 5×5, where $k = 6$ if the full connection way is adopted. So there are 41,600 connections in the C2 layer. Each feature map in C2 contains $6 \times 5 \times 5 = 150$ weights and biases. This means that there are $16 \times (150 + 1) = 2,416$ trainable parameters.

S2 is the subsampling layer containing 16 feature maps and each feature map consists of 5×5 neurons. S2 contains 400 neurons. There is a one-to-one correspondence between the feature maps in S2 and the feature maps in C2. The window of subsampling S2 is a matrix of size 2×2. So there are $16 \times 25 \times (2 \times 2 + 1) = 2,000$ connections in the S2 layer. Each feature map in S2 contains a weight and a bias. This means that there are 32 trainable parameters in the S2 layer.

F1 is a full connection layer containing 120 neurons. Each neuron in F1 is connected to the 400 neurons in S2. So the number of connections or the trainable parameters are $120 \times (400 + 1) = 48,120$. F2 is a full connection layer and the output layer, which contains 10 neurons, 1,210 connections and 1,210 trainable parameters.

In Figure 8.18, the number of feature maps in the convolutional layer increases layer by layer. This can supplement the loss caused by sampling. On the other hand, the convolutional cores make the convolutional operation on the feature maps of the former layer to produce the current convolutional feature maps. The different features produced expand the feature space and make the feature extraction more comprehensive.

The error back-propagation (BP) algorithm is mostly used to train CNN in a supervised way. In the gradient descent method, the error is back propagated to constantly adjust the weights and biases. This allows the global sum of squared error on the training samples to reach a minimum value. The BP algorithm consists of four processes: the network initialization, the information flow feed-forward propagation, the error BP, the update of the weights and the biases. In error back-propagation, we need to compute the local variation value of the gradient on the weights and the biases.

In the initial process of training CNN, the neurons in each layer need to be initialized randomly. The initialization of the weights has a great influence on the convergence rate of the network and so the process of initializing the weights is very important. There exists a strong relationship between the initialization of the weights and the selection of the activation function. The weights should be assigned by the fastest changing parts of the activation function. The selection of big weights or small weights in the initialization process will lead to a small change in the weights.

In the feed-forward propagation of the information flow, the convolutional layer extracts the basic primary features of the input to make up several feature maps.

Then the subsampling layer reduces the resolution of the feature maps. After the convolution layer and the subsampling alternatively complete the feature extraction, then the network obtains the high order invariance features of the input. These high order invariance features will be transmitted to the fully connected neural network and used to classify. After the information transformation and computing in the hidden layer and output layer of the fully connected neural network, the network finishes the forward propagation process of the learning. The results are then given by the output layer.

The network starts the error BP process when the actual output is not equal to the expected output. The errors are propagated from the output layer to the hidden layer and then propagated from the hidden layer to the subsampling layer and the convolutional layer in the feature extraction stage. The neurons in each layer start to compute the changed value of the weights and biases when they get their output errors. At last the network will enter the weights update process.

1. Feed-forward propagation of the convolutional layer

Each neuron in the convolutional layer extracts the features in the local accepted field of the same location of all feature maps in the former layer. The neurons in the same feature map share the same weight matrix. The convolutional process can be viewed as the convolutional neurons seamlessly scanning the former feature maps line by line through the weight matrix. The output, $O_{(x,y)}^{(l,k)}$, of the neuron located in line x column y in the kth feature map of the lth convolutional layer can be computed by Equation (8.41), where $\tanh(\cdot)$ is the activation function:

$$
O_{(x,y)}^{(l,k)} = \tanh\left(\sum_{l=0}^{f=1}\sum_{\gamma=0}^{kh}\sum_{c=0}^{kw} W_{r,c}^{k,l} O_{x+r,y+c}^{l-1,t} + \mathbf{Bias}^{j,k}\right). \tag{8.41}
$$

From Equation (8.41), we need to traverse all neurons of the convolutional window in all the feature maps of the former layer to compute the output of a neuron in the convolutional layer. The feed-forward propagation of the full connection layer is similar to the convolutional layer. This can be viewed as a convolutional operation on the convolutional weight matrix and the input with the same size.

2. Feed-forward propagation of subsampling

There are similar number of feature maps and one-to-one correspondence relationship between the subsampling feature maps and the convolutional feature maps. Each neuron in the subsampling layer is connected to the subareas with the same size neuron but the non-overlapping happens through the subsampling window. The output, $O_{(x,y)}^{(l,k)}$, of the neuron located in line x column y in the kth feature map of the *l*th subsampling layer can be computed by Equation (8.42).

$$\mathbf{O}_{(x,y)}^{(l,k)} = \tanh \left(\mathbf{W}^{(k)} \sum_{r=0}^{\text{sh}} \sum_{e=0}^{\text{sw}} \mathbf{O}_{\text{xsh}+r,\text{ysw}+c}^{t-1,k} + \mathbf{Bias}^{j,k} \right). \qquad (8.42)$$

3. Error BP of the subsampling layer

Error BP starts from the output layer and enters the subsampling layer through the hidden layer. The error BP of the output layer needs to first compute the partial derivative of the error of the neurons in the output layer. Suppose the output of the *k*th neuron is o_k for the training sample *d*. The expected output of the *k*th neuron is t_k for the sample *d*. The error of the output layer for the sample *d* can be represented as $E = 1/2 \sum_k (o_k - t_k)^2$. The partial derivative of the error *E* about the output o_k is $\partial E/\partial o_k = o_k - t_k$. Similarly, we can solve the partial derivatives of the error of all neurons in the output layer. Then we solve the partial derivatives of the error of the input in the output layer. Set $d(o_k)$ is the partial derivative of the error of the input of the *k*th neuron in the output layer. $d(o_k)$ can be computed by Equation (8.43), where $(1+o_k)(1-o_k)$ is the partial derivative of the activation function tanh(·) of the input of the neuron. Then we start to compute the partial derivatives of the error all the neurons in the hidden layer. Suppose the neuron *j* in the hidden layer is connected to the output neuron through the weight w_{kj}. The partial derivative $d(o_j)$ of the error of the output of the neuron *j* can be computed by Equation (8.44). When we obtain the partial derivative of the error of the output of the hidden layer, the error is back propagated to the hidden layer. Through a similar process, the error will be back propagated to the subsampling layer. For the convenience of expression, the partial derivatives of the error of the outputs of the neuron are called as the output errors of the neuron. The partial derivatives of the error of the inputs of the neuron are called as the input errors of the neuron:

$$d(o_k) = (o_k - t_k)(1 + o_k)(1 - o_k), \qquad (8.43)$$

$$d(o_j) = \sum d(o_k) w_{kj}. \qquad (8.44)$$

There are similar number of feature maps and one-to-one correspondence relationship between the subsampling feature maps and the convolutional feature maps. So, it is an intuitive process that the error is propagated from the subsampling layer to the convolutional layer. Equation (8.43) is used to compute the input errors of all neurons in the subsampling layer. Then the above input errors are propagated to the former layer of the subsampling layer. The subsampling layer is set to the *l*th layer, then the output error of the neuron located in line *x* column *y* in the *k*th feature map of the $(l-1)$th layer is computed by Equation (8.45).

$$d(o_{x,y}^{l-1,k}) = d(o_{([x/sh],[y/sw])}^{l,k}) W^{(k)}. \tag{8.45}$$

All neurons in a feature map of the subsampling layer share a weight and a bias. So, the local gradient variations of all weights and biases are related to all neurons in the subsampling layer. The weight variation $\Delta W^{(k)}$ and the bias variation $\Delta \mathrm{Bias}^{(l,k)}$ for the kth feature map in the lth subsampling layer can be computed by Equations (8.46) and (8.47). In Equation (8.47), f_h and f_w respectively indicate the height and the width of the feature map in the lth subsampling layer:

$$\Delta W^{(k)} = \sum_{x=0}^{fh} \sum_{y=0}^{fw} \sum_{r=0}^{sh} \sum_{c=0}^{sw} o_{x,y}^{l-1,k} d(o_{([x/sh],[y/sw])}^{l,k}), \tag{8.46}$$

$$\Delta \mathrm{Bias}^{(l,k)} = \sum_{x=0}^{fh} \sum_{y=0}^{fw} d(O_{x,y}^{l,k}). \tag{8.47}$$

4. Error BP of the convolutional layer

There exists two error BP ways in the convolutional layer: "push" and "pull". The "push" way (the left figure in Figure 8.21) can be considered as the neurons in the lth layer actively propagating the errors to the neurons in the $(l-1)$th layer. This is suitable for serial implementation. There is the "write conflict" problem in parallel implementation. The "pull" way (the right figure in Figure 8.21) can be considered as the neurons in the $(l-1)$th layer actively obtaining the errors from the neurons in the lth layer. It is difficult to implement the "pull" way. Due to the border effect of the convolutional operation, we need to confirm which neurons in the feature map of the former layer are connected to the neurons in the current layer.

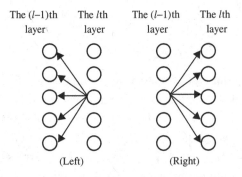

Fig. 8.21.   Two ways of error BP

Here the "pull" way is used to describe the error BP process of the convolutional layer. Equation (8.43) is employed to compute the input error of each neuron in the convolutional layer. Then the input error is propagated to the neurons in the former layer of the convolutional layer, like Equation (8.48):

$$d(O_{(x,y)}^{(l-1,k)}) = \sum_{t=0}^{m-1} \sum_{(p,q)c,d} d(O_{(p,d)}^{(l,t)})w, \qquad (8.48)$$

where A is the coordinate set of the neuron located in line x column y in the kth feature map of the lth layer and the neurons in the lth layer. w indicates the connected weight between the two neurons. The serial computational process that the error in the convolutional layer is back propagated to the former subsampling layer is described as the following:

> **for** each neuron i in the former layer of the convolutional layer
> Confirm which neurons in the convolutional layer are connected to the
> neuron i
> 'Pull' the error from the relevant neurons in the convolutional layer using
> equation (8.48)
> **end for**

The local gradient variation of the line r and the column y of the weight matrix describing the connection between the k-th feature map in the convolutional layer and the tth feature map in the former layer can be computed using Equation (8.49):

$$\Delta W_{(r,c)}^{(k,t)} = \sum_{x=r}^{fh-kh+r} \sum_{y=c}^{fw-wc+c} d(O_{x,y}^{l,k})O_{r+x,c+y}^{l-1,t}. \qquad (8.49)$$

All neurons in a feature map of the convolutional layer share a bias. The computational method is same to the subsampling layer.

With the complication of solving the problem and the higher performance requirement for CNN, the training data needs to be more complete and larger. So we need to train the network with stronger capability. This means that the network will have more trainable parameters. As the famous ImageNet dataset contained 14,197,122 labeled images [221]. The CNN containing 650,000 neurons in the library [247] was used to classify the ImageNet dataset. There were 60,000,000 trainable neurons in the above mentioned CNN. A large amount of training data and training parameters will significantly increase the computational time and especially the scrial computation will cost a few months of computational time [93]. Therefore, the researchers have started to research the parallel CNN. There exist at least five parallel ways, namely the parallelism of the samples, the parallelism between the former back layers, the parallelism between the feature maps in the same layer, the parallelism between the neurons in the feature map and the parallelism of the neuron weights [399].

8.4 Introspective Learning

8.4.1 Introduction

Introspection refers to investigating a person's own thought or emotion, i.e., self-observation. It also refers to observing sensation and perception experience under the control of the experiment condition. Introspection is opposite to appearance. The appearance is to investigate and observe the situation with the exclusion of oneself. Introspection method is an early psychological research approach. It investigates the psychological phenomena and process according to the report of the tested person or the experience described by himself. Introspection learning introduces the introspection concept into machine learning. i.e., by checking and caring about knowledge processing and reasoning methods of intelligence systems itself and finding out problems from failure or poor efficiency. The introspection learning forms its own learning goal and then improves the method of solving problems.

A learning system with the ability of introspection learning will improve learning efficiency as well. When a system is in a complicated world, it is difficult to tell all the possible relevant information and deduce the method of the system in advance. A very difficult question is how to predict the situation that the system will face and what information will be important and what response condition will be needed. Hence better flexibility and adaptability are required for the system, making it more sophisticated to deal with all kinds of situations. The system should be of the ability to improve the system's knowledge and know how to operate. But most learning systems do not possess the ability to change knowledge processing and reasoning methods. In a learning system with multi-policy, the central issue is to choose and arrange the learning algorithms for the particular situation. It requires the intelligence system to automatically choose and arrange the appropriate algorithm from the algorithm storehouse. By using introspection learning, the learning system can determine its goal based on analyzing successes and failures of the executed task. In other words, its goal is not one that the designer of the system or user provides. The system can clearly determine what is needed and what should be learned. In other words, the introspection learning system can understand the causes of the failure and related reasoning and knowledge in the process of operating the system. The system has its own knowledge and the ability to check its reasoning. In this way, the system can learn effectively. And the learning is less effective without such introspection. Therefore, introspection is necessary for effective learning.

The introspection learning involves four subproblems:

(a) There are standards that determine when the reasoning process should be checked, i.e., monitoring reasoning process;
(b) Determine whether failure reasoning takes place according to the standards;
(c) Confirm the final reason that leads to the failure;
(d) Change the reasoning process in order to avoid similar failure in the future.

In order to find and explain the failure, introspection learning system is required to be able to visit the knowledge about its reasoning process until the present moment. It needs a rough or clear expectation about the field result and its internal reasoning process. It is capable of discovering the failure of expectation in the reasoning process and in problem solving. In addition, it can also use reasoning failure to explain expectation failure and determine how to change the reasoning process and then correct the error thereafter. The introspection learning process includes three steps:

(a) Judge a failure. Determine whether a disappointed expectation should be generated;
(b) Explain the failure. Introspection learning system can find out the cause of the error of reasoning line before the failure and give the explanation to the reasoning failure. The system provides the definite goal of introspection learning so as to change its knowledge and reasoning process;
(c) Correct the failure. The system carries out the tactics of introspection learning according to the goal of introspection learning.

From the above, an introspection learning system must possess in itself an intact learning structure, such as a knowledge base, an algorithm base and an inference engine, etc. In addition, it requires a set of meta reasoning representations in order to track and confirm the realized process of reasoning. The system also requires a set of evaluation standards for reasoning, including explanation, efficiency analysis, mistake, failure, etc. It requires an introspection mechanism that is used to check the reasoning, form goals and execute the policy as well.

Cox applied the explanation pattern (XP) to explain anomaly and then created an accident understanding system Meta-AQUA [103]. It is a goal-driven learning system. The system chooses algorithms from an algorithm toolbox and combines them with the multi-learning method, so as to repair the erroneous part that leads to the failure of the system. The input of the system is dataflow of the incident concept entity, while the executing task is to generate an interaction model of the person and the incident. As a system prophesies a certain explanation that is tenable in an incident, a different explanation might appear after the incident and a failure will happen. The system will explain why the system fails and form a knowledge learning tactic which can change the failure. Hence, the system can learn through its failures.

When Meta-AQUA has not succeeded in understanding a story passage, it then uses the introspective Meta-XPs (IMXPs) to repair its reasoning process. An IMXP describes the tactics that are related to reasoning failure and repairing reasoning. An IMXP can be considered as the template matched with the description of the real reasoning process. It determines whether the reasoning will fail. But the real reasoning process is expressed by trace meta-XPs (TMXPs). For different reasoning failures, meta-AQUA has summed up the failure's symptom categories, both reason type and goal type. The symptom of reasoning failure can be used to confirm the reason of the failure and the reason of the failure can also be used to confirm the related learning goal.

ROBBIE is a route planning system proposed by Fox [154]. Its task is to produce a route planning from one place to another place under the conditions of several streets, possessing limited map knowledge and a small amount of initial samples. It examines the quality of planning by carrying out the planning in one simulation world. ROBBIE is a case-based system. Its knowledge can accrue from increasing cases, i.e., when the cases increase, it will understand the map better. ROBBIE's introspective unit monitors the reasoning of the planning device and compares the expected performance of the real reasoning process with that of the case-based reasoning process. When expectation failure takes place, the introspective unit will stop planning the task and will attempt to explain the failure and correct the system. If there is enough information to prove that the failure may occur, the system will continue carrying out the task. When necessary information is ready, explanations and modifications will resume from the suspended place. The feature of ROBBIE's system is to apply introspection learning in a case-based retrieval reasoning module and realize the refining of the case index. When retrieval fails, the reason of failure can be found through the introspective unit and the retrieval process is corrected. In addition, the system has provided the frame for applying introspection learning to intact the process of case-based reasoning.

8.4.2 General model of introspection learning

The general introspection course is divided into three parts: judge the failure, explain the failure and correct the failure [434]. Judge the failure: based on the establishment of definite and finite expectations of the reasoning process, compare the expectation with the real executing process of the system and then find the difference. The difference between expected behavior and real behavior is explanation failure. To determine whether the failure takes place means that there is a group of definite expected values about the reasoning state of the system. Expectation failure is monitored in the process of reasoning. When every step of the reasoning process is going on, compare the related result with the related expectation. If expectation is found, then failure will take place. Explain the failure: based on the standard of expectation failure and the trace of reasoning, explain the failure. After finding the reason, a definite correcting suggestion related to the reasoning process should be presented, in order to avoid the same failure again. Correct the failure: related corrective action of the reasoning process can be appended to a particular expectation. For example, when an expectation failure takes place, the appended method can also be presented at the same time. The description of the corrective method is not detailed enough. So, the system should also include forming the mechanism of revision tactics. The revision module carries out the real revision tactics, real modification according to the description of failure and the suggestion of revision.

The general model [452] of introspection learning is shown in Figure 8.22. Besides judging the failure, explaining the failure and correcting the failure, the model also includes knowledge base, reasoning trace, reasoning expectation model and monitor protocol, etc. The monitor protocol is used to standardize the monitoring of the reasoning process. It prescribes where and how the reasoning process should be monitored and where and how the control of the system should be transferred.

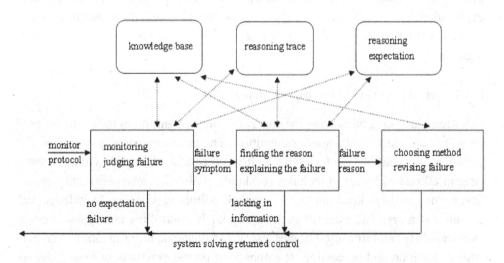

Fig. 8.22. Introspection learning model

The knowledge base includes the knowledge relevant to reasoning. It is not only the foundation of reasoning but also the grounds for judging and explaining the failure at the same time. The reasoning trace has recorded the reasoning process. It is specially used in introspection learning and is also important ground for judging, explaining and correcting the failure. The reasoning expectation model is an ideal model of the system's reasoning process. It has provided the standard for reasoning expectation and therefore, is the main grounds for judging the failure. The introspective learning unit of the system uses monitor protocol, an already existing background, reasoning expectation and reasoning trace to check whether the current state shows expectation failure.

The emergence of expectation failure includes two cases. One is when a model expectation about the current ideal state of reasoning process does not fit the current real reasoning process, expectation failure will take place. The other one is, when the system cannot continue because of disastrous failure, expectation failure takes place certainly. If there is no expectation failure in the reasoning unit, then all the expectations fit the real process and the system is informed that everything is all right and then the system regains the power control again. If a failure is found, the reasoning will use background, reasoning trace and the ideal expectation model to look for the initial reason for the failure and explain the failure. It is possible that the obtained information is not enough to diagnose and correct the failure when a failure is found. At this time, the introspection learning unit can suspend its explanation and revision tasks until there is abundant information. When the necessary information is already obtained, the explanation and revision tasks will resume from the suspended place. The explanation of the failure can provide a clue to correct the failure. After explanation, the learning goal of correcting the failure is generated and the revision method is also formed according to the learning goal. After revision, the system will regain power control.

8.4.3 Meta-reasoning of introspection learning

Meta-reasoning originates from the concept of meta-cognition in the cognitive process. It is also called self-monitor cognition. The meta-cognition is viewed as the cognition of cognition. It refers to a cognitive process about oneself and the knowledge of all related things. It includes two kinds of abilities, awareness and control. The former refers to knowing one's own ability limiting, concept, knowledge and cognitive strategy. The latter refers to appropriately controlling and applying one's own knowledge and strategy. The past learning system paid more attention to knowledge acquisition and processing. It emphasized on the exactness of knowledge as well as that of the reasoning process. This makes a demand for reasonably expressing the reasoning process based on knowledge representation. Similar to the meta-data of warehouse, i.e., data about the data, meta-reasoning is used in the introspection learning system. By using meta-reasoning, the learning system can acquire the cognition of knowledge and knowledge processing and further finish the proper control and usage of its own knowledge and tactics.

Meta-reasoning involves reasoning about the reasoning. As one of the main goals of introspection learning is to revise the reasoning process according to reasoning failure or execution, expressing the reasoning process through the basic level is a basic condition of introspection learning. The introduction of meta-reasoning requires reaching two goals. The first goal is to record the reasoning process of the system and form the reasoning trace. The second goal is to explain the reasoning process and provide a causal chain for reasoning failure. And the final goal is to offer expression for the reasoning process of monitoring and offer essential information for explaining and revising reasoning failure.

The expression of meta-reasoning can be realized by both external and internal ways. The external way is to establish one ideal model for the reasoning process and design different evaluation standards at different stages. The internal way is to use the expression with meta-explanation to internally record the reasoning process and explain an anomaly. For instance, the Meta-AQUQ system applies XP theory to express the transition of the mind state and names this kind of expression structure as the meta-explanation pattern (MXP). Its meaning is an XP of one mode about another explanation mode. Since the standard explanation mode is the expression method of a cause and effect structure, MXP can explain its own explanation process. According to the difference in functions, there are two kinds of meta-explain patterns. One is used for tracking the explanation process and it is called as TMXP. Another one is to use introspective explanation and it is called as IMXP.

8.4.4 Failure classification

Another important problem of the introspection learning system is failure classification. Meta-AQUA system has listed the types of symptoms, reasons for failure and the related learning goal. The failure symptom is classified according to whether actual value (A) and expected value (E) exist and whether they are the same or not including contradictory, unexpected, deadlock, strange affair, false proposition, expect proposition, degradation, etc. Each symptom is expressed by the association of various failure marks. The system has proposed two kinds of wrong marks such as, inference expectation failure and amalgamation failure. It also has four kinds of omission mark, such as, overdue prophecy, search failure, structure failure and input failure. ROBBIE system classifies the abnormity according to different modules in the model and combines with related assertion, which is the main ground for explaining failure. The failure is divided by the reasoning process. The reasoning process is divided into several stages, such as index example, search case, adjusting case, second retrieval case, executing case and keeping case. The failure is also divided into several stages.

The failure classification is a key element of introspection learning. It is the ground for judging failure and provides an important clue toward explaining the failure and at the same time forming the corrected learning goal. The failure classification also determines the ability of introspection learning to a certain extent. Hence, it is necessary to set up a rational failure classification for the introspection learning system. Failure classification considers two important factors. One is the granularity of failure classification, while the other is association among failure classification, failure explanation and the goal of introspection learning. The granularity of failure classification can decide whether the contradiction of classification is too thin or too thick. For big failure classification, we can abstractly describe the failure as well as finish the classifying quickly according to the different stages of the reasoning process. In this way, we cannot only include some unpredictable situations and increase the adaptability of the systematic introspection, but can also accelerate the contrasting process according to the different stages. The thin classification can describe the failure in detail. This can provide valuable clues for failure explanation. Appropriately dealing with association between failure classification and failure explanation will also raise systematic introspection ability. The system not only requires the finding of the failure reason through failure symptom and forming introspective learning goal, but also has the ability (adaptability) to deal with all kinds of different problems. The failure explanation can also be divided into different levels. The granularity of failure classification facilitates forming a reasonable relationship between failure symptom and failure explanation.

The method of failure classification includes common failure approach and reasoning process module approach. The common failure approach proceeds with common characteristics of failure and finishes the classification. For instance, lack of input information can come down to input failure; inference machine's failure in inducing or creating a solution for a problem comes down to creation failure; knowledge failure is regarded as knowledge contradiction and so on. The common approach considers the failure classification with respect to the whole system. This approach is suitable for introspection learning in the distributed environment. The module approach is to classify the reasoning process into several modules and creates a partition according to the module. For example, case-based reasoning can be divided into several modules, such as retrieval, adjustment, evaluation and storage. Retrieval failure refers to the anomaly appearing in the retrieval process. The module approach is suitable for the reasoning in a modular system. In some cases, the two kinds of approaches can be combined.

8.4.5 Case-based reasoning in the introspective process

Case-based reasoning is obtaining the source case in the memory through suggestion of the goal case and then guiding the goal case by using the source case. In this reasoning, facing problems and situations is called goal case and the question or situation in the memory is called source case. Its advantage lies in simplifying knowledge acquisition, improving the efficiency and quality of problem solving. The process of case-based reasoning is to form case's retrieval characteristics according to the current goal and then search related cases in the memory case base by using the retrieval feature. Then it selects a case that is most similar to the current situation, judges the case in order to suit the current situation, forms a new case and evaluates the new case and finally stores the new case to the base for further usage.

The case-based reasoning and model-based reasoning are important ways to realize introspection learning. On the contrary, introspection learning can also improve the process of case-based reasoning. A key link in the introspection learning process is to find out the reason for failure according to the failure features. Introspection not only concerns the executing failure or reasoning failure, but should also contain less effective execution or reasoning process. Besides finding the error, the system needs to evaluate reasoning. From the perspective of expectation, the failure judgment is also called supervision and evaluation. The expectation value is considered as the criterion of supervision and evaluation. At the same time, the evaluation factor can be used for quantitative evaluation. Supervision is oriented to the reasoning process while evaluation is oriented to reasoning result. A series of processes, such as case-based reasoning retrieval, adjustment, evaluation and storage, finishing of judgment failure and explanation failure may show the effectiveness of judgment and explanation. Hence, case-based reasoning is an effective method. In the Meta-AQUA system, the process from checking errors to forming learning goals is a case-based reasoning process. The system can find out the reason of failure and then form the learning goal using the failure symptom. On the other hand, the usage of introspection learning in different modules of case-based reasoning, such as retrieval and evaluation, has improved the adaptability of the system and its accuracy. The evaluation of the case is an important step in the case-based reasoning system. Quantitative case evaluation enables the case to automatically modify the case weight, so as to improve the effectiveness of case retrieval.

8.5 Brain Cognitive Data Analysis

8.5.1 Brain function imaging

Human brain is the center to obtain, store, process, integrate internal and external environment information from the human body and is a very ingenious and perfect information processing system. In recent years, the human brain planning research has employed the modern information tools to analyze, compare, integrate, model and simulate a large number of different levels of the human brain data. The research then drew the brain structure mapping and built the neuroinformatics database and the global knowledge manage system about the neural system data. This promotes humans to understand the human brain from the molecular level to the overall system level.

With the emergence and application of the brain function imaging technology, we can carry out the brain research in the living body and the overall system level. Like a window prying into the brain, we can obtain all kinds of functional activities of the brain, especially the advantageous activities, through watching the cerebral blood flow and the glucose metabolism under the atraumatic condition. At present, the common brain imaging technologies are functional magnetic resonance imaging (fMRI), positron emission tomography (PET), magneto-encephalography (MEG), etc. The comparison of the brain functional imaging technology is shown in Table 8.1.

With the development of the brain functional fMRI technology, the ability to research the brain has been greatly improved and has resulted in massive amount of data collection. A large amount of knowledge behind the data cannot be found only through the computers as they simply store, query and calculate those experiment data. So the researchers employ machine learning and data mining to integrate the brain functional imaging data into the ordering data and further analyze process, integrate and model the ordering data by combining it with psychology, linguistics and brain science. Only then will the new rules and the deep mechanisms of the advantageous cognitive activities be revealed.

8.5.2 Brain nerve semantics

In 2001, Mitchell from Carnegie Mellon University started to observe the activities of the images and the characters in the human brain through fMRI and captured the functional magnetic resonance results of the brain [357]. In 2008, Mitchell introduced five scientific problems in his paper that was published in *Science* [324]:

Table 8.1. Comparison of brain functional imaging technology

	fMRI	PET	EEG
Image-forming principle	The detected MR signal can show the oxyhemoglobin saturation and the blood flow volume, and indirectly reflect the amount of energy expenditure of the brain. This reflects the activity of the neurons to some extent.	The isotope intake of the brain is used to measure the glucose metabolic rate in the different positions, the regional cerebral blood flow, the brain metabolism, the brain biochemistry, the drug dynamics change and the oxygen and sugar metabolism in the blood.	This measures the electronic physiological function of the external electric current of the nerve cells.
Temporal resolution	Second	Minute	Millisecond
Spatial resolution	Millimeter	10 millimeters	10 millimeters
Invasive injury	The intense radio frequency and the high magnetic field can produce a few harmful effects.	The radiation of the radioisotope can produce seriously harmful effects.	No invasive injury occurs
Preparation time of measuring	Short	Long	Long
Measuring time	Long	Secondary	Short
Cost	The equipment cost is expensive, while the consultation cost is cheap.	Both equipment cost and the consultation cost are expensive.	The equipment cost is cheap and the consultations cost is expensive.

(1) Can we get the mental state from the functional magnetic resonance image, or forecast the mental state in terms of the structure of the functional magnetic resonance image?

(2) Can we get the semantics of the stimulation about the neural activity code though the classifier?

(3) Are the representations of the human mental state similar? That is, the representations of the human mental state similar when we research things with common nature? For example, is there the same mental state for the word "indeterminacy" in the brains of different people?

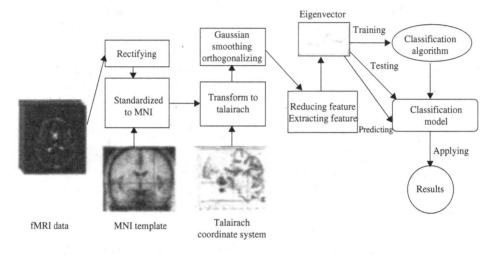

Fig. 8.23. Functional magnetic resonance image classification processing

(4) Can the basic principle of the neural expression be found? If we input any word, is there a universal theory for the neurons to predict the activities of the brain?

(5) What is the semantic foundation of neural combination coding? How do I predict the neural expression by extracting the semantic feature and then predict the neural state and the brain state?

Mitchell *et al.* employed the support vector machine, the dynamic Bayesian network and the nearest neighbor algorithm to research the cognitive state, and made some progress.

The brain cognitive state recognition process based on the fMRI classification includes four parts as given in Figure 8.23:

(1) Preprocessing procedure: The preprocessing of the original experiment data includes head motion correcting, image standardizing, coordinate system transforming, Gaussian smoothing and data orthogonalizing etc.

(2) The extracting and reducing feature dimension: Since the number of the voxel points of the functional magnetic resonance image is of several hundred thousands orders magnitude and there are a large number of non-activated voxel points, the redundancy of the data is very high. So, we need to extract the low dimensional feature to effectively represent the original data.

(3) Modeling and validating procedure: The original data with the class label is split into training data and testing data. The appropriate classification algorithm is used to train the model and evaluate the effectiveness of the model.

(4) Applying and recognizing procedure: The data without the label is put into the trained model. The model will classify the functional magnetic resonance and recognize the connotative brain cognitive state information.

8.5.3 Brain functional connectivity analysis

The early research on brain functional connectivity was mainly carried out through cognitive experiments or by locating the interested regions in *a priori* anatomical structure. The interested static fMRI data is served as "seed" and the other encephalic region data is served as the correlation analysis. Then, we can get the collaborative consistency of the specific encephalic region activity in the resting state, and propose the concept of the default mode. As the research continued, the scientists found a group of encephalic regions that were negatively correlated to the encephalic regions in the task state. There exists the low-frequency oscillation hemodynamic response and the high correlation in these encephalic regions in the resting state. As the static data processing method research continues, the concept of the default mode continuously develops and the analysis of the static function connection is gradually introduced into the difference analysis research between the psychopath and the non-psychopath. In addition, the functional connectivity in the resting state is the foundation for the functional connectivity of the human brain. There exists no difference because of the different cognitive mental tasks. A large number of the cognitive and physiological disorders may be closely related to the brain functional connectivity disorders.

After the data driver algorithms are introduced into the functional connectivity analysis, some researchers used principle component analysis (PCA) and independent component analysis (ICA) to split the static human brain into five relatively independent functional networks and to propose the inside and outside combination hypothesis that the five networks, respectively take charge of the specific functions of the human brain [122].

The general model of ICA is

$$x = f(s), \tag{8.50}$$

where $x = (x_1, x_2, \ldots, x_N)^r$ is the observed random variable vector, $s = (s_1, s_2, \ldots, s_N)^r$ is the independent principle hidden variable vector, known as the source vector as well. At most there can be one Gaussian component in s. $f : R^M \to R^N$ is an unknown function. If f is a linear function, we can get a linear ICA. Otherwise we can get a nonlinear ICA. The common problem is to evaluate the mixed function f and the source vector s.

The aim of ICA is to search for a linear transformation W of the observation signal x. The transformed signal is independent as much as possible:

$$u(t) = Wx(t) = WA_{s(t)}, \tag{8.51}$$

where u is an estimate of the source signal. In order to reduce computation, we need to make a preprocessing on the data before the ICA. The preprocessing operation includes centralizing and whitening. The centralizing means the original data minus its average value, which makes it the zero mean value. The so-called whitening is to linearly transform the centralized data, which makes the transformed data uncorrelated and the variance as 1. There are a large number of ICA learning algorithms, including the non-Gaussian maximization, the mutual information minimum, the maximum likelihood estimation, etc. However, those algorithms are equivalent in some conditions and can be transformed as each other.

PCA is an effective way to solve the problems such as the model has too many parameters, the parameters are related to each other, and that the parameter information is overlapped. In multi-variate analysis, the measurement in high dimension space has many limitations. PCA is the method to simplify those problems. As far as possible, PCA can convert the multiple parameters into a few primary parameters to avoid reducing the information of the original parameters. This makes the original related variables change into a few unrelated factors and each factor has a comprehensive meaning. The principle of PCA is to search an optimal linear transformation to transform the related variances into unrelated new variances with the same number. Then the new variances with the maximum variance are retain and they reflect the primary information of the data. These new variances are the principle components. Of course, there is the actual means in the specific field as well.

We can know from the mathematical knowledge that the total variance is not changed after the principle component transformation. This means that the variance of the original data has the principle component representation. Furthermore, each eigenvalue of a matrix is the variance of each principle component and the eigenvectors corresponding to the eigenvalues are the coefficients of the original variables in the principle components. The transformed principle components will be sorted in a non-incremental way. The top k principle components reflect the maximum information. The first principle component or the top k principle components can represent the information of the original data and reach the goal of reducing the dimension of the data. Furthermore, because the principle components are not related to each other, the correlation degree is higher and the performance of reducing the dimension is better.

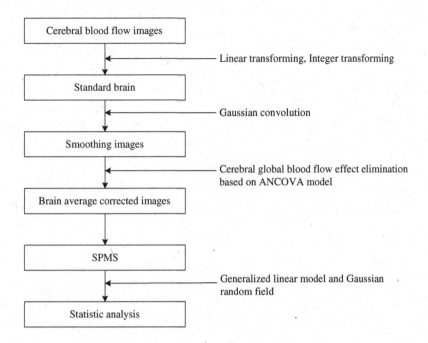

Fig. 8.24. The analysis process of SPM

In order to analyze the brain functional imaging data, Friston from the Hamas Smith Hospital in UK in 1994 first developed the statistical parametric mapping (SPM) called as SPM94. The first version of SPM was based on Matlab. The later version, SPM95, not only processes the PET data but also processes the fMRI data. The analysis flow chart of SPM is shown in Figure 8.24.

The image processing method is employed to obtain the called pixel value of SPM represented by the statistics in the analysis process of SPM. Then, those pixel values are used in the statistic analysis. The whole procedure can be viewed as two steps: the space preprocessing and the statistical analysis and the inference. The details, about this content is stated in literature [27].

Chapter 9

Brain-Like Computing

Through cross-collaboration in the fields of brain science, cognitive science and artificial intelligence, we should strengthen basic and original research in the inter-disciplinary subject of intelligence science, solve the major basic theory problems of brain-like computing and innovate brain-like computing intelligent systems.

This chapter focuses on the latest progress of brain-like computing and proposes a roadmap for the development of intelligence science.

9.1 Overview

In 1936, Turing put forward the great idea of the Turing machine, which is based on the prototype of the human brain's information process and laid the theoretical foundation of the modern computer [493]. Turing tried to build "a brain" and first noted that putting programs into a machine can make a single machine play multiple functions.

Since the 1960s, Von Neumann's architecture had been mainstream computer architecture. In classic computers, the place of data processing and the place of data saving were separated. The memory and the processor were divided by a data channel that existed between the area of data saving and the area of data processing, i.e., the bus. Fixed channel capacity showed that only finite quantity of data could be "checked" and processed at any time. Processors were configured with a few memories in order to save data when computing. After having accomplished all the necessary computation, the processor wrote results back to the memory by the data bus. Generally, this procedure does not cause a problem. Most of the modern processors use a cache at the time of enlarging the memory, in order to minimize the flow in the data bus with fixed capacity and to offer a temporary save at the place adjacent to the spot of calculation. If a computation frequently needs many pieces of data, the processor will save them in the cache, while accessing the cache faster than the main memory. However, the architecture of the cache does not work on this computing challenge of the simulative brain. Even a relatively simple brain consists of millions of neurons that are connected by billions of synapses. So imitating such a big and relative brain needs to cost the cache capacity that is as big as the computer's main memory, which will lead to a machine that cannot work immediately. The following problems exist in the development of computer technologies:

(1) Moore's law shows that the device will reach the limit of physical miniature in the coming 10–15 years.
(2) Limited by the structure of the data bus, programming is hard and causes high energy consumption when we process large-scale and complex problems.
(3) There is no advantage according to the analysis that it is complex, varied, real-time and dynamic.
(4) Cannot meet the demand of processing the information of the "digital world" greatly. In the sea of data produced every day, 80% of the data is original without any processing, while the majority of original data's half-life period is only 3 hours.
(5) After a long-term endeavor, the calculating speed of the computer is up to one quadrillion times, but the level of intelligence is low.

We can study from the human brain that researching the method and algorithm of the human brain process and developing analogous-brain-calculate have become urgent requirements at present. Now, the study of brain science has been attached greater importance in the world. On January 28, 2013, EU launched the "Human Brain Project", investing 1 billion euros as funds for research and development in the next decade. The goal was to use a super computer to multi-stage and multi-layeredly simulate the human brain completely and help people to understand the function of the human brain. American President Obama announced an important project on April 2, 2013, which would take about 10 years and cost a total amount of 1 billion dollars. This project, called "Brain Research through advancing innovative neuro technologies (BRAIN)", was launched in order to study the functions of billions of neurons and explore the human's perception, behavior and consciousness, and find out methods to cure diseases related to the brain, such as Alzheimer's disease.

IBM promised to use 1 billion dollars for its cognitive computing platform Watson. Google purchased nine robot companies and one machine learning company, including Boston Dynamics. The father of high-throughput sequencing

Rothberg and Yale university professor Xu Tian established a new biotech company, combining deep learning with biomedical tech in research and development for new medicine and the technology of diagnostic instruments.

As Europe, America and other countries have launched a variety of projects of the human brain, China also launched its own brain science project. The "China Brain Plan" has been prepared over two years and has formed an initial research pattern, which is the basis of brain cognitive principle, serious diseases of the brain and brain-like AI. The study of brain-like computing and AI is a significant part of the "China Brain Plan" and taking the research and development and industrialization of brain-like AI as core, they develop from four directions of "humid", "soft", "hard" and "large-scale service". The research fields include the following factors: building big data of brain science and a platform for brain simulation, parsing mechanism of the brain's cognitive and information process, which is generally biological lab (humid); developing core algorithms of brain-like AI and software systems about brain-like AI, such as algorithm of deep learning (soft); from various intelligent wearable devices to robots of industry and service, designing brain-like chips, robots and hardware systems of brain-like AI (hard); carrying out applied research in the field of early diagnosis of critical diseases including brain diseases, researching new medicines and intelligent navigation, public security, intelligent city, new technology of aeronautics and cultural transmission and so on. The "China Brain Plan" has been approved by the State Council and has been listed as one of the "important science technology projects about the country's future development".

Robin Li, Chairman of Baidu, realized that AI is one of the most advanced technologies of the 21st century, the development of which will improve and extend the border of human ability greatly. AI will take a profound effect on promoting tech-innovation, enlarging the country's competing advantage and even motivating the development of the human society. In the national committee 2015, he suggested to set up "China brain" plan and to investigate intelligent human–computer interaction, prediction for big data analysis, automatic driving, intelligent medical diagnosis, intelligent unmanned aircraft and robots used by military and civil. Baidu will invest 350 million dollars to advance the "Baidu brain" project.

9.2 Blue-Brain Project

9.2.1 Brain neural network

The blue-brain project involves the usage of the IBM blue gene supercomputer to simulate the various functions of the human brain, such as cognition, perception, memory and so on. Blue-brain project is the first comprehensive attempt using detailed simulations to understand brain function and dynamic function with reverse engineering methods to research the mammalian brain.

The size of the human brain is only $1,400\,\text{cm}^3$ and its weight only has 20 W power, but the computing power is far beyond today's supercomputers. Twenty billion neurons of the cerebral cortex and million kilometers long axons, which are connected to their cerebral white matter, provide most advanced human brain functions, like emotions, planning, thinking and the main memory. Recent ongoing research has produced a large number of scientific data on neurons, but the interaction of neurons, the structure of the neocortex and the information processing mechanism are still unclear. Neuroscience research has shown that the brain's neural network is a multi-scale sparse directed graph. In particular, local short-distance connections can be regulated through repeated statistical changes to descriptions and global remote connection. Brain behavior is entirely formed by individual functional units of non-random and associated interactions and this is a key factor of organized complexity.

Markram, director of the Institute of Brain and Mind, Swiss Institute of Technology in Lausanne and his experimental group spent more than a decade building up a database of nerve centers, so they have the largest single nerve cell database around the world.

In July 2005, the Swiss federal Institute of Technology in Lausanne and IBM together announced to develop research on the blue-brain project [282], make progress in understanding the function of the brain and the function disorders and provide the way to solve mental health and intractable problems about neuropathy. At the end of 2006, the blue-brain project had created a basic unit model of the cortical function column. In 2008, IBM used a blue gene supercomputer to simulate 55 million neurons and 500 billion synapses of the rat brain. IBM gained 4.9 million dollars from DARPA to study neuromorphic compute. IBM Almaden Research Center and IBM Watson Research Center, along with Stanford University, University of Wisconsin-Madison University, Cornell University, Columbia University Medical Center and the University of California Merced have participated in the program study.

9.2.2 Cerebral cortex model

One of the earliest discoveries found that cortical structures include six different levels of cortical thickness. Researchers had found a layer and special network of connections within the cortex and obtained patterns between different characteristics [56]. For the purpose of simulation, IBM translates this typical layered gray matter in the cortico-hypothalamic structure into a prototype of gray matter network (see Figure 9.1) [325].

Connections between layers are primarily vertical and only a small amount of lateral spread in a diametric cylindrical structure called "cortical function column" exists. In many cortical regions, the functional neurons in the column share the same features, which show that features include not only the structural entities, but also functions. Cylinder range measurements of collected information will help us to build a scale model, as shown in Figure 9.1.

The cortical function column usually occupies only a few millimeters and seems to be responsible for specific functions, including motor control, vision and planning. According to the change of cell density in the six cortex levels, the brain is divided into cortical areas. Each function corresponds to a special possibility of cortical circuits [230]. For example, Brodmann area is clearly associated with the core vision processing functions. Over the course of time, there have been hundreds of scientists, who focused on understanding how each cortical region of the brain plays a corresponding function and how it carries out structural functions.

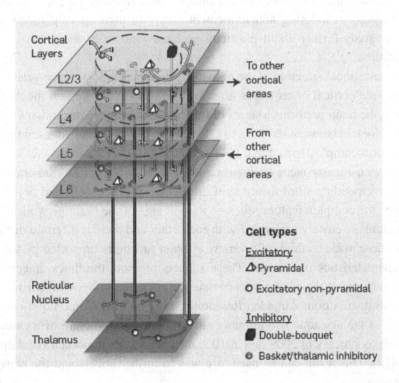

Fig. 9.1. A circuit diagram of the thalamocortical system simulated on the C2 cortical simulator

In the 20th century, a lot of research showed overwhelming evidences in support of the cortical areas associated with a view of specific function, and that the brain also demonstrates an alarming degree of plasticity. At present, research has proved the fact that in the process of ferret brain development, visual pathways in the white matter connect to the auditory cortex and auditory pathways are simultaneously connected to the visual cortex. They are specialized for the corresponding auditory area and can also be modified for the corresponding visual area and vice versa. This amazing natural reconstruction allows us to expect that the core algorithm of neural computation may not depend on the morphology of specific sensory organs or motor neurons, while the observed changes in the cortical structure of the regions may indicate the fine typical neural circuits. We expect these typical circuits to carry out reverse engineering. The existence of such a typical microloop is an important hypothesis. Although a large number of local cortical circuit layouts have been estimated, the exact form of the microloop is still unknown and its role in neural computing has not been confirmed. Even if we could find a basis for typical circuits, in order to unlock its potential mechanism, we must identify and implement with plasticity mechanisms. Such mechanisms ensure that the development and the mature stage in the process of a typical circuit of tailoring and refinement complete their specific functions. We will later study further about plasticity problems and its possible local synaptic mechanisms.

Organizational structure of the nervous system in the most coarse-grained scale and multiple cortical areas forms a network to deal with complex functions. For example, the brain performs a series of intricate dexterity eye movements when we read. We look in between the lines to select a series of lines and edges, which combine to form complex spatial and temporal patterns. These patterns can be seen as a key to open a masterpiece of linguistic knowledge, which makes the brain bathed in the corresponding word meaning of the sights, sounds, smells and objects. Surprisingly, the complex feature relies on a small area of the brain network. Regions on structure are closely connected with each other and there is a certain distance in space. These made us think of a variety of brain functions supported by the whole brain characteristics of subnets. These subnets promote the flows, integration of information and at the same time promote the cooperation between existed differences and distribution. Almaden Research Center of IBM Corporation conducted research of the macaque and human brain white matter structure of measurement and analysis process in 2009 and 2010 and achieved two important breakthroughs [326, 412]. This result can be used as a way to further understand the network of brain regions.

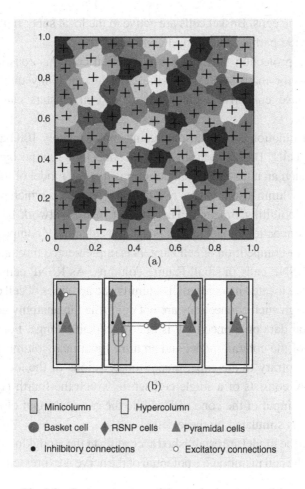

Fig. 9.2. System structure of the cerebral cortex model

Different connections of the six layers of the cerebral cortex indicate their different functions. For example, the input connection is usually sent to the fourth layer, the second layer or the third layer. According to the document [280] of the rat cortex model, the model of the cerebral cortex is presented in Figure 9.2 [119, 121].

The model of Figure 9.2(a) represents the geometric distribution about a plane of the cortex. The plane includes 100 super functional columns, each column is distinguished by different colors and each super functional column is formed by 100 small feature columns. Figure 9.2(b) represents the connectivity of the model. Each small functional column contains 30 conical cells activated by a short distance to neighboring cells. Cone cells project onto the local cell belonging to the same cluster of other small feature columns of core cells and other clusters of conventional spikes of non-cone cells. Basket cells are active in the local super functional column and RSNP provide partial inhibition of cone cells.

Long-range projection between small function columns constitute the memory of the attractor matrix and define the cell clusters. Only the small function columns that have collective memory mode or cell clusters can be of mutual encouragement.

Each super function column also contains approximately 100 basket cells activated by cone cells. Basket cells make the connection routine by inhibiting the conical cells. Such an ultra-functional column is like the model of the winner-take-all. Each small column also includes two partial RSNP cells which connect conical cells and have inhibiting function. The abstract neural network based on current long-distance connection model indicates that the cell cluster competition has additive property. The competition of cell clusters is implemented through the cone cells and the other RSNP cells in small feature columns. As RSNP cells would inhibit cone cells that are located in local small columns, the activities of cell clusters will be affected. Although such connections are not confirmed in anatomy and physiology, the experimental data of connectivity is in an acceptable range. For simplicity, the small features of the column model and an ultra-functional column are more obvious, which is contrary to the experimental observations of the local Gauss model [68]. The model consists of a single cell set, in which the fourth layer of the cortex provides the input of the cone cells, while the external input of the memory of synaptic events is simulated by these cells.

The cells in the model are established according to the Hodgkin–Huxley formula [130, 215] and the cell membrane's potential of the nerve is expressed as a differential equation

$$C_{\mathrm{m}} \frac{\mathrm{d}V}{\mathrm{d}t} = I_{\mathrm{comp}} + I_{\mathrm{cond}} + I_{\mathrm{syn}}, \tag{9.1}$$

where C_{m} denotes membrane capacitance, I_{comp} denotes the total current adjacent compartments, I_{cond} denotes the total ion current in the cell membrane channel and I_{syn} represents the sum of synaptic currents. The electrical behavior of cells is described by the active and inactive variables of ion current. For example, the delay of potassium ions carrying plastic electric current can be expressed as:

$$I_{Kr} = (E_{Kr} - V(t))G_{Kr}n^4, \tag{9.2}$$

where n is an activation variable and can be expressed as:

$$\frac{\mathrm{d}n}{\mathrm{d}t} = \alpha_n(1 - n) - \beta_n n, \tag{9.3}$$

where α_n and β_n are nonlinearly dependent on $V(t)$. A cone cell in the model is composed of six compartments. Each compartment has a state variable corresponding to cell membrane potential and one or two state variables representing ion current (each compartment at most has five ion currents). Some booths with the flow of intracellular calcium ion will have more than one state variable. In addition, some synapses carry other calcium ion flows and want to add other variables. In general, the synapse is determined by three state variables: one represents the degree of opening and the other two represent synaptic strength (facilitation and inhibition) of short-range change.

In order to achieve the simulation, a project team of IBM created a mode collection about non-overlapping vertical memory: picking a small column to form a pattern in each column with super function. Two long distances in the same pattern of small function columns will be randomly connected by remote. In this way, each cone cell only receives a pattern of remote activation. Similarly, each RSNP cell receives conical cell excitation of the small functional column from the external model.

9.2.3 Super computing simulation

Basic elements of the simulator include: neurons used to display a large number of behaviors like the presentation model, the communication of peak potential, the dynamic channel of synapses, the synaptic plasticity, the structure in plastic, the stratification, the microfunction column, the ultrafunctional column and the cortical network consisting of regional and multi-regional network architecture (as shown in Figure 9.2). Each of these elements is modular and can be configured individually, so we have flexibility to test a large number of brain structures and dynamics of biological thought-provoking hypotheses. Correspondingly, its possible combination is a great space and this requires the simulator to run at a certain rate, so as to achieve rapid user-driven exploration.

The history of neural simulation can be traced to 1950. Since then, studies on cortical simulation (as shown in Figure 9.1) have been developed along two lines: the detail and the scale. Several publicly available simulators, including NEURON and GENESIS, are applied to the detail simulation of a small number of neurons [64]. Unfortunately, biophysics of the fine details can lead to near real-time simulation of mammals and the size of this task is computationally impossible. Regrettably, such fine details in biophysics will lead to a mammalian scale, and near real-time simulation tasks cannot be achieved in calculation. On the other hand, other studies have used compact imaging neurons, which demonstrate the simulation for millions of neurons and billions of synapses. The research goal is close to real-time simulation

Table 9.1. Several mammalian neurons and synapses

	Mouse	Rat	Cat	Monkey	Human
Billions of Neurons	0.016	0.055	0.763	2	20
Trillions of Synapses	0.128	0.442	6.10	16	200

speed and at the same time, along the direction of model scale and neuroanatomical detail in the direction of expanding the boundaries of cutting-edge research.

A simulation meets the requirements of size, speed and detail at the same time, corresponding to the three resources of the computing system: storage, computation and communication. Obviously, it is a serious challenge. For example, cats' cerebral cortex has nearly 1 billion neurons and more than 6 trillion synapses (as shown in Table 9.1). As the number of synapses is more than 10,000 times, the amount of memory needed to support is proportional to the number of synapses. Therefore, even if we can use one byte of storage space to describe the state of a synapse, a cat simulation will need at least 6TB memory space. Each synapse's efficient synaptic data structure requires about 16 bytes of storage space. In addition, each neuron is assumed to be updated frequently and the dynamic differential equation describing the evolution of the neuron state is 1 trillion times per second. The biological neurons excite at an average rate of 1 time per second and most synapses will receive 1 spike per second. So there will be 6 trillion peak messages delivered in a neural network. In order to meet this demand, we will accelerate the development of super-computing, algorithms and software architecture, which are critical for the pace of innovation.

From the aspects of hardware, the blue gene supercomputer system offers many computing processors, a large amount of distributed memory and a high bandwidth communication subsystem. From the software aspect, the IBM project team has developed a cerebral cortex called C2 simulator. The simulator adopts the distributed storage multi-processor architecture. The analog scale continues to expand and constraints in the simulation of neurophysiology and neuroanatomy continue to increase.

Since 2007, the work was aimed at understanding the cerebral cortex of rats and mice. The simulations of the IBM project team has maintained a steady growth. In May 2009, the team used the Dawn Blue Gene/P supercomputer system in cooperation with the Lawrence Berkeley National Laboratory and got the latest results of the research (as shown in Figure 9.3). The research results make full use of the storage capacity of the supercomputer system and they are a valuable milestone regarding the cat scale cortical simulation (roughly equivalent to 4.5% of the size of

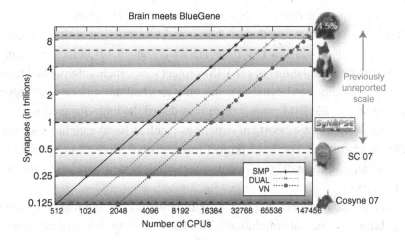

Fig. 9.3. Scalabel cerebral cortex simulation by C2

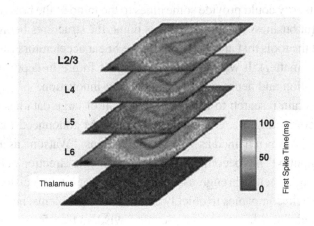

Fig. 9.4. Simulation response to a triangle stimulate hypothalamus loop

the human brain) [14]. These analog networks show neurons that are reproducible and have the lock feature asynchronous packet by self-organization [15].

Analog to the frequency of α (8–12 Hz) and γ (>30 Hz), mammals' neural activity recurs showing frequent vibration in large areas of the neural cerebral cortex. In a similar visual stimulation paradigm, the analog network displays that specific population response delay is consistent with the observation in the mammalian cerebral cortex [14]. Simulator allows us to analyze thousands of nerve tissue, but animal memory is limited and can record only dozens of nerve groups. With this advantage, we can construct a stimulus-evoked detailed picture, of events in the network communication. Figure 9.4 summarizes the following activities: passing from the thalamus to the fourth and sixth floors of the cerebral cortex and then passing to the layers 2, 3 and 5, while there is horizontal transmission within the layers.

C2 Simulator provides a key integrated workbench for detecting brain algorithms. So far, the simulations of the IBM project team, including the key feature of a lot of nerve structure and dynamics, has only touched the surface of neuroscience data. For example, the IBM project team introduced the long-distance white matter project, other important subcortical structures (such as basal ganglia) and structural plasticity mechanisms. The IBM project team always adopted an open attitude to deal with emerging technologies in detail that brought new measuring methods for cortical circuits.

It's unrealistic to expect that cognitive function can be automatically generated from the biological neural simulations. The IBM project team expected that a simulator could be consistent with brain background and that it can form and perform the neural computing theory. Through studying behavioral simulation, a complete mathematical theory could provide some clues to the mind of the brain and for developing intelligent business machines. On this point, the structures being built are not the answer but the tools that are used to find, like linear accelerators (used to explore the structure of matter). It will lay a foundation for future in-depth understanding of brain calculation and neuromorphic engineering innovation.

Cognitive brain research to promote the arrival of large data has accompanied the cognitive computing era. On March 6, 2014, IBM announced that its big data analytics platform was renamed as Watson foundations. "Watson" as a synonym for "cognitive computing" has become IBM's future strategic direction of big data. Cognitive computing systems through assistance, understanding, decision, insight and discovery, can help companies to quickly discover new problems, new opportunities and new value and to achieve customer-centric wisdom transformation.

On January 29, 2015, at the 29th American Artificial Intelligence Conference, Sellmann from the Thomas J. Watson Research Center of IBM, was invited to speak on "intelligent decision". The report noted that recent advances in artificial intelligence had provided a commercially viable collaborative strategic decision support system for vision. These cognitive systems integrate information retrieval, knowledge representation, interactive modeling, social learning ability and logical reasoning probabilistic decision under uncertain conditions.

9.3 Human Brain Project of the EU

9.3.1 Introduction

On January 28, 2013, the European Commission announced the election results of the "future and emerging technologies (FET) flagship project," and two representatives of frontier science and technology in the future multinational research projects — Graphene and the human brain plan (human brain project, HBP) won from 21 candidates. Each plan is to receive 1 billion euros as research funding in the next 10 years.

The human brain project hopes to create an integrated research platform, which aims at developing the most detailed model of the human brain based on information communication. Under the coordination of Markram who is in EPFL Lausanne, 87 organizations, including universities from 23 countries (including 16 EU countries), research institutions and industry organizations will collaborate using computer simulation methods to study the human brain. The study is expected to promote the development of artificial intelligence, robots and neuromorphic computing systems, to lay the foundations for medical advances in science and technology, and to contribute to the nervous system and related diagnosis, treatment and drug tests.

The human brain project aims to explore and understand the human brain's running processes, to study the human brain's low-power, high-efficiency mode of operation and its learning function, the association function, innovative features, etc. to simulate the human brain through information processing, modeling and supercomputing technologies and to develop human brain energy efficient supercomputers through supercomputing technology for diagnosis and treatment of the human brain, human interface and the human brain controlled robot research [283].

The human brain project is divided into five areas and each area is based on existing work requiring further research [205].

1. Data

It is necessary to collect and filter out the necessary strategic data to draw the human brain atlas and to design the human brain model and at the same time to attract research institutions to contribute data outside the project. Nowadays, neural cognitive science has accumulated massive experimental data and a lot of original research brings new discoveries. Even so, the vast majority of core knowledge, which constructs a multi-level brain atlas and a unified brain model, is still needed. So the primary task of the human brain plan is to collect and describe strategic data, which are filtered and are valuable. The human brain project points out three key points about the research of data:

(1) The multilevel data of the rat brain. Earlier studies have shown that the results of the research about the rat brain also applies to all mammals. So it will provide a key reference for the system research about the relationship between the different levels of the rats' brain tissue.

(2) The multilevel data of the human brain. The research data of the rat brain can provide important reference in the study of the human brain to a certain extent, although there are fundamental differences between them. In order to define and explain the differences, the plan of the human brain's research team is to collect the strategy of the human brain and accumulate the existing rat brain data as much as possible.

(3) The structure of human cognitive systems. It is one of the important goals for the HBP to make clear the association between the structure of the human brain and the function of the human brain. The HBP will focus on the structure of neuron regarding about specific cognitive and behavioral skills, from other non-human species' simple behavior to the human-specific advanced skills, like language.

2. Theory

The mathematical and theoretical basis of the human brain's research. It is necessary to define a mathematical model, which tries to explain internal relations between different brain tissue levels such as the acquisition of the information, the description of the information and the storage function of the information. If it lacks uniform and reliable theoretical basis, it will be difficult to solve the problem regarding the data of neuroscience and the problem of fragmentation in the research. So the HBP should have a coordinate institution studying the mathematical theories and models to explain the inner relationship in the different brain levels in order to achieve information acquirement, description and storage function. As a part of this coordinate institution, the human brain plan should establish an open "European Institute for Theoretical Neuroscience" to attract more outstanding scientists, who will be involved in this project and act as incubators for innovative research.

3. The Technology Platform of Information and Communication

In order to improve research efficiency to provide services for neuroscientists, clinical researchers and technology developers, it is necessary to establish comprehensive information and communication platforms, including six big platforms: neural information system, human brain simulation system, medical information system, high-performance computing system, neuromorphic computing system and neural robotics system.

(1) Neural information system. The neural information platform of the human brain project provides an effective technical method for neuroscientists, analyzes the structure of the brain and the data of function easily, and indicates the directions for the multi-levels of the human brain mapping. These platforms also include many tools about neural predictive information. These tools help to analyze the

data of different brain levels that describe brain tissue and also help to evaluate some parameter values, which cannot be arrived at from natural experiment. Before this study, the lack of data and knowledge was an important obstacle that blocked us from systematically understanding the brain. While the tools function, these problems are solved.

(2) The simulation system of the human brain. The human brain project can establish a sufficient scale for the human simulation platform, aiming to establish and simulate the multi-level and multi-dimension of the human model to tackle many kinds of specific issues. This platform plays a key role in the whole project. It provides modeling tools, workflows and simulators for researchers and helps them get large and diverse data to process dynamic simulation from the brain models of rats and humans. It makes "computer simulation experiment" possible. With all kinds of tools in the platform, we can generate a variety of input values, which are essential for medical research (disease models and drug effects model), neuromorphic computing and neural robot research.

(3) High-performance computing system. The high-performance computing platform of the human brain project provides sufficient computing power to establish and simulate the human brain model. It not only has advanced supercomputer technology, but also has new interactive computing and visual performance.

(4) Medical information system. The medical information system of the human brain project gathers clinical data from hospital archives and private databases (but strictly protects patient information security as a precondition). These functions can help the researcher to define the disease's "biological signature" in each stage, to find a key breakthrough. Once researchers have detection and classification methods on biological basis, they will find the original disease easily and study the related effective treatment.

(5) Neuromorphic computing system. The neuromorphic computing platform of the human brain project provides researchers and application developers with hardware and at the same time provides a variety of equipment and software prototype for modeling the brain. Using the platform, developers can develop many compact low-power equipment and systems, which are closer to human intelligence.

(6) Neural robotics platform. The neural robotics platform of the human brain project provides tools and workflow for researchers, so that they can use sophisticated brain models to connect to the virtual environment in physical simulation. But they had to rely on the study in human and animal natural environment to get a similar conclusion as before. The system provides a brand new research strategy for neuro-cognitive scientists and helps them to discern many kinds of

principles under human behaviors. From the technical standpoint, the platform will provide developers with the necessary development tools, and help them develop some robots that have human potential. This goal was not achieved in the previous studies, due to the lack of a central controller for the "type of brain".

4. Applications

The fourth major goal of the human brain project is that it can reflect a variety of practical values for cognitive science research, clinical research and technology development.

(1) Principle of unified knowledge system. "Simulation system of the human brain" and "neural robot platform" are detailed explanations for the neural circuits of specific behavior, so that researchers can use them to implement specific applications, such as the effect of genetic defects, analyzing the result of different level tissue cells and setting up a drug effect evaluation model. A human brain model can be used to distinguish humans and animals in nature. For example, the model can show the human language skill. This model will allow us to change our mind about the knowledge of the brain, and it can also be applied in the field of specific medical and technical development.

(2) The awareness, diagnosis and treatment of brain diseases. Researchers can make full use of medical information systems, neuromorphic computing systems and brain simulation systems to find the biological signatures in the process of the evolution of various diseases, conduct in-depth analysis and simulation of these processes, to finally get new disease prevention and treatment options. This project will be fully embodied with the practical value of HBP. New diagnostic techniques, which can predict diseases before they cause irreversible harm, can advance the diagnosis and achieve "customized medicament", and they will ultimately benefit patients and reduce health care costs. A better understanding of the disease and diagnosis will optimize the drug development process and it is beneficial to improve the success rate of experiments and to reduce the cost of new drug research.

(3) The future computing technology. Researchers can use high performance computing systems, neuromorphic computing systems and neural robots in the human brain plan to develop new computing technologies and applications. High-performance computing platforms will be equipped with supercomputing resources and they will integrate the technologies of a mixture of multiple neural morphological tools. With the help of neuromorphic computing systems and neural robot platform, researchers can make a software prototype that has great market potential. These prototype includes house robots and service

robots, which are inconspicuous, but have a strong technical capability, including data mining, motor control, video processing, imaging and information communications.

5. Social Ethics

Considering the huge impact of the research technique of the human brain plan, it will set up an important social ethics group to finance the research on the potential impact socially and economically. This group affects the human brain plan's researcher in ethics, and improves the level of ethics and social responsibility in him. Its primary task is to engage in positive dialogue between stakeholders and community groups, which have different methodologies and values.

The roadmap of the human brain project is shown in Figure 9.5 [508].

9.3.2 Spike-timing-dependent plasticity

Learning and memory of the brain are core issues in neurosciences. Nowadays, brain synaptic plasticity is the key to study the information storage of the brain. The concept is affected by Hebb's hypothesis. Hebb's guess is described as follows: repeated and continuous active cells together act as a store memory trace, also called memory imprinting, which is able to increase the bonding strength between

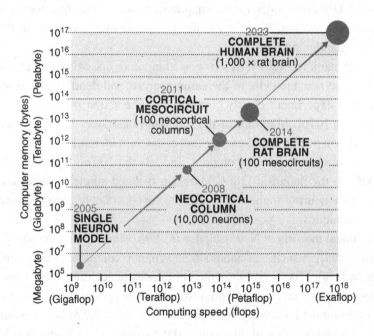

Fig. 9.5. The roadmap of the human brain project

the groups of interconnected neurons [206]. In recent years, a new concept in the study of cells has emerged and it emphasizes on timing rather than frequency. This kind of new learning paradigm is called as spike-timing-dependent plasticity. This paradigm arouses great interest in studying, because of its simplicity, biological rationality and computing capacity.

Hebb's principle is essentially a causal selection principle which is based on award synapse so as to drive the postsynaptic neuron successfully. It's also a natural neural mechanism that is a simultaneously associated and sequential perception event. Between 1850 and 1867, Hebb's thought inspired a number of researchers, who tried to explain how synaptic plasticity explains Pavlov and Watson's classical conditioning and Skinner's operational conditions.

The discovery of hippocampal plasticity caused excitement in research. Douglas and Goddard showed that repeated high frequency is a more effective burst in long-term potentiation (LTP) than in a single long ankylosing training. It is an important milestone in the history of synaptic plasticity. LTP became a popular protocol induced by repeated short bursts and it confirmed the importance of the simulation of the induction of LTP and persistent time. Hebb predicted and elaborated this conclusion in the 20th century. Douglas and Goddard named LTP under the recommendation of Andersen. Large amount of experimental and theoretical studies based on Hebb's assumption combined potential cells, synapse and network mechanisms. Debate changes in presynaptic or postsynaptic trajectories and bring the focus on competition, Synapse can be changed in many ways, including presynaptic, postsynaptic and both.

In the Sakmann laboratory, Stuart won a landmark discovery that records information from the somatic cells of the same neurons and dendrites by patch-clamp recording. The experiment clearly confirms that the action potential spreads back to the dendrites [470]. Markram of the Sakmann laboratory suggested that single subthreshold synaptic potential energy causes calcium increment of low-level influx [285], lets a large single action potential, and lets the 100 ms long trail of calcium reverse back to the dendritic [286]. Markram isolated single synaptic connection between conical neurons in the cortex and developed a matching pair of patch clamp recording technique.

In the annual meeting of Neuroscience in 1995, Markram had presented the first experimental study, which was about single synaptic connections between neurons in the cerebral cortex, demonstrating the importance of accurate time by presynaptic and postsynaptic neuron peak potential timing of the spiking [286]. Single spiking peak potential marked a turning point in relative time of the millisecond timescale. It's opposite to the decision of direction and the size of relative time of competition type and general depolarization or simulation sequence [284]. Back-propagation peak potential can be viewed as the sum of all synaptic input, therefore the ideal correlation between individual synaptic inputs is generated along dendrites. Post-synaptic timing of peak potential is spread by direct current injection to produce, so these changes are not heterogeneous. Postsynaptic timing of peak potential can play along an associated diaphragm and it has identical discovery with the previous polarized synaptic input diaphragm. The study reveals that the LTP is a causal relationship of presynaptic preceding postsynaptic timing of peak potential, instead of 10 ms instantaneous time. However, long-term depression is inspired by the presynaptic of the non-causal relationship of postsynaptic timing. In other words, the distribution of cells is not always electrified together because of the time. The bigger time of 100 ms will not cause any plasticity, named STDP. These experiments also showed that the block of postsynaptic peak potential destroys LTP because of the resistance of the NMDA receptors.

Two theories about STDP were published in 1996. Gerstner [173] extended his old theory, which was based on the timing of the peak potential of Herb's potential difference, to the potential difference of the causality peak potential timing and suppression of non-causation. Although there is still a 1 ms's window of time, to explain how the barn owl's auditory system in the receptive field generates very detailed transient accuracy. The article builds on peak potential timing level, including drawing the STDP function. Abbott and Blum published a model about plastic temporal correlation and applied it to the model of hippocampus to explain the rodents' navigation experiment [2]. Under their study, Blum and Abbott [58], proposed a possible method to reduce the transmission efficiency in the condition of presynaptic electric pulse after postsynaptic electrical pulse. According to the speed of the construction, it is also very simple to re-explain the study of Blum and Abbott in the STDP framework.

Markram and Tsodyks developed a widely used synaptic stimulation test, beyond the single shock test, revealed the connection of short-term plasticity and reported that Hebb's pairing is not necessary to change the effect of synapses and their short-time dynamics. This revives the Eccles's test about high-frequency stimulation in the synaptic transmission path. For long-term plasticity to increase to the new research level, the short-term plasticity can be changed to long-term plasticity, which they call as the redistribution of synapse effect or RSE [288]. Tsodyks and Markram have also developed a dynamic model of synaptic transmission, which demonstrates how simple changes in various synaptic parameters change the transmission of synaptic and introduces the possibility of release and synaptic inhibition and encourages these concepts to determine the transmission signal coding [491]. Markram and his colleagues studied the STDP in 1997 [284].

In 1999, Guoqiang Bi and Muming Poo verified the causal SDTP windows by making a lot of time sequence in detail [54]. For example, using paired recording of split neurons, Guoqiang Bi and Muming Poo recovered the long time window with 40 ms at a very alarming speed between LTP and LTD and reached the almost perfect consistency between presynaptic and postsynaptic activity. This rapid variations between LTP and LTD is called instantaneous effect on biology, but it is resurrected in the cerebral cortex [71] and regarded as one feature of STDP.

Some of the recent studies on STDP are clustered in STDP factors such as speed, high order peak potential sequence motif and parametric aspects of dendritic location. Another important area of experimental study in future is the relationship between STDP and short-term plasticity. To a great extent, the model of STDP and dependency rate only change the strength of synaptic. This change in the transient sensitivity is still completely unknown about how the STDP recombines activity patterns in a recurrent local loop.

Future research is needed to clarify the relationship between synaptic learning rules and internal equilibrium plasticity. Paying attention to the nature of Hebb's plasticity algorithm indicates that it is not stable. Persistent relevant release among connected neurons can cause synaptic enhance, which in turn leads to the increase of the degree of relevant release and causes a positive feedback and leads to uncontrolled growth of synapses. Although some form of STDP retains the issuance rate of the postsynaptic in a stable state, the stability of the inherent characteristics in a highly connected network may not be fast enough to track the rate of rapid increase.

Future studies need to clarify the network topology of Hebb's collection. I guess this is a problem that needs the methods of graph theory. An important question is whether the topology is uniquely determined by the experience, or by an experience mechanism independent of the experience. After Hebb's hypothesis was published, theorists pointed out that if the synapse is saturated, these collections for storing a plurality of memory are not very helpful. Therefore synaptic inhibition must also exist, taking into account the better storage.

9.3.3 Unified brain model

The human brain project aims to set up a uniform brain model which can simulate supercomputers, covering all the current understanding of the human brain. Prototype of the human brain project is the blue brain project given in Figure 9.6 [508], which starts with a neuron model to establish the cortex of the simulation area from the bottom to the top.

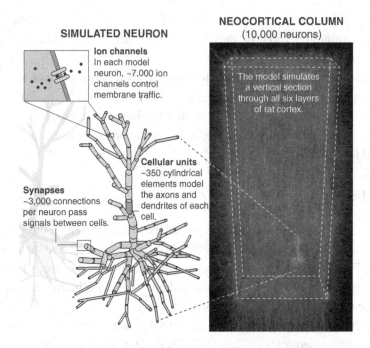

Fig. 9.6. Blue brain simulation

In the human brain project, Markram wants to put all the points together for a unified modeling and completes their countless ion channels. He is not only modeling a neural circuit for the related sense of smell, but also modeling the whole brain. We understand how these levels are combined and make it clear on how the brain controls behavior and cognition, including the genetic level, the molecular level, the neuron and the chromosomes, the principle of microcircuit, the big loop, the middle loop and the brain region.

It was a fable in the 1980s to research on a complete unified theory of the brain, which needed a computer performing 10^{18} calculations per second. But Markram was not afraid of difficulties, since computing power doubles every 18 months. This means that a computer of million trillion level will appear in 2020. At the same time, he also believed that neuroscientists should be ready for it.

Since the 1980s, Markram and his students collected data from the perspective of the cerebral cortex of rats, including the results obtained from different laboratories by performing the experiment 20,000 times. Information included morphology, three-dimensional (3D) restructuring, electrical properties, the communication of synapses, the location neuron synapses, the behavior of synapses and even of the genes involved in gene expression data. By the end of 2005, Markram's team let part of the related information integrate into a single neuron model. In 2008, researchers

did about 10,000 models, composed of tubular model cortex that is known as cortical function column. Currently, they have simulated 100 units of connection using
a more advanced blue gene computer.

The unified model can be used to preserve data about cortical structure and
function. In fact, the majority of the team's efforts is to set up "basic framework and
software for large-scale ecosystem", so that the blue brain is useful for all of the
scientists. The system will contain tools that auto convert the data into simulation
and a tool for information.

9.4 The US Brain Project

In April 2, 2013, the White House announced the "Brain Research through Advancing Innovative Neurotechnologies (BRAIN)" program, referred to as "BRAIN
Project". The program is comparable to the human genome project, and it will
explore mechanisms of the human brain, draw the whole brain activity map and
develop new therapies for incurable brain diseases.

After the "BRAIN project" of the United States was released, the National Institutes of Health immediately set up a "BRAIN Project" working group. The "BRAIN
Project" working group proposed nine funding areas: statistical brain cell types; the
establishment of brain structure diagram; the development of large-scale neural network recording technology; the development of neural circuits operations tools;
understanding the contact between nerve cells and individual behavior; integrating
the neuroscience experiments and theory, models, statistics; describing the mechanism of the human brain's imaging techniques; the establishment of mechanisms to
collect human data for scientific research; knowledge dissemination and training.

The United States carried out in-depth research in brain science and brain-like
computing and made progress.

9.4.1 Human connectome project

The Human Brain Atlas is one of great challenges of the 21st century. The Human
linker project (Human Connectome Project, HCP) will clarify the neural pathways
underlying brain the function and behavior, which is a key factor to face this challenge. Decrypting this amazing yet complex connection diagram will reveal what
makes us unique and makes everyone different.

The research project (WU-Minn HCP consortium) was led by the University of
Washington, the University of Minnesota and the University of Oxford and its goal
was to use non-invasive imaging of cutting-edge technology to create an integrated
human brain circuit atlas of 1,200 healthy adults (twins and their non-twin siblings).

This research will produce valuable information on brain connectivity and reveal the relationship between behavior and the contribution of genetic and environmental factors to the individual difference of brain behavior. The Van Essen laboratory of the University of Washington developed the connection group workbench, which provided a flexible user-convenient access, mass data stored in ConnectomeDB database for free and played a leading role in the development of other brain atlas analysis methods. The beta version of the connection group workbench has been published on the website, www.humanconnectome.org.

9.4.2 MoNETA

The school of cognition and nervous system of the Boston University carried out long-term studies of the brain neural model in the US. As early as 1976, Grossberg proposed an adaptive resonance theory (ART) [181,182]. Top-down mechanism controls forecasting of encoding and matching and effectively triggers rapid learning, resisting the total oblivion. Achieving the goal of rapid and stable study but not the total oblivion is usually attributed to the stability/plasticity dilemma. Stability/plasticity dilemma states that each brain system requires fast and stable learning. If the brain system design is too safe, then we should expect to find a similar principle that can run in all brain systems. The principle can be based on the whole life process of changing conditions in making different responses to learn the growing knowledge stably. ART presets some basic features of human and animal perception and cognition, which is part of the answer to solve the brain stability/plasticity dilemma. In particular, the human being is a conscious creature, which can learn about the expectation of the world and make inferences of what is going to happen. Human beings are a kind of attention-type creatures as well. The data processing resources are concentrated on a limited number of available information at any time. Why are human beings conscious and attention-type creatures? Stability/plasticity dilemma and the solution of making use of the resonance state provide a unified framework for understanding this problem.

ART assumes that there is a close connection between the processing mechanism that makes us learn quickly and steadily for the changing world and the other processing mechanism that focuses on the information we are interested in. Only the resonance state can drive new rapid learning process in order to solve the stability/plasticity dilemma, which is the origin of the name of this theory.

The recent ART model, known as the LAMINART, shows that ART predictions may be specific [193] in the thalamus cortical circuit. The LAMINART model makes the integration of visual development, learning, perception, attention and 3D vision. However, it does not include the control mechanisms of the dynamics of the peak potential on learning, higher-order-specific thalamic nuclei, non-specific thalamic nuclei, regularity resonance and reset and the pharmacological modulation.

In 2008, Grossberg put forward the SMART (Synchronous Matching Adaptive Resonance Theory) model [195], in which the brain coordinates a multi-stage thalamus and cortex learning process and stabilizes important information out of the memory. The SMART model shows both bottom-up and top-down paths that work together and coordinate the several processes of learning expectations, focus, resonance and synchronize to complete the above objectives. In particular, the SMART model explains how to achieve needs about concentrating on learning through the brain subtle loop, especially the cell hierarchical organization in the new cortex loop.

The SMART model explains how to naturally coexist in the LAMINART structure and so, it is beyond the ART and the LAMINART models. In particular, the SMART model explains and simulates that shallow cortical circuits may interact with the specific primary and higher thalamic nuclei and non-specific thalamic nuclei, in order to control process of matching or non-specific thalamic nucleus that is used to control cognitive learning and resist complete forgetting. Based on the process of acetylcholine, it is possible to make the nature of the predicted alertness control crystallized. Nature only makes use of the local computation signal control via learning from the continuous environment data.

The SMART model is the first work to link cognitive and brain vibration, especially in the frequency domain γ and β, which are obtained from a series of cortical and subcortical structures. The SMART model shows why β vibrations can become a modulated top-down feedback and resetting symbol. The SMART model developed earlier simulation work, and explained how the gamma vibration is generated when the modulated top-down expectation is matched with the consistent bottom-up input. Such a match makes the cell more efficient across its incentive threshold to stimulate action potentials, which leads to the overall enhancement of the local gamma frequency synchronization in the shared top-down modulation.

The SMART model made different vibration frequencies associated with the spike timing-dependent plasticity (STDP) together. If the average incentive of presynaptic and postsynaptic cells is 10–20 ms, in other words, in the STDP learning window, learning scenarios will be more easily restricted to the matching conditions. This model predicts that STDP will further strengthen sync excitement in the regions of the related cortical and subcortical and the long-term memory weights can be matched with synchronous resonance to prevent or quickly reverse fast learning rules. In the matched condition, the amplified γ vibration makes the presynaptic excitement compress into a narrow time-domain window, which will help excitement to spread over the cortex hierarchical structure. The prediction is consistent with the rapid reduction of effects and postsynaptic excitatory of the observed lateral geniculate nucleus.

Different oscillation frequency and matching/resonance (γ frequency) or mismatch/reset (β frequency) are associated with these frequencies, not only for the selection of learning, but also for discovering the active search process of the cortical mechanisms that support new learning. No match can predict the expressed fact in the components of ERP N200, which pointed out that new experiments can be used to combine ERP and oscillation frequency as a cognitive process index for dynamic regularity learning.

Funded by the US National Science Foundation, the Institute of Cognitive and Neural Systems, in the Boston University, set up the Center of Excellence for Learning in Education, Science and Technology (CELEST). In CELEST, the designers of the calculation model, neuroscientists, psychologists, engineers and researchers from the Cognitive and Neurological Department of the Harvard University, the Massachusetts Institute of Technology, the Brandeis University and the Boston University carried out communication and collaboration. They researched on the basic principles of how to plan, organize, communicate and memorize, especially the brain model of application learning and memory, and they wanted to construct a low power consumption, high density neural chip, to achieve increasingly complex large scale brain circuits, and to solve the problem of challenging pattern recognition.

The Institute of Cognitive and Neural Systems, in the Boston University, designed a software called MoNETA (Modular Neural Exploring Traveling Agent) [499], which is the brain of a chip. MoNETA will run on the brain inspired microprocessor, which was developed by the US California HP Labs. Its basic idea is the principle that distinguishes us from a high-speed machine with no intelligence quotient (IQ). MoNETA happens to be the name of the roman goddess of memory in mythology. "MoNETA" will do that which other computers have never done before. It will perceive the surrounding environment and decide what information is useful and then this information will be added to the structure of reality taking shape in some applications. It will develop a plan to ensure its own survival. In other words, MoNETA will have the same motivation as cockroaches, cats and people. The place of MoNETA distinguished from other artificial intelligence is that it does not need to be explicitly programmed with the same as the mammalian brain and can be in a variety of environments for dynamic learning.

9.4.3 Neurocore chip

Stanford University's Boahen and his research team developed 16 custom Neurogrid chips. Each chip can simulate 65,536 neurons. These chips can simulate

1 million neurons and billions of synaptic connections. By design, the Neurocore chip has a very high energy efficiency. Strategy made by Bergen *et al.* is to make an assured synaptic share hardware circuit. The size of the Neuro-grid is comparable to an iPad and the number of neurons and synapses that can be simulated is far more than other brain simulations performed on a tablet computer under the same conditions of energy consumption. The development of the Neuro-grid obtains funding from the US National Institutes of Health.

The operating speed of the circuit board is 9,000 times higher than the average personal computer, while the power consumption is far lower than the PC. It is used for humanoid robots, artificial limb control and other purposes. The Neuro-grid named "Neurocore" used 16 dedicated IC. With these IC, it can reproduce the action of about 1,050,000 neurons in the brain and billions of synapses. Stanford University said that the Neurocore made use of semiconductor technology about 15 years ago for manufacturing. The Neurogrid's development cost is $40,000. Bergen said that if we can use the latest manufacturing process, the manufacturing cost can be reduced to only $400 for the current 1/100. Stanford University said that the strategy is making use of a small number of circuits to reproduce a large number of synaptic action obtain a success and so they used the older process technology in the IC package. This strategy is particularly large in the low power consumption of IC.

9.4.4 HP memristor

It is a challenge to integrate the memory and the computation to construct a brain-inspired structure. Memristor is the best technology to achieve this task, because it has enough energy consumption efficiency, storage density and can equal the human biological memory. With this device, the artificial intelligence system, which is close to the size and energy consumption of the mammalian brain, can be constructed.

When the HP team led by HP Senior Fellow Williams researched silica, they accidentally discovered the silica with Latch Crossbar function, which can be used to make a memristor. Memristor is a piece of thin TiO_2 sandwiched between two electrodes (above platinum) as an intermediate. The titanium piece is divided into two parts: one half is normal TiO_2, and the other half is slightly "hypoxic" with less several oxygen atoms. The Hypoxic half is positively charged, so the current through the resistor is relatively small and the current leads from the side of the hypoxia to the normal side. Hypoxic "hole" will gradually vacillate to the normal side under the influence of an electric field. To the piece of material, the part of gas shortage will be in a relatively high proportion, but the resistor of the system will be reduced. Anyway, when the current flows from the normal side to the anoxic

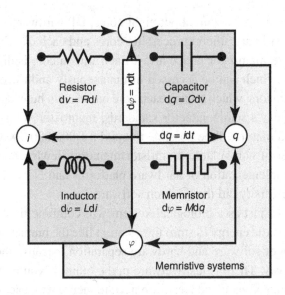

Fig. 9.7. The theoretical model of the memristor

side, the electric field will push the oxygen hole back and the resistor will increase. The state of the resistor is the state of being frozen after the power is cut off. The theoretical model of the memristor is shown in the bottom right corner in Figure 9.7. Memristor can be considered similar to synapses as synaptic's status depends on how close the connection is between any two neurons, which is a key part of the mammal's ability to learn new information.

Defense Advanced Research Projects Agency (DARPA) began a program in 2008, which is called systems of neuromorphic adaptive plastic scalable electronics (SyNAPSE). In the same year, HP labs developed a functional memristor, which is reputed to be the fourth basic electronic component after resistors, capacitors and inductors. This concept is not new. In 1971, Professor Leon Chua of the University of California at Berkeley speculated that the memristor will behave like a resistor whose conductance changes the function of its internal state and the applied voltage. Since the memristor can remember how much current flows through, it can work as an essentially non-volatile memory. But because the memristor cannot consume any power to remember its past status, its greatest potential is still a practical element simulating brain synapses.

HP has generated a more complex memristor under the auspices of the US Department of DARPA. The architecture of the brain inspired microprocessor developed by HP labs can be considered as a multi-core chip based on the memristor. Today, high-end microprocessors have multiple cores, or processing units. But unlike the typical microprocessor with about eight cores, HP hardware will include hundreds of simple, ordinary silicon processing cores and each core has its own high-density jungle-like memristor lattice array. Each silicon core is directly connected to its Mbit cache which can be accessed instantaneously and the cache consists of millions of memristors, which means each core has its own huge dedicated memory pool. Even by today's semiconductor standards, memristor volume is very small. Williams claimed that it will be possible to build a 1,000,000,000,000,000 bits per square centimeter of non-volatile memristor memory. Hewlett-Packard completed the design and implementation of hardware platforms and Nerve Morphology Lab at the Boston University did the work on software.

The memristor just as a biological system will combine tight calculation and data and use very little energy to store information like the human brain. We need to abandon the idea of software and hardware separation, because the brain does not function in that way. There is just wetware in the brain. If you really want to copy a mammal's brain, software and hardware need to merge with each other. Although memristor is intensive, cheap and tiny, its failure rate is high and it is similar to the characteristics of the brain synapses. This means that the architecture must allow a single circuit defect, just like the brain. When there is a synapse loss, it will not cause a system failure but reduce the quality in a fault-tolerance way.

9.5 Brain Simulation System Spaun

The human brain is a highly complex organ. If scientists want to build an artificial brain model, they must first understand the working principle of our brain. Specifically, they should first understand every part of brain responsible computing tasks, as well as the principles of these operations and functions of the neural network system. In November 2012, *Science* published the research of Eliasmith *et al.* [135], which introduces a large-scale human brain model, as shown in Figure 9.8. The brain model is capable of simulating a variety of complex human behavior, which indicates that the scientists in the field of artificial intelligence research have also taken a big step forward.

Eliasmith *et al.* developed the brain simulation model, which is called the Semantic Pointer Architecture Unified Network, referred to as Spaun. The system is able to observe images and uses the corresponding model of the arm to make appropriate action. Eliasmith *et al.* developed the Spaun system that can complete eight kinds of different tasks. Each task will include the introduction of a variety of graphics (mainly digital graphics) in all of the eight tasks and based on the graphics the appropriate action is made (artificial arm to draw "saw" numbers). These tasks

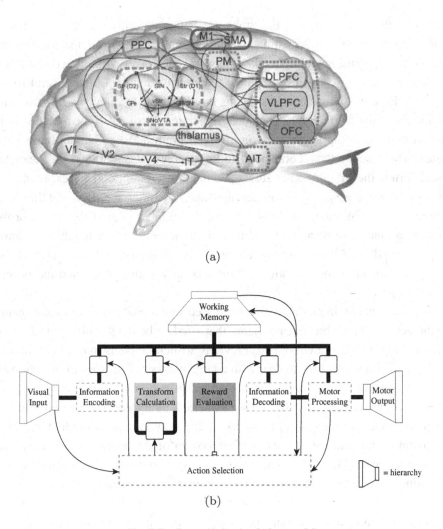

(a)

(b)

Fig. 9.8. Spaun brain simulation model

include some simple image recognition tasks and also include some memory tasks (see figures in accordance with the order to re-write it again), but also strengthen the learning task (such as gambling task) and more complex cognitive tasks (similar to a class of IQ tests). The Spaun system will rely on its own 2.5 million neurons to complete these tests. These neurons in accordance with the composition of our human brain form a number of subsystems, which correspond to the different areas of the human brain. Finally, they are linked to each other between these subsystems with the most basic functions of the brain [281].

The visual image information which is seen by the artificial brain will first be "compressed", removing irrelevant or redundant information. Eliasmith and team used a multi-level Restricted Boltzmann Machine algorithm in the compression processing of graphics information. The algorithm belongs to an operation mechanism of feedforward neural network system and each layer with limited Boltzmann machine processing can get a graphical feature information. After several rounds (layer) of Boltzmann machine processing, it will be able to get all the relevant information about the entire graph. Then the graphic information will be assigned to the various corresponding subsystems in artificial brain and real human brain visual cortex. These subsystems correspond to the primary visual cortex, the secondary visual cortex, the striatum outer cortex and the inferior temporal cortex. In terms of motor function, the Spaun system has also taken a similar approach and they make simple action commands, such as painting the number of 6. This can be broken down into many simple actions and then these actions are put together to draw a "sophisticated" 6. All relevant operations are based on the optimal control theory, which also includes the operations of the auxiliary motor center and the primary motor center.

The artificial brain model, with compressed signal processing and accompanied by the action, solves breadth problems that need to be dealt with when the brain is interacting with the environment. Previous artificial models in dealing with such problems do not know how to deal with a large number of sensory information and also how to make options in the face of numerous action alternatives.

The cognitive device of the Spaun system actually consists of two intersecting parts, which correspond to the working memory system of the human brain's prefrontal cortex and the action selection system of the human brain's basal ganglia and thalamus [133]. The action selection system controls the current state of the artificial brain and at the same time, the part is also inspired by the reinforcement learning theory and the current popular basal ganglia model. The working memory system of Spaun adopts a new algorithm. This algorithm draws from the nervous system of the neuroscience field and the convolution memory theory from the field of mathematical psychology. The nervous system algorithms make Spaun to have a networking information storage mechanism, while the convolution memory theory makes Spaun to combine effectively previous information with the latest information received. So Spaun can effectively make repetitive behaviors, such as writing a figure in the first number and the last digit, which is not comparable to the other human brain models. Eliasmith *et al.* also use another memory working system to presume automatical relationship between past and current signals. These automated reasoning capabilities mean the most elementary syntactic function. Spaun presents function of digital recognition and reproduction, which indicates that this syntax function will be realized some day in the future. This reproductive function is directly related to symbolic computation, which is very common in computer science and also in the theory of the association. The Spaun system uses these calculation methods incredibly and has adopted the most basic IQ test.

In the Spaun system, the subsystem corresponding to the region of the prefrontal cortex plays a role in connecting the subsystem abstract arithmetic, symbolic computation and a single neuron activity. About convolution memory function, Elia Smith *et al.* made a very interesting prediction. They estimated that the neuronal cell activation rate (average number of action potentials in unit time) will gradually accelerate with complete constant and continuous memory working.

In each module of the Spaun system, the actual information is processed by a large number of activated nerve cells. Under physiological conditions, the contact between the high-level operation carried out by means of neural network and low-level operation relying on single neurons rely on the so-called "Neural Engineering Framework" to rebuild in the Spaun system [134]. The architecture of the nervous system is especially good at achieving the arbitrary mathematical vector operation in the active neural networks. The system assumes that the information will be read at the speed of nerve activation and then the information will be converted into neural activity function in a nonlinear way. The processed information in each subsystem will be assigned to each of the neuronal cells and this model is also very consistent with the conclusions obtained from brain electrophysiological research working. For example, the response speed of our brain for different sensory stimuli (input) signals or the output signal of the motor are not the same.

When the Spaun system does not do well in simulated real brain situations in some aspects, we are not surprised. For example, several parts of the response activity of the system in several aspects (including the most basic statistical category) are clearly different from the actual situation of the brain. We do not know how much these problems can be improved in the future, and we are also unclear about the extent to which these deviations of the inconsistencies of our brain's internal basic response level are a true reflection. The biggest problem of the Spaun system is the nature of it being hard-wired and the fact that it cannot be learned for new tasks (functional). However, the structure of Spaun has great flexibility. It does not rigidly adhere to one particular task and multiple parts are equipped with learning function in the Spaun system, such as graphic information multi-processing system and action selection system. As for the broader learning ability, such as learning a new task, it may be a blank that Elia Smith *et al.* deliberately left. In fact, the drawback of Spaun is precisely the parts where we lack understanding of the brain. Eliasmith *et al.* had brought a great deal of brain research into the Spaun system.

This work itself has already brought a working brain theory for us. However, it does not include mechanisms associated with learning. In addition, Eliasmith *et al.* also provided the possibility of a large, top-down development of an artificial intelligence system. The emergence of the Spaun system has set up a new benchmark for this work and also provides a new way. That is, we should not think about how to concentrate as many nerve cells as possible and the amount of information together, but we should focus on reproducing the brain function and exercising more complex behavior.

9.6 Neuromorphic Chip

The essential difference between the "Von Neumann architecture" and the "human brain architecture" is that the human brain achieves storing and processing information by synapses and there is no obvious boundary between storing and processing. Due to the plasticity of one quadrillion synapses, nerves change after various factors and conditions, thus affecting the functions of the human brain.

Imitating the understanding, action and cognitive ability of the human brain becomes a significant bionic researching goal. The latest achievement of this field is the neuromorphic chip. On April 23, 2014, *MIT Technology Review* published an article named "Top Ten Breakthrough Science Technology" and the neuromorphic chip of Qualcomm was in it.

9.6.1 The development history of neuromorphic chip

In 1990, honorable professor, Mead of the California Institute of Technology gave the definition of the neuromorphic chip, as "simulating chips are different from data chips which only have binary results. It can obtain various results like the real world and simulate the electrical activity of the human brain neurons and synapses." However, Mead did not complete the design of the simulating chip.

The chip company of speech signal processing, Audience, studied the characteristics of the nervous system, such as learning plasticity, fault-tolerance, avoiding programming and low energy consumption. Audience has researched and developed the neuromorphic chip based on the human cochlea. The chip simulates human ears that can suppress noise and apply to the smartphone. Thus, Audience has become the top company in the field of speech signal processing.

Qualcomm's "neural-network processor" is different from usual processors in the aspect of the working principle. In essence, it is a typical computer chip made up of silicon crystal materials, but it can complete "qualitative" functions and not "quantitative". The software tool developed by Qualcomm can simulate the brain's activities and the "neural-network" of processors designed according to the way of information passed by the human neural network. The tool can permit developers to write programs based on "Biological Excitation". Qualcomm assumed that his "neural-network processor" can accomplish the cognitive task of "Classification" and "Prediction".

Qualcomm named his "neural-network processor" as "Zeroth". Zeroth derives from the "Zeroth Law". The law rules that a robot should not harm humanity, or allow humanity to harm by inaction. The R&D team of Qualcomm is working toward developing a new computing architecture that can break the traditional model. They hope to build a new computing processor, which simulates the human brain and the nervous system and lets terminals own the embedded cognition. There are three goals for Zeroth: "Bionic learning", "Make the terminal observe and know the world like the human" and "Create and define the Neural Processing Unit (NPU)". According to "Bionic learning", Qualcomm completed it based on the studying of dopamine which is a neurotransmitter substance, rather than coding.

Since the time when IBM created the first human brain simulator in 1956, it has been working on the study of the brain-like computer. Developing the neuromorphic chip based on the large nervous-system-like group went into its vision, after the chip imitated the synaptic transmission lines. Among them, IBM developed the first generation of neurosynaptic chips used in the development of the "cognitive computer". Although the "cognitive computer" cannot code like the traditional computers, it can learn by accumulating experience, finding relationship between things and simulating brain structure and the plasticity of synapses.

In 2008, under the funding of DARPA, IBM developed the second phase of the "SyNAPSE" project by working on creating the system that can both simultaneously process multi-source information and update constantly by itself according to environment, achieving the characteristics of the nervous system like learning, plasticity, fault-tolerance, avoiding programming and low energy consumption. The project leader Modha thought that the neuromorphic chip would be another milestone during the evolutionary history of the computer.

In the beginning of August 2013, IBM announced the brain-like system TrueNorth and hoped it would replace today's computer in some application scenarios. Deep Blue and Watson of IBM defeated the human, but depended on speed and memory space, rather than intelligence. Watson stored 4TB text database, including the whole Wikipedia and internet database like WordNet, when it took part in the contest. Deep Blue is capable of examining 200 million moves per second and chooses the fittest one at the contest of international chess games. Nevertheless, it only won by the advantage of one round when confronted by Kasparov. Efficiency of computers are not high, for example, Watson, formed by 90 servers, consumed 85,000 W, while the adults' brain consumed about 20 W.

On August 8, 2014, IBM published the chip that could simulate the human brain in the journal *Science*. The chip can simulate the functions of the human brain neurons and synapses and other brain functions, so that it can complete the computing function. This was a great progress in the field of the chip of brain simulation. IBM said that, this microchip named the TrueNorth was good at completing the missions of pattern recognition and object classification, etc. and so on, and its power consumption was greatly lower than traditional hardware.

In 2003, British ARM began to develop hardware of the brain-like neural network, called SpiNNaker. In 2011, the company officially launched the SpiNNaker chip containing 18 ARM cores. In 2013, ARM began to develop spiking interface based on UDP that can be used in the communication of the heterogeneous neuromorphic system. In 2014, the company joined hands with the Waterloo University, in the supporting hardware calculation of the Spaun model.

In 2011, Heidelberg University in Germany launched a four-year program called BrainScales on the basis of FACTS under the funding of Proactive FP7 [398]. In 2013, they joined the EU's "Human Brain Plan". In the International Super Computer Meeting held in Leipzig, which ended on June 20, 2013, Professor Meier, one of the human brain researching program's coordinators in of Heidelberg University, introduced the researching progress gained by the Germany scientists. Meier announced that the neuromorphic system would appear on silicon chips or wafer. This is not only a kind of chip, but also a complete silicon wafer. There are 200,000 neurons and 5 million synapses integrated on the chip. The size of this silicon wafer is like a big plate. These silicon wafers are the cornerstones of the new type of brain-like computer architecture that will be developed by the Brain Research Project of the EU in the next 10 years.

9.6.2 IBM's TrueNorth neuromorphic system

DARPA began a plan named SyNAPSE in 2008. IBM was the first to launch the chip prototype of a single core that contained 256 neurons, 256 times 256 synapses and 256 axons in 2011. The prototype had already processed complex missions like playing Ping Pong at that time. But it was relatively simple and the brain capacity of such a single core was equal to an insect in terms of scale.

After three-year endeavor, IBM had made a breakthrough at the aspect of complexity and usability, and launched TrueNorth chip, as shown in Figure 9.9 [309].

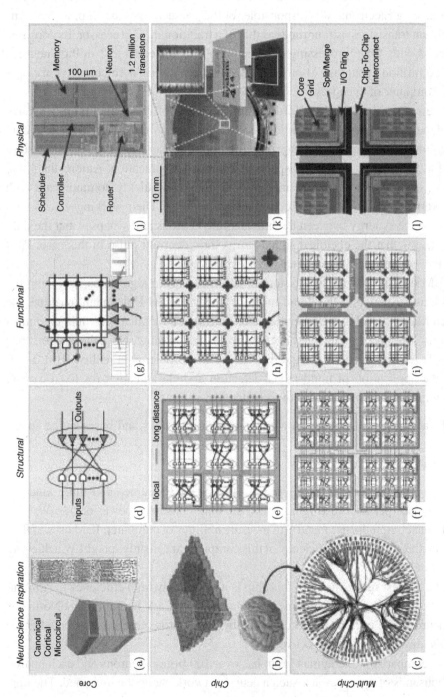

Fig. 9.9. IBM's TrueNorth chip

This chip can simulate the functions of neurons and synapses to execute computing. Samsung Electronic was responsible for the production of the chip, which owns 5. 4 billion transistors, is four times as that of a traditional PC processor. Its core area is packed with 4,096 processing cores and the effect is equal to 1 million neurons and 256 million synapses. At present, IBM has already used 16 chips to develop a super computer of synapses.

The structure of the TrueNorth is similar to that of the human brain and each kernel includes about 1.2 million transistors. Among the transistors, the part of data processing and dispatching occupies a little, but the majority of the transistors are used for data storage and other aspects of kernel communication. Among the 4,096 kernels, each kernel has native memory and they can quickly communicate with other kernels through a special communication mode. Their working way is very similar to the synergy between the human brain neurons and synapses, but the only difference is that the chemical signals turns into a current pulse in this case. IBM calls the structure, as "Synapses Kernel Architecture".

IBM used a software eco-system to add well-known algorithms, including the convolutional network, the liquid machine, the restricted Boltzmann machine, the hidden Markov model, the support vector machine, the optical flow and the multimodality classification, into architecture by off-line learning. Now, these algorithms in the TrueNorth need no change. In order to test problems in reality, IBM developed the application of multi-target detection and classification for fixed camera configuration. The mission has two challenges:

(1) To accurately detect the crowd, bicycles, cars, trucks and buses in the sparse image.
(2) To accurately identify items.

Operating under 400 pixels times 240 pixels, 30 frames and three kinds of colors videos per second (Figure 9.10), the chip consumes power of 63 mW. Like traditional computers use FLOPS to measure abilities of computer, IBM uses SOP to measure the abilities and efficiency of this computer. It can only spend 1 W achieving 46 billion SOP.

The biggest selling point of this chip is its extremely high efficiency in communication, thus, greatly reducing power consumption. Each kernel of TrueNorth has 256 neurons and each nerve is connected by 256 neurons that are distributed at the nerve's inner and outer, respectively.

By comparison, the human brain has over 100 billion neurons and each neuron has thousands of synapses and such a neural network cannot be imagined. The final

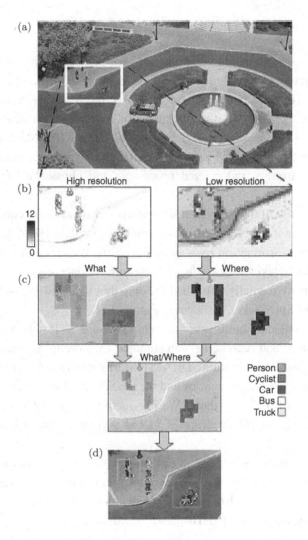

Fig. 9.10. Detection and classification of multi-target

goal of IBM is to build a computer that contains 10 billion neurons and 100 trillion synapses. The functions of such a computer are 10 times stronger than the human that brain, while power consumption is only 1,000 W.

On March 29, 2016, the Lawrence Livermore National Laboratory (LLNL) announced that it has purchased the first brain-like super computing platform developed by IBM based on the TrueNorth neuromorphic chips. The platform contains 16 chips and only needs to consume about a tablet computer power of 2.5 W and the processing amount of calculation can be equivalent to about 16 million neurons and 40 million synapses.

9.6.3 British SpiNNaker

SpiNNaker is the program that was launched jointly by many universities in Manchester, Southampton, Cambridge and Sheffield and enterprises. It obtains investment from EPSRC. The leader is Professor Furber of the Manchester University, who has worked on the study of the human brain functions and structure for many years. He is one of the union designers for the Acorn RISC Machine, which was the ancient form of the ARM processor. After the project got permission, ARM supported this strongly and offered processors and physical IP to the scientific team.

There are about 100 billion neurons and up to 1 quadrillion connections in the human brain, even if 1 million processors can only simulate 1% of the human brain. Neurons transmit information by way of simulating the electron's peak electronic pulse, while SpiNNaker uses the way of describing data package to simulate. In 2011, the company formally published the chip that included 18 ARM cores [349]. The structure of SpiNNaker is shown in Figure 9.11.

A single SpiNNaker multi-processor chip contains 18 low-power-consumption ARM 986 kernels, and each kernel can simulate 1,000 neurons. Each chip also has 128 MB low-power-consumption SDRAM to store the information of the connecting weight of synapses between neurons and the time delay of synapses. A single chip's power-consumption is lower than 1W. The method of partial synchronization in the chip and usage of the measure of global asynchronization between chips is followed.

There is no central timer in the SpiNNaker system, and this means, that the sending and receiving of signals will not be synchronous and these signals will interfere with each other. Also, the output will change by millions of micro random changes. It sound like disorder and it actually needs high precision for some missions, like mathematical calculations. But this system can calmly deal with fuzzy operating calculations. For example, when you should lose your hands in order to throw a ball easily, or choosing a word at the end of one sentence. After all, brains do not give the calculated results in 10 decimal places and the human brain is more like a disorderly system. A large amount of SpiNNaker processors were connected by Ethernet and were asynchronously interconnected. Each SpiNNaker contains a router made specially, which is used to achieve the communication of inner neurons and chips' neurons of SpiNNaker.

In 2013, Manchester University developed interface of spike potential based on UDP, which can be used in the communication of the heterogeneous neuromorphic system. This interface shows the mixed communication of SpiNNaker and Brain-Scale system, thereby developing large-scale neuromorphic network.

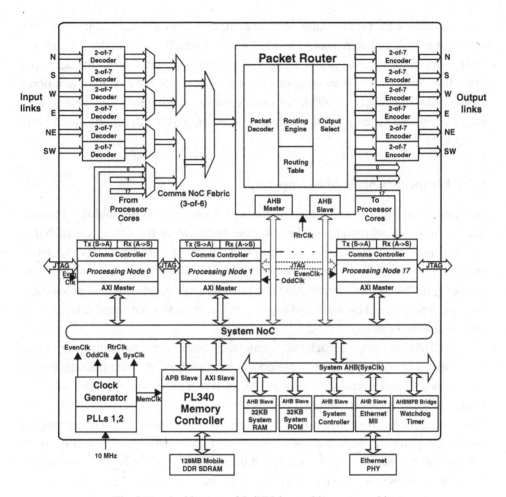

Fig. 9.11. Architecture of SpiNNaker multi-processor chip

9.7 Development Roadmap of Intelligence Science

Through the crossing cooperation of the fields of brain science, cognitive science and artificial intelligence, we should strengthen our nation's research of basic and original crossing field of intelligence science, solve the significant basic theory problems at the development of cognitive science and information science, drive the development of intelligent information processing key technology relating to the nation's economy, society and national safety and put forward theoretical basis for the prevention and treatment of brain disease and disorders.

On October 29, 2013, in the Chinese Association for Artificial Intelligence "Innovation–driven–the Era of Big Data Artificial Intelligence" Summit Forum, the author depicted the development "roadmap" of intelligence science: In 2020, we must achieve the primary class of brain computing, namely elementary brain-like computing and computers should achieve the goal which is to complete precise listening, speaking, reading and writing and in 2035, we must enter the advanced brain-like computing, where computers not only have IQ, but also have emotional intelligence and finally in 2050, we must combine intelligence science and nanotechnology and develop a neuromorphic computer, which will achieve super-brain computing.

9.7.1 Elementary brain-like computing

In recent years, the organic combination and fusion of nanotechnology, biology, information and cognition have become the highlight of the world, called NIBC converging technologies. Any converging technology of these four fields will accelerate the development of science and society. The development of brain and cognitive science will drive a new breakthrough in information's expressing and processing. Intelligent tech based on brain and cognitive science will drive a new revolution of information technology.

By 2020, in order to achieve elementary brain-like computing and make machines to hear, speak, read, write and even communicate with humans conveniently, we should overcome the difficulty of semantic processing. The semantic meaning is the data's meaning. There is no meaning for the data itself and only when the data is given meaning data turn into information and the meaning of the data is semantic. Semantics is the interpretation of data symbols and it can be regarded as the meaning of the concept of things standing for what they are in reality. Corresponding data and the relationship between semantics is data's explanation and logical expressing. Semantics have the characteristic of territoriality and there is no semantic that does not belong to any domain. For computer science, semantic meaning usually aims at users for the explanation of computer expressing which is used to depict reality, i.e., the method used to connect computer expressing with reality by users.

Computer data appears in many forms, such as text, voice, graphics, pictures, videos and animation. In the elementary phase, if scientists want to make robots to understand the content of media like humans, they must breakthrough robots' semantic processing.

1. Natural Language Processing

Text semantic processing is essentially natural language processing. Natural language processing is not studying usual natural language, but studying a computer system that can efficiently achieve natural language communication, especially soft systems. So, it is a part of computer science. Natural language communication between humans and computers means that computers can understand the meaning of natural language text and express the given intention and idea in natural language. The former is called natural language understanding, which the latter is called natural language generation. So, natural language processing generally includes natural language understanding and natural language generation.

Natural language processing, natural language communication or natural language understanding and natural language generation, are very difficult. The root reason is the widespread variable ambiguity in natural language text and dialog. From format, a Chinese text is a string formed by characters (including punctuation). Characters can form words, words can form sentences and then some sentences form a paragraph, section, chapter and article. Whether it is a variety of levels, or at the shift from a low level to a higher up level, there is the phenomenon of ambiguity. That is, a string with the same format, can be understood as different strings under the different scenes or context and have different meanings. Under normal circumstances, the majority of these problems can be solved according to the rules of the corresponding context and scenes. In other words, overall there is no ambiguity. This is the reason we do not think about the ambiguity of the natural language and we can communicate correctly by using natural language. On the other hand, as we can see, in order to eliminate, it's necessary to need much knowledge and inference. It is important to collect and sort out the knowledge completely; to find a fit form to save computer science; and to efficiently use them to eliminate ambiguity. All of them are very difficult work and the workload is extremely high. It cannot be finished by a few people in a short term and it remains a long-term systematic work.

From recent theory and technology, universal and high-quality natural language system is also a goal that needs a long-term effort. However, the aim of certain application and some practical systems with ability of natural language processing have emerged. Some of them have been commercialized and even industrialized, for example, natural language interface of data base and experts systems, all kinds of machine-translation systems, full text information retrieval systems, automatic abstracting systems and so on.

2. Image Semantics Generation

With the development of image processing technology, multi-media technology and network technology, the amount of image information is increasing. How to auto-generate image semantic meaning and understand image semantics is a significant scientific problem about image retrieval and pattern recognition.

Due to the inherent characteristics of images, if we want to auto-generate image's semantic meaning, we must combine the image's feature, research level and cultural environment. We can build the semantic meaning mode by the study of image semantic meaning and then depict the image by the semantic meaning mode and promote the improvement of image semantic meaning research level.

Image semantic meaning is divided into three layers, i.e., the bottom features layer, the object layer and the concept layer. The bottom features, in essence, is no image semantics information and its basic idea is to extract the relationship of the image's colors, texture, shape and space. At present, content-based retrieval is on this layer. The object layer mainly considers the problems about the objects and objects' space in images. Perception feature extraction is based on a biological mechanism. The concept layer mainly solves the meaning expressed by images through scene, knowledge and emotion. Scene semantics refers to the scene of the image. Knowledge semantics combines scene semantics with knowledge base, rationalizing the knowledge in images and focuses on the action expressed in the images. Emotion semantics is included by the image from the perspective of people, such as the romantic image and the horror image. Semantics concept layer usually involves abstract attributes of image. It is built on the basis of image recognition and the extraction of bottom features and needs a high-level reasoning of the object and the meaning and the goal of the scene, achieving the association of bottom physical features and high-level semantics, building the index of concept semantics layer and achieving the retrieval of the concept semantics layer.

3. Speech Recognition

Auto speech recognition is high-tech and makes the machine turn the speech signal to the corresponding text or command after recognizing and understanding it. ASR includes extraction and determination of the acoustic feature, acoustic model and language model. The extraction and determination of acoustic feature is a significant part of speech recognition. The extraction and determination of acoustic feature is a procedure of information compression, as well as a procedure of signal deconvolution.

The acoustic model is the calculation from speech to syllable probability. The acoustic model in speech recognition usually uses HMM for modeling of the element recognition and a speech element is a three to five status HMM. A word is a HMM formed by a string of speech elements that form this word. All models of continuous speech recognition are a HMM combined with word and mute.

Language model is the calculation from speech to word probability, mainly divided into the statistical model and the rule model. The statistical language model uses probability statistics to show the inner statistic regulars, in which N-Gram is simple and efficient and is widely used. The regular model refers to some rules or the grammatical structure.

Due to the diversity and complexity of the speech signal, present speech recognition system can only be satisfied based on performance under certain conditions, or used in some specific occasions. Speech recognition system roughly depends on four factors: recognizing the size of vocabulary and acoustic complexity, the quality of speech signal, single speaker or speakers and hardware platform. Speech is the most natural communicating media in the present communicating system. With the development of computer and voice processing technology, the voice–voice translation between different languages will become the hot spot of speech research. The research hot spots of speech recognition include: design data base of natural language; speech features extraction; use of corpus for processing the acoustic model; algorithm of speech recognition research; language translation; speech synthesis and dialog processing research.

Deng co-work with Hinton found that the deep network can improve the precision of speech recognition. The fruit was further deepened by Microsoft Research Asia. They built some huge neural network, which includes 6.6 million neural connections, as shown in Figure 9.12. This is the biggest model in the research history of speech recognition. This model's error recognition rate reduced by a third from the lowest error rate in the Switchboard standard data sets. After all, in the field of speech recognition, the lowest error rate in these data sets has not been updated for many years.

4. Language Cognitive

The development of psychological science has already revealed that the understanding and generation of language is an extremely complex problem. Language offers a unique condition of understanding the relationship between heredity and environment for us. The study of language cannot only make us understand the function of heredity and environment in the understanding and generation of language, but also make us further understand learning and heredity's role in other various cognitive functions and related important revelations. This research gives us a great opportunity to reveal the essence of various human cognitive and intelligence procedures.

The characteristics of the Chinese language is the perfect combination of speech, shape and meaning. Understanding these characteristics can create a new way of natural language processing.

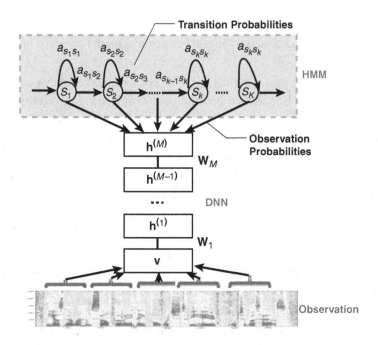

Fig. 9.12. Speech recognition model combined with deep network

9.7.2 Advanced brain-like computing

By 2035, the goal of intelligent science is to achieve advanced brain-like computing, and making artificial systems with high-IQ and high EQ.

IQ refers to the abilities of number, space, logic, vocabulary, memory and it is the ability of humans to understand objective things and to apply knowledge to solve practical issues. The discretion of IQ is used to mark the development level of intelligence. The test of IQ was invented by French Binet and his students. The calculating formula is:

$$IQ = 100 \times \frac{MA}{CA},$$

MA = Mental Age,
CA = Physical Age.

If someone's MA is the same as his CA, his IQ is 100, implying that his IQ is medium. The majority of person's IQ is between 85 and 115.

EQ is the ability of self-knowledge, self-understanding and emotion-control. EQ was first presented by two American psychologists Salover and Mayer in 1990. After being put forward in 1990, it did not arouse attention worldwide until 1995. In 1995, Goleman, a scientific journalist of *New York Times* published a book *EQ:*

Why EQ Is More Important Than IQ and aroused global research and discussion of EQ. So Goleman was honored as "the father of EQ".

Goleman summarized EQ as the possession five abilities: "self-awareness ability; self-regular ability; self-motivation ability; the ability of knowing other emotions; the ability of managing interpersonal relationships". The connotation of EQ can be divided into inner and outer: the inner EQ refers to the ability of knowing one's own talent, gift, clearly perceiving one's own emotion and high tolerance when facing setback; the outer EQ refers to the ability of acute observation to distinguish others' motivation, reading others' emotional effect, knowing how to work with others to achieve team goals.

From the definition of EQ, the core of EQ includes knowing and managing emotion, self-motivation and dealing with interpersonal relationship correctly. They are embodied in the following respects:

1. The perception, assessment and presentation of emotion

(1) Identify one's self-mood from own physical status, emotional experience and thought.
(2) Identify mood from others' art, design by language, voice, appearance and action.
(3) Present mood and present the necessity related to the mood.
(4) Distinguish the authenticity and veracity in mood presenting.

2. Promote emotion in the process of thinking

(1) The ability of guiding mood and thought.
(2) Mood imparts the direction of attention to information.
(3) Positive emotion affects positive work to judge the related emotion and memory procedure.
(4) Prompt individual thinking from multi-perspectives through the change of mood in making an individual's from being positive attitude to being negative.
(5) Emotional status makes promotion to certain problem solutions.

3. The understanding and feeling of emotion

(1) Tag on mood, know the relationship between mood and presentation; such as the knowledge of the difference between "Love" and "Like".
(2) Understand the meaning presented by emotion.
(3) Know and analyze the reason of emotion generation.
(4) Understand complex mood, such as the emotion of love–hate.

(5) Know the possibility of emotional transformation, like anger can convert to satisfy, or shame.

4. Adjust maturely to emotion

(1) Accept any mood with an open spirit.
(2) Maturely immerse in or depart from a certain mood according to the known information and judgment.
(3) Maturely supervise the emotion related to self and others.
(4) Process the emotion of self and others, mitigate negative emotions, enhance positive emotions and do not depress or exaggerate.

5. Maintain the harmonious interpersonal relationship

(1) Accurately express and properly control self-emotion.
(2) Basic skills of interpersonal communication.
(3) Co-work with others.
(4) The strain capacity of processing any problem arising in interpersonal communication.

6. Deal with frustration

(1) Objectively know frustration.
(2) Rationally reason the frustration.
(3) Form the mechanism of frustration defense and regulatory mechanism.

9.7.3 Super-brain computing

By 2050, the goal of intelligent science is to reach super-brain computing, in which artificial systems have the characteristics of high-intelligence, high-performance, low-power-consumption, high-fault-tolerance and all-consciousness.

1. High-intelligence

High-intelligence is the intelligence of the human level expressed by artificial systems. On the basis of understanding the biological intelligence mechanism, high-intelligence gives out accurate and testable computing models for the working principle of the human brain and makes machines perform the functions that need human intelligence to achieve it. Researchers should investigate intelligent science and build mind models, adopt the view of information to study all of the human's mental activities, including feeling, perception, appearance, language, learning, memory, thinking, emotion and consciousness. A brain-like computer, in essence, is a kind of nerve computer that simulates the function of human neural information processing by way of parallel distribution processing and self-organizing and it is a system connected by a large amount of basic processing units. Such systems build the mental model of the brain system by the reverse program of the brain's structure, dynamics, functions and actions and then achieve the mental-like intelligent machine in the program. Intelligent science will offer theoretical basis and key technology to brain-like computers, such as building neural function column, cluster coding model, mental model of brain system, exploring the mechanism of learning memory, language cognition, co-work of different brain areas, emotional computing and intelligent evolution and achieve intelligent machine as the same level as the human brain.

2. High-performance

High-performance mainly refers to running speed. The performance of the computer will increase between 10^8 and 10^9 times in 40 years and the speed will be up to 10^{24} time per second. Traditional information devices have met huge obstacles at the aspects of complexity, cost and power-consumption. The chip tech based on CMOS has come close to the physical limit and hence we are eager in expecting new subversive technology. On the other hand, the chip will assemble the multi-function of computing, memory and communication and satisfy the features of multi-type, short-term design.

Silicon microelectronics devices, evolving from micron to nanometer, get a huge success according to the Moore Law and the Scaling Law. Now, 65 nm silicon CMOS technology has already achieved large-scale production and 45 nm silicon CMOS technology has begun production, in which integrating scale of single chip is more than 800 million transistors. In 2007, Intel and IBM successfully researched high k gate dielectric and metal gate technology, and applied in 45 nm silicon CMOS technology. By combining strained silicon technology and SOI structure, 32 nm silicon CMOS technology has been tried to be produced. Some companies like Intel and Samsung have successfully researched the devices whose sizes are below 10 nm. Experts predict when line width is below 11 nm, silicon CMOS technology will reduce the limit regarding the aspects of speed, power-consumption, integration, cost and reliability. So the solution for continuous innovation of the basic research field of nm devices physics and new materials will become one of the most significant scientific technology problems of the 21st century.

In January 2009, IBM developed the Graphene transistor whose gate is 150 nm and the cut-off frequency is 26 GHz. Graphene has extremely high mobility, with a saturated speed between six times and seven times to Si and its coefficient of thermal conductivity is high. Graphene is fit for high-speed, low-power-consumption, high-integration low-noise and microwave circuit. At present, the operating frequency of a graphene MOS transistor with 150 nm gate can reach 26 GHz. If the gate is down to 50 nanometer, the frequency graphene transistor is expected to exceed 1 THz. By 2020, we can successfully develop the graphene material and transistors with great performance and solve the technological problems of interconnection and integration. By 2025, the graphene system chip can be successfully developed and form large scale production.

In addition to electronic computing technology based on CMOS chip, quantum computing, spinning electron computing, molecular computing, DNA computing and optical computing, there are prospective system technology researches that are developing vigorously as well.

3. Low-energy-consumption

When the human brain operates, it only consumes power similar to igniting a 20 W bulb. Even if we reproduce the function of the brain on an advanced huge computer, it needs a dedicated power plant. Of course, this is not the only difference. The brain owns some effective components that we cannot reproduce. The key is that the brain can run under the voltage of about 100 mV. But CMOS logic circuit needs higher voltage to make it operate correctly. The higher working voltage means that the power lost is caused when the wires transmit the signal.

In computers today, the consumption on circuit level is Pico-joule, while the consumption on system layer is microjoule. Both of them are far above the lower limit theory given by physics. There is a big space to decrease the consumption of the system. Technologies of low energy consumption are related to many aspects, such as material, devices, system architecture, system software and management mode. Technologies breaking through low energy consumption would be a great challenge of chip and system designed in the next decades.

4. High fault-tolerance

When the system breaks down internally the system can still offer correct services to the outer environment. This ability is referred to as fault-tolerance. The concept of fault-tolerance technology was first put forward by Avizienis in 1967, i.e., a program of a system can still be correctly processed in case of logical problems.

Both the human brain and the neural network have the feature of fault-tolerance. When the parted units become invalid, they can still continue working correctly. So the super-brain computing system must have a highly reliable performance.

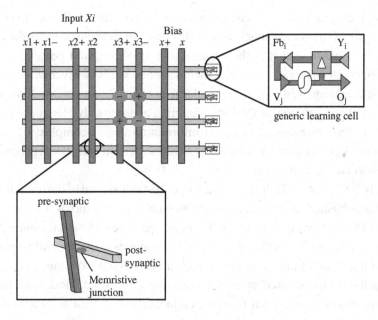

Fig. 9.13.   Single layer memristor crossing switch array

In future, the probability of manufacturing defects in widely expected adapting nanoscale electronic equipment will increase. Article [72] puts forward a novel and high fault-tolerance crossing switch architecture. The neural network can reliably implement this based on the architecture of the memristor crossing switch. Figure 9.13 shows a single layer memristor crossing switch array. Article [72] presents rapid convergence for the single layer crossing switch that adapts the Delta rule to study the Boolean function. The architecture can learn Boolean function and have a manufacturing defect rate as much as 13% and have reasonable redundancy. Compared with other technology, such as cascaded triple modular redundancy, reuse and reconfigure of Von Neumann architecture, this shows the greatest fault-tolerance performance.

5. All consciousness

Consciousness may be one of the biggest secrets and the highest achievement of the human brain. Consciousness is the organisms' perception of the outer world and the objective things of self-psychology and physiological action. The brain mechanism of consciousness is the object studied by all kinds of brain science, and it is also the core problem of psychological research. The human brain is the organ that conducts conscious activities in humans. In order to reveal regular science and build the brain model with consciousness, we not only need to research conscious cognitive processes, but also need to research non-conscious cognitive processes. At the same time, self-consciousness and circumstancial-consciousness are also problems that need great importance attached to. Self-consciousness is the individual's of the existence of oneself and it is the organization system of self-perception and the method in which one treats oneself. It includes three kinds of psychological components: self-cognition, self-experience and self-control. Circumstance-consciousness is the inner representation of the individual in a continuously changing outer environment. In the environment of social information that is complex, dynamic and changeable, circumstance-consciousness is the key reason that affects people regarding decision and performance.

In July 2005, in the 125th anniversary of the establishment of the journal *Science*, the journal published in its special issue "Questions: what do not we know?", and put forward 125 questions that needed to be answered. The second question is "what is the biological basis of consciousness?" [314]. Descartes, a French philosopher of the 17th century, said "I think, therefore I am." It is observed that consciousness is the topic that has been discussed by philosophers for a long time. Modern scientists say that consciousness springs out from the collaboration of billions of neurons in the brain. But it is too ambiguous. In particular, how do neurons generate consciousness? Recently, scientists have found the methods and tools that can conduct objective research to the most subjective and the most individual thing and help patients whose brain is injured. Besides being clear on the concrete operating method of consciousness, scientists also want to know the answer of a deeper level question: why does it exist and how does it originate?

Professor Stephen Hawking, one of Britain's pre-eminent scientists, has said that primitive forms of artificial intelligence developed so far have already proved very useful, but he fears the consequences of creating something that can match or surpass humans [203].

References

1. Abbott, A. and Schiermeier, Q. (2013). Graphene and virtual brain win billion-euro competition. *Nature*, 493: 585–586.
2. Abbott, L. F. and Blum, K. I. (1996). Functional significance of long-term potentiation for sequence learning and prediction. *Cerebral Cortex*, 6: 406–416.
3. Abbott, L. and Dayan, P. (1999). The effect of correlated variability on the accuracy of a population code. *Neural Computation*, 11: 91–101.
4. Albin, R. L., Young, A. B. and Penney, J. B. (1989). The functional anatomy of basal ganglia disorders. *Trends in Neurosciences*, 12(10): 366–375.
5. Albright, T. D., Kandel, E. R. and Posner, M. I. (2000). Cognitive neuroscience. *Current Opinion in Neurobiology*, 10(5): 612–624.
6. Albus, J. S. (2002). 4D/RCS: A reference model architecture for intelligent unmanned ground vehicles. In *Proceedings of the SPIE 16th Annual International Symposium on Aerospace/Defense Sensing, Simulation and Controls*, Orlando.
7. Alderfer, C. (1972). *Existence, Relatedness and Growth* (Free Press, New York).
8. Aleksander, I. (2014). *Impossible Minds: My Neurons, My Consciousness* (Revised Edition) (World Scientific Publishing Co., Singapore).
9. Aleksander, I. and Morton, H. (2012). *Aristotle's Laptop: The Discovery of our Informational Mind* (World Scientific Publishing Co. Pte. Ltd., Singapore).
10. Amabile, T. M. (1996). *Creativity in Context* (Boulder, CO, USA).
11. Amari, S. (1985). *Differential Geometrical Methods in Statistics, Springer Lecture Notes in Statistic*, 28 (Springer, New York).
12. Amari, S. (1994). Information geometry and manifolds of neural networks. In *From Statistical Physics to Statistical Inference and Back*, (eds.) Grassberger, P. and Nadal, J. P. (Kluwer Academic Publishers Dordrecht, the Netherlands), pp. 113–138.
13. Amari, S. (2005). Population coding, Bayesian inference and information geometry. *Advances in Neural Networks*, 3496: 1–4.
14. Ananthanarayanan, R., Esser, S. K., Simon, H. D. and Modha, D. S. (2009). The cat is out of the bag: Cortical simulations with 10^9 neurons and 10^{13} synapses. Gordon Bell Prize Winner. In *Proceedings of the ACM/IEEE Conference on Supercomputing* (Portland, OR, November 14–20).
15. Ananthanarayanan, R. and Modha, D. S. (2007). Anatomy of a cortical simulator. In *Proceedings of the ACM/IEEE Conference on Supercomputing* (Reno, NV, November 10–16). ACM, New York, NY, 3–14.
16. Anderson, J. R. (1976). *Language, Memory, and Thought* (Erlbaum Hillsdale, NJ).
17. Anderson, J. R. (1983). *The Architecture of Cognition* (Harvard University Press, Cambridge, MA).
18. Anderson, J. R. (1991). The adaptive nature of human categorization. *Psychological Review*, 98: 409–429.

19. Anderson, J. R. (1992). Automaticity and the ACT* theory. *American Journal of Psychology*, 105: 165–180.

20. Anderson, J. R. (1993). *Rules of the Mind* (Erlbaum Hillsdale, NJ).

21. Anderson, J. R. (2005). Human symbol manipulation within an integrated cognitive architecture. *Cognitive Science*, 29(3): 313–341.

22. Anderson, J. R. (2007). *How Can the Human Mind Occur in the Physical Universe?* (Oxford University Press, New York).

23. Anderson, J. R. (2010). *Cognitive Psychology and Its Implications* (Seventh Edition) (Worth Publishing, New York).

24. Anderson, J. R. and Lebiere, C. L. (2003). The Newell test for a theory of cognition. *Behavioral and Brain Science*, 26: 587–637.

25. Andrieu, C., De Freitas, N., Doucet, A., *et al.* (2003). An Introduction to MCMC for machine learning. *Machine Learning*, 50(1): 5–43.

26. Ashburner, J., Friston, K. and Penny, W. (eds.) (2004). *Human Brain Function* (Second Edition) Elsevier Inc., Amsterdam).

27. Ashburner, J., Barnes, G., Chen, C., *et al.* (2009). SPM8 Manual (Functional Imaging Laboratory, Institute of Neurology, London, UK), November 10.

28. Ashby, F. G., Prinzmetal, W., Ivry, R., *et al.* (1996). A formal theory of feature binding in object perception. *Psychological Review*, 103(1): 165–192.

29. Atkinson, J. W. and Feather, N. T. (1966). *A Theory of Achievement Motivation* (Wiley, New York).

30. Atkinson, R. C. and Juola, J. F. (1973). Factors influencing the speed and accuracy of word recognition. In *Attention and Performance IV*, (ed.) Kornblum, S. (Academic Press, New York) pp. 583–612.

31. Attneave, F. (1954). Some informational aspects of visual perception. *Psychological Review*, 61: 183–193.

32. Aydede, M. (2004). Language of thought hypothesis. In *Stanford Encyclopedia of Philosophy*, http://plato.stanford.edu/entries/language-thought/, First published May 28, 1998; substantive revision, July 27.

33. Baader, F., Lutz, C., Milicic, M., Sattler, U. and Wolter, F. (2005). Integrating description logics and action formalisms: first results. In *Proceedings of the 12th National Conference on Artificial Intelligence* (AAAI'05) (AAAI Press/MIT Press) pp. 572–577.

34. Baars, B. J. (1988). *A Cognitive Theory of Consciousness* (Cambridge University Press, New York, USA).

35. Baars, B. J. (1997). *In the Theater of Consciousness: The Workspace of the Mind* (Oxford University Press, USA).

36. Baars, B. J. (2002). The conscious access hypothesis: Origins and recent evidence. *Trends in Cognitive Science*, 6(1): 47–52.

37. Baars, B. J. (2003). How brain reveals mind: Neuroimaging supports the central role of conscious experience. *Journal of Consciousness Studies*, 10(9–10): 100–114.

38. Baars, B. J., Banks, W. P. and Newman, J. B. (2003). *Essential Sources in the Scientific Study of Consciousness* (A Bradford Book, MA).

39. Baars, B. J. and Franklin, S. (2007). An architectural model of conscious and unconscious brain functions: Global workspace theory and IDA. *Neural Networks*, 20(9): 955–961.

40. Baars, B. J. and Franklin, S. (2009). Consciousness is computational: The LIDA model of global workspace theory. *International Journal of Machine Consciousness*, 1(1): 23–32.

41. Baars, B. J. and Gage, N. M. (eds.) (2010). *Cognition, Brain and Consciousness* (Second Edition) (Elsevier Academic Press, Burlington, MA, USA, Oxford, UK).

42. Baars, B. J. and Edelman, D. E. (2012). Consciousness, biology and quantum hypotheses. *Physics of Life Reviews*, 9: 285–294.

43. Bach, J. (2011). A motivational system for cognitive AI. *Artificial General Intelligence LNAI*, 6830: 232–242.

44. Baddeley, A. D. and Hitch, G. J. (1974). Working memory. In *The Psychology of Learning and Motivation*, (ed.) Bower, G. A. (Academic Press, New York) pp. 47–89.

45. Baddeley, A. D. (2000). The episodic buffer: A new component of working memory? *Trends in Cognitive Sciences*, 4: 417–423.

46. Baddeley, A. D. (2001). Is working memory still working? *American Psychologist*, 11: 851–864.

47. Baddeley, R., Abbott, L. F., Booth, M. C., Sengpiel, F., Freeman, T., *et al.* (1998). Response of neurons in primary and inferior temporal visual cortices to natural scenes. *Proceedings of Royal Society of London: Series B*, 164: 1775–1783.

48. Balduzzi, D. and Tononi, G. (2009). Qualia: The geometry of integrated information. *PLoS Computational Biology*, 5(8): 1–224.

49. Barnard, P. J. and May, J. (1999). Representing cognitive activity in complex tasks. *Human–Computer Interaction*, 14(1): 93–158.

50. Barlow, H. B. (1961). Possible principles underlying the transformation of sensory messages. In *Sensory Communication*, (ed.) Rosenbluth, W. A. (MIT Press, Cambridge, MA) pp. 217–234.

51. Barlow, H. B. (1972). Single units and sensatioperceptual psychology? *Perception*, 1: 371–394.

52. Beaton, M. and Aleksander, I. (2012). World-related integrated information: Enactivist and phenomenal perspectives. *International Journal of Machine Consciousness*, 4(2): 439–455.

53. Berardi-coletta, B., Buyer, L. S. and Dominowski, R. L. (1995). Metacognition and problem — Solving: A process-oriented approach. *Journal of Experimental Psychology*: *Memory and Cognition*, 21(1): 205–223.

54. Bhumbra, G. and Dyball, R. (2004). Measuring spike coding in the supraoptic nucleus. *Journal of Physiology*, 555: 281–296.

55. Bi, G. Q. and Poo, M. M. (1998). Synaptic modifications in cultured hippocampal neurons: dependence on spike timing, synaptic strength, and postsynaptic celltype. *Journal of Neuroscience*, 18: 10464–10472.

56. Binzegger, T., Douglas, R. J. and Martin, K. A. (2004). A quantitative map of the circuit of cat primary visual cortex. *Journal of Neuroscience*, 24(39): 8441–8453.

57. Block, N. and Fodor, J. (1972). What psychological states are not. *Philosophical Review*, 81: 159–181.

58. Blum, K. I. and Abbott, L. F. (1996). A model of spatial map formation in the hippocampus of the rat. *Neural Computation*, 8: 85–93.

59. Blumstein, S. E. (2004). Phonetic category structure and its influence on lexical processing. *Proceedings of the Texas Linguistic Society* (Cascadilla Press, Somerville, USA).

60. Blumstein, S. E. and Milberg, W. P. (2000). Language deficits in Broca's and Wernicke's aphasia: A singular impairment. In *Language and the Brain: Representation and Processing*, (eds.) Grodzinsky, Y., Shapiro, L. and Swinney, D. (Academic Press Cambridge, Massachusetts).

61. Bobrow, D. G. and Collins, A. M. (eds.) (1975). *Representation and Understanding: Studies in Cognitive Science* (Academic Press, New York).

62. Bohm, D. and Hiley, B. J. (1993). *The Undivided Universe: An Ontological Interpretation of Quantum Theory* (Routledge, London).

63. Bock, K. and Levelt, W. (1994). Language production: Grammatical encoding. In *Handbook of Psycholinguistics*, (ed.) Gernsbacher, M. A. (Academic Press, San Diego, CA) pp. 945–984.

64. Brette, R., *et al.* (2007). Simulation of networks of spiking neurons: A review of tools and strategies. *Journal of Computational Neuroscience*, 23(3): 349–398.

65. Brown, R. D. (1996). Example-based machine translation in the pangloss system. In *Proceedings of the Sixteenth International Conference on Computation Linguistics*, pp. 169–174.

66.   Bruner, J. S. (1996). *The Process of Education* (Harvard University Press, Cambridge, MA).

67.   Burks, A. W. (1986). An architectural theory of functional consciousness. In *Current Issues in Teleology*, (ed.) Rescher, N. (University Press of America, Lanham, Maryland).

68.   Buzas, P., Kovacs, K., Ferecsko, A. S., Budd, J. M. L., *et al.* (2006). Model-based analysis of excitatory lateral connections in the visual cortex. *Journal of Comparative Neurology*, 499(6): 861–881.

69.   Cairns-Smith, A. G. (1998). *Evolving the Mind: On the Nature of Matter and the Origin of Consciousness* (Cambridge University Press, Cambridge).

70.   Calvin, W. H. (1997). *How Brains Think: Evolving Intelligence, Then And Now* (Basic Books, USA).

71.   Celikel, T., Szostak, V. A. and Feldman, D. E. (2004). Modulation of spike timing by sensory deprivation during induction of corticalmap plasticity. *Nature Neuroscience*, 7: 534–541.

72.   Chabi, D. and Klein, J. (2010). High fault tolerance in neural crossbar. 5th *International Conference on Design and Technology of Integrated Systems in Nanoscale Era* (DTIS), 1–6.

73.   Chalmers, D. J. (1996). *The Conscious Mind: In Search of a Fundamental Theory* (Oxford University Press, UK).

74.   Chalmers, D. J. (2000). What is a neural correlate of consciousness? In *Neural Correlates of Consciousness: Empirical and Conceptual Issues*, (ed.) Metzinger, T. (MIT Press, USA).

75.   Chalmers, D. J. (2002). *Philosophy of Mind: Classical and Contemporary Readings* (Oxford University Press, UK).

76.   Chalmers, D. J. (2008). Mind and consciousness: Five questions. In *Mind and Consciousness: 5 Questions*, (ed.) Grim, P. (Automatic Press, New York).

77.   Chang, L., Lin, F. and Shi, Z. (2007). A dynamic description logic for representation and reasoning about actions. In *Knowledge Science, Engineering and Management* (Springer, Heidelberg) pp. 115–127.

78.   Chang, L., Shi, Z., Qiu L. and Lin, F. (2008). A tableau decision algorithm for dynamic description logic. *Chinese Journal of Computers*, 31(6): 896–909.

79.   Chang, L., Shi, Z., Gu, T. and Zhao, L. (2012). A family of dynamic description logics for representing and reasoning about actions. *Journal of Automated Reasoning*, 49(1): 1–52.

80.   Chen, L. (1982). Topological structure in visual perception. *Science*, 218: 699–700.

81.   Chen, L. (2005). The topological approach to perceptual organization. *Visual Cognition*, 12: 553–637.

82.   Chen, Y., Han, C., Wang, C., *et al.* (2006). The application of a convolution neural network on face and license plate detection. In *Proceedings of the 18th International Conference on Pattern Recognition* (IEEE Computer Society, Hong Kong) pp. 552–555.

83.   Chomsky, N. (1957). *Syntactic Structures* (The Hague, Mouton).

84.   Chomsky, N. (1959). On certain formal properties of grammars. *Information and Control*, 2: 137–167.

85.   Chomsky, N. (1963). *Formal Properties of Grammar* (Wiley, New York, USA).

86.   Chomsky, N. (1968). *Language and Mind* (Harcourt, Brace and World, New York).

87.   Chomsky, N. (1996). Language and evolution (letter). *New York Review of Books*, February 1.

88.   Chomsky, N. and Miller, G. A. (1963). *Introduction to the Formal Analysis of Natural Languages* (Wiley, New York, USA).

89.   Chomsky, N. and Schützenberger, M. P. (1963). The algebraic theory of context-free grammars. In *Computer Programming and Formal Systems* (North-Holland Publishing Company, Amsterdam).

90.   Churchland, P. (1995). *The Engine of Reason, The Seat of the Soul: A Philosophical Journey into the Brain* (MIT Press, Cambridge, MA).

91.   Churchland, P. S. (1996). The Hornswoggle problem. *Journal of Consciousness Studies*, 3(5–6): 402–408.

92. Churchland, P. S. and Sejnowski, T. (1992). *The Computational Brain* (MIT Press, Cambridge, MA, USA).
93. Ciresan, D. C., Meier, U., Gambardella, L. M., *et al.* (2010). Deep big simple neural nets excel on handwritten digit recognition. *Neural Computation*, 12: 3207–3220.
94. Clark, A. (1998). *The dynamic challenge. Cognitive Science*, 21(4): 461–481.
95. Clark, A. (1999). Where brain, body, and world collide. *Journal of Cognitive Systems Research*, 1: 5–17.
96. Cohen, J. D. and Schooler, J. W. (eds.) (1997). *Scientific Approaches to Consciousness: 25th Carnegie Symposium on Cognition* (Erlbaum, UK).
97. Collins, A. M. and Quillian, M. R. (1969). Retrieval time from semantic memory. *Journal of Verbal Learning and Verbal Behavior*, 8: 240–247.
98. Collins, A. M. and Loftus, E. F. (1975). A spreading activation theory of semantic memory. *Psychological Review*, 82: 407–428.
99. Collins, J. J., Chow, C. C. and Tmhoff, T. T. (1995). Stochastic resonance without tuning. *Nature*, 376: 236–238.
100. Coltheart, M., Curtis, B. Atkins, P. and Haller, M. (1993). Models of reading aloud: Dual-route and parallel-distributed-processing approaches. *Psychological Review*, 100: 589–608.
101. Coltheart, M., Rastle, K., Perry, C., Langdon, R. and Ziegler, J. (2001). The DRC model: A model of visual word recognition and reading aloud. *Psychological Review*, 108: 204–258.
102. Cosmides, L. and Tooby, J. (2000). The cognitive neuroscience of social reasoning. In *The New Cognitive Neurosciences*, (Second Edition) (ed.) Gazzaniga, M. S. (MIT Press, USA).
103. Cox, M. T. and Ram, A. (1999). Introspective multistrategy learning on the construction of learning strategies. *Artificial Intelligence*, 112: 1–55.
104. Creem, S. H. and Proffitt, D. R. (2001). Defing the cortical visual systems: "what", "where", and "how". *Acta Psychologica*, 107: 43–68.
105. Crick, F. (1994). *The Astonishing Hypothesis* (Scribner, New York).
106. Crick, F. and Koch, C. (1992). The problem of consciousness. *Scientific American*, September, pp. 152–159.
107. Crick, F. and Koch, C. (1998). Consciousness and neuroscience. *Cerebral Cortex*, 8: 97–107.
108. Crick, F. and Koch, C. (2003). A framework for consciousness. *Nature Neuroscience*, 6: 119–126.
109. Dahl, G., Yu, D., Deng, L., *et al.* (2012). Context-dependent pre-trained deep neural networks for large-vocabulary speech recognition. *IEEE Transactions on Audio, Speech, and Language Processing*, 20(1): 30–42.
110. Delclos, V. R. and Harrington, C. (1991). Effects of strategy monitoring and proactive instruction on children problem-solving performance. *Journal of Educational Psychology*, 83(1): 35–42.
111. Dell, G. S. (1986). A spreading activation theory of retrieval in language production. *Psychological Review*, 93: 226–234.
112. Dell, G. S., Schwartz, M. F., Martin, N., Saffran, E. M. and Gagnon, D. A. (1997). Lexical access in aphasic and non-aphasic speech. *Psychological Review*, 104: 801–837.
113. Dennett, D. C. (1991). *Consciousness Explained* (Little Brown and Company, Boston).
114. Deneve, S. (2007). Bayesian spiking I: Inference. *Neural Computation*, 20: 91–117.
115. Deneve, S. (2007). Bayesian spiking II: Inference. *Neural Computation*, 20: 118–145.
116. Desjardins, G., Courville, A., Bengio, Y., *et al.* (2010). Tempered Markov chain monte carlo for training of restricted Boltzmann machine. *Proceedings of Artificial Intelligence and Statistics*, pp. 145–152.
117. Deutsch, J. and Deutsch, D. (1963). Attention: Some theoretical considerations. *Psychological Review*, 70: 80–90.

118. DiGiovanna, J., Mahmoudi, B., Fortes, J., *et al.* (2009). Coadaptive brain–machine interface via reinforcement learning. *IEEEs Transaction on Biomedical Engineering*, 56(1): 54–64.

119. Djurfeldt, M. (2012). The connection-set algebra — A novel formalism for the representation of connectivity structure in neuronal network models. *Neuroinformatic*, 10(3): 287–304.

120. Djurfeldt, M., Johannes, H., Jochen, M. E., Niraj, D., *et al.* (2010). Run-time interoperability between neuronal network simulators based on the music framework. *Neuroinformatics*, 8(1): 43–60.

121. Djurfeldt, M., Lundqvist, M., Johansson, C., Rehn, M., Ekeberg, O., and Lansner, A. (2008). Brain-scale simulation of the neocortex on the IBM Blue Gene/L supercomputer. *IBM Journal of Research and Development*, 52(1/2): 31–41.

122. Dodel, S., Herrmann, J. M. and Geisel, T. (2002). Functional connectivity by cross-correlation clustering. *Neurocomputing*, 44–46: 1065–1070.

123. Dominowski, R. L. (1990). Problem solving and metacognition. In *Lines of Thinking*, (eds.) Gilhooly, K. J., Keane, M. T. G., Logie, R. H. and Erdos, H. (Wiley, New York, USA).

124. Dong, Q. and Shi, Z. (2011). A Research on introspective learning based on CBR. *International Journal of Advanced Intelligence*, 3(1): 147–157.

125. Dorigo, M. and Gambardella, L. (1997). Ant colony system: A cooperative learning approach to the traveling salesman problem. *IEEE Transaction on Evolutionary Computation*, 1(1): 53–56.

126. Edelman, G. M. (2003). Naturalizing consciousness: A theoretical framework. *Proceedings of the National Academy of Sciences of the United States of America*, 100(9): 5520–5524.

127. Edelman, G. M. (2004). Biochemistry and the sciences of recognition. *Journal of Biological Chemistry*, 279: 7361–7369.

128. Edelman, G. M. (2007). Learning in and from brain-based devices. *Science*, 318(5853): 1103–1105.

129. Edelman, G. M. and Tononi, G. (2000). *A Universe of Consciousness*: *How Matter Becomes Imagination* (Basic Books, New York).

130. Ekeberg, O., Walle, P., Lansner, A., Traven, H., Brodin, L. and Grillner, S. (1991). A computer based model for realistic simulations of neural networks. I: The single neuron and synaptic interaction. *Biological Cybernetics*, 65(2): 81–90.

131. Eliasmith, C. (1996). The third contender: A critical examination of the dynamicist theory of cognition. *Philosophical Psychology*, 9(4): 441–463.

132. Eliasmith, C. (1997). Computation and dynamical models of mind. *Minds and Machines*, 1997(7): 531–541.

133. Eliasmith, C. (2013). *How to Build a Brain*: *A Neural Architecture for Biological Cognition* (Oxford Press, London, UK).

134. Eliasmith, C. and Anderson, C. H. (2003). *Neural engineering*: *Computation, Representation, and Dynamics in Neurobiological systems* (MIT Press, Cambridge, MA).

135. Eliasmith, C., Stewart, T. C., Choo, X., Bekolay, T., DeWolf, T., Tang, Y. and Rasmussen, D. A. (2012). Large-scale model of the functioning brain. *Science*, 338: 1202–1205.

136. Ernst, G. and Newell, A. (1969). *GPS*: *A Case Study in Generality and Problem Solving* (Academic Press, USA).

137. Engel, A. K. and Singer, W. (2001). Temporal binding and the neural correlates of sensory awareness. *Trends in cognitive Sciences*, 5(1): 16–25.

138. Esser, S. K., Andreopoulos, A., Appuswamy, R., *et al.* (2013). Cognitive computing systems: Algorithms and applications for networks of neurosynaptic cores. In *The International Joint Conference on Neural Networks* (*IJCNN*) pp. 1–10.

139. Everett, H. (1957). *On the Foundations of Quantum Mechanics*. PhD Thesis, Princeton University, Department of Physics.

140. Fairhall, A., Lewen, G., Bialek, W., *et al.* (2001). Effciency and ambiguity in an adaptive neural code. *Nature*, 412: 787–792.

141. Fan, J., Xu, W., Wu, Y., *et al.* (2010). Human tracking using convolutional neural networks. *IEEE Transactions on Neural Networks*, 21(10): 1610–1623.

142. Farber, I. B. and Churchland, P. S. (1995). Consciousness and the neurosciences: Philosophical and theoretical issues. In *The Cognitive Neurosciences*, (ed.) Gazzaniga, M. S. (MIT Press, Cambridge, Massachusetts) pp. 1295–1306.

143. Farwell, L. A. and Donchin, E. (1988). Talking off the top of your head: Toward a mental prosthesis utilizing event-related brain potentials. *Electroencephalography and Clinical Neurophysiology*, 70(6): 510–523.

144. Feldman, J. and Ballard, D. (1982). Connectionist model and their properties. *Cognitive Sciences*, 6: 205–254.

145. Field, D. J. (1987). Relations between the statistics of natural images and the response properties of cortical cells. *Journal of Optical Society of America A*, 4(12): 2379–2394.

146. Flavell, J. H. (1976). Metacognitive aspects of problem solving. In *The Nature of Intelligence*, (ed.) Resnicked, L. B. (Erlbaum, Hillsdale, NJ).

147. Fodor, J. A. (1975). *The Language of Thought* (Thomas Crowell, New York, USA).

148. Fodor, J. A. (1981). *Representations* (Bradford/MIT Press, Cambridge, MA, USA).

149. Fodor, J. A. (1983). *The Modularity of Mind* (MIT Press, Cambridge, MA, USA).

150. Fodor, J. A. (1987). *Psychosemantics* (Bradford/MIT Press, Cambridge, MA, USA).

151. Fodor, J. A. (1987). *The Elm and the Expert* (Bradford/MIT Press, Cambridge, MA, USA).

152. Fodor, J. A. (2000). *The Mind Doesn't Work That Way* (MIT Press, USA).

153. Forgas, J. P., Williams, K. D. and Wheeler, L. (eds.) (2003). *The Social Mind: Cognitive and Motivational Aspects of Interpersonal Behavior* (Cambridge University Press, UK).

154. Fox, S. (1996). Introspective multistrategy learning: Constructing a learning strategy under reasoning failure. PhD Thesis, Technical Report No. GIT-CC-96-06, Georgia Institute of Technology, College of Computing, Atlanta, GA.

155. Frackowiak, R. S. J., Ashburner, J. T., Penny, W. D., *et al.* (eds.) (2004). *Human Brain Function* (Second Edition) (Elsevier Inc., Amsterdam).

156. Franklin, S., Kelemen, A. and McCauley, L. (1998). IDA: A cognitive agent architecture In *Proceedings of the IEEE Conference on Systems, Man and Cybernetics* (IEEE Press).

157. Franklin, S. and Patterson, F. G. Jr. (2006). The LIDA Architecture: Adding new modes of learning to an intelligent, autonomous, software agent. *Integrated Design and Process Technology*, IDPT-2006, Society for Design and Process Science, San Diego, CA.

158. Franco, L. and Rolls, E. T. (2004). The use of decoding to analyze the contribution to the information of the correlations between the firing of simultaneously recorded neurons. *Experimental Brain Research*, 155: 370–384.

159. Friederici, A. D., Pfeifer, E. and Hahne, A. (1993). Event-related brain potentials during natural speech processing: Effects of semantic, morphological and syntactic violations. *Cognitive Brain Research*, 1: 183–192.

160. Friederici, A. D., Steinhauer, K. and Pfeifer, E. (2002). Brain signatures of artificial language processing: Evidence challenging the critical period hypothesis. *Proceedings of the National Academy of Sciences of the United States of America*, 99: 529–534.

161. Fujii, H. and Ito, H. (1996). Dynamical cell assembly hypothesis: Theoretical possibility of spatio-temporal coding in the cortex. *Neural Network*, 9: 1303–1350.

162. Fukuyama, O., Suzuki, T. and Mabuchi, K. (2010). RatCar: a vehicular neuro-robotic platform for a rat with a sustaining structure of the rat body under the vehicle. *Annual International Conference of the IEEE Engineering in Medicine and Biology Society*.

163. Furber, S. (2004). *ARM System-on-Chip Architecture* (Second Edition) (Addison-Wesley Professional).

164. Fuster, J. M. (2004). Upper processing stages of the perception-action cycle. *Trends in Cognitive Sciences*, 8: 143–145.

165.   Fuster, J. M. and Bressler, S. L. (2012). Cognit activation: A mechanism enabling temporal integration in working memory. *Trends in Cognitive Sciences*, 16: 207–218.

166.   Gao, X. and Chu, Z. (2002). *The Philosophy of Mind (in Chinese)* (Commercial Press, Beijing, China).

167.   Gardner, H. (1993). *Multiple Intelligences: The Theory in Practice* (Basic Books, New York, USA).

168.   Gardner, H. (1999). *Intelligence Reframed* (Basic Books, New York, USA).

169.   Gardner, H. (2004). *Frames of Mind: The Theory of Multiple Intelligences* (Basic Books, New York, USA).

170.   Gardner, H. (2006). *Multiple Intelligences: New Horizons* (Basic Books, New York, USA).

171.   Gazzaniga, M. S., Ivry, R. B. and Mangun, G. R. (2009). *Cognitive Neuroscience: The Biology of the Mind* (W. W. Norton & Company Inc.).

172.   Ge, Y. and Jiang, W. (2006). On Consistency of Bayesian inference with mixtures of Logistic Regression. *Neural Computation*, 18: 224–243.

173.   Gerstner, W., Kempter, R., van Hemmen, J. L. and Wagner, H. (1996). A neuronal learning rule for sub-millisecond temporal coding. *Nature*, 383: 76–81.

174.   Geschwind, N. (1967). Brain mechanisms suggested by studies of hemispheric connections. In *Brain Mechanisms Underlying Speech and Language*, (eds.) MiUiken, C. H. and Darley, F. L. (Gruen and Stratton, New York, USA).

175.   Gilhooly, K. J., Logie, R. H., Wetherick, N. E. and Wynn, V. (1993). Working memory and strategies in syllogistic reasoning tasks. *Memory and Cognition*, 21: 115–124.

176.   Goleman, D. (1995). *Emotional Intelligence: Why It Can Matter More Than IQ* (Bantam Books, USA).

177.   Gordon, H. W. and Levelt, R. (1988). Importance of specialized cognitive function in the selection of military pilots. *Journal of Applied Psychology*, 73(1): 38–45.

178.   Gottlieb, J., Oudeyer, P.-Y., Lopes, M. and Baranes, A. (2013). Information seeking, curiosity and attention: Computational and neural mechanisms. *Trends in Cognitive Science*, 17(11): 585–596.

179.   Green, R. G., Beatty, W. W. and Arkin, R. M. (1984). *Human Motivation: Physiological, Behavioral and Social Approaches* (Allyn and Bacon, Inc., Massachusetts, USA).

180.   Greeno, J. G. (1989). Situations, mental models and generative knowledge. In *Complex Information Processing: The Impact of Herbert*, (eds.) Simon, A., Klahr, D. and Erlbaum, K. K. (Psychology Press, New Jersey).

181.   Grossberg, S. (1976). Adaptive pattern classification and universal recoding: I Parallel development and coding of neural detectors. *Biological Cybernetics*, 23: 121–134.

182.   Grossberg, S. (1976). Adaptive pattern classification and universal recoding: II. Feedback, expectation, olfaction, illusions. *Biological Cybernetics*, 23: 187–202.

183.   Grossberg, S. (1977). Pattern formation by the global limits of a nonlinear competitive interaction in n dimensions. *Mathematical Biology*, 4: 237–256.

184.   Grossberg, S. (1978). Decision, patterns, and oscillations in the dynamics of competitive systems with application to Volterra–Lotka systems. *Journal of Theoretical Biology*, 73: 101–130.

185.   Grossberg, S. (1978). Competition, decision, and consensus. *Journal of Mathematical Analysis and Applications*, 66: 470–493.

186.   Grossberg, S. (1980). How does a brain build a cognitive code? *Psychological Review*, 87: 1–51.

187.   Grossberg, S. (1982). *Studies of Mind and Brain* (Reidel, Boston, USA).

188.   Grossberg, S. (1987). Competitive learning: From interactive activation to adaptive resonance. *Cognitive Science*, 11: 23–63.

189.   Grossberg, S. (1988). Nonlinear neural networks: Principles, mechanisms, and architectures. *Neural Networks*, 1: 17–61.

190. Grossberg, S. (1988). *Neural Networks and Natural Intelligence* (MIT Press, Cambridge, MA, USA).

191. Grossberg, S. (1988). Competitive learning: from interactive activation to adaptive resonance, In *Neural Networks and Natural Intelligence*, (ed.) Grossberg, S. (MIT Press, Cambridge, MA, USA).

192. Grossberg, S. (1990). Content-addressable memory storage by neural networks: A general model and global Liapunov method. In *Computational Neuroscience*, (ed.) Schwartz, E. L. (MIT Press, Cambridge, MA, USA).

193. Grossberg, S. (2003). Laminar cortical dynamics of visual form perception. *Neural Networks*, 16(5–6): 925–931.

194. Grossberg, S. (2007). Consciousness CLEARS the mind. *Neural Networks*, 20(9): 1040–1053.

195. Grossberg, S. and Versace, M. (2008). Spikes, synchrony, and attentive learning by laminar thalamocortical circuits. *Brain Research*, 1218: 278–312.

196. Grossberg, S. (2011). Foundations and new paradigms of brain computing: Past, present, and Future. *Artificial Intelligence Around Man and Beyond* (Springer) pp. 1–7.

197. Gurney, K., Prescott, T. J. and Redgrave, P. (2001). A computational model of action selection in the basal ganglia I: A new functional anatomy. *Biological Cybernetic*, 84(6): 401–410.

198. Gurney, K., Prescott, T. J. and Redgrave, P. (2001). A computational model of action selection in the basal ganglia II: A new functional anatomy. *Biological Cybernetic*, 84(6): 411–423.

199. Hagoort, P. (2005). On Broca, brain, and binding: A new framework. *Trends in Cognitive Sciences*, 9(9): 416–423.

200. Hagoort, P. (2014). Nodes and networks in the neural architecture for language: Broca's region and beyond. *Current Opinion in Neurobiology*, 28: 136–141.

201. Hagoort, P., Hald, L. A., Bastiaansen, M. C. M. and Petersson, K. M. (2004). Integration of word meaning and world knowledge in language comprehension. *Science*, 304(5669): 438–441.

202. Harnish, R. M. (2001). *Minds, Brains, Computers: An Historical Introduction to the Foundations of Cognitive Science* (Wiley-Blackwell, USA).

203. Hawking, S. W. (2014). *Is Artificial Intelligence a Threat to Human Existence?* (BBC World Service, 12.3).

204. Hawkins, J. and Blakeslee, S. (2004). *On Intelligence* (Times Books, New York, USA).

205. HBP Sub-subprojects: https://www.humanbrainproject.eu/discover/the-project/sub-projects.

206. Hebb, D. O. (1949). *The Organization of Behavior: A Neuropsychological Theory* (Wiley, New York, USA).

207. Heider, F. (1958). *The Psychology of Interpersonal Relations* (John Wiley & Sons, New York, USA).

208. Hennessey, B. A. and Amabile, T. M. (1998). Reality, intrinsic motivation, and creativity. *American Psychologist*, 53(6): 674–675.

209. Hernández, D. (1994). *Qualitative Representation of Spatial Knowledge* (Springer-Verlag, New York).

210. Hinton, G. E. (2002). Training products of experts by minimizing contrastive divergence. *Neural Computation*, 14: 1771–1800.

211. Hinton, G. E. (2010). *A Practical Guide to Training Restricted Boltzmann Machines* (Springer, New York).

212. Hinton, G. E. (2015). Deep Learning. Invited Speaker, 29th AAAI Conference on *Artificial Intelligence*, (Austin, Texas, USA), January 24–30.

213. Hinton, G. E., Oindero, S. and Ten, Y. W. (2006). A fast learning algorithm for deep belief nets. *Neural Computation*, 18(7): 1527–1554.

214. Hinton, G. E. and Salakhutdinov, R. R. (2006). Reducing the dimensionality of data with neural networks. *Science*, 313(5786): 504–507.

215.   Hodgkin, A. L. and Huxley, A. F. (1952). A quantitative description of ion currents and its applications to conduction and excitation in nerve membranes. *Journal of Physiology* (London), 117: 500–544.

216.   Hopfield, J. J. (1982). Neural networks and physical systems with emergent collective computational abilities. *Proceedings of the National Academy of Sciences of the USA*, 9(2554).

217.   Horst, S. (2009). *The Computational Theory of Mind. Stanford Encyclopedia of Philosophy* (Stanford University Press, Palo Alto, CA).

218.   Huang, X. and Weng, J. (2002). Novelty and reinforcement learning in the value system of developmental robots. In *Second International Workshop on Epigenetic Robotics: Modelling Cognitive Development in Robotic Systems*, (eds.) Prince, C. G., Demiris, Y., Marom, Y., Kozima, H. and Balkenius, C. (Edinburgh, Scotland, Conference Paper) pp. 47–55.

219.   Humphries, M. D. (2002). *The basal ganglia and action selection: A computational study at multiple levels of description.* (Department of Psychology, University of Sheffield, Sheffield UK).

220.   Humphreys, G. W., Cinel, C., Wolfe, J., *et al.* (2000). Fractionating the binding process: Neuropsychological evidence distinguishing binding of form from binding of surface features. *Vision Research*, 40(12): 1569–1596.

221.   ImageNet (2014). http://www.image-net.org/, Stanford Vision Lab, Stanford University.

222.   Jackendoff, R. (2007). *Language, Consciousness, Culture: Essays on Mental Structure* (MIT Press).

223.   Jitendra, F., Serge, B., Thomas, L. and Jianbo, S. (2001). Contour and texture analysis for image segmentation. *International Journal of Computer Vision*, 43(1): 7–27.

224.   Johnson-Laird, P. N. (2010). Mental models and human reasoning. *Proceedings of the National Academy of Sciences of the United States of America*, 107: 18243–18250.

225.   Jones, R. M., Laird, J. E., Nielsen, P. E., Coulter, K. J., Kenny, P. and Koss, F. V. (1999). Automated intelligent pilots for combat flight simulation. *AI Magazine*, 20: 27–41.

226.   Jonides, J., Smith, E. E., Koeppe, R. A., Awh, E., Minoshima, S. and Mintun, M. A. (1993). Spatial working memory in humans as revealed by PET. *Nature*, 363: 623–625.

227.   Just, M. A. and Carpenter, P. A. (1985). Cognitive coordinate system: Accounts of mental rotation and individual difference in spatial ability. *Psychological Review*, 92(2): 137–172.

228.   Kaelbling, L. P., Littman, M. L. and Cassandra, A. R. (1998). Planning and acting in partially observable stochastic domains. *Artificial Intelligence*, 101: 99–134.

229.   Kahneman, D. (1973). *Attention and Effort* (Prentice-Hall, Englewood Cliffs, NJ, USA).

230.   Kandel, E. R., Schwartz, J. H. and Jessell, T. M. (2000). *Principles of Neural Science* (Fourth Edition) (McGraw-Hill Medical, New York, USA).

231.   Kang, K. and Sompolinsky, H. (2001). Mutual information of population codes and distance measures in probability space. *Physics Review Letters*, 86: 1–4.

232.   Kaplan, F. and Oudeyer, P. Y. (2003). Motivational principles for visual know-how development. In *Proceedings of the 3rd International Workshop on Epigenetic Robotics: Modeling Cognitive Development in Robotic Systems*, (eds.) Prince, C. G., *et al.* (Lund University Cognitive Studies) pp. 73–80.

233.   Karmiloff-Smith, A. (1992). *Beyond Modularity, A Developmental Perspective on Cognitive Science* (MIT Press, Cambridge, MA).

234.   Kaye, L. (1998). *The Language of Thought.* http://host.uniroma3.it/progetti/kant/field/lot.htm.

235.   Kelly, K. (1994). *Out of Control: The New Biology of Machines, Social Systems, and the Economic World* (Basic Books, New York, NY).

236.   Kirsh, D. (1991). Foundations of AI: The big issues. *Artificial Intelligence*, 47: 3–30.

237.   Kleene, S. C., Shannon, C. and McCarthy, J. (1996). Representation of events in nerve nets and finite automata. In *Automata Studies*, (eds.) Shannon, C. E., McCarthy, J. and Ashby, W. R. (Princeton University Press, Princeton, USA).

238. Knill, D. C. and Pouget, A. (2004). The Bayesian brain: The role of uncertainty in neural coding and computation. *Trends in Neuroseiences*, 27(12): 712–719.

239. Knobe, J. and Nichols, S. (2008). *Experimental Philosophy* (Oxford University Press, UK).

240. Kober, J. and Peters, J. (2012). *Reinforcement Learning in Robotics: A Survey. Adaptation, Learning, and Optimization* (Springer, New York).

241. Kohonen, T. (1982). Self-organized formation of topologically correct feature maps. *Biological Cybernetics*, 43: 59–69.

242. Kohonen, T. (1993). Things you haven't heard about the self-organizing map. *Proceedings of IEEE International Conference on Neural Networks*, (San Francisco) 1147–1156.

243. Kohonen, T. (1997). *Self-Organizing Maps* (Second Edition) (Springer-Verlag, Berlin, Germany).

244. Kohonen, T. and Kashi, S. (2000). Self-organization of a massive document collection. *IEEE Transactions on Neural Networks*, 11(3): 574–585.

245. Kosslyn, S. M. (1990). Components of high-level vision: A cognitive neuroscience analysis and accounts of neurological syndromes. *Cognition*, (2).

246. Kosslyn, S. M. (2005). Mental images and the brain. *Cognitive Neuropsychology*, 22(3/4): 333–347.

247. Krizhevsky, A., Sutskever, I. and Hinton, G. E. (2012). ImageNet classification with deep convolutional neural networks. In *Annual Conference on Neural Information Processing Systems*, (Lake Tahoe), 1106–1114.

248. Kuypers, H. G. J. M. (2011). Anatomy of the descending pathways. In *Handbook of Physiology, The Nervous System, Motor Control* (Wiley, New York).

249. Lafferty, J., McCallum, A. and Pereira, F. (2001). Conditional random fields: Probabilistic models for segmenting and labeling sequence data. In *International Conference on Machine Learning*, pp. 282–289.

250. Laird, J. E., Newell, A. and Rosenbloom, P. (1987). SOAR: An architecture for general intelligence. *Artificial Intelligence*, 33(1): 1–64.

251. Laird, J. E. (2012). *The Soar Cognitive Architecture* (MIT Press, USA).

252. Lake, B. M., Salakhutdinov, R. and Tenenbaum, J. B. (2015). Human-level concept learning through probabilistic program induction. *Science*, 350(6266): 1332–1338.

253. Langley, P. (2006). Cognitive architectures and general intelligent systems. *AI Magazine*, 27: 33–44.

254. Lathrop, S. D. (2008). *Extending Cognitive Architectures with Spatial and Visual Imagery Mechanisms*. PhD dissertation, University of Michigan.

255. Lathrop, S. D. and Laird, J. E. (2009). Extending cognitive architectures with mental imagery. In *Proceedings of the Second Conference on Artificial General Intelligence* (Arlington).

256. Lawler III, E. E. and Porter, L. W. (1967). The effect of performance on job satisfaction, industrial relations. *A Journal of Economy and Society*, 7(1): 20–28.

257. Le, Q. V., Ranzato, M., Monga, R., *et al.* (2012). Building high-level features using large scale unsupervised learning. *ICML2012*, Edinburgh, 81–88.

258. LeCun, Y., Boser, B., Denker, J. S., *et al.* (1989). Handwritten digit recognition with a back-propagation network. In *Advances in Neural Information Processing Systems* (Morgan Kaufmann, Denver) pp. 396–404.

259. LeCun, Y., Bottou, L., Bengio, Y., *et al.* (1998). Gradient-based learning applied to document recognition. *Proceedings of the IEEE*, 86(11): 2278–2324.

260. Lee, G. (2015). Facebook AI Director Yann LeCun on his quest to unleash deep learning and make machines smarter. *IEEE Spectrum*, 18: 21–24.

261. Leng, G., Brown, C., Bull, P., *et al.* (2001). Responses of magnocellular neurons to osmotic stimulation involves coactivation of excitatory and inhibitory input: An experimental and theoretical analysis. *Journal of Neuroscience*, 21(17): 6967–6977.

262. Levelt, W. J. M. (1989). *Speaking*: *From Intention to Articulation* (MIT Press, Cambridge, USA).

263. Levelt, W. J. M. (ed.) (1993). *Lexical Access in Speech Production* (Blackwell, Cambridge).

264. Levelt, W. J. M. (1999). Language. In *Encyclopedia of Neuroscience*, (eds.) Adelman, G. and Smith, B. H. (Second revision and enlarged edition) 1005–1008 (Elsevier Science, Amsterdam, Netherlands).

265. Levelt, W. J. M. (1999). Models of word production. *Trends in Cognitive Sciences*, 3(6): 223–232.

266. Levelt, W. J. M. (1999). Producing spoken language: A blueprint of the speaker. In *The Neurocognition of Language*, (eds.) Brown, C. M. and Hagoort, P. (Oxford University Press, Oxford, UK).

267. Levelt, W. J. M. (2001). Relations between speech production and speech perception: Some behavioral and neurological observations. In *Language, Brain and Cognitive Development*: *Essays in honor of Jacques Mehler*, (ed.) Dupoux, E. (MIT Press, Cambridge, MA, USA).

268. Levelt, W. J. M. (2001). Defining dyslexia. *Science*, 292(5520): 1300–1301.

269. Levelt, W. J. M. (2001). Spoken word production: A theory of lexical access. *Proceedings of the National Academy of Sciences*, 98(23): 13464–13471.

270. Levelt, W. J. M. and lores, d' Arcais, G. B. (eds.) (1978). *Studies in the Perception of Language* (Wiley, New York, USA).

271. Levelt, W. J. M. and Indefrey, P. (2001). The speaking mind/brain: Where do spoken words come from. In *Brain*, (eds.) Marantz, A. Miyashita, Y. and O'Neil, W. Image, Language (MIT Press, Cambridge, MA, USA).

272. Levelt, W. J. M., Roelofs, A. P. A. and Meyer, A. S. (1999). A theory of lexical access in speech production [target paper]. *Behavioral and Brain Sciences*, 22(1): 1–37.

273. Levelt, W. J. M., Roelofs, A. P. A. and Meyer, A. S. (1999). Multiple perspectives on lexical access. Reply to commentaries. *Behavioral and Brain Sciences*, 22(1): 61–76.

274. Li, Q. Shi, J. and Shi, Z. (2005). A model of attention-guided visual sparse coding. *ICCI2005*, 120–125.

275. Li, Z., Shi, Z., *et al.* (2013). Learning semantic concepts from image database with hybrid generative/discriminative approach. *Engineering Application of Aritifical Intelligence*, 26(9): 2143–2152.

276. Liaw, J. and Berger, T. (1999). Dynamic synapse: Harnessing the computing power of synaptic dynamics. *Neurocomputing*, 26–27: 199–206.

277. Lin, L.-J. and Mitchell, T. M. (1992). Memory approaches to reinforcement learning in non-Markovian domains. Technical report, CMU-CS-92-138, Carnegie Mellon University.

278. Lindenmayer, A. and Rozenberg, G. (eds.) (1976). *Automata, Languages, Development* (North-Holland, Amsterdam, Netherlands).

279. Littman, M. L., Sutton, R. S. and Singh, S. P. (2001). Predictive representations of state. *Advances in Neural Information Processing System*, pp. 1555–1561.

280. Lundqvist, M., Rehn, M., Djurfeldt, M. and Lansner, A. (2006). Attractor dynamics in a modular network model of the neocortex. *Network Computation in Neural Systems* 17: 253–276.

281. Machens, C. K. (2012). Building the human brain. *Science*, 338 (6111): 1156–1157.

282. Markram, H. (2006). The blue brain project. *Nature Reviews Neuroscience*, 7: 153–160.

283. Markram, H., Meier, K., Lippert, T., *et al.* (2011). Introducing the human brain project. *Procedia Computer Science*, 7: 39–42.

284. Markram, H., Lübke, J., Frotscher, M. and Sakmann, B. (1997). Regulation of synaptic efficacy by coincidence of postsynaptic APs and EPSPs. *Science*, 275: 213–215.

285. Markram, H. and Sakmann, B. (1994). Calcium transients in dendrites of neocortical neurons evoked by single subthreshold excitatory postsynaptic potentials via low- voltage-activated calcium channels. *Proceedings of National Academy of Science USA*, 91: 5207–5211.

286. Markram, H. and Sakmann, B. (2007). Action potentials propagating back into dendrites triggers changes in efficacy of single-axon synapses between layer V pyramidal cells. *Society for Neuroscience Abstract.*

287. Markram, H. W. and Sjöström, P. J. (2011). A history of spike timing dependent plasticity. *Front Synaptic Neuroscience,* 3: 1–24.

288. Markram, H. and Tsodyks, M. (1996). Redistribution of synaptic efficacy: A mechanism to generate infinite synaptic input diversity from a homogeneous population of neurons with out changing absolute synaptic efficacies. *Journal of Physiology Paris,* 90: 229–232.

289. Marr, D. (1982). *Vision: A Computational Investigation into the Human Representation and Processing of Visual Information* (W. H. Freeman, San Francisco, USA).

290. Marsland, S., Nehmzow, U. and Shapiro, J. (2000). A real-time novelty detector for a mobile robot. *EUREL European Advanced Robotics Systems Masterclass and Conference.*

291. Maslow, A. H. (1943). A theory of human motivation. *Psychological Review,* 50: 370–396.

292. Maslow, A. H. (1954, 1970, 1987). *Motivation and Personality* (Addison Wesley, USA).

293. Matthews, P. (1996). Relationship of firing intervals of human motor units to the trajectory of post-spike after-hyperpolarization and synaptic noise. *Journal of Physiology,* 492: 597–628.

294. Mayer, J., Wildgruber, D., Riecker, A., *et al.* (2002). Prosody production and perception: Converging evidence from fMRI Studies. *Proceedings of Speech Prosody 2002, Aix-en-Provence,* France, April, 11–13, 487–490.

295. Mayeux, R. and Kandel, E. R. (1991). Disorders of language: The aphasias. In *Principles of Neural Science,* (eds.) Kandel, E. R., Schwartz, J. H. and Jessell, T. M. (Third Edition) (Elsevier, Netherlands) pp. 840–851.

296. McCallum, R. A. (1993). Overcoming incomplete perception with utile distinction memory. In *The Proceedings of the Tenth International Machine Learning Conference* (Morgan Kaufmann Publishers, Inc.).

297. McCallum, R. A. (1995). Instance-based state identification for reinforcement learning. *Advances in Neural Information Processing System,* 7: 377–284.

298. McCarthy, J. (1980). Circumscription a form of non-monotonic reasoning. *Artificial Intelligence,* 13(1–2): 27–39.

299. McClelland, J. L. (1991). Stochastic interactive processes and the effect of context on perception. *Cognitive Psychology,* 23: 1–44.

300. McClelland, J. L. (1994). The organization of memory: A parallel distributed processing perspective. *Revue Neurologique (Paris),* 150(8–9): 570–579.

301. McClelland, J. L. and Rumelhart, D. E. (1981). An interactive activation model of context effects in letter perception: Part 1. An account of basic findings. *Psychological Review,* 88: 375–407.

302. McClelland, J. L. and Rumelhart, D. E. (1986). *Parallel Distributed Processing: Explorations in Parallel Distributed Processing* (MIT Press, USA).

303. McClelland, J. L., Mirman, D. and Holt, L. L. (2006). Are there interactive processes in speech perception? *Trends in Cognitive Sciences,* 10(8): 363–369.

304. McClelland, D. C., Atkinson, J. W., Clark, R. A. and Lowell, E. L. (1953). *The Achievement Motive* (Appleton-Century-Crofts, NY, USA).

305. McCulloch, W. S. (1988). *Embodiments of Mind* (MIT Press, Cambridge, MA, USA).

306. McCulloch, W. S. and Pitts, W. (1943). A logic calculus of the ideas immanent in nervous activity. *Bulletin of Mathematical Biophysics,* 5: 115–133.

307. McMillan, G. R., *et al.* (1995). Direct brain interface utilizing self-regulation of steady — state visual evoked response (ssver). *Proceedings of RESNA,* 693–695.

308. Mehrotra, K., Mohan, C. K. and Ranka, S. (1994). *Fault Tolerance of Neural Networks.* RL-TR-94-93 (Syracuse University, Syracus, New York).

309. Merolla, P. A., Arthur, J. V., Alvarez-Icaza, R., *et al.* (2014). A million spiking-neuron integrated circuit with a scalable communication network and interface. *Science*, 345(6197): 668–672.

310. Merrick, K. E. (2007). *Modelling Motivation for Experience-based Attention Focus in Reinforcement Learning*. Thesis, The University of Sydney.

311. Merrick, K. E. (2012). Intrinsic motivation and introspection in reinforcement learning. *IEEE Transactions on Autonomous Mental Development*, 4(4): 315–329.

312. Meyer, D. E. (1970). On the representation and retrieval of stored semantic information. *Cognitive Psychology*, 1: 242–300.

313. Miller, S. M. (ed.) (2015). *The Constitution of Phenomenal Consciousness*. Advances in Consciousness Research, 92 (John Benjamins Publishing Company).

314. Miller, G. (2005). What is the biological basis of consciousness? *Science*, 1 July, 309: 79.

315. Minsky, M. (1967). *Computation: Finite and Infinite Machines* (Prentice-Hall, Inc. Upper Saddle River, NJ, USA).

316. Minsky, M. and Papert, S. (1969). *Perceptrons* (MIT Press, USA).

317. Minsky, M. (1975). *A Framework for Representing Knowledge. The Psychology of Computer Vision*, (ed.) Winston, P. H. (McGraw-Hill, USA).

318. Minsky, M. (1985). *The Society of Mind* (Simon and Schuster, New York, USA).

319. Minsky, M. (1989). *Semantic Information Processing*, (ed.) Hall, R. P. (MIT Press, Cambridge, MA, USA).

320. Minsky, M. (1991) Machinery of consciousness. *Proceedings, National Research Council of Canada, 75th Anniversary Symposium on Science in Society*.

321. Minsky, M. (2006). The emotion machine: Commonsense thinking, artificial intelligence and the future of the human mind. *Psychology & Psychotherapy, Science, Barnes & Noble.com*.

322. Mitchell, T. M., Hutchinson, R., Just, M., Niculescu, R. S., Pereira, F. and Wang, X. (2003). Classifying instantaneous cognitive states from fMRI data. *American Medical Informatics Association Symposium*, Washington D.C.

323. Mitchell, T. M., Hutchinson, R., Niculescu, R. S., Pereira, F., Wang, X., Just, M. and Newman, S. (2004). Learning to decode cognitive states from brain images. *Machine Learning*, 57(1–2): 145–175.

324. Mitchell, T. M., Shinkareva, S. V., Carlson, A., Chang, K. M., Malave, V. L., Mason, R. A. and Just, M. A. (2008). Predicting human brain activity associated with the meanings of nouns. *Science*, 320: 1191–1195.

325. Modha, D. S., Ananthanarayanan, R, Esser, S. K., *et al.* (2011). Cognitive computing. *Communications of the ACM*, 54(8): 62–71.

326. Modha, D. S. and Singh, R. (2010). Network architecture of the long-distance pathways in the macaque brain. *Proceedings of the National Academy of Sciences of the USA*, 107: 13485–13490.

327. Mook, D. G. (1987). *Motivation: The Organization of Action* (W. W. Norton and Company, Inc., New York).

328. Moto-oka, T. (1983). Overview to the fifth generation computer system project. *ISCA '83 Proceedings of the 10th Annual International Symposium on Computer Architecture*, (ACM New York, NY, USA), 417–422.

329. Moto-oka, T. and Stone, H. S. (1984). Fifth-generation computer systems: A Japanese project. *Computer*, 17(3): 6–13.

330. Musliner, D. J., Durfee, E. H. and Shin, K. G. (1993). CIRCA: A cooperative intelligent real-timecontrol architecture. *IEEE Transactions on Systems, Man, and Cybernetics*, 23(6): 1561–1574.

331. Newell, A. (1980). Physical symbol systems. *Cognitive Science*, 4: 135–183.

332. Newell, A. (1981). Physical symbol systems. In *Perspectives on Cognitive Science*, (ed.) Norman, D. A. (Lawrence Erlbaum Associates, Hillsdale, N. J).

333. Newell, A. (1982). The knowledge level. *Artificial Intelligence*, 18: 87–127.
334. Newell, A. (1990). *Unified Theories of Cognition: The William James Lectures* (Harvard University Press, USA).
335. Newell, A. (1991). Reasoning, problem solving and decision processes: The problem space as a fundamental category. In *Attention and Performance VIII*, (ed.) Nickerson, N. R. S. (Erlbaum, New York).
336. Newell, A. and Simon, H. A. (1972). *Human Problem Solving* (Prentice–Hall, USA).
337. Newell, A. and Simon, H. A. (1976). Computer science as empirical inquiry: Symbols and search. *Communications of the Association for Computing Machinery*, 19(3): 113–126.
338. Ng, A., Ngiam, J, Foo, C. Y., Mai, Y. and Suen, C. Deep learning lecture. http://deeplearning.stanford.edu/wiki/index.php/UFLDL_Tutorial.
339. Nguyen, M. and Oudeyer, P.-Y. (2014). Socially guided intrinsic motivation for robot learning of motor skills. *Autonomous Robots*, 273–294.
340. Nigel, J. T. (1999). Are theories of imagery theories of imagination? *Cognitive Science*, 23(2): 207–245.
341. Nirenberg, S., Carcieri, S. M., Jacobs, A. L. and Latham, P. E. (2001). Retinal ganglion cells act largely as independent encoders. *Nature*, 411: 698–701.
342. Nuxoll, A. and Larid, J. E. (2007). Extending cognitive architecture with episodic memory. In *Proceedings of the 22nd AAAI Conference on Artificial Intelligence*, 1560–1564.
343. O'Doherty, J. E., Lebedev, M. A., Ifft, P. J., *et al.* (2011). Active tactile exploration using a brain–machine–brain interface. *Nature*, 479(7372): 228–231.
344. Ornstein, R. E. (1977). *The Psychology of Consciousness* (Second Edition) (Harcount Brace Jovaovich, New Work).
345. Osadchy, M., LeCun, Y. and Miller, M. (2007). Synergistic face detection and pose estimation with energy-based models. *Journal of Machine Learning Research*, 1197–1215.
346. Oudeyer, P.-Y. (2010). On the impact of robotics in behavioral and cognitive sciences: From insect navigation to human cognitive development. *IEEE Transactions on Autonomous Mental Development*, 2(1): 2–16.
347. Oudeyer, P.-Y. and Kaplan, F. (2004). Intelligent adaptive curiosity: A source of self-development. *Fourth International Workshop on Epigenetic Robotics*, Lund University, 127–130.
348. Oudeyer, P.-Y., Kaplan, F. and Hafner, V. (2007). Intrinsic motivation systems for autonomous mental development. *IEEE Transactions on Evolutionary Computation*, 11(2): 265–286.
349. Painkras, E., Plana, L. A., *et al.* (2013). SpiNNaker: A 1-W 18-core system-on-chip for massively-parallel neural network simulation. *IEEE Journal of Solid-state Circuits*, 48(8): 1943–1953.
350. Paninski, L. (2003). Estimation of entropy and mutual information. *Neural Computation*, 15: 1191–1253.
351. Papalexakis, E. E., Fyshe, A., Sidiropoulos, N. D., Talukdar, P. P., Mitchell, T. M. and Faloutsos, C. (2014). *Good-enough brain model: Challenges, algorithms and discoveries in multi-subject experiments* (KDD 2014, Conference Paper, New York, NY, USA) pp. 95–104.
352. Pavlov, I. P. (1998). http://www.iemrams.spb.ru:8101/english/pavlov.htm.
353. Penrose, R. (1989). *The Emperor's New Mind* (Oxford University Press, UK).
354. Penrose, R. (1994). *Shadows of the Mind* (Oxford Press, London, UK).
355. Penrose, R. and Hameroff, S. R. (1996). Conscious events as orchestrated space-time selections. *Journal of Consciousness Studies*, 3(1): 36–53.
356. Penrose, R. and Hameroff, S. (2011). Consciousness in the universe: Neuroscience, quantum space-time geometry and Orch OR Theory. *Journal of Cosmology*, 14: 1–36.
357. Pereira, F., Just, M. and Mitchell, T. (2001). *Distinguishing Natural Language Processes on the Basis of fMRI-measured Brain Activation* (PKDD 2001, Freiburg, Germany).

358. Perus, M. (1996). Neuro-quantum parallelism in brain–mind and computers. *Informatica*, 20: 173–183.
359. Perus, M. (1997). Mind: neural computing plus quantum consciousness. In *Mind Versus Computer.* (eds.) Gams, M., Paprzycki, M. and Wu, X. (IOS Press, Amsterdam) pp. 156–170.
360. Perus, M. (2010). Visual conscious experience. In *The Complementarity of Mind and Body*, (ed.) Amoroso, R. (Nova Science Publ., New York) pp. 75–113.
361. Petrovici, M. A., Vogginger, B., Meier, K., *et al.* (2014). Bridging the gap between software simulation and emulation on neuromorphic hardware: An investigation of causes, effects and compensation of network-level anomalies in a mixed-signal waferscale neuromorphic modeling platform. CoRR abs/1404.7514.
362. Pfeil, T., Scherzer, A., Schemmel, J. and Meier, K. (2013). Neuromorphic learning towards nano second precision. *IJCNN* 2013: 1–5.
363. Pfurtscheller, G., *et al.* (1992). Prediction of the side of hand movements from single trial multichannel EEG data using neural networks. *Electroencephalography Clinical and Neurophysiology*, 82: 313–315.
364. Picard, R. W. (1997). *Affective Computing* (MIT Press, London, England).
365. Pinker, S. (1994). *The Language Instinct: How the Mind Creates Language* (Morrow, New York).
366. Porter, L. and Lawler, E. (1968). *Managerial Attitudes and Performance* (Richard Irwin, Homewood, Illinois).
367. Posner, M. I. (1978). *Chronometric Explorations of Mind* (Erlbaum, Hillsdale, NJ, USA).
368. Posner, M. I. (1994). Attention: the mechanism of consciousness. *Proceedings of National Academy of Sciences of the United States of America*, 91(16): 7398–7402.
369. Posner, M. I. (2003). Imaging a science of mind. *Trends in Cognitive Sciences*, 7(10): 450–453.
370. Posner, M. I. (2004). The achievements of brain imaging: Past and present. To appear in *Attention and Performance XX*, (eds.) Kanwisher, N. and Duncan, J. (Oxford University Press, USA) pp. 505–528.
371. Posner, M. I. (ed) (2004). *Cognitive Neuroscience of Attention* (Guilford, New York, USA).
372. Posner, M. I. and DiGirolamo, G. J. (2000). Attention in cognitive neuroscience: An overview. In *The New Cognitive Neurosciences*, (ed.) Gazzaniga, M. S. (Second Edition, MIT Press, Cambridge, MA), 621–632.
373. Posner, M. I. and Raichle, M. E. (1994). *Images of Mind* (Freeman, New York, USA).
374. Pouget, A., *et al.* (1998). Statistically efficient estimation using population codes. *Neural Computation*, 10: 373–401.
375. Pouget, A., Dayan, P. and Zemel, R. (2003). Inference and computation with population codes. *Annual Review of Neurosceience*, 26: 381–410.
376. Prescott, T. J., Gonzalez, F. M. M., Gumey, K., Humphries, M. D. and Redgrave, E. (2006). A robot model of the basal ganglia: Behavior and intrinsic processing. *Neural Network*, 19: 31–61.
377. Putnam, H. (1960). Minds and machines. In *Dimensions of Mind,* (ed.) Hook, S. (New York University Press, New York).
378. Putnam, H. (1967). The nature of mental states. In *Mind Language and Reality*, Philosophical Papers, 2 (Cambridge University Press, Cambridge) 37–48.
379. Quillian, M. R. (1968). Semantic memory. In *Semantic Information Processing*, (ed.) Minsky, M. (MIT Press, Cambridge, MA) pp. 227–270.
380. Rao, A. S. and Georgeff, M. P. (1991). Modeling rational agents within a BDI-architecture. KR, 91: 473–484.
381. Rieke, F., *et al.* (1997). *Spikes: Exploring the Neural Code* (MIT Press, Cambridge, USA).
382. Roco, M. C. and Bainbridge, W. S. (eds.) (2002). Converging technologies for improving human performance. NSF/DOC-Sponsored Report.

383. Roelofs, A. (1997). The WEAVER model of word-form encoding in speech production. *Cognition*, 64(3): 249–284.

384. Rolls, E. T., Aggelopoulos, N. C., Franco, L. and Treves, A. (2004). Information encoding in the inferior temporal visual cortex: Contribution of the firing rates and the correlations between the firing of neurons. *Biological Cybernetics*, 90: 19–32.

385. Rosenblatt, F. (1962). *Principles of Neurodynamics* (Spartan Books, New York).

386. Rumelhart, D. E., Lindsay, P. H. and Norman, D. A. (1972). A process model for long-term memory. In *Organization of Memory*, (eds.) Tulving, E. and Donaldson, W. (Academic Press, New York, USA).

387. Rumelhart, D. E. and Ortony, A. (1977). The representation of knowledge in memory. in *Schooling and the Acquisition of Knowledge*, (eds.) Anderson, R. C., Spiro, J. J. and Montague, W. E. (Erlbaum, Hillsdale, New Jersey).

388. Rummery, G. A. and Niranjan, M. (1994). On-line Q-learning using connectionist systems. Technical Report CUED/F-INFENG/TR 166, Engineering Department, Cambridge University.

389. Rusu, P., Petriu, E. M., Whalen, T. E., Cornell, A. and Spoelder, H. J. W. (2003). Behavior-based neuro-fuzzy controller for mobile robot navigation. *IEEE Transactions on Instrumentation and Measurement*, 52(4): 1335–1340.

390. Salakhutdinov, R. (2010). Learning deep Boltzmann machines using adaptive MCMC. *Proceedings of the 27th International Conference on Machine Learning*.

391. Santos, E. S. (1976). Fuzzy automata and languages. *Information Science*, 10(3): 193–197.

392. Saunders, R. (2001). *Curious Design Agents and Artificial Creativity*. PhD Thesis, University of Sydney, Sydney.

393. Saunders, R. and Gero, J. S. (2001). *Designing for interest and novelty: Motivating design agents*. CAAD Futures 2001 (Kluwer, Dordrecht) pp. 725–738.

394. Saunders, R. and Gero, J. S. (2002). Curious agents and situated design evaluations. In: *Agents In Design. Key Centre of Design Computing and Cognition*, (eds.) Gero, J. S. and Brazier, F. M. T. (University of Sydney, Sydney) pp. 133–149.

395. Saunders, R. and Gero, J. S. (2004). Situated design simulations using curious agents. *Artificial Intelligence for Engineering Design, Analysis and Manufacturing*.

396. Schacter, D. L., McAndrews, M. P. and Moscovitch, M. (1988). Access to consciousness: Dissociations between Implicit knowledge in neuropsychological syndromes. In *Thought without Language*, (ed.) Weiskantz, L. (Oxford, Oxford University Press) pp. 242–278.

397. Schank, R. C. (1972). Conceptual dependency: Theory of natural language understanding. *Cognitive Psychology*, (4)3: 532–631.

398. Schemmel, J., Brüderle, D., Meier, K., *et al.* (2010). A wafer-scale neuromorphic hardware system for large-scale neural modeling. *ISCAS*, 2010: 1947–1950.

399. Schmidhuber, J. (2014). *Deep Learning in Neural Networks: An Overview*. http://www.idsia.ch/~juergen/deep-learning-overview.html.

400. Schmidhuber, J. (1997). *What's interesting*. TR-35-97 (Lugano, Switzerland).

401. Schmidhuber, J. (1991). A possibility for implementing curiosity and boredom in modelbuilding neural controllers. In *The International Conference on Simulation of Adaptive Behaviour: From Animals to Animats*, (eds.) Meyer, J. A. and Wilson, S. W. (MIT Press/Bradford Books) pp. 222–227.

402. Seidenberg, M. S. and McClelland, J. L. (1989). Visual word recognition and pronunciation: A computational model of acquisition, skilled performance, and dyslexia. In *From Neurons to Reading*, (ed.) Galaburda, A. (MIT Press, Cambridge, MA) pp. 255–305.

403. Seife, C., Miller, G., Pennisi, E., *et al.* (2005). What don't we know? *Science*, 1 July 309: 78–102.

404. Selfridge, O. G. (1959). Pandemonium: A paradigm for learning. In *Proceedings of a Symposium on the Mechanization of Thought Processes* (H. M. Stationery Office, London), 511–526.

405. Sellmann, M. (2015). Intelligent Decisions. Invited Speaker, *29th AAAI Conference on Artificial Intelligence* (Austin, Texas, USA), January 24–30.

406. Sha, F. and Pereira, F. (2003). Shallow parsing with conditional random fields. *Proceedings of HLT- NAACL*, 213–220.

407. Shannon, C. E. (1948). A mathematical theory of communication. *Bell System Technical Journal*, 27: 379–423 and 623–656.

408. Shannon, C. E. and McCarthy, J. (eds.) (1956). *Automata Studies* (Princeton University Press, Princeton N J., USA).

409. Shen Kuo (1994). *Chinese tone and intonation types of construction (in Chinese) Dialects*.

410. Shepard, R. N. and Metzler, J. (1971). Mental rotation of three-dimensional objects. *Science*, 171: 701–703.

411. Shepard, R. N. and Cooper, L. (1982). *Mental Images and Their Transformations* (Cambridge MA, MIT Press) pp. 26–90.

412. Sherbondy, A. J., Dougherty, R. F., Ananthanaraynan, R., *et al.* (2009). Think global, act local: Projectome estimation with BlueMatter. In *Proceedings of the Medical Image Computing and Computer Assisted Intervention Society*, Lecture Notes in Computer Science (London, September 20–24). (Springer, Berlin) pp. 861–868.

413. Sherrington, C. S. (1961). *The Integrative Action of the Nervous System, 1961 Edition* (Yale University Press, New Haven, CT, USA).

414. Shi, J. and Shi, Z. (2005). On intelligence (in Chinese). *Computer Science*, 32(6): 109–111.

415. Shi, Z. (1992). *Principles of Machine Learning* (International Academic Publishers, Beijing, China).

416. Shi, Z. (ed.) (1992). *Automated Reasoning. IFIP Transactions A-19* (North-Holland, Netherlands).

417. Shi, Z. (1993). *Neural Computing* (in Chinese) (Electronic Industry Press, Beijing, China).

418. Shi, Z. (1998, 2006, 2011). *Advanced Artificial Intelligence* (in Chinese). (Science Press, Beijing, China).

419. Shi, Z. (2000). *Intelligent Agent and Application* (in Chinese) (Science Press, Beijing, China).

420. Shi, Z. (2002, 2011). *Knowledge Discovery* (First and Second Editions) (in Chinese) (Tsinghua University Press, Beijing, China).

421. Shi, Z. (2003). Prospect of intelligent science (in Chinese). *Scientific Chinese*, 8: 47–49.

422. Shi, Z. (2003). *Consciousness System Model* (in Chinese). In *Consciousness and Brain*, (eds.) Wang, Y. and Yang, Y., *et al.* (Beijing, People's Publishing House, China).

423. Shi, Z. (2006,2013). *Intelligence Science* (in Chinese) (Tsinghua University Press, Beijing, China).

424. Shi, Z. (2006). On intelligence science and recent progresses. *IEEE ICCI*, 16: 2006.

425. Shi, Z. (2008). *Cognitive Science* (in Chinese) (University of Science and Technology of China Press, Hefei, China).

426. Shi, Z. (2009). On intelligence science. *International Journal on Advanced Intelligence*, 1(1): 39–57.

427. Shi, Z. (2009). *Neural Networks* (in Chinese) (High Education Press, Beijing, China).

428. Shi, Z. (2009). Research on brain-like computer. *Brain Informatics*, 5.

429. Shi, Z. (2011). Foundations of intelligence science. *International Journal of Intelligence Science,* 1(1): 8–16.

430. Shi, Z. (2011). *Advanced Artificial Intelligence* (World Scientific Publishing Co., Singapore).

431. Shi, Z. (2012). *Intelligence Science* (World Scientific Publishing Co., Singapore).

432. Shi, Z. (2013). Computational model of memory in CAM. Keynote Speaker, AGI–13, Workshop on Formal MAGIC.

433. Shi, Z. (2013). Intelligence science is the road to human-level artificial intelligence. Keynotes Speaker, IJCAI–13, *Workshop on Intelligence Science* (Beijing, China).

434. Shi, Z. (2013). Intelligence science and technology innovation driven development- from large data to intelligence science (in Chinese). Invited Speaker, Chinese Association for artificial intelligence, "Innovation Driven Development — artificial intelligence in the era of big data", (Shenzhen, China).

435. Shi, Z. (2015). *Mind Computation* (in Chinese) (Tsinghua University Press, Beijing, China).

436. Shi, Z. (2015). CAM is a General Framework of Brain-Like Computing. Invited Speaker. 1st World Congress of Robotics (WCR-2015), Shenyang, China.

437. Shi, Z. (2016). *Artificial Intelligence* (in Chinese) (China Machine Press, Beijing, China).

438. Shi, Z., Dong, M. Jiang, Y. and Zhang, H. (2005). A logic foundation for the semantic web. *Science in China, Series F, Information Sciences*, 48(2): 161–178.

439. Shi, Z., Ma, G., Xi, Y. and Lu, C. (2015). Motivation learning in mind model CAM. *International Journal of Intelligence Science*, 5(2): 63–71.

440. Shi, Z. and Wang, X. (2010). A mind model CAM: Consciousness and memory model. *Proceedings of Cognitive Science, ICCS 2010*, 148–149.

441. Shi, Z. and Wang, X. (2011). A mind model CAM in intelligence science. *Progress of Advanced Intelligence*, 2: 20–27.

442. Shi, Z., Wang, X. and Yue, J. (2011). Cognitive cycle in mind model CAM. *International Journal of Intelligence Science*, 1(2): 25–34.

443. Shi, Z. and Wang, X. (2011). A mind model CAM in intelligence science. *International Journal of Advanced Intelligence*, 3(1): 119–129.

444. Shi, Z., Wang, X. and Xi, Y. (2014). Cognitive memory systems in consciousness and memory model. *IEEE WCCI 2014*, 3887–3893.

445. Shi, Z. and Yu, Z. (1990). *Cognitive Science and Computer* (in Chinese) (Scientific Popularization Press, Beijing, China).

446. Shi, Z. Yue, J. and Ma, G. (2014). A cognitive model for multi-agent collaboration. *International Journal of Intelligence Science*, 4(1): 1–6.

447. Shi, Z., Yue, J. and Zhang, J. (2013). Mind modeling in intelligence science. *IJCAI*, WIS-2013, 30–35.

448. Shi, Z., Yue, J. and Ma, G. (2014). Visual awareness in mind model CAM. Cognitive 2014, Venice, Italy, pp. 262–268.

449. Shi, Z., Zhang, J., Yang, X., Ma, G., Qi, B. and Yue, J. (2014). Computational cognitive models for brain–machine collaborations. *IEEE Intelligent Systems*, November/December, 24–31.

450. Shi, Z., Zhang, J., Yue, J. and Qi, B. (2013). A motivational system for mind model CAM. *AAAI Symposium on Integrated Cognition* (Virginia, USA), 79–86.

451. Shi, Z., Zhang, J., Yue, J. and Yang, X. (2014). A cognitive model for multi-agent collaboration. *International Journal of Intelligence Science*, 4(1): 1–6.

452. Shi, Z. and Zhang, S. (2005). Case-based introspective learning. *IEEE ICCI'05. Proceedings of the 4th IEEE International Conference on Cognitive Informatics*, Irvine, USA, pp. 43–48.

453. Shi, Z. and Zheng, Z. (2007). Tolerance granular space model (in Chinese). In *Granular Computing: Past, Present and Future*, (eds.) Teqian, M., *et al.* (Science Press) pp. 42–82.

454. Shi, Z., Han, Z. and Jun, W. (1997). Applying case-based reasoning to engine oil design. *Artificial Intelligence in Engineering*, 11: 167–172.

455. Silver, D., Huang, A., Maddison, C. J., *et al.* (2016). Mastering the game of Go with deep neural networks and tree search. *Nature*, 529(7587): 484–489.

456. Simon, H. A. and Newell, A. (1958). Heuristic problem solving: The next advance in operations research. *Operations Research*, 6(1): 1–10.

457. Simsek, O. and Barto, A. G. (2004). Using relative novelty to identify useful temporal abstractions in reinforcement learning. *The 21st International Conference on Machine Learning*, Banff, Canada.

458. Simsek, O. and Barto, A. G. (2006). An intrinsic reward mechanism for efficient exploration. *The 23rd International Conference on Machine Learning*, University of Pittsburgh, Pennsylvania, USA, 833–840.

459. Singer, W. and Gray, C. M. (1995). Visual feature integration and the temporal correlation hypothesis. *Annual Review of Neuroscience*, 18: 555–586.

460. Singh, S., Barto, A. G. and Chentanex, N. (2005). Intrinsically motivated reinforcement learning. *Advances in Neural Information Processing Systems*, 17: 1281–1288.

461. Skinner, B. F. (1954). The science of learning and the art of teaching. *Harvard Educational Review*, 24(2): 86–97.

462. Smith, A. G. (1996). *Evolving the Mind: On the Nature of Matter and the Origin of Consciousness* (Cambridge University Press, UK).

463. Smith, E. E., Shoben, E. J. and Rips, L. J. (1974). Structure and process in semantic memory: A featural model for semantic decisions. *Psychological Review*, 81: 214–241.

464. Smolensky, P. (1986). Information processing in dynamical systems: Foundations of harmony theory. *Parallel Distributed Processing*, 1: 194–281.

465. Snaider, J., McCall, R. and Franklin, S. (2012). Time production and representation in a conceptual and computational cognitive model. *Cognitive Systems Research*, 13(1): 59–71.

466. Sompolinsky, H., *et al.* (2001). Population coding in neuronal systems with correlated noise. *Physics Review E*, 64: 1–9.

467. Squire, L. R. (1992). Memory and the hippocampus: A synthesis from findings with rats, monkeys, and humans. *Psychological Review*, 99: 195–232.

468. Stagner, R. (1977). Homeostasis, discrepancy, dissonance: A theory of motives and motivation. *Motivation and Emotion*, 1: 103–138.

469. Stanley, J. C. (1976). Computer simulation of a model of habituation. *Nature*, 261: 146–148.

470. Stuart, G. J. and Sakmann, B. (1994). Active propagation of somatic action potentials into neocortical pyramidal cell dendrites. *Nature*, 367: 69–72.

471. Suchman, L. A. (1987). *Plans and Situated Actions: The Problem of Human–Machine Communication* (Cambridge University Press, UK).

472. Sun, R. (1997). Learning, action and consciousness: A hybrid approach towards modeling consciousness. *Neural Networks*, 10(7): 1317–1331.

473. Sutskever, I. and Tielemant, T. (2010). On the convergence properties of contrastive divergence. *Journal of Machine Learning Research — Proceedings Track*, 9: 789–795.

474. Sutter, E. E. (1992). The brain response interface: Communication through electrical brain response. *Microcomputer Applications*, 15: 31–45.

475. Sutton, S., Bramn, M., Zabin, J. and John, E. R. (1965). Information delivery and the sensory evoked potential. *Science*, 155: 1436–1439.

476. Tao, J., Zhao, S. and Cai, L. (2002). Study on Chinese speech synthesis system based on statistical prosodic model. *Chinese Journal of Information*, 16(1): 1–6.

477. Thagard, P. (2005). *Mind: Introduction to Cognitive Science* (MIT Press, USA).

478. Thagard, P. (2012). *The Cognitive Science of Science* (MIT Press, USA).

479. Tieleman, T. (2008). Training restricted Boltzmann machines using approximations to the likelihood gradient. *Proceedings of the 25th international conference on Machine learning*, 1064–1071.

480. Tieleman, T. and Hinton, G. (2009). Using fast weights to improve persistent contrastive divergence. *Proceedings of the 26th Annual International Conference on Machine Learning* (New York, NY, USA).

481. Tononi, G. (2008). Consciousness as integrated information: A provisional manifesto. *The Biological Bulletin*, 215: 216–242.

482. Tononi, G. and Sporns, O. (2003). Measuring integrated information. *BMC Neuroscience*, 4: 31.

483. Toyoizumi, T., Aihara, K. and Amari, S. (2006). Fisher information for spike-based population decoding. *Physics Review Letters*, 97: 1–4.
484. Trados. (2005). http://www.translationzone.com/cn.
485. Treisman, A. (1960). Contextual cues in selective listening. *Quarterly Journal of Experimental Psychology*, 12: 242–248.
486. Treisman, A. (1982). Perceptual grouping and attention in visual search for features and for objects. *Journal of Experimental Psychology: Human Perception and Performance*, 8: 194–214.
487. Treisman, A. (1996). The binding problem. *Current Opinion in Neurobiology*, 6: 171–178.
488. Treisman, A. (1998). Feature binding, attention and object perception. *Philosophical Transactions of the Royal Society, Series B*, 353: 1295–1306.
489. Treisman, A. M. and Gelade, G. (1980). A feature-integration theory of attention. *Cognitive Psychology*, 12(1): 97–136.
490. Treisman, A. and Gormican, S. (1988). Feature analysis in early vision: Evidence from search asymmetries. *Psychological Review*, 95: 15–48.
491. Tsodyks, M. (2002). Spike-timing-dependent synaptic plasticity — the long road towards understanding neuronal mechanisms of learning and memory. *Trends Neuroscience*, 25: 599–600.
492. Tulving, E. (1983). *Elements of Episodic Memory* (Oxford Clarendon Press, London, UK).
493. Turing, A. M. (1936). On computable numbers with an application to the Entscheidungs problem. *Proceedings of the London Mathematical Society, Series-2*, 42: 230–265.
494. Turing, A. M. (1950). Computing machinery and intelligence. *Mind*, 59: 433–460.
495. Ungerleider, L. G. and Mishkin, M. (1982). Two cortical visual systems. In *Analysis of Visual Behavior*, (eds.) Ingle, D. J., Goodale, M. A. and Mansfield, R. J. W. (MIT Press, Cambridge, MA), pp. 549–586.
496. Van Essen, D. (1985). Functional organization of primate visual cortex. In *Cerebral Cortex*, Vol. 3, (eds.) Peters, A. and Jones, E. G. (Springer, New York), pp. 259–329.
497. Van Essen, D. (2013). The Human Connectome Project: Progress and Perspectives. Keynotes Speaker, IJCAI-13 Workshop on Intelligence Science, http://www.intsci.ac.cn/WIS2013/.
498. van Steveninck, de Ruyter, Lewen, R., Strong, G., *et al.* (1997). Reproducibility and variability in neural spike trains. *Science*, 275: 1805–1808.
499. Versace, M. and Chandler, B. (2010). The brain of a new machine. *IEEE Spectrum* December 2010, 28–35.
500. Victor, J. (2002). Binless strategies for estimation of information from neural data. *Physical Review E*, 66: 051903 1–15.
501. Vidal, J. J. (1973). Toward direct brain–computer communication. *Annual Review Biophysics*, 157–180.
502. von der Malsburg, C. (1995). Binding in models of perception and brain function. *Current Opinion in Neurobiology*, 5(4): 520–526.
503. von Neumann, J. (1941). The general and logical theory of automata. In *Cerebral Mechanisms in Behavior* (John Wiley and Sons, New York, NY, USA).
504. von Neumann, J. (1945). First draft of a report on the EDVAC. *Technical Report*, University of Pennsylvania.
505. von Neumann, J. (1951). The general and logical theory of automata. In *Cerebral Mechanisms in Behavior: The Hixon Symposium*, California Institute of Technology, Hixon Fund (Wiley, New York).
506. von Neumann, J. (1958). *The Computer and the Brain* (Yale University Press, New Haven, CT, USA).
507. von Neumann, J. (1966). *Theory of Self-Reproducing Automata* (University of Illinois Press, IL, USA).

508. Waldrop, M. M. (2012). Computer modelling: Brain in a box. *Nature*, 482: 456–458.
509. Wang, Y. M., Lu, M. L., Wu, Z. H., *et al.* (2013). Ratbot: A rat "understanding" what humans see. *International Workshop on Intelligence Science, in conjunction with IJCAI-2013*, 63–68.
510. Watanabe, W., Nakanishi, K. and Aihara, K. (2001). Solving the binding problem of the brain with bidirectional functional connectivity. *Neural Networks*, 14: 395–406.
511. Watkins, C. J. C. H. (1989). Learning from delayed rewards. PhD thesis, University of Cambridge.
512. Watson, J. B. (1913). Psychology as the behaviorist views it. *Psychological Review*, 20: 158–177. http://psychclassics.yorku.ca/Watson/views.htm.
513. Welford, A. T. (1967). Single-channel operation in the brain. *Acta Psychologica*, 27: 5–22.
514. Weng, J. (2012). *Natural and Artificial Intelligence: Introduction to Computational Brain–Mind* (BMI Press, Okemos, Michigan, USA).
515. Weng, J. (2015). Brain as an emergent finite automaton: A theory and three theorems. *International Journal on Intelligence Science*, 5: 2.
516. Weng, J. and Hwang, W. (2000). An incremental learning algorithm with automatically derived discriminating features. *Fourth Asian Conference on Computer Vision*, Taipei, Taiwan, pp. 426–431.
517. Weng, J. and Luciw, M. (2012). Brain-like emergent spatial processing. *IEEE Tranactions on Autonomous Mental Development*, 4(2): 161–185.
518. Weng, J., Luciw, M. and Zhang, Q. (2013). Brain-like temporal processing: Emergent open states. *IEEE Transactions on Autonomous Mental Development*, 5(2): 89–116.
519. Weng, J., McClelland, J., Pentland, A., Sporns, O., Stockman, I., Sur, M. and Thelen, E. (2001). Autonomous mental development by robots and animals. *Science*, 291(5504): 599–600.
520. Weng, J., Paslaski, S., Daly, J., Van Dam, C. and Brown, J. (2013). Modulation for emergent networks: Serotonin and dopamine. *Neural Networks*, 41: 225–239.
521. Wetmore, D. and Baker, S. (2004). Post-spike distance-to-threshold trajectories of neurones in monkey motor cortex. *Journal of Physiology*, 555: 831–850.
522. Wiener and Norbert. (1948). *Cybernetics, or Control and Communication in the Animal and the Machine* (The Technology Press, New York).
523. Wintermute, S. (2009). An Overview of Spatial Processing in Soar/SVS. Technical Report CCA-TR-2009-01, Center for Cognitive Architecture, University of Michigan.
524. Wintermute, S. (2010). Abstraction, imagery, and control in cognitive architecture. PhD Dissertation, University of Michigan.
525. Wintermute, S. and Laird, J. E. (2007). Predicate projection in a bimodal spatial reasoning system. In *Proceedings of the 22nd AAAI Conference on Artificial Intelligence* (Vancouver).
526. Wintermute, S. and Laird, J. E. (2008). Bimodal spatial reasoning with continuous motion. In *Proceedings of the 23rd AAAI Conference on Artificial Intelligence*, Chicago.
527. Winograd, T. (1972). *Understanding Natural Language* (Academic Press, USA).
528. Winograd, T. and Fernando, F. (1986). *Understanding Computers and Cognition: A New Foundation for Design* (Ablex Publishing Corporation, Norwood, New Jersey, USA).
529. Wolpaw, J. R., *et al.* (1991). An EEG-based brain–computer interface for cursor control. *Electroencephalography and Clinical Neurophysiology*, 78: 252–259.
530. Woods, W. A. (1970). Transition network grammars for natural language analysis. *Communications of the ACM*, 13(10): 591–606.
531. Wu, B., Su, Y., Zhang, J., Li, X., Zhang, J., Chen, W. and Zheng, X. (2009). BCI Chinese input virtual keyboard system Based on P300 (in Chinese). *Chinese Journal of Electronics*, 37(8): 1733–1738, 1745.
532. Yang, J. and Yang, Y. (2004). The rhythm generation in speech production (in Chinese). *Psychological Science*, 12(4): 481–488.
533. Zadeh, L. A. (1965). Fuzzy sets. *Information Control*, 8: 338–353.

534. Zadeh, L. A. (1994). Soft computing and fuzzy logic. *Software, IEEE*, 11(6): 48–56.

535. Zemel, R. S., Peter, D. and Alexander, P. (1998). Probabilistic interpretation of population codes. *Neural Computation*, 10: 403–430.

536. Zhang, B. and Zhang, L. (1992). *Theory and Application of Problem Solving* (Elsevier Science Publishers, North-Holland, Netherlands).

537. Zhang, J. and Shi, Z. (1995). An adaptive theoretical foundation toward neural information processing NFT. *Proceeding of ICONOP'95*, 217–220.

538. Zhang, J., Shi, Z. and Liu, J. (1998). Topology approximation correction approach — A learning mechanism of neural field theory. *Proceedings of International Conference on Neural Network and Brain*, 421–424.

539. Zhang, K., Ginzburg, I., McNaughton, B. L. and Sejnowski, T. J. (1998). Interpreting neuronal population activity by reconstruction: Unified framework with application to hippocampal cells. *Neurophysiology*, 79: 1017–1044.

540. Zhong, Y. (2014). *Principles of Advanced Artificial Intelligence: Concepts, Methods, Models and Theories* (in Chinese) (Science Press, Beijing, China).

541. Zhou, Z. (2016). *Machine Learning* (in Chinese) (Tsinghua University Press, Beijing, China).

Index

Printed in the United States
By Bookmasters